COMMANDING FIRE

An Officer's Life in the 151st Machine Gun Battalion, 42nd Rainbow Division During World War I

COMMANDING FIRE

An Officer's Life in the 151st Machine Gun Battalion, 42nd Rainbow Division During World War I

Narrative by Lieutenant N. P. Parkinson
151st Machine Gun Battalion

Edited by Joel R. Parkinson
Director and Curator,
World War History & Art Museum, Alliance, Ohio

Schiffer Publishing Ltd
4880 Lower Valley Road • Atglen, PA 19310

Library of Congress Control Number: 2013951934

Printed in China
ISBN: 978-0-7643-4582-1

We are interested in hearing from authors with book ideas on related topics.

Published by Schiffer Publishing Ltd.
4880 Lower Valley Road
Atglen, PA 19310
Phone: (610) 593-1777
FAX: (610) 593-2002
E-mail: Info@schifferbooks.com.

Visit our web site at:
www.schifferbooks.com
Please write for a free catalog.
This book may be purchased from the publisher.
Try your bookstore first.

CONTENTS

FOREWORD

Nellis Paul Parkinson was born January 26, 1890, in Marion County, Illinois. Later in life, he would entertain his grandchildren with tall and truthful stories rendered with his characteristically broad grin.

One factual story took place in his boyhood. In retrospect, the incident is noteworthy for its prescience. As he recalled: "My mom sent me to the store with 15 cents to buy some beefsteak. I ran to the store, which was only a few blocks away. I ran everywhere in those days. I bought a big slice of beefsteak, and was walking home with this slice of beefsteak under my arm when I saw a train with troops bound for the Philippines parked at the railroad station. Then a sergeant asked me how much I paid for the steak." The intimidated youngster barely looked up. Yet the profiteer in him managed to mumble "Thirty cents" in reply. Apparently, Nellis sensed an opportunity and meant to exploit it. Then the sergeant responded, "I'll give you fifty cents for it!" These soldiers had been traveling for several hours without food. Another man asked the sergeant how he would cook the beef on the train. He retorted that he would eat it raw if he had to. Then, reaching into his pocket, he found a silver dollar. The train was about ready to pull out and none of the other men had change for his silver dollar. Grabbing the beefsteak from the young boy, the man boarded the coach. The sergeant stood on the steps, holding the meat in one hand and the silver dollar in the other. Nellis was sure that he had lost out and would have to return home empty-handed. As the train slowly pulled away, the famished soldier flashed a smile. Flipping the silver dollar to the lad he hollered, "Here sonny! Keep the change! Join the army someday!"

That is exactly what he did. Following America's entry into the Great War, Nellis P. Parkinson signed up on July 4, 1917, at 27 years of age. He wound up in the newly-formed 42nd "Rainbow" Division. This was to become one of the most effective and famous U.S. divisions of World War I. The outfit was uniquely composed of National Guard units drawn from 26 states and the District of Columbia, making it the darling of the public back home. It was committed to each major American operation. The 42nd Rainbow emerged as one of the most battle-hardened combat divisions of the war, sustaining some of the heaviest casualties.

The story Parkinson tells in this book is his account of experiences commanding machine guns in the Rainbow Division during the First World War. Parkinson typed this narrative in 1930 for future reference by his sons Tom (then nine) and Robert (seven). What Parkinson intended as a private memoir turns out to be a fascinating historical record of America in the Great War.

Parkinson's record is remarkable for both its breadth and detail. He gives us a first-hand look at significant American engagements in the World War, including action in Lorraine, Champagne, Chateau-Thierry, St. Mihiel, Meuse-Argonne, and service in the Army of Occupation. As a platoon commander, Lieutenant Parkinson saw warfare at the front, not from the rear. As an officer, Lieutenant Parkinson was at times privy to some of the bigger picture in a way that enlisted men were not.

From this vantage point he describes defense and attack, trench and open warfare, night and day operations, waiting and marching, monotony and terror, daily life, and deadly action. What Clausewitz aptly termed the "fog" and "friction" of war are amply exemplified. Lieutenant Parkinson himself displayed calculated initiative, having learned to seize windows of opportunity as he had done with the beefsteak (minus the fibbing). He was no daredevil, but neither would he let an opening slip away. Also notable is previously unknown anecdotal material about Douglas MacArthur that illuminates his early career as Chief of Staff and later as Parkinson's brigade commander in the Rainbow Division. This is all the more interesting, because these impressions were written well before MacArthur became a household name.

Unusual happenings within the 42nd Division are recounted that are not covered by other histories. Parkinson unmasked a couple of spies at Pexonne whom he placed under arrest. The 168th Infantry unleashed their rockets' red glare against fellow Americans in a small-scale "civil war." MacArthur unwound with the officers of the 151st Machine Gun Battalion at their New Year's Eve party in occupied Germany. Nothing of interest is ignored.

Some of Parkinson's stories are the stuff that fiction is made of, except that they are true. The unlikely sighting on a clear day of an artificial rainbow just before the Rainbow Division was thrown against Cote de Chatillon would qualify as the inspiring turning point before a valiant assault in a war movie. The episode of two German high explosive shells hitting the dung heap he was standing on could have been taken from a far-fetched cartoon, but it was not very funny at the time.

Lieutenant Parkinson comprehensively captured the mundane as well as the momentous. Yes, his account brings to life the heroic and the horrific. Yet he also dwells on details of their day-to-day struggle that have often gone unnoticed. Soldiers got hungry, bored, tired, muddy, cold, wet, lousy, sick, lost, and homesick in the unsung intervals between fighting heralded by popular history. Parkinson wrote vividly about all this from personal experience. As with the bygone sergeant on the troop train, food was the infantry's preoccupation at the front. Occasions of scrounging barely a mouthful of scraps or moldy bread crumbs on the battlefield are telling. The weather was their relentless enemy, never giving quarter when hostile. At times, Parkinson reminisces about these lesser fortunes of war with wry humor punctuated by resounding understatement.

A windfall for us today is Parkinson's custody of words which were not his own. His manuscript incorporated a history of Company D written by its commander, Captain Monroe A. Means. He also included the history of the entire 151st Machine Gun Battalion by two NCOs from its headquarters. Apparently, these unpublished accounts informally circulated among the former comrades in arms just after the war. Parkinson also passed down a couple of books containing marginal notes by Lieutenant John H. Geiszel, a fellow officer from Company D. Parkinson's preservation of these primary sources is a singular gain for posterity.

Taking a step back and looking at the whole, a couple of underlying themes stand out. Major Cooper D. Winn conceived tactics in the 151st Machine Gun Battalion that proved to diminish their own casualties, boost the success of infantry attacks, and ultimately win adoption by their brigade, division, and corps. The lessons they learned the hard way dispel some of the oversimplified myths people hold today of lone machine guns sweeping open ground and cutting down waves of infantry. Direct fire may have been potent in defense, but overhead fire became the norm in the attack. In either mode, careful coordination among massed machine guns was vital to their survival and mastery of the field. Isolated machine gunners were more likely to be dead than deadly.

It also becomes evident throughout that casualties among machine gunners were mainly inflicted by artillery and gas. This was true whether they were dug in or on the move. On the other hand, aircraft had almost no effect on the ground for either side, except for their role in artillery observation. Though strafed and bombed time and again, *none* of Company D's 112 casualties were sustained from air attacks. Apparently, few if any of the 151st Machine Gun Battalion's nearly 500 casualties were inflicted from the skies. Billy Mitchell's unprecedented and celebrated fleet of 1,481 planes was nowhere to be seen in the crucial first hours of punching through German lines into the St. Mihiel Salient. Apparently they were rained out. Thus, any perpetuated myth of effective close air support in World War I goes down in flames.

However they were caused, mounting casualties were the leading tragedy of the War to End All Wars. At several junctures, Parkinson names officers with him in early settings, only to grimly mention how most or all of them were later killed here or there in the war. Had snapshots been taken, he would often have been the sole survivor from group photos. Parkinson himself cheated death through several close calls when he could have or should have been killed in action. Indeed, the casualty rate in his company reached 65 percent through about eight months of fighting in 1918. Yet Lieutenant Parkinson came through it all in one piece. We later generations of Parkinsons are decidedly glad about that!

Following the war, N. P. Parkinson married Florence North. "Park" and Florence had two sons, five grandchildren (of whom I am the youngest), and eleven great-grandchildren. After protecting his country, the veteran turned his pistol in for a briefcase and offered protection of a different kind. He was an insurance agent for seventeen years. Then the Governor of Illinois appointed him as Assistant Director of the Illinois Department of Insurance (1941-1944) and later Director of the same department (1944-1949). Upon leaving this post, Parkinson served in several executive capacities of insurance companies. Diligent and hard working, he did not retire until he was 80 years old.

One would never know from his easy-going manner that in 1918 he saw so much death and destruction. He led men in war, but somehow led a peaceful life with peace of mind thereafter. I never heard Grandad (as he liked to be called) speak of his own valor or about real fighting. He only told stories of what incidentally happened to him during the war. N. P. Parkinson died August 4, 1978, at the age of 88.

For years his memoirs were tucked away in obscurity. Only about a decade ago did I learn that the manuscript existed when my older brother mentioned something about it and later showed it to me. I was thrilled by what I read. I had distinct memories as a boy of hearing Grandad's stories about the lucky ricochet hitting the bull's-eye, about the lone asparagus sprout, and about the manure pile mishap that should have blown him up. Now I could read these and similar stories in black and white, placed in their larger context. I held the rest of the story in my hands.

It was not long before I resolved that Grandad's story should be published. Off I went transcribing, researching, footnoting, illustrating, and reveling all the way. It is my distinct privilege to bring N. P. Parkinson's World War memoirs to light for today's readers.

Commanding Fire carries an intentional double meaning. This book is one officer's account of commanding machine gun fire on the battlefields of northern France in 1918. Yet, it also records the command that machine gun fire itself held over those battlefields. As the narrative unfolds, it grows from a personal memoir into a history of the entire 151st Machine Gun Battalion. Parkinson was not absorbed with himself, but tells about what his men and peers were up to. When they began to fight as a unit instead of piecemeal among the infantry, Parkinson's story truly embodies the battalion's story. The brief company and battalion histories included at the end widen the scope further. The other combat units of the 42nd Rainbow Division had their stories told shortly after the war. To my knowledge, this is the first published history of the 151st Machine Gun Battalion.

The running narrative is Lieutenant Parkinson's. I have taken the liberty to edit some punctuation and spellings. The photos, maps, charts, insets, captions, footnotes, bibliography, and index are my additions. I trust that the format clearly distinguishes what is original from what adorns it.

Illustrations put a face on Parkinson's words. Footnotes correlate events that Parkinson relates with records of the same events in other sources. These independent confirmations lend credibility to the many circumstances Parkinson reports that are not known elsewhere. Transfers, promotions, and casualties meant that the chain of command was in regular flux. Accordingly, I have reconstructed the chain of command for each battle and presented it in a chart to assist the reader in following who was in command of what at any time. Parkinson's movements can be generally traced on maps that are furnished.

In some ways, this endeavor has been a family affair. I would like to thank my wife, Darla Parkinson, for her encouragement throughout this project. She is not particularly zealous for military history, yet she was more than favorable to the endeavor after recognizing the merits of publishing Grandad's story. I am grateful to my cousin, Richard Parkinson, for providing a missing page of text from the D Company history by Captain Means. I also thank my mom, Marilyn Parkinson, for proof reading the manuscript.

I am especially indebted to my brother, Greg Parkinson. First and foremost, he generously gave me the original manuscript from which I worked. He also supplied a couple of key original photographs which I used for illustrations. To top it off, Greg was my principle cheerleader and closest confidant through this project. During the tedious work of transcription he prodded me along and offered constructive suggestions. Thanks, big brother!

The final product is offered as a tribute to the men of the 151st Machine Gun Battalion, especially those who did not come home because they were buried "over there".

Joel R. Parkinson
Editor of *Commanding Fire*

CHAPTER 1: ENLISTMENT & COMMISSION

World War Begins in Europe, U.S. Drawn In, Ft. Sheridan, Colonel Roosevelt, A Commission, Ordered Overseas, Hoboken, The St. Louis.

During the last week of July 1914, I went on a fishing trip on the Okaw River east of Centralia, Illinois, and for a week saw no newspapers. When I returned home August 1st, I was astounded to learn that war had been declared and that the armies of the European countries were mobilizing. I realized it was the greatest war known in the history of the world and appreciated the fact that I was living at a time which would be set down as one of the most important in all history. At the same time, it all seemed distant to me and it did not appear possible that such an event could ever draw America into it.

My sympathies the first few weeks were with Germany[1] because of her reputed efficiency, but only for a short time, because public opinion gradually turned in favor of France, England, and Belgium. Some people predicted that we would be drawn into it, but I never agreed. Even when the *Lusitania* was sunk in 1915, it seemed to me out of the question even to think that our country would be drawn into such a terrible conflict. However, dating from that event, public opinion seemed to be more uniform. The presidential elec-

1. Such sympathies were more or less typical of American public opinion until the reality of German violation of Belgian neutrality and British propaganda about alleged German atrocities set in.

tion of 1916, while won by President Wilson on the slogan of "Peace, Prosperity and Preparedness," seemed to bring the matter to an issue.

Fort Sheridan, Illinois, 1917. The fog came in from Lake Michigan on the left. *Editor's collection.*

In February 1917, the Germans commenced unrestricted warfare on merchant ships entering British or French ports. In view of the previous notices by President Wilson, this was interpreted by our public as a virtual declaration of war on the United States. I could not fully realize the situation, although with my roommate and most intimate friend, Dr. Chester B. Parkinson, who was also a distant cousin, I discussed this situation every day. He foresaw the coming of war and joined a Preparedness League, whereby, as a dentist, he was studying in advance for service in the army. The two of us discussed the situation with the other friends of our group: Dr. Jesse T. McDavid; his brother Joel McDavid, an attorney; Byron Merris; Carl Nulty; and others. They all seemed to be preparing for war, but I still could not realize that it was coming.

When war was actually declared by Congress in April 1917, the newspapers stated that it was not the intention of our War Department to send a large army to France. It intended to send only a few divisions of regular army troops as moral support. I did not care to enlist to be one of a few who should spend a year or two in France. I did resolve, however, that I would see to it that when the war was over, no one would have anything on me as to the manner in which I had served.

Within another two or three weeks it was decided that the United States should raise a large national army. The papers announced that beginning the first week of May, officer training camps would open in many parts of the country to train officers for the army. Applications were being received, five or six for each one that could be accommodated in these camps. My work at Millikin University,[2] where I was employed, was just six weeks from finishing the college year. When I discussed the advisability of applying for admission to the First Officers' Training Camp, I was persuaded to finish out my year until commencement and close up the business of the office, then try to enter the second camp, which was to begin in August.

Fort Sheridan, Illinois, 1917. Interior of typical quarters. *Editor's collection.*

Following out the above program, on July 4, 1917, I formally applied for admission to the Second Officers' Training Camp beginning August 27th. July 28th, I received notice to report to Springfield, Illinois, for examination August 2nd. There were over a hundred men from Decatur who received similar notice. Only eight, however, were finally ordered to report to the second training camp. I was fortunate to be one of the eight.

Why I should be selected in preference to many who were not was more than I could understand, excepting that, during the interview with Colonel Stacey, the examining officer, I claimed a reading knowledge of German and admitted having taken a few private French lessons. I also had the recommendation of my good friend Admiral C. B. T. Moore of Decatur. He had spent his life in the Navy and had retired a year or two previously. At any rate, I considered myself very fortunate in being ordered to report to Fort Sheridan August 27, 1917.

On the above date, I traveled to Fort Sheridan. The other men from Decatur were William Collins; William J. Armstrong, a Spanish War Veteran; Verne E. Rogers, Athletic Director of Decatur High School; Ralph Tenney; Herbert

2. Located in Decatur, Illinois.

Hessler; and Louis Fisher. Also Arden Hamman and Henry Currie were two Decatur boys who remained over from the first camp. In addition, Wallace Holcombe and many others of my acquaintance throughout the state were in this second camp.

On arriving at Fort Sheridan, we lined up in front of the gymnasium and at a certain point in the line were told to fall out and join one of four lines forming ahead: one each for those who wished to join the Infantry, Artillery, Coast Artillery, or Engineers. Bill Collins, Bill Armstrong, and I were in line together, and we all stepped into the line that was registering for Infantry training. The three of us, along with Verne Rogers, were assigned to Company 22 and directed to the barracks, where we received second-hand uniforms and were assigned to cots in the barracks room.

Sour Note. B-Flat bugle of D Company, 151st Machine Gun Battalion. A similar bugle left an impression on Parkinson his first night at Fort Sheridan. He listened intently as "Taps" slowly signaled that the day was done. Then some wise guy in the barracks punctuated the tune with a sour note: "That's what they'll play over your grave." *World War History & Art Museum (WWHAM) collection, Alliance, Ohio.*

That night at 9:30, for the first time I heard the bugle sound "Taps" as a signal that the day's work was done. It made quite an impression on me, and the impression was greatly deepened by a wise crack from one of the men in the Company who said, "Listen, there goes 'Taps'!" And after it had finished he said, "That's what they'll play over your grave."[3]

Next day, the company formed on the drill ground of the barracks and all lined up according to height, the tallest on the right. There was only one man to my right, so I had the position of the second tallest man in the company. This put me in the First Squad. Will Collins was also in this same squad, together with Clark Donnigan, Chicago; Tom Heffron, Chicago; William Sweeny, Chicago; Ed Clarkson, Rock Island; and Irving Crego, Aurora. These men formed the First Squad. Each of us took turns for a week at a time being the Corporal of the squad.

The company commander was Captain Gresham Griggs, formerly of Bloomington, Illinois. He had been commissioned in the first school, and he was assisted by Captain George Des Loge and First Sergeant Davanon. Former

3. On a similar note, before assaulting Belleau Wood in June of 1918, Marines of the 2nd Division could be heard singing their own dark parody of George M. Cohan's hit song: *The Yanks are coming! The Yanks are coming! But we won't come back, We'll be buried over there.*

Lieutenant Governor of Illinois Barratt O'Hara was a Private in this company and Elmer Doocy, a former football star of Wesleyan University at Bloomington, was also in Company 22.

After a period of several weeks training, the entire regiment formed on the drill field, staked out trenches, and began digging. We dug all day in the hot sun and then occupied the trenches that night while part of the regiment attacked in a sham battle. The next day was also spent digging, and again the next night standing guard in expectation of another attack from the other half of the regiment.

We also spent several days on the rifle range. I proved to be a very poor marksman. On one occasion, the First Squad was shooting against another squad. Owing to my poor marksmanship, I waited until last to fire. The score was very close, and on my last shot the bullet hit the dirt halfway to the target, but the man in the pits at the target signaled that I had made a bull's-eye. The shot was a ricochet.[4] After it struck the ground, it glanced straight to the center of the bull's-eye. This shot won the match for our squad by two points. On the final score for the range I ranked about 109th out of 114 men in the company. On other work, however, such as mathematics and written tests, I usually was among the first dozen.

Lucky Shot. The rifle range at Fort Sheridan, Illinois, 1917. This is where a ricochet by Parkinson won a shooting match for his squad. *Editor's collection.*

4. Parkinson cleverly embellished this story by omission when he told it to his grandson (the editor) as a boy. With a broad grin he would punctuate hitting the bull's-eye by saying, "*So they made me a lieutenant*". He conveniently left out the rest of his training to make it sound like this lucky shot won his commission, not just the contest.

During the camp, we were frequently honored by the attendance of famous personages. Governor Lowden once spoke to the entire regiment. I recall, when in a grand burst of eloquence, he made the statement, "Men of Illinois, I envy you!" Then someone of the crowd yelled, "Why don't you join up? There's still lots of room." This was an uncalled-for remark, because Governor Lowden had served in the Spanish American War and was at that time almost sixty years of age.

Digging In. Troops digging a trench at Fort Sheridan, Illinois, 1917. *Editor's collection.*

On another occasion, ex-President Roosevelt came to our camp. All three regiments passed in review in honor of the ex-Commander-in-Chief of the army. Afterward, we assembled in close formation to hear an address by him. I was in the First Squad, and therefore in the first rank immediately in front of the Colonel. Newspaper photographers snapping from behind included me in the picture. I cherish the copies of these prints which I have obtained.

It was thought by the instructors that if a man were taught to mix it with the boxing gloves he would develop an aggressive spirit which would be beneficial in a bayonet fight. Therefore, James J. Delaney, the man who trained James J. Jeffries into a heavyweight championship, was engaged to train us in boxing. The company marched to the drill field and lined up in company front. The front line about faced, and there each man looked into the eyes of his opponent. Boxing gloves were distributed, and all the men of the company practiced leading and blocking according to instructions of J. J. Delaney from a high platform. Meanwhile, the men of all other companies stood around and watched until it became their turn with the gloves.

Zig-Zag. Overhead view of the trench system at Fort Sheridan, Illinois, 1917. *Editor's collection.*

When I faced about, I found before me Tom Heffron, a young man not quite twenty-one who had won some amateur boxing championship at the University of Chicago. He was a good boxer, and he proceeded to demonstrate the fact to the audience at my expense. Jim Delaney had coached us to lead once with the left hand while blocking with the right hand and had coached to go no farther, but to repeat this one drill until it was perfected. Heffron did not stop, however. He began mixing it at once and soon had me outclassed. We attracted the notice of Jim Delaney, who stopped the whole drill and had all of them watching the two of us.

I did not enjoy being so conspicuous, but since we were on trial for commissions I was not going to show a yellow streak. I took my medicine standing up and at the same time landed a few telling blows on him. Since we mixed it so heavily, the men of our company thought we were angry and tried to get us into a grudge fight. This was a month before camp ended, and during the remaining month other men of the camp tried to get Heffron and me to fight it out. Neither of us wanted to, as we had no grudge. He was satisfied when he attracted the attention of the higher officers. The fight occurred just before noon. Although he had outclassed me, by the time he reached the barracks he was so sick he did not eat any dinner. He was tired and had a cut lip. I was tired and had been pounded around a good bit, but it did not affect my appetite and next day I was O.K.

I go into detail about this fight because we later greeted each other on the field of the Second Battle of the Marne on Hill 212, just a short time before he was killed in action.

During the later part of October, our regiment again went into the trenches. It was cold and rainy, and a heavy mist came off Lake Michigan and chilled us through to the marrow. The trenches were knee deep in mud everywhere. We could not show our heads above the parapets because we were supposed to be simulating battle conditions. We were ordered to keep below the surface under penalty of losing our chance at a commission. Three days of this hardship on the shores of Lake Michigan, twenty-eight miles from Chicago, were the most severe test on my physique of everything that I actually experienced, even later on the battlefields. The difference, of course, was that at Fort Sheridan, we were not under hostile fire.

Teddy Roosevelt Addressing Troops at Fort Sheridan, Illinois, Fall 1917. N. P. Parkinson is wearing sunglasses in the front row. He received this position in the First Squad by virtue of being the second tallest man in Company 22. *Photo courtesy of Greg T. Parkinson.*

The camp ended November 27th. On the night of November 26th, our Company had a farewell banquet at the Union League Club in Chicago. E. P. Christopherson, in our company, was an ex-regular army man and, because of his experience with routing paperwork, had been working at headquarters, assisting in getting out final orders. That night at the Union League Club he called me to one side and told me that he had seen an order on which my name appeared at the head of a list that was ordered to overseas duty in France. I had realized all the time the possibility of being sent to France, but I had

Getting the Point. Company 22 in bayonet training at Fort Sheridan, Illinois, late 1917. In front on the far right is N. P. Parkinson wearing the moustache. The neat formation was artificial, staged as it was for a photo opportunity. *Photo courtesy of Greg T. Parkinson.*

Commissioned. Second Lieutenant Nellis Paul Parkinson upon his commission at Fort Sheridan in 1917. *Editor's collection.*

never dared hope that I would be selected. He also told similar news to Donnigan, Carlson, Collins, and Rogers. We were all delighted at our assignments.

Next day, November 27th, the final day of the camp, sure enough, I received a commission as Second Lieutenant and an order directing me to report at Hoboken, New Jersey, January 15, 1918, for duty overseas. This meant that I had the time between November 27th and January 15th to prepare for the trip.

Immediately I began buying my equipment and uniforms. It required several hundred dollars, but through the thoughtfulness of several wealthy men of Chicago, the Fort Sheridan Association was formed for the purpose of making loans to members to buy officer equipment. In this way I borrowed $150, which enabled me to finish out my equipment which cost, all told, approximately $400. We had been paid $100 per month during the three

Army Officers' Clothing

Officers' Dress Uniforms.

Made of a good grade navy blue all wool uniform cloth. Well finished in all details. Shipping weight, 4¾ pounds.

No. 6L20001½ Price of coat, with braid trim and collar devices, and pants **$45.00**

Plain White Cotton Duck Uniform. Shipping weight, 3¾ pounds.

No. 6L20002½ Price of coat and pants, collar devices included **$10.00**

Officers' Service Uniforms.

Olive drab wool serge cloth (Summer weight). Shpg. wt., 4¾ lbs.

No. 6L20003½ Price of coat and pants, collar devices included **$35.00**

Olive drab wool serge cloth (Winter weight). Shipping weight, 5¼ pounds.

No. 6L20004½ Price of coat and pants, collar devices included **$45.00**

Uniform, made of olive drab cotton khaki cloth. Shpg. wt., 3¾ lbs.

No. 6L20005½ Price of coat and pants, collar devices included **$15.00**

Enlisted Men's Uniform, made same style as No. 6L20005½, except not as good in quality.

No. 6L20014½ Price of coat and pants (without collar devices and sleeve stripes).... **$8.50**

Officers' 16-Ounce Meiton Olive Drab Wool Work Suit. Shpg. wt., 5 lbs.

No. 6L20016½ Price of coat and pants, collar devices included **$35.00**

Always state style of collar devices or ornaments wanted on coats.

Our prices on uniforms include collar ornaments and sleeve stripes only, unless otherwise stated. State style of ornaments wanted on collar. Caps, insignia, belts, sabers, leggings and shoes are quoted separately on this and other pages.

Every garment is made to order and cut to individual measurement. We require ten to fourteen days for making uniforms. On caps allow us five to seven days. In ordering use special order blank enclosed.

Officers' Caps.

For dress uniforms. White Duck Cap, complete with extra white cover and ornament. Matches Uniform No. 6L20002½. Sizes, 6¾ to 7¾. **State size wanted.** Shipping weight, 1½ pounds.

No. 6L20022½ Price, each.... **$6.50**

Navy Blue Uniform Cloth Cap with ornament. Matches Uniform No. 6L20001½. Sizes, 6¾ to 7¾. **State size wanted.** Shipping weight, 1½ pounds.

No. 6L20023½ Price, each.... **$6.50**

Service Cap.

For all army officers. Olive Drab Wool Serge Cap with ornament. Cloth matches Uniforms Nos. 6L20003½ and 6L20004½. Can also be worn with Uniforms Nos. 6L20005½, 6L20014½ and 6L20016½. Sizes, 6¾ to 7¾. **State size wanted.** Shipping weight, 1½ pounds.

No. 6L20024½ Price, each... **$3.00**

Same style as above, made of better quality cloth. Shipping weight, 1½ pounds.

No. 6L20021½ Price, each... **$4.50**

Waterproof Cap Cover.

Olive drab, rubberized cloth. Fits over top of officers' cap, thereby making top of cap waterproof; cover can be folded and carried in your pocket. Shipping weight, 3 oz.

No. 6L20208 Price, each...... **38c**

Canvas Army Puttees.

U. S. Army Regulation Canvas Puttees. Also used by Home Guards. Olive drab color. Sizes, 13 to 17 in. calf measurement. **State size wanted.** Shipping weight, 12 ounces.

No. 6L20083

Price, per pair.. **$1.30**

Army Service Hat.

Regulation Montana Peak Army Service Hat. A good grade felt. Sizes, 6¾ to 7¾. **State size.**

No. 33L06279 Each...... **$2.50**

Same as above, but made of strictly first quality felt.

No. 33L06360 Each...... **$5.00**

Hat Cords.

No. 6L20042 Officers' Gilt and Black Silk Hat Cord. Price, each.......... **$1.25**

No. 6L20025 As above, but better quality. Price, each.......... **$1.75**

No. 6L20026 Cords for infantry, engineer, artillery, signal, quartermaster, hospital, cavalry and rookie. **State which is wanted.** Price, each. **.20c** Shipping wt., 4 oz.

Hat Strap.

Leather Hat Strap for Montana peak hat. Shipping wt., 2 ounces.

No. 6L20027 Price, each.............. **10c**

Wool Cap.

Rough Finish Wool Cap; outside pulldown band. A warm, comfortable cap for general wear. Small, medium and large in size. **State which is wanted.** Shpg. wt., 6 oz.

No. 93L04632 Gray mixture. Price...... **$1.00**

No. 93L04633 Brown mixture. Price...... **$1.00**

Canvas Leggings.

The latest U. S. Regulation style. Olive drab color canvas. Full side lace legging with canvas strap. Sizes, 13 to 17 in. **State size wanted.** Shpg. wt., 1 pound.

No. 6L20088

Price, per pair.. **$1.40**

Leather Army Puttees.

First quality heavy tan color grain cowhide leather. Sizes, 14 to 17 in. calf measurement. **State size wanted.** Shipping weight, 1¾ pounds.

No. 6L20084

Price, per pair.............. **$7.00**

As above, split cowhide leather, pigskin grain, waterproof finish...

Spring Style Leather Army Puttees.

First quality heavy brown color grain cowhide leather. Spring fastener; no calf strap. Sizes, 14 to 17 inches calf measure. **State size wanted.** Shipping wt., 1¾ lbs.

No. 6L20098

Price, per pair.. **$8.00**

Knit Puttees.

The latest style Knit Puttee, with cuff. Mostly used while reposing. Can also be worn under regular Puttees. Olive drab wool yarn; tie string top and bottom adjustable to any size. Shipping weight, 9 ounces.

No. 6L20089

Per pair. **$2.95**

Spiral Cloth Puttees.

Olive Drab Color Woven Wool Cloth Spiral Puttees. Snug fitting and easily adjusted. Officially adopted by the Government. Shipping weight, 12 ounces.

No. 6L20086

Price, per pair **$4.00**

...ntee Every Article Purchased From Us to Satisfy You Perfectly.

Uniforms For Sale. Page from the Sears, Roebuck Military Equipment Catalog, circa 1917-1918. *World War History & Art Museum (WWHAM) collection, Alliance, Ohio.*

Cover of Sears, Roebuck Military Equipment Catalog, circa 1917-1918. American officers outfitted themselves at their own expense during World War I. They purchased their gear from retailers like Sears. *World War History & Art Museum (WWHAM) collection, Alliance, Ohio.*

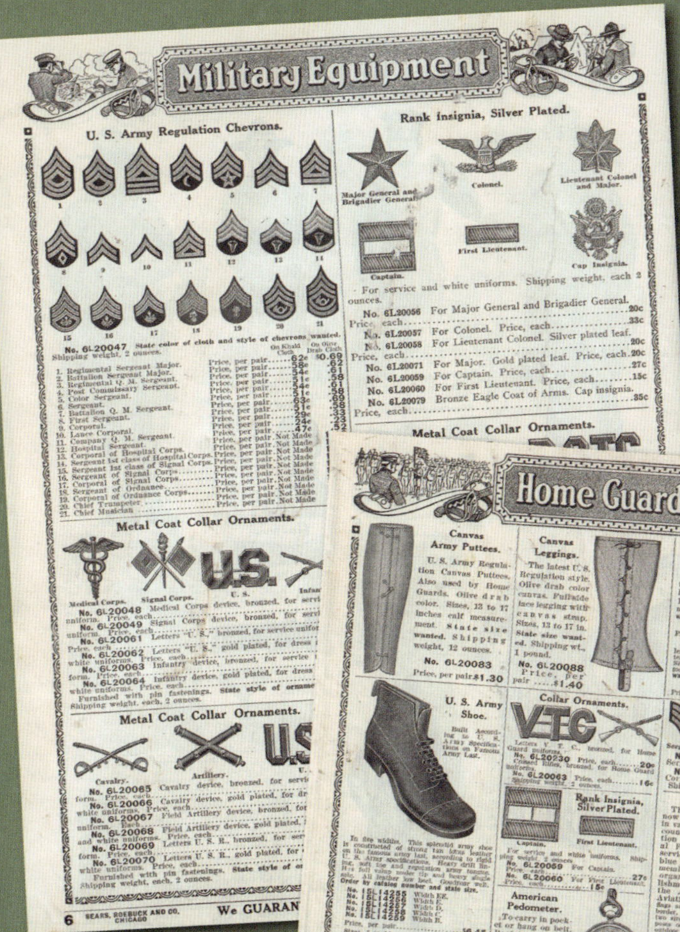

Military Equipment

U. S. Army Regulation Chevrons.

No. 6L20047 State color of cloth and style of chevrons wanted. Shipping weight, 2 ounces.

1. Regimental Sergeant Major.
2. Battalion Sergeant Major.
3. Regimental Q. M. Sergeant.
4. Post Commissary Sergeant.
5. Color Sergeant.
6. Sergeant.
7. Battalion Q. M. Sergeant.
8. First Sergeant.
9. Corporal.
10. Lance Corporal.
11. Company Q. M. Sergeant.
12. Hospital Sergeant.
13. Corporal of Hospital Corps.
14. Sergeant 1st class of Hospital Corps.
15. Sergeant 1st class of Signal Corps.
16. Sergeant of Signal Corps.
17. Corporal of Signal Corps.
18. Sergeant of Ordnance.
19. Corporal of Ordnance Corps.
20. Chief Trumpeter.
21. Chief Musician.

Rank Insignia, Silver Plated.

Major General and Brigadier General. Colonel. Lieutenant Colonel and Major. Captain. First Lieutenant. Cap Insignia.

For service and white uniforms. Shipping weight, each 2 ounces.

No. 6L20056 For Major General and Brigadier General. Price, each ... 20c

No. 6L20057 For Colonel. Price, each ... 33c

No. 6L20058 For Lieutenant Colonel. Silver plated leaf. Price, each ... 20c

No. 6L20071 For Major. Gold plated leaf. Price, each 20c

No. 6L20059 For Captain. Price, each ... 27c

No. 6L20060 For First Lieutenant. Price, each ... 15c

No. 6L20079 Bronze Eagle Coat of Arms. Cap insignia. Price, each ... 35c

Metal Coat Collar Ornaments.

Metal Coat Collar Ornaments.

6 SEARS, ROEBUCK AND CO. CHICAGO — We GUARAN

Insignia For Sale. Page from the Sears, Roebuck Military Equipment Catalog, circa 1917-1918. *World War History & Art Museum (WWHAM) collection, Alliance, Ohio.*

Home Guard Equipment

Canvas Army Puttees. Canvas Leggings. Leather Army Puttees. Army Slip-On Sweater.

No. 6L20083 Price, per pair ... $1.30

No. 6L20088 Price, per pair ... $1.40

No. 6L20084 ... $6.75

No. 6L20085 ... $4.40

No. 6L20188 Price, each ... $3.50

U. S. Army Shoe. Collar Ornaments. Chevrons. For Home Guard Officers. Officers' Leather Belt.

Rank Insignia, Silver Plated. Service Flags. Police Whistle.

No. 6L20199 Price, ea. $1.60

American Pedometer. No. 6L25229 Price, each ... 95c

Men's Pocket Knife. Jungle Mosquito Protector.

Vacuum Bottles. Vacuum Food Canteen.

The Colt Machine Gun.

No. 6L20145½ Price ... $865.00

Leather Preservative. Preserves Harness by Keeping It Pliable. Makes Two Pairs of Shoes Do the Work of Three.

For Parcel Post Rates and Information, See Inside Front Cover.

SEARS, ROEBUCK AND CO. CHICAGO 11

Machine Gun Anyone? For $865.00 one could order a Colt-Marlin machine gun from a Sears catalog in 1917 and have the weapon delivered to your doorstep. *World War History & Art Museum (WWHAM) collection, Alliance, Ohio.*

months of school, but from that our meals had been deducted, so it required more than our entire three months' pay to buy our equipment.

I visited Centralia and Decatur and prepared to travel overseas, although I was not permitted to divulge my sailing date, nor the place where I was to report.

On January 8th, while in Decatur on my way to the port of embarkation, I received news that Mother had fallen on the ice the day before and broken her hip. I knew to return to see her would make another hard farewell for her. I merely telephoned her and made no change in my plans.

On the night of January 9th, I took the Pennsylvania train for New York City in the midst of a blizzard, with ten inches of snow and the temperature 22 degrees below zero. The train arrived in New York City nineteen hours late, but as we were travelling in Pullman cars we were comfortable.

The USS St. Louis. The ship that transported Lieutenant N. P. Parkinson from Hoboken to England. *Editor's collection.*

On arriving in New York City I reported immediately, on January 15th, to the Embarkation Officer at Hoboken, N.J. and was told to return January 19th to receive orders. This gave me four days in New York City. I stayed at the McAlpin Hotel, and Lieutenant Verne Rogers and I shared the same room. Across the hall, Lieutenants Ed Carlson and Adrian C. Edwards shared a room. Adjoining us were Lieutenant Paul Derrickson and Edward J. Veasey sharing a third room. All of these men, except Lieutenant Veasey, were from Company 22. The six of us spent much time together during the five days in New York. It was well we could not see into the future, because Lieutenants Derrickson, Veasey, and Edwards were killed in action.

On January 19th, we reported for sailing orders and were told to report the next day to Vessel 529, Pier No. 62, at the foot of West 32nd Street, ready to go on board ship. The ship proved to be the American Line mail steamer *St. Louis*. During the time of the Spanish-American War, it was the fastest vessel afloat. So it was converted from a merchant ship to an auxiliary cruiser. I recall as a boy having read a story of the Spanish War in which the hero was a member of the crew of the Auxiliary Cruiser *St. Louis*. The ship was now painted in camouflage. Six-inch guns were mounted fore and aft and manned by U.S. Navy gunners. I was assigned to stateroom #252 on the second deck, first class, berth #2, with Lieutenants Ed Carlson, Nels W. Peterson, and a fourth man whom I do not recall. I believe it was either Lieutenant Clyde H. Wasson or William Hale. The ship hove anchor about noon on Sunday, January 20, 1918, and I was off for France traveling as a casual officer on a passenger liner.

CHAPTER 2: ARRIVAL IN FRANCE

THE SUBMARINE ZONE, LIVERPOOL, SOUTHAMPTON, ACROSS THE CHANNEL, LE HAVRE, CHATILLON-SUR-SEINE, TROYES, CHALONS, NANCY, HOÉVILLE, RANSEY WOODS, 12TH FRENCH INFANTRY, THE GERMAN DRIVE MARCH 21, 1918.

When the *St. Louis* was ready to sail, all military passengers were ordered below the deck so that German spies in the harbor would not know that the ship was carrying troops. I was greatly disappointed in not having a sight of the Statue of Liberty as we pulled out. We were kept below deck for about two hours. At the end of that time we were allowed to come on deck again, but there was no land in sight. The sun was just sinking on the ocean horizon, and off to the north a Belgian relief ship with a large red cross painted on it was sailing east.

That night, in the main dining room of the ship, all officers were introduced to each other and assigned regular places at the table. After our first meal, we were given a splendid talk by Dr. Harry Emerson Fosdick,[1] a passenger on this ship, on the subject, "Don't Be a Little Man In a Big Age." (The following May, I again heard Dr. Fosdick when he came to our battalion on the front at Pexonne as a Y.M.C.A. speaker.)

1. Fosdick was a prominent Presbyterian pastor of liberal persuasion.

On the morning of January 21st, I began to be seasick. Of course, it was no fun, but I recall that I was pleasantly surprised that seasickness was no worse. I had always been led to believe that when seasick, a man felt about ready to die. Although I was uncomfortable and kept only a part of my meals down, it did not keep me from enjoying the trip. We sailed 390 miles the first day and 411 miles the second. Because of rainstorms and squalls the sea got pretty rough on this date. At five P.M. it was reported that the steering gear was broken. The vessel appeared to drift with the wind for several hours until repairs were completed at four A.M. next morning. Without the power of the engine to cut through the waves it made sailing rougher, and of course those of us inclined to seasickness were still more uncomfortable.

By January 24th, which was Thursday, I enjoyed sitting on the deck. The moonlight evening and the salt sea air gave a very pleasant setting for the sea voyage. We had a vaudeville show in the dining room that night and another address by Dr. Fosdick. We also heard a speech by Col. Farmer, the ranking Army officer.

January 26th was my birthday. For dinner that night the menu cards showed roast turkey. It was canned, but good nevertheless. All cooking was by English chefs. The seasoning was not popular, but it was all first class. I wrote several letters home on this night using ship stationary, but in order to get through censorship, I, myself, cut the name *St. Louis* off of each sheet that I used. I mailed the letters at the ship post office, and as soon as we reached Liverpool they were started by British mail back to the U.S.A.

On January 27th, the Captain of the ship wirelessed ahead for a convoy of destroyers to escort us through the submarine zone. He then gave us a scare by calling our attention to the fact that, of course, the Germans too would intercept the message, decipher it, and be waiting for us at the appointed meeting place. Since these were the closing days of the first year of unrestricted submarine warfare – and also the Kaiser's birthday – it was expected that the enemy submarines would be making a special effort to sink Allied ships. In addition, the *St. Louis* was a marked ship, not only because of her size, but because she had driven off a German submarine that attacked on a previous voyage, for which exploit the newspapers gave the crew much favorable publicity. We were sure that the enemy would be "laying for us".

On January 28th, we were met by the destroyers at the rendezvous and escorted up the Irish Coast toward England. We were expecting to sight land anytime, dock that night, and disembark early Tuesday morning. The sea was quiet, and we could see fish playing in the waves. We entered Liverpool harbor at 3:45 A.M. January 29th, after steaming up the Mersey River and "crossing the bar" made famous by Lord Tennyson's poem. About noon, we left the *St. Louis* and were ferried ashore. One of the guards on the ferry boat was a British veteran of the Marne. As we stood on the boat we noticed a conspicuous building with a large dome. "What building is that?", one of the Americans asked. "That is the Globe Building," the guard answered. "It is quite new. In fact, it has only been built about thirty years."

Our baggage passed through customs without inspection and, as quickly as we could identify our own and buy a lunch, we were guided aboard a train headed for Southampton. They were small coaches, with doors opening on the sides like cabs. In our coach there were seats for only thirteen. The train moved very rapidly, however, even though the coaches were small.

We had lunch at Birmingham, passed through Oxford and Reading, and arrived at Southampton about midnight. After we detrained at the station, a Marine Sergeant guided our group of about 100 officers to a rest camp. It was a cold, frosty night. The moon was shining brightly as we stood under a great spreading oak tree in this rest camp to draw three blankets each. After I had drawn three, I realized that they would not be enough to keep me warm. Therefore, I again stood in line at the end and got three more, so that I had six blankets. Next day, we went downtown and saw an old Roman arch and several other historical landmarks. We were not permitted to buy food, but I did buy a Sam Brown belt. There were many holly trees and big English oaks growing in this region.

Our breakfast was served by the British and consisted of a cup of muddy coffee and potatoes boiled with the jackets on and laid in the center of the table in a small net of a sack with each man to help himself. Likewise, a plate of bacon, about a slice for each man, was placed in the center of the table, and we each had two slices of whole wheat bread.

At four P.M., after returning the blankets we had drawn, we reported at the dock and embarked on British transport No. 221, which proved to be the *Atrim*. Shortly afterward, the ship hove anchor and started out through the shoals. Buoys appeared everywhere, showing where mines had been laid. A mine-laying ship with a destroyer convoy was also going out to sea. Many castles and fine homes appeared on the banks as we went down this smooth channel from Southampton leading to the rough English Channel.

During the two days we were in England, we saw the food question was becoming serious due to the many vessels being sunk by the enemy submarines. I did not have a single meal where I did not leave the table almost as hungry as when I first sat down. I anxiously looked forward to supper on the ship, hoping that it would at least be as good as on the *St. Louis*. None of the army officers, however, could enter the dining room until the ship's crew had finished. Then we entered according to rank. It was almost 7:00 when the colonels and lieutenant colonels first sat down. Only a few could be accommodated at a time, and there were so many majors, captains, and 1st lieutenants who outranked me that it looked like it would be almost breakfast time before my turn would come.

Even outside the dining room there were seats for only about half of us, so the other half had to stand. These seats were in the salon, where the air soon became foul because it was packed so full of men. It was too chilly out on deck to sleep, but by pacing the deck we could keep warm and get fresh air. It was very tiresome, however, pacing the deck on a gnawing stomach when I knew that I would have nothing to eat until the colonels, majors, captains, and 1st lieutenants leisurely finished their meal. It gave me an idea, however.

So when my turn did come at 10:00, I went to the foot of the list so that I would not have to give up my seat at the table to someone else. I planned to sleep there until morning. Finally, about 11:00 P.M., I went into the dining room with the last bunch. There were only three or four of us, and all the tables were served freely with a supper of whole wheat bread, coffee, jam, cold smoked tongue, and cold roast beef and ham. Since there were only three or four of us, we all were able to eat our fill. We then laid our heads over the table and slept until 6:00 in the morning, when the steward awakened us to spread the table for breakfast. We were served a good breakfast at the first table before the colonels and majors were ready to get up.

Between naps, while sleeping in the dining room, I realized that the ship was no longer in motion. It had entered the mouth of the Seine River and docked at Le Havre. At 7:30 A.M., we strode down the gangplank and set foot on French soil. As our baggage was unloaded from the ship it was loaded on a truck, while we officers formed a column and marched to a rest camp, the location of which I do not remember, except that it was uphill all the way. As about 100 of we officers marched through the streets, French children ran before us singing "Tipperary" and begging for pennies. Halfway up the long steep hill a window opened and a lady unfurled an American flag, the first we had seen since leaving the United States. We answered with a cheer, then saluted and passed on.

At the rest camp, we were each issued six blankets and assigned two together in a small cone-shaped tent with board floors. Lieutenant Forward and I slept in the same tent. We put six blankets under us and six over us and slept warm. We had meals at the British officers' club, where wine and tea were plentiful at all hours. I was thoroughly disgusted with a few of the American officers who, in my opinion, disgraced themselves here by drunkenness. So far, I had never tasted liquor, wine, or beer, and did not until Chatillon-sur-Seine, when I learned I was going to spend two weeks with the French. Then deliberately, on separate evenings, I tried out wine, beer, champagne, and cognac so I would at least know what to expect while with the French.

At this British rest camp, we became acquainted with some veteran British officers and saw many Negro troops from British East India. Of course, they spoke a different language.

We were aroused at 2:00 next morning, February 1st, to prepare to entrain. We turned back in our borrowed blankets, and while it was still dark marched to the railroad station at Le Havre. Of course, we were way ahead of time. We loaded our baggage on the train and stood for hours on the siding. Finally, after much worrying by a nervous engineer colonel who tried to command the train, all were aboard and the train pulled out at 7:30 A.M.

The route of travel was through Rouen and Mantes to Versailles, around Paris, then through Esternay, Sezanne, Soummesous, Vitry, Blesme, Joinville, and Chaumont, then back to Chatillon-sur-Seine. At Mantes, while the train stopped, two French girls called through the iron fence. Several of us went over and tried out our knowledge of the French language. As the train prepared to move on we obtained their addresses and later exchanged post cards with them.

At St. Dizier, British ladies of the Red Cross served us cheese sandwiches and hot coffee with cognac. The country through which we passed was beautiful, but east of Versailles it was marked with the scars of battle. Shot-up buildings, stumped trees, and French and German soldiers' graves told us that the war zone was not far away. The train stood all night in the yards at Chaumont after a two-day trip across France. Next morning, a detachment of officers from Chaumont[2] and Langres boarded our train as it pulled out for Chatillon. Among these were Lieutenants Chapman, Nusser, Eastman, and Sundvall of Company 22 at Fort Sheridan. At Chatillon, we were all assigned to the Second Corps School for special training in infantry weapons.

We were quartered in a reclaimed chateau bearing the date 1688 on a gable window. During the First Battle of the Marne, this building had been used for military headquarters by Marshall Joffre. It was shaped like a "U" and had a moat around it and a dungeon below. We could have no lights at night other than candles, concealed lanterns, and our own pocket flashes. On rising each morning, all of us would go down to the moat and break the ice to shave and wash in ice water in February.

On Monday, February 4th, all officers were lined up to be divided into classes. So far as possible, we were to be permitted to select the weapon on which we were to specialize. As we all stood in company front, those who wanted to take special training in machine guns were ordered to step three paces forward. About half of the entire group stepped forward. This was several times the number there was room for, so they started counting from the right. There was room for 94. I was number 93 and barely got in the class of my choice. About a hundred or more were disappointed.

At this school we were given instructions on the Hotchkiss machine gun and the Colt pistol. We passed many written examinations and practical tests on the field and range. The entire theme of this school was to train to break through the trenches into open warfare[3] at all costs. The streets in this village were narrow and dark. The sidewalk in one place was 18 inches wide and was built flush against a stone building on one side and the curbing on the other. This was exceptionally narrow, however. I noted at this time that I made good progress with the French language.

2. Chaumont was where General Pershing had his headquarters for the A.E.F.

3. General Pershing was a strong advocate of open warfare (by fire and movement over open ground) as opposed to static trench warfare.

After the school had been underway some time, Major Scott (the chief instructor of our school and son of General Hugh L. Scott) and Lieutenant Siberling selected the best crews for a night field problem. I was one of the four. This special night problem was to be in conjunction with all other branches of the infantry, and the machine guns were to fire an overhead barrage while the infantry, Stokes mortars, grenade throwers, and other branches of the infantry were to advance under cover of our barrage and their own fire.

Old Faithful. U.S. Marines of the 77th Company, 6th Machine Gun Battalion, 2nd Division dug in with their French Hotchkiss machine gun. Twelve American divisions in France (including the 42nd) were equipped with French Hotchkiss machine guns. For the most part, the Hotchkiss machine gun was a reliable weapon, much less prone to jamming than the earlier French St. Etienne. *Photo courtesy of David Fisher.*

When firing machine guns at an invisible target, the range is regulated by instruments known as "bubbles," or gun levels. They are built on somewhat the same principle as a carpenter's level and were laid on the sights of the machine guns in order to assure the right elevation for correct range. It is unsafe to shoot overhead fire without testing with a level. Just a few minutes before the demonstration was to begin, they discovered there was no gun level in the group. It was really Major Scott's oversight, but he passed the buck to someone else. Meanwhile, there we stood with zero hour almost at hand. He roared to Lieutenant Chance to send someone after that bubble. Lieutenant Chance turned to Lieutenant Hutchinson and asked him to go. "Not Hutchinson," roared Major Scott, "He's too old."

At this time, I saw the opportunity to attract favorable attention that I had been waiting for. Therefore, I spoke up and volunteered to get a gun level and started off on a three- or four-mile run back to the Patronage. At Fort Sheridan, those officers who were always making themselves conspicuous seemed to get the higher commissions. Those of us who assumed that the Captain would call on us when he wanted to hear from us got the lower assignments. Therefore, on entering the school at Chatillon, I resolved that I would not do much of it, but at my opportunity, I would do it a few times very decidedly. This was one occasion, and apparently it worked, because I received one of the most favorable assignments after this school closed.

In about forty minutes, I came back on the run. I handed two levels to Major Scott and received a gracious "thank you". Meanwhile, the maneuver had started. Major Scott had estimated the range and taken a chance. The bullets were a little wild and drove the observers to cover, but no damage was done. He was relieved now to have levels so as to be able to lay the guns accurately. After the maneuver was over we carried the guns back to the barracks and cleaned them as best we could by candle light. We machine gunners worked an hour after all others had gone home, but next morning, Major Scott found some dirt on the guns and ordered the entire class of 94 men under arrest and confined to quarters over Sunday. Word of this must have reached Colonel Bamford, the School Commander, because that afternoon Major Scott rescinded the order.

Standard Equipment. A crew from an American machine gun company of an infantry regiment with their French Hotchkiss machine gun. The Hotchkiss machine gun, along with the M1915 St. Etienne tripod as shown here, was standard equipment for the 151st Machine Gun Battalion. However, men of the 151st Machine Gun Battalion were not issued rifles. They needed their hands free to carry ammo boxes. *Editor's collection.*

In the chateau where we were billeted that night, we came home tired out from the demonstration. Lieutenant Nels W. Peterson, whose bunk was in the same room as mine, had made a fire in the fireplace. Those of us who occupied this room were Lieutenants L. H. Gray, Carthage, Missouri; Joseph H. Ware, Jr., Kansas City; William Murphey, St. Louis and Chicago; George R. Forster, Carthage, Missouri; Nels W. Peterson, Detroit; Wm. Hale, St. Louis and Arkansas; and Lieutenant Fanta of Wisconsin. I wrote letters home, but I received my first mail February 24th. On March 5th, I received a cablegram addressed to Lieutenant Parkinson, but it was intended for some other Lieutenant Parkinson. It was much delayed, as it had been sent on St. Valentine's Day. Lieutenant Richard D. Chapman, one of the lieutenants in this school, had married a Moss girl who lived next door to McKees in Centralia. He lived in Carbondale, but at one time he had been a teller in the Merchants State Bank in Centralia. We now spent a good deal of time together, and I helped him a good deal with his problems on indirect machine gun fire.

On the last Sunday in February came my turn for a bath in the one shower bath that had been improvised several weeks before. It was my first tub bath since leaving the *St. Louis*. The water was cold, but it was refreshing after I had shivered through.

On Monday, March 4th, the school was nearing an end. We were given a lecture on gas and two days' instruction and training in defense against gas, including the wearing of gas masks. On Friday, March 8th, I went on sick report because of a callous on the ball of my foot that had been giving me a great deal of trouble. While on sick report, I saw my name on a list of 23 that were to be sent to the French front as observers at the close of the school. Sunday, March 9th, was the final exhibition day of the school. I had no active part in the final exhibition because I had been on sick report the two days previous.

That night, at the evening meal, the list of 23 names was read and we were ordered to have baggage packed, downstairs, and out doors ready to leave for the French front at 3:00 A.M. Of course, we all arose about 2:00 A.M. and were ready at the appointed hour. We waited until 10:30 A.M. before any word came. Then, at 10:45, we rode in trucks to the railroad station, where we had orders to report to the Fourth French Army at Nancy for a two-week tour of duty, after which we were to report to the Rainbow Division.

The train pulled out at 1:00 P.M. En route, I sat with Lieutenant Sundvall. He seemed to have the war on his mind. Likewise. Lieutenant Adrian C. Edwards was rather pessimistic about chances at the front. I realized the danger, but was light-hearted about it. Both Sundvall and Edwards were killed in action, but I was never scratched. Nevertheless, Captain Taylor was the most jovial man on our train and he, too, was killed in action.

At 7:00 P.M. we were in Troyes, and stayed here until eleven. We had four hours to go about the city and to do a little bit of shopping. Next morning we were in Chalons, went to a hotel, and downtown had a view of the Cathedral. Then we took the Paris Express at 10:45 A.M. through Gondrecourt and arrived at Nancy at 4:30 P.M. Here we saw where German Gothas had dropped bombs and damaged the station and many nearby buildings.

At the station at Nancy we were met by a French Lieutenant and his chauffeur, who took us in a big fifteen-passenger French camion to the headquarters of his brigade. There the party divided, and some were taken on to the headquarters of the 12th French Regiment at Hoéville. We arrived at dark, after the

French officers had finished their evening meal. They immediately prepared food for the six American officers in our party. As we sat around the table eating, we became acquainted with these French officers at Regimental Headquarters. One of them was Lieutenant La Coste and another was Lieutenant Grostarzu. Lieutenant Grostarzu was the interpreter. The Colonel of this regiment had lived in the city of Lens before the war. When the Germans over-ran that city, all his property was destroyed and his family was held captive until they died. He was left alone, bitter in his hatred of the Germans and vitriolic in his denunciations against them.

While we were eating, a battery of French artillery nearby opened up with some harassing fire. It was the first firing that I had heard that I knew to be actual warfare. That night, we six American officers slept in hospital beds in the infirmary. Besides Lieutenant Noxon and me, there were Lieutenants Wasson and Sutherland. Lieutenant Sutherland had left a family and seemed especially serious-minded this night. It was the last time I saw him, but after the war, I learned that he was blown to pieces by a shell while on a raid with the 32nd Division.

There was another lieutenant, whose name I do not remember, who had just been married before leaving for France. He was blue and despondent. So much so that I remember commenting to Wasson that I was awfully glad that I was not leaving a wife or even a sweetheart behind. I knew that my father, mother, and sisters were much concerned about my welfare, but that would be enough for one to have on his mind without having to leave a wife and family.

Next morning, after breakfast, Lieutenant Grostarzu guided us farther forward to the headquarters of the battalion under the command of *Commandant* (Major) Esquilat. This was to be our first location. Halfway there we were met by Lieutenant Eugene Etienne. He had been notified by telephone that we were on the way. He was a splendid young French officer who spoke English perfectly and was assigned as our interpreter and guide. He was relieved of all other duties in order that he could give Lieutenant Noxon and me full attention and show us the plan of trench fortification and system of defense pertaining especially to machine gunners. He was a splendid fellow, a veteran of the Marne, Somme, Champagne, and Verdun, and wore the *Croix de Guerre* with a star and palm.

We spent the morning getting acquainted with the other French officers who ate at this battalion mess. They were Lieutenant Laval, who was the Adjutant, and Lieutenant La Coste, whom we had met the night before and who was the machine gun officer of this battalion, while Captain Roccascera, the regular machine gun officer, was on leave. There were also Lieutenants Le Deuc and Calmet. The last two were medical officers. Lieutenant Le Deuc and Captain Roccascera were natives of Algeria.

At noon on March 12th, we ate our first meal with this company of French officers. It was served in true French style by a first class chef in courses of one dish at a time. They had only a light meal at noon. The main meal was in the evening. It was rather a warm day, and when Lieutenant Noxon asked for a glass of water with his meal all laughed, and the chef brought him a glass of red wine. Throughout our stay I hardly tasted water. The water in this location was not considered safe to drink unless mixed half and half with wine. Red wine was served with each meal, and with the coffee a flask of cognac was brought in. I enjoyed the wine, but one attempt at the cognac was enough.

This regiment had been resting in this quiet sector, recuperating from losses sustained in the attack they made at Verdun seven months previous. They had been located in this area long enough to establish good communications to the rear. Therefore, they had excellent food and drink. While eating the noonday meal on this March 12th, the Germans began shelling a wooden barracks built in the woods across the road from the hut where we were eating. It had been the intention of *Commandant* Esquilat to have Lieutenant Noxon and I sleep in this same barracks, but the Germans demolished it with two or three well-directed 77s before we entered. We were therefore assigned bunks in the main dugout. This was the first hostile firing I had heard. The shells burst about 100 yards away.

In the afternoon of Tuesday, March 12th, Lieutenant Etienne guided Lieutenant Noxon and me through a portion of the front line. We went to the farthest outpost and looked across a small ravine at the German trenches on the other side. As we watched, we could see shovels of dirt being thrown from the trench on the parapet above. German troops were cleaning out the trench. We could not, however, see any helmet above the parapet. But just the same, one of the men on guard at the outpost turned his Chauchat machine gun on the spot and, of course, the digging ceased. On this day, we also visited a place where the French were running a sap from the front line under No Man's Land to where it would be underneath the German trench with the intention of setting off a mine under the enemy positions. On the way back to headquarters, German shells broke overhead and I picked up a few fragments of hot steel and mailed them home.

During the first few days, Lieutenant Etienne inquired about the cause of my decided limp. When he learned that it was a callous on the ball of my foot, he instructed his orderly to half sole my shoes, French hobnail fashion. That was my first set of hobnails, but my callous healed at once. The hard stiff sole protected the bruise until it could heal.

Each morning and afternoon, Lieutenant Etienne took us to a different part of the front line and showed us the plan of machine gun defense. On the night of March 14th, he took us to a place where French machine gunners were firing overhead on the German rear areas. First I loaded while Lieutenant Noxon fired 100 rounds, and he, in turn, loaded while I fired 100 rounds. Of course, we could not see our target and we had no idea where we were shooting. But the French sergeant in command told us we were firing on a place where the Germans were accustomed to distributing rations each evening.

While the firing continued we went through the trenches, and at the point where the fire passed over our front lines we stood under the abaque[4] to hear the crack of the machine gun bullets as they passed over our heads going toward the enemy. Later on, when my guns were firing over the advancing troops, I recalled the sound of bullets cracking overhead and knew what it meant to attacking troops to hear the sound of a protective machine gun barrage overhead.

On March 18th, while we were eating our evening meal, the Germans opened harassing fire on our positions in Ransey Woods. A shell made a direct hit on our kitchen and wounded a corporal. We all took to the cover of the trench, except Lieutenant Etienne. He dashed to the kitchen to care for the corporal. As we stood in the trenches shells began falling nearer. This was the most severe shelling I had yet been under and I was somewhat uneasy. However, I was much reassured by the easy manner in which the French officers with me faced the situation. On looking up after ducking a shell that came too close for comfort, I glanced at a poilu in the trench beside me. He seemed to be wearing a gas mask. I held my breath and put on my own mask hurriedly, but a second look at the poilu[5] showed me that he was merely wearing a beard. In the dusk, the shape of his beard was much the same shape of the style of mask used by the French.

On Sunday, March 17th, we had a special dinner celebrating St. Patrick's Day. I do not know whether the French celebrate this day very strongly or not, but they had the impression that the Americans did. Therefore, *Commandant* Esquilat bought the champagne for the dinner. I remember that at this meal they served an omelet in flaming brandy sauce. That afternoon, we went to a spot in the woods where the French were putting on a musical entertainment. We could not understand any part of it, except that I was greatly thrilled at the way they sang "Madelon."

Suddenly, two German planes dropped out of the sky to surprise and shoot down a French observation balloon. We hurried to the edge of the woods in time to see the balloon coming down in smoke and saw the white puffs of shrapnel bursting all around the two planes as they were fleeing back to Germany. The day before, a German plane had been brought down by a French plane and this attack on the observation balloon was in retaliation.

Spring flowers were blooming in the woods, and I collected a bunch of violets and mailed them home to several friends in letters.

It was on Wednesday, March 20th, that Captain Roccascera returned from leave. As was the French custom, he brought a supply of champagne and there was a jovial entertainment that evening at dinner.

4. "Abaque" is French for an arch or top of the capital of a column. Lieutenant Parkinson probably meant the height or apex of the trajectory of shells.

5. "*Poilu*" was the nickname for a French infantryman, similar to "doughboy" for an American soldier. The designation probably derives from the French for "hairy" and refers to the unshaven quality of Frenchmen stuck in the trenches for long periods.

During the night of March 21st, we were awakened by heavy artillery firing. We learned a few days later that this was the date on which the first big German offensive of 1918 had started.[6] As reports came from the front that it was only harassing fire all again went back to sleep, except *Commandant* Esquilat, who sat at the telephone for almost an hour, taking calls as they came in from headquarters of his several company commanders. I realized then, for the first time, the responsibility of an officer commanding troops in battle.

During our stay with the French officers, our only breakfast was a cup of cocoa and a piece of toast. It was always served in bed. It seemed that these French officers could not get out of bed until they had their cup of chocolate. There was never anything more until noon, and on some days there would be nothing more until the middle of the afternoon and then one final big meal. Nevertheless, we were well fed, and although we always had good appetites, we were not hungry.

On the night of March 21st, we again stood under the abaque[7] of French machine gun fire and heard the sound. The Frenchmen were firing at a point where the Germans were known to be building wire entanglements. As we stood in the front line listening, a German machine gunner opened up firing in bursts and, between bursts, yelled across No Man's Land in what was said to be perfect French, cursing and mocking the French and calling them "French fools." A French patrol next night reported that the Germans seemed to be preparing a gas cylinder attack by setting up projectors on the front line. We received no verification of this, however, and so far as I know, the gas attack never came off.

Another day, the three of us visited the artillery position of a French battery of 75s. The lieutenant in charge greeted us cordially, showed us around the position, and invited us to take a shot at the enemy. Therefore, just before leaving, Lieutenant Noxon and I each pulled the lanyard of a 75 to send a shell to Germany. We did not know what our target was, but in just a few minutes, when we were only a short distance down the road, we heard the swish of shells over our heads and looked back to see great geysers of dirt and dust rising in the air at the battery position. The Germans were retaliating for our two shots. They fired about a dozen on this battery without causing any casualties, then continued their "strafing" by shifting their range to other nearby positions.

On Sunday, March 24th, Lieutenants Etienne, Noxon, and I moved our headquarters from the battalion headquarters of Major Esquilat to the headquarters of one of the companies in another battalion. We were quartered in a dugout so deep in the ground it was reached by descending forty-two steps. The two weeks' time that we were supposed to spend with the French had

6. The German offensive against the British along the Somme was from March 21 through April 5, 1918

7. "Abaque" is French for an arch or top of the capital of a column. Lieutenant Parkinson probably meant the height or apex of the trajectory of shells.

elapsed and we were expecting any day to be ordered back to our own troops. We did not mind the front line duty, however, with a deep dugout for us to sleep in. The entrance of this dugout was also in a forest.

One evening, after the meal, Lieutenant Noxon and I took a walk through the paths in this forest where we were not under observation by the enemy. Suddenly, we found ourselves in the midst of German machine gun fire clipping through the trees about us. We immediately flattened on the ground and waited for it to stop. Although most of the firing passed overhead, several bullets came dangerously near.

The Soixante-Quinze. A French 75mm field gun on the Western Front, 9 April 1918. The French "75" was mobile, reliable, accurate, and quick-firing. Parkinson's French hosts in Lorraine gave him the honor "to send a shell to Germany" from one of their 75s. *Editor's collection.*

Another day at this post, an enemy shell exploded in the trench not 20 feet behind me. Only the zig-zag construction of the trenches saved me. I brought home the nose of this shell as a souvenir.

For Sunday dinner March 24th, which was Palm Sunday, we were invited to Company One, where Captain Barb entertained all the American officers at dinner. One of his lieutenants had just returned from leave and brought a supply of champagne and Bordeaux wine. There was also plenty of *penole*, which was the name of the regular issue of French wine. The Frenchmen put out a real party, and several of them had more to drink than was good for them. Besides Lieutenants Noxon, Wasson, and me, there were three other Americans whose names I do not remember.

One American in particular refused to take any drink whatever. The Frenchmen didn't understand such action and took it as an insult to their hospitality. The rest of us did not hesitate to accept their hospitality in the form of Bordeaux wine and Champagne. In addition to their wine, they had roast chicken, mushrooms, honey, and omelets with many delicate trimmings. It was as good a meal as I ever ate.

Lieutenant Wasson was one of the American officers at this dinner, and during the feasting, one of the Frenchmen boasted about how much he could drink. He poured out a glass of cognac for everyone present and yelled, "*Que's sec*!", which means, "It's dry!" When this magic phrase is uttered, good Frenchmen are supposed to drink their glasses dry at a single gulp. Lieutenant Wasson knew that a glass of cognac would be more than I could drink, so he spoke to me in English and told me to empty the small glass into my mouth before swallowing any, and then gulp it all down. All the Americans of the party gulped their cognac in this way without difficulty. But all the Frenchmen drank their cognac in small swallows, and by the time their glasses were dry tears were running down the cheeks of all.

This drinking performance won the admiration of the French. When the party broke up in the middle of the afternoon they bade us goodbye and assured us that if the Americans could fight as well as they could drink, the Germans were whipped already. I do not say this in a boastful way; I did not taste cognac again for many months. But since American officers were on trial, I was glad that we conducted ourselves in a way that won their approval, even if they did test our manhood by our ability to drink.

On the day following Palm Sunday, the French newspapers which came to us at the front carried news of a German long range gun fired on Paris at a range of 110 kilometers.[8] None of us could believe it, but the newspapers reported it as a fact and the paper the next day confirmed it.

Meanwhile, the newspapers carried news of the advance of the Germans near Montdidier, showing that they were advancing from fifteen to thirty kilometers a day through the British Army. The French were much downcast at this defeat of the British and felt it unfair that it was necessary to send French troops to stem the German advance. Every Frenchman we met asked us how many American troops were in France and we told them from 200,000 to 500,000. "Where are they?" they would ask. "We need them at the front. It is time they were getting into the fight." I always answered that they were being trained in the rear, ready to spring a surprise on the Germans. Lieutenant Etienne frequently asked me this question. I told him of the 1st, 2nd, 26th, 42nd, and 32nd Divisions that I knew of. I also told him it would be only a short time

8. The "Paris Gun" (distinct from the road-mobile Big Berthas) was actually a battery of three guns based on the German navy's 380mm design but lengthened and tubed down to 210mm. They were elevated at a fixed 50-degree angle and the range of the projectiles was set by the number of bagged powder charges used. By firing high into the thin atmosphere, where air drag was negligible, ranges of up to 75 miles or about 110 kilometers were achieved.

until he would hear of performances of American troops that would dishearten the Germans and give the Allies due cause for rejoicing.

Shock and Awe. Damage to a building in Paris, France, from bombardment by German long range gun. With a range of 110 kilometers (75 miles), the so-called "Paris Gun" initially stunned the French and Americans in March 1918, but had little lasting military impact. *Editor's collection.*

On the morning of Wednesday, March 27th, at 6:30, we left Charne Post, which was the dugout forty-two steps down. We bade farewell to Captain Barb and then to Major Esquilat and reported to regimental headquarters, where we paid our respects to the Colonel in command and Lieutenant Grostarzu. From there we went to Brigade Headquarters, where all the Americans in this sector were being assembled to be sent back to Nancy.

When all of us were assembled at Brigade Headquarters, we went in to the commanding officer to pay our respects and bid him goodbye. On the wall hung a military map. The Colonel showed us the progress of the German Army in the Montdidier Sector. As we thanked this Brigade Commander for his hospitality, he answered in English, "I am glad to have met you American officers and to have had the privilege of extending you the hospitality of the French Army. We believe you are going to give a good account of yourselves when you get into action." Then he pointed to the map and said, "But you are too late. The British Army has collapsed and the French are bled white. The Germans will be in Paris before you can prevent it."

There were about a dozen American officers listening. All of us assured him that we were going back to our troops only because General Pershing was ready to start something with the troops that he had been training in the rear. We shook hands with the Brigade Commander and told him not to give up; that he would live to see the truth of our statements demonstrated. I made a mental note right there that as soon as any number of Americans got into action, I would recall those words to Lieutenant Etienne.

Lieutenant Etienne walked down the road with us for about a kilometer. Lieutenants Noxon, Wasson, and I bade him goodbye and thanked him for his many courtesies and the splendid hospitality of the French. I made mental note that I would want to see this Frenchman again, and that I would keep up this friendship throughout the war and afterward. It was the last time I saw him. (One day, after the Armistice, I received a letter from his aunt living in Paris in reply to one that I had written to him immediately after the American victory on the Marne. It stated that he had been killed in action August 1918. I knew, however, that he had lived long enough to see the tide of the war turned by the dash of the American troops.)

At Lieutenant Etienne's suggestion, I introduced him by mail to two or three American girls back home. One of these girls was Florence,[9] and she exchanged several letters with him before his death.

9. This was Florence North, whom Parkinson would marry after the war.

CHAPTER 3: BADONVILLER

PEXONNE, NEUFMAISON, FENNVILLER, A-14, CHAMOIS, VILLAGE NEGRE, A-13, A-15.

Following the tour of duty with the French regiment north of Nancy, Lieutenant John F. Noxon and I reported at the headquarters of the 42nd Division at Luneville. We were given billets for the night, and next day received orders assigning us to the 151st Machine Gun Battalion stationed at Badménil. At about 3:00 P.M., we loaded our baggage in a truck loaded to capacity with officers who had been with the French. It was an open truck and rain was falling. We had a hard ride through several towns in this region. At each town some of the officers would get off with their baggage and report to the unit stationed there.

We arrived at Badménil at 7:00 P.M. and reported promptly to Major Winn, who was in command of the 151st Machine Gun Battalion. He assigned us to D Company, commanded by Captain J. H. Lightner. As we had had nothing to eat supper was prepared for us and, while eating, we became acquainted with the other officers of the company: 1st Lieutenant Monroe A. Means, 2nd Lieutenant John Geiszel, and 2nd Lieutenant William P. Andres.

This company had been Company B of the 149th Machine Gun Battalion, which had been formed from the 4th Regiment of Pennsylvania Infantry National Guard. They had just received orders[1] which transferred them from the 149th Machine Gun Battalion to the 151st Machine Gun Battalion, which formerly was made up of three companies of National Guard from Georgia. Our company then became Company D, 151st Machine Gun Battalion, and

1. This order came on March 28. Parkinson and Noxon were assigned to this newly designated Company D just three days later on March 31 (Means).

retained this designation throughout the war. The other companies were Companies B, C, and F from the Second Georgia Infantry.

The following day, Lieutenant Noxon and I were issued U.S. gas masks and Colt automatics which completed our equipment. I was assigned to command the 3rd Platoon and at 3:30 P.M., took command of my first body of troops as the company fell in to march to the front. As we marched to the front in the rain the sun suddenly broke forth in the west and a beautiful rainbow appeared. So on my first day with the troops of the Rainbow Division we were cheered by a rainbow on the eve of going to the front.[2] Unquestionably this must be a good omen.

Sergeant Harry Peacock was my platoon sergeant. We marched approximately twelve miles that night to the village of Pexonne. This was regimental headquarters for the 168th Infantry. Our Company D was attached to the Third Battalion of this regiment under command of Major Brewer.[3] On arriving at Pexonne, the three combat platoons took position in the support line. Captain Lightner ordered me to remain in Pexonne and sent the 3rd Platoon into the line under command of Lieutenant Noxon, whose headquarters was at the position known as B-2.

Major Cooper D. Winn. Commander of the 151st Machine Gun Battalion. Winn is in the middle, wearing the campaign hat. He is shown with officers of the French 32nd Division in Lorraine, February 10, 1918. As the war progressed, Major Winn championed more effective machine gun tactics that would eventually win over his brigade, division, and corps commanders. *Photo courtesy of U.S. Army Military History Institute.*

2. Parkinson mentions eight rainbows that cheered the Rainbow Division before combat as well as their psychological impact on the men.
3. Normally Companies A and B were assigned to the 167th Infantry Regiment while Companies C and D were attached to the 168th Infantry. Company D would always act with the 168th's Third Battalion until August when MacArthur reorganized the 84th Brigade.

The 42nd Rainbow Division

The Secretary of War, Newton D. Baker, called the Rainbow Division "both an accident and an inspiration." In 1917, he asked General William Mann if a composite division could be formed out of surplus National Guard units from the various states. Mann affirmed this was possible and suggested some of the states from which units could be drawn. In that meeting, then-Major Douglas MacArthur described it as, "stretching like a rainbow clear across the United States." That is how the 42nd Division was conceived and received its nickname from its future Chief of Staff.

There was a dispute at the time within the War Department whether National Guardsmen would be useful combat troops. MacArthur was a strong advocate in favor of using the National Guard. He knew that local militias comprising able-bodied men of all kinds had mixed results in history. Yet MacArthur pointed out that men joined the National Guard voluntarily and tended to be the more militant of the populace; the passive and the cowardly were absent. The combat record of the 42nd Division would later prove MacArthur right.

Composed of National Guard units from 26 states and the District of Columbia, the fighting elements of the Rainbow Division included:

83rd Infantry Brigade	84th Infantry Brigade	67th Field Artillery Brigade
165th Infantry (NY)	167th Infantry (AL)	149th Field Artillery (IL)
166th Infantry (OH)	168th Infantry (IA)	150th Field Artillery (IN)
150th MG Bn. (WI)	151st MG Bn. (GA)	151st Field Artillery (MN)
[1 Company from PA]	[Company D from PA]	117th Trench Mortar (MD)

Also, the 149th MG Bn. (PA) was the Division's reserve machine gun battalion.

After a rush to organize, train, and ship out, the 42nd Rainbow Division was one of the first American divisions to arrive in France. It was the very first U.S. division assigned to hold a sector of the front by itself and the first to raid German trenches (led by Douglas MacArthur).

The following morning, I was assigned to move the supplies and ammunition from a building which was under observation by the Germans to another building 300 yards down the main street. I was assigned a detail of men whom I did not know. I was at a great disadvantage, because the men, wanting to try out a new officer, would carry one load of equipment to the new location and not return. As I did not know their names, I could not check up on them. I was not going to fall down, however, in this first assignment from my new company commander. I helped carry the material to the new location, and each time I went I rounded up every enlisted man in sight and brought him back and put him to work so that I got the equipment all moved. This was all on Easter Sunday, March 31st.

The 151st Machine Gun Battalion

Companies B and C originated in the Confederate Army and fought at Chancellorsville and Gettysburg. With Company F, they formed the 1st Battalion under the command of Major Cooper D. Winn in the 2nd Georgia Infantry in 1917. This Battalion was assigned to the 42nd Division as the 151st Machine Gun Battalion. Early in 1918, Company K from the 149th Machine Gun Battalion became Company D of the 151st. From then on, the battalion was four companies strong: three were from Georgia, and one from Pennsylvania. Replacements eventually diversified them further.

The night previous, Lieutenant Noxon had been unable to locate the position to which he had been assigned. This was due to no fault of his, as he had never been there, but it seemed that Captain Lightner was trying us both out. Lieutenant Noxon came back and admitted his inability to locate the post. He would have made a better impression with the Captain had he sent back a messenger.

It was Lightner's plan that Lieutenant Noxon and I should alternate daily in command of the Third Platoon at Position B-2. Therefore, on April 1st, I relieved Lieutenant Noxon at noon and stayed in position that night. We alternated each day at this position. The gun positions were in a forest on top of a hill overlooking the Badonviller Sector. The men were quartered in a dugout on the reverse slope of this hill. A small stone building of one room was used for officers' quarters. It had formerly been a game keeper's lodge in this forest region, but was now entirely bare, with the exception of two sleeping bunks made from rough timber and chicken wire netting. About 50 yards up this road was a battery position of the 150th Field Artillery of our division under command of Lieutenant Inman, with whom I soon became acquainted and spent a good deal of time with during the day.

Captain Monroe A. Means. Commander of D Company, 151st Machine Gun Battalion from early June 1918 until the Company was disbanded in 1919. Means was gassed June 18, 1918, but refused to leave his men. He also neglected to mention this incident in his own account of D Company's history. *World War History & Art Museum (WWHAM) collection, Alliance, Ohio.*

This position was about two kilometers from Pexonne. Therefore, Captain Lightner invited Lieutenant Noxon and me, as well as the other officers of this company, to return to Pexonne during the day for officers' mess. Accordingly, we ate our three meals at Pexonne and reported at sundown to the line, where we stayed overnight and well after sunrise each morning. This was a support position. The first line trenches were several hundred yards in front of us, so we did not have to be as alert as if we were in the first line. Neither did we suffer any shell fire while I was at this position.

One afternoon, while coming to my post, I passed by an unoccupied artillery position at the intersection of the main road leading east from Badonviller with a trail through the forest. Shell holes all around showed where the Germans had fired while the Americans occupied the position two months previous. It was now deserted, but the Germans thought it was occupied and, just as I passed, sent about a dozen 77 shells over in rapid succession. I was caught directly in the cone of fire and dirt was thrown all over me as I ran to get away from this marked position. All of these shells seemed to fall within about 50 yards or less of me. They came over in rapid succession and gave me the worst scare I had yet experienced.

Lieutenant John H. Geiszel. Geiszel normally commanded the Supply Train for D Company, 151st Machine Gun Battalion. At St. Mihiel, he commanded a combat platoon and was severely wounded in the neck by shrapnel. *World War History & Art Museum (WWHAM) collection, Alliance, Ohio.*

On arriving at Badménil, where I reported to Captain Lightner the first day, Lieutenant Noxon and I were very much surprised to find Lieutenants Ackley and Baumet also assigned to this company. They had been with us at the 2nd Corps Machine Gun School at Chatillon-sur-Seine. They knew that Lieutenant Noxon and I had been among the highest in rank and gave us the laugh at beating us to the front line for some time. They were not kept, however, by Captain Lightner, but were sent back to Division Headquarters and in turn assigned to the machine gun company of the 168th Infantry. We then had the laugh on Ackley and Baumet, because the machine gun company of an infantry regiment has a much harder time than the companies of a brigade battalion.

After Lieutenant Baumet was relieved, I was permanently assigned to the post at Fennviller, which was a small village between Pexonne and Badonviller. I had different personnel to command: a section or half a platoon which was composed of two machine gun crews. I immediately inspected my command and gave gas mask drills. Two gas masks in bad condition were repaired or replaced. Our men slept in the buildings in Fennviller, ready to take nearby battle positions in case of alarm. Our only duties at Fennviller were to guard a 10-gallon glass jar of cognac which the French regiment before us had left behind and taken a receipt for. Each officer relieved at the post required his successor to give a receipt. Many an American gazed on its contents with longing eyes, but none dared to take the responsibility of opening it. Three months later, after the French and the 77th Division had relieved us, a strong German raiding party penetrated to Fennviller. I often wondered what became of that big jar of cognac. It was at Fennviller that I picked up the large-caliber shell fragment that I sent home.

One day, while sitting in the doorway of my billet at Fennviller, I saw Lieutenant Edward Veasey coming down the road. I had known him well at Hotel McAlpin while waiting in New York for sailing orders. He told me of letters from Lieutenant Paul Derrickson, now with the 1st Division. Lieutenant Veasey was billeting officer for the 168th Infantry.

Another day while on duty here, a private belonging to headquarters company of the 168th Infantry came running into my post and stated that two civilians had been taking photographs of some deserted battery positions up the road toward Badonviller. They were now on their way back to Pexonne. I sent a man on ahead at double time to intercept them when they reached Pexonne. The private from headquarters company and I followed them quickly, although we did not run. We overtook them at Pexonne and took them into the office of the Town Major, where we found a French interpreter.

These men had a camera which folded up to resemble a book and a tripod wrapped in paper and concealed under their coats. They claimed to be members of a new military class, just called to the colors, and were taking some souvenir photographs. I was not satisfied with their story and took them back up the road to the headquarters of Col. Bennett, regimental commander. One of the men turned and offered resistance. I could not understand him and he probably could not understand me. I was somewhat excited, and when he resisted I struck him with my open hand. Meanwhile, I kept my right hand on my automatic. The blow sent him staggering, and thereafter both prisoners went peaceably until I turned them over to the Colonel. He commended me for arresting these men, and I in turn commended the private who had first called it to my attention. I did so to his commanding officer, Colonel Bennett. When Major Winn learned of these events, he also commended me warmly. The prisoners were turned over to the Divisional Intelligence Section. I never heard further about them, but presume they must have given a satisfactory explanation,[4] as I was never called to testify.

After twelve days in the support positions of the B line, the Third Battalion of the 168th Infantry, to which we were attached, was ordered to relieve one of the other Battalions in the A line. On Friday, April 12th, I went forward to the

4. Their story was not credible. New military class or not, they were not in uniform, they concealed their equipment, they resisted arrest, and local commanders were not informed of any authorized photographers in their sector. Besides, troops did not normally take souvenir snapshots using a tripod. The fact that Lieutenant Parkinson heard nothing more about them does not prove the two were not spies. Captain W. E. Talbot of the 42nd Division caught a spy red-handed trying to signal submarines from the *Mount Vernon* en route to France. Yet Washington ordered his release for diplomatic reasons. The French later caught and executed this same spy, diplomatic status notwithstanding (Reilly, 76-77).

first line to familiarize myself with my new post, which was A-14. Lieutenant Stratford of C Company was in command. I spent the morning at the post with him. I took Sergeant Stark with me, who was my section sergeant. This post was in the C. R. Chamois, which was one of the positions in the front line trench ("C. R." being an abbreviation for "Center of Resistance").

While with Lieutenant Stratford, I saw my first American planes in action. We had seen previously quite a number of German and French planes in combat and many German planes under fire from our anti-aircraft artillery. On this day, we suddenly heard two strange sounding motors which we felt must be the famous new Liberty motors. There had been two German planes in the air directing the fire of their guns against our positions. These two Americans came suddenly, chased the Germans back home, then turned their own machine guns on the German trenches and took a number of aerial photographs. We learned afterwards they hurried back to Luneville, developed the photographs, and within a few minutes had the American artillery firing on positions discovered through those photographs.

On the night of April 13th, which was Saturday, my section marched from Fennviller with guns and ammunition loaded on mule carts. We marched through Badonviller and took the road out toward the Village Negre Sector. When immediately behind the ridge between A-14 post and the road, the equipment was unloaded and we started to climb over the hill under cover of darkness without passing through the trenches.

I had approached the position in daytime and had gone through the trenches, so I did not know the overland route. Sergeant Stark insisted on the overland route because under cover of darkness it would be safe, and it would be much easier to handle the equipment than through the narrow trenches. At the top of the ridge he lost his way. For some time we did not know where we were. The Germans were sending over rockets and magnesium flares which made the woods light as day until they burned out. This was rather trying on our nerves until we located ourselves and proceeded to A-14. There, early in the morning of Sunday April 14th, we relieved C Company.

In the front line positions, it was a rule for all hands to "stand to" one hour before dawn and until sunrise. Also from one hour before sunset until an hour after dark. Other times, we kept guards posted in pairs at each machine gun position and one at the dugout entrance. They stood guard two hours at a time and were in turn relieved. Persons not on duty were to keep out of sight, and for the most part stayed in the dugout, where bunks were built in tiers from rough timber and wire netting. During the 21 days in this post I became well acquainted with the two squads under my command while we all lived together in the same dugout.

One day, we saw a rocket go up from one of our own front line positions. Immediately our own artillery began firing, even before the rocket struck the ground. We afterward learned that some important inspecting officer wanted to try out our artillery. He ordered the lieutenant at this infantry post to call for a barrage by sending up the proper signal rocket, but he did not take any steps to stop the barrage. This continued for about half an hour, wasting many thousands of dollars of ammunition and giving away the location of all our division batteries, where they had been concealed carefully and at much effort. Another time a week later, I was called by the guards early in the morning, as a heavy barrage had started down the line somewhat to our left. The Alabama Regiment of our division was putting over a raid. We watched these fireworks and listened to the roar for about half an hour, all about a mile to our left.

One night at G. C. 8 in front of us I heard a grenade explode where it was thrown by a watching sentinel. Then an American voice from No Man's Land called, "Don't throw any more. For God's sake, let me come in!" He had been lost from a patrol the night before. He lay in a shell hole until morning. Then by daylight he regained his bearings so as not to enter the enemy trenches, waited for darkness again, then came home.

During our stay at A-14, soldiers came from all nearby trenches to view a 10-inch German shell that had fallen on the Chamois ridge in front of us. It stood on end, three feet high, near the mouth of the dugout on the slope sheltered from enemy view. We later saw many, but this was our first big-caliber dud.

Usually the nights were illuminated by magnesium flares which, after a crack of a Very pistol, ascended high in the air like a rocket and descended slowly, attached to small parachutes. These flares were shot by both sides at every suspicious noise in front. At the warning crack of the pistol we instinctively flattened on the ground or froze in our tracks, because under these flares the enemy shot at every moving object. In the dugout at A-14 was a Very pistol for shooting these rockets. It had a strange fascination for me and I wished for an excuse to shoot it. But, as there was an outpost line in front of us, I never had the opportunity.

At night, our patrols dominated No Man's Land. Each front line battalion sent scouts and patrols creeping toward the enemy trenches to observe what had happened during the day. Each night we would receive written orders telling what time they were expected in front of our post and for our sentinels to be careful and not fire on them or embarrass them by shooting illuminating flares. Also, each night we received the official sign and countersign. It was usually two similar words, such as EPERNAY for the sign and EPINAL for the countersign, or VERDUN and VERPEL or PARIS and PERONNE. We first used the same as the French, but later patriotism led the boys of Georgia, Alabama, and Iowa to insist on names from our own state geographies.

Near the end of our tour of duty, the Americans began a three-day bombardment of the Salient-de-Feys, a wooded point in the German trench system. We watched this barrage continually for three days as shell after shell landed in the woods, exploded, threw a geyser of dirt and debris in the air, and settled down as another explosion would occur nearby. Several times I saw trees thrown in the air, as they had been uprooted by large shells exploding under their roots. After the third day, the Ohio Regiment (166th) of our division made a raid on this point.

Often times we would hear a German battery open up harassing fire. Large guns located to the left of our position seemed to open up on our rear area and sweep to their left as they harassed one position after another. These guns, firing rapidly, made a metallic, belching roar which reverberated through our ravine and on over succeeding ridges behind us. As the guns swung around so that the shells passed directly over us, it was thrilling to see the flash on the sky from the woods near us and then hear the sound of the discharge, which traveled more slowly than the flash and the projectile. We often then would hear the American artillery retaliate with their French 75s.

It was reputed to be a rule in our artillery brigade to return two shots for every one sent over by the Germans. Men from the intelligence section counted the number of shells sent over by the Germans and with delicate instruments figured out the location of the firing enemy batteries. Our own artillery then answered as quickly as possible, and we were told that they made it a practice to return to each German battery firing exactly twice the number of shells that the Germans had fired. Most of the time it was possible to count these shells, but of course during a real barrage, when there was rapid drum fire from both sides, it was out of the question to count them.

During the twenty-one days we were in this position, no hostile artillery fire came close enough to be dangerous, but we were frequently harassed by machine gun fire and snipers. Our machine gun emplacements had been used by the French for years and were undoubtedly known to the Germans. As a matter of defense, I began building, or rather digging, reserve emplacements so that we would have places to operate our guns if the German artillery fire should drive us from our present places.

One evening, while Corporal Erb and I were laying out a new emplacement, we were driven in by sniper's bullets. Another time with a squad, we were cleaning out trenches near the spring in the ravine nearby when the Germans opened up with indirect machine gun fire which fell all around us and drove us to shelter. They swept the hill for fifteen minutes with perfect enfilade fire through our trenches. Had we not quickly taken shelter, we would have suffered heavy casualties. Once a machine gun bullet falling at a high angle from long range punctured a tin wash basin held by Raymond Proffit just as he picked it up to start shaving.

The personnel of my section was made up partly of original men of this Battalion from Pennsylvania and partly of replacements from Idaho and Montana. At this post with me were Sergeants Stark and Kiphorn, Corporals Erb and Pennell, and Privates Zimmerman, McGinnis, Holbrook, and Kissinger from Pennsylvania. Also Privates Boden, Clark, Proffit, Currier, Dickson, Roberts, Graves, and Schmidt, who were from the western states. As I became acquainted with these men I developed a great deal of confidence in them, particularly in those who came from the western states. They were the rough and ready and well-met class that we have always heard about in the far west.

The Communication Trench.

PROBLEM—Whether to walk along the top and risk it, or do another mile of this.

Cartoon by Captain Bruce Bairnsfather. Infantry of all nations in the World War wondered whether the enemy or the elements caused the greater suffering. During one of Lieutenant Parkinson's stints in the trenches, "It rained nineteen of the twenty-one days we were in this sector." Among other hardships were knee-deep mud, uniforms alive with lice, and sharing dugouts with rats. The bright side of the rain was that rainbows followed. The Rainbow Division always saw one before a fight (Parkinson recorded some eight instances) and their pot of gold was always victory. *Cartoon from Bruce Biarnsfather, Fragments From France, 1917.*

In the dugout, while not on guard, we learned some new songs from each other, and I had reason to believe from their attitude that I had won the confidence of the men under my command.

It rained nineteen of the twenty-one days we were in this sector. On one occasion, we saw five German aeroplanes attack a French machine. Although greatly outnumbered, the Frenchman maneuvered his plane so that he was not shot down, landing within the American lines.

During this tour at A-14, the bunks in which we slept were creeping with lice. Every day we "read our undershirts" and removed as much lice as we could find, but the next day more would hatch, and we were constantly annoyed by their creeping. Almost every day I would take a bath, or rather wash with a pint of water in a tomato can, which was the largest utensil available, but we had no clean clothing and no other place to sleep.

Rats abounded. We heard them at all hours, digging or squealing behind the board walls of our dugouts. The minute it became quiet in a dugout, the rats would peek out from a dozen holes and steal forth, foraging for scraps of food. We wondered why poison gas did not exterminate them, but they seemed to be immune.[5] One time, when we had been wearing our masks for half an hour, one of the men in our section suddenly jerked off his mask and exclaimed, "Well if the gas don't kill that rat, it won't kill me!"

Rats are natural comedians, if one has the opportunity and time to observe them. But our greatest source of fun from the animal kingdom was from the cuckoo birds that abounded in this Badonviller region. We heard them calling every day. For a long time, their call itself set us laughing, but later these birds timed their calls most appropriately to pass as comment on what someone had just said. It happened almost invariably when someone became emphatic in a statement. He could then depend on having some bird in the forest nearby brand him "cuckoo." One day, I had just finished a reprimand to three negligent members of my section when the seriousness of the occasion was irrecoverably destroyed by a bird almost directly overhead calling, "Cuckoo! Cuckoo!", and maybe he was right. I would not deny it.

On the night of May 2nd at 10:30 P.M., we were relieved by a platoon under command of Lieutenant Smith of the Regimental machine gun company. We went back to the support area, and I was again stationed with this same section at B-2 on the road east of Badonviller. This post was a wooded ridge. The trees were half-leaved out. Birch, pine, oak, and beech made a fine blending of colors. Across the road was a bubbling spring of cold water which we used for drinking purposes after treating it with lime. At the top of the ridge, where our machine gun positions were, we viewed the entire country from the highest point around. A ladder was built into a high tree for concealment, so that

5. Some accounts say that rats were killed by gas, but these were earlier in the war. By 1918 three years of natural selection in the static front lines of Lorraine may have preserved those rats possessing a resistance to certain kinds of gas.

when the leaves were out in full we could view not only our own lines, but the German lines, as well.

With the exception of the deserted battery position, where I was caught once in shell fire a few weeks previous, this valley had not been ravaged by hostilities. But 500 yards across another road and on into the front line near A-14, shell fire had made mud out of sod, snags out of large trees, and stumps out of smaller ones. To our right was the Village Negre Sector, which was also in a beautiful timbered ridge. This was not a real village, but derived its name from the many dugouts and partly-sheltered shacks built on the reverse slope of this hill. This Village Negre Sector was occupied by another battalion of the 168th Infantry. The top of the hill was level and rolling, but the reverse slope and the forward slope were very steep and gave a good military position.

One day, going down the road on the way to Pexonne as I passed through Fennviller, I observed two officers in the open field, examining the wire entanglements. They were under German observation, but the road on which I was walking was concealed by camouflage. These two officers completed their inspection and started walking to the road so as to reach it about the time I would intersect their path. They had been observed by the Germans, who were waiting for them to reach the road, where they would have an accurate range. As we all three arrived together, the Germans opened fire with half a dozen 77s which fell right in our midst and caused us all to scatter. Miraculously, no one was injured.

After returning from the tour of duty at A-14 post, the entire company, including myself and the other officers, put our clothes and blankets through the delousing plants, where they were thoroughly steamed and renovated. We had a good shower and felt clean again.

On the night of May 9th, we went forward between 8:00 and 11:00 P.M. and took over the position A-13, in the Village Negre Sector. This was a machine gun post on the ridge behind A-14. We had a field of fire flanking the line to the west so that we would have enfilade fire on the enemy should they break through the first line of resistance. We had a splendid dugout for the entire section. It was probably fifteen feet deep and protected by a solid stone ceiling, which in turn was covered by a thick layer of natural soil. The ridge was covered by small growth of pine and birch trees which partially concealed us from the enemy, but our positions were well known to the enemy, having been detected by photographs made while the trees were free from leaves.

One day, while at this point, one of the men was shaving when machine gun fire broke his mirror for him. Another day, our own artillery was firing high into the air on hostile planes at such an angle that the fragments of the shells showered our position so that we had to take cover quickly. This post, A-13, was connected by a trench to P. A. 5, which was the post of command of the infantry company occupying this sector under Lieutenant Cotter of the 168th Infantry.

On the evening of May 14th, a battery of the 150th Field Artillery opened fire, with the German trenches in front of the Village Negre Sector as its target. Their guns were new 155mm caliber, and because they were new (or perhaps from faulty ammunition or faulty calculations) the shells fell short and landed in our own front lines. For several hours these big shells skimmed over our heads at Post A-13 and landed on the front line positions before us. The infantry withdrew to shelter and sent distress signals to the rear to increase the range. The firing stopped about midnight, but before dawn it started again.

At 6:00 A.M., a shell made a direct hit in the rear entrance of P. C. at G. C. 8. Men who had just been relieved from duty were sleeping and when the shell exploded they had no chance. Lieutenant Francis McIlvain, Sergeant Clem Hobbs, and Private Max Hubbell were killed immediately and Private McConnell was fatally wounded. It also wounded Privates Leuth and Bolts. The latter was blown out through another entrance of the dugout and burned so severely that he never returned to duty. The explosion set off a supply of signal rockets that were stored in the dugout. It became an inferno which burned for an hour, so that none could enter to recover the bodies. By the time our own guns were stopped, the commotion had attracted the attention of the Germans, who now opened a severe bombardment on these positions that wounded three infantrymen and killed Corporal Remel.

On the evening of May 25th, after we had been in this sector for sixteen days, I went down this trench to spend a few minutes with Lieutenant Cotter, discussing the relief which was planned for that night. On the way back, a German aeroplane overhead spotted me in this trench, nose dived, and sprayed the trench with machine gun fire. I hugged the side of the trench and then ran back to my post at A-13 just in time to see that whole post swept by machine gun fire.

A small patrol of Germans had attacked the infantry outpost ahead of us. All their fire that did not strike the infantry line landed right in our midst, but that did not make their machine gun fire any less harmful. In this attack on the outposts, the Germans first advanced about forty in number with their hands in the air, calling "Kamerad." Lieutenant Doocy, in command of that platoon, ordered them to come in one at a time if they wanted to surrender. They continued coming in a body, whereupon the American infantry opened fire. The Germans immediately took cover and returned fire. They were driven off by the Americans with heavy casualties, but with no losses to the Americans.

I remembered this Lieutenant Doocy as one of my comrades in Company 22 at Fort Sheridan Officers Training Camp. Prior to that time he was a star half-back on the Illinois Wesleyan Football Team at the same time that I was a student at Millikin. I later came in contact with this lieutenant in battle at Sergy and in the Champagne, and found him to be a high type officer, always ready for contact with the enemy. The post occupied by Lieutenant Doocy's platoon was known by the code name "G. C. 8," meaning in French, "GROUPE de COMBAT 8."

We were to be relieved that night at eleven o'clock. Germans were shelling heavily in the rear areas and the relief was late. We did get away, however, at 12:30 A.M., being relieved by Lieutenant Swift of the Regimental machine gun company. I had known him at the 2nd Corps School at Chatillon-sur-Seine. We made our way back to Pexonne for the night, but were assigned to combat positions at B-3 and B-3-1/2. We immediately went to bed on arriving at Pexonne, but at 1:30 the entire area, including the village of Pexonne, was rocked by a tremendous explosion. We quickly dressed and prepared to take our positions for battle.

Two Exploded Gas Drums. These were used in the German gas projector attack against the 168th Infantry at Village Negre May 27, 1918. Groups of 100 drums, each holding about two gallons of liquified gas, were fired together by electrical detonation. There was little time to react, especially for those asleep. *Photo from Taber, The Story of the 168th Infantry.*

We could tell that the action was at the front lines in the Village Negre Sector. The Germans, apparently knowing about the relief, had inaugurated a great projector gas attack on the newly-arrived troops on the theory that the they would not yet be familiar with this sector. It proved to be the heaviest concentration of gas thus far experienced in the war by any body of troops. The Germans had secretly placed a large number of gas projectors in their front line trenches which threw large steel balls filled with concentrated phosgene, chlorine, and mustard gas. These projectors were fired simultaneously by electricity and deluged the Village Negre Sector with gas before the sleeping men could be warned. They followed it up with a tremendous bombardment of high explosive shells and gas shells.

This battalion suffered over 150 casualties.[6] Captain Fleur, of the machine gun company which relieved my company, was killed. Lieutenants Priddy, Sevier, and Green of the infantry were killed. Two men of the Y.M.C.A. attached to these two battalions distinguished themselves for services far beyond duty: Hedley Cooper and Halliday Smith. No present-day critic of the record of the Y.M.C.A. in the war can get far with me in criticizing the services of this organization. The services of these two men alone overshadow all shortcomings of the Y.M.C.A. for the entire A.E.F. They both gave their lives carrying in wounded in the midst of the bombardment and heavy gas concentration.

Immediately on the outbreak of this tremendous explosion we started to our combat positions. As we were starting, we received orders from Major Brewer of the 3rd Infantry Battalion telling us to do just what we had already started. On the way to my positions at B-3 and B-3-1/2, we turned to the right at Fennviller and found the road drenched with gas from gas shells, so we wore our gas masks through this region. The shell fire was heavy up in the direction of Village Negre, but at that moment none was falling near us, although the gas was heavy. It was pitch dark. With difficulty, we could follow the road with which we were familiar. Suddenly, our section of two squads was bracketed by an outburst of firing from the German artillery. Gas and high explosive shells burst all around us and in our midst. We ran to the top of the hill, still wearing our gas masks, and took shelter in a trench. Just as I dived into the trench, Jim Walters jumped into the same trench on top of me. I had really fallen into this trench and he thought I was wounded and kept trying to help. I thought he was wounded and kept trying to help him. Neither could talk with his mask on. We soon found that both were all right.

After the Germans raised the range, we proceeded on our way to our combat positions, still having to wear our masks. Making our way cautiously through the trenches and wire, and then through the timber and wire, we arrived at combat position B-3. I had tested several times for gas, but when we arrived at B-3 we were met by Sergeant Coover and Privates Mud Main and Wayne McLaughlin, who were not wearing masks. We therefore removed our masks. It was beginning to break daylight. I had no information as to the result up front, so I ordered all men to their combat posts, where we stayed until we knew that the Germans were not attempting to advance.

I noticed that I was in a high fever and feared that I had been gassed. I knew that exercise was fatal to a man who had been badly gassed. I also knew that I would not be able to return to this post for several days. So I had Sergeant Coover guide me down to B-3-1/2, which was a new post being constructed. I went very slowly, so as to avoid as much as possible the effects if I had been

6. About 100 of these men of the 168th Infantry were killed outright by the gas as they were sleeping in their dugouts. They had no chance to get their masks on. The gas was followed by a fierce German raid which the infantry repulsed. According to the 84th Brigade's adjutant, this incident filled survivors of the regiment with utter contempt for the Germans. In battles to follow, the 168th Infantry would fight with "Cromwellian austerity" (Wolf, 18).

gassed. I soon felt a little better and realized that if I had been gassed it was not serious. Shortly after sunrise we returned to Pexonne, where I was down for three days with a high fever which had been running through the personnel of the battalion.[7] I spent three days in bed and was treated by the battalion physician, but did not consent to going to the hospital.

Lieutenant Noxon, during this same night, had been gassed and went to the hospital. He never again joined our company, but was transferred to the Tank Corps. After the war, Lieutenant Ralph Tenney of Decatur told me of having met Lieutenant Noxon in Paris. He was from Pittsfield, Massachusetts, and had been a student of Harvard and a graduate of the Plattsburg Officers Training Camp. He was twenty-one years of age in November 1917, just a few days prior to the time he was commissioned.

After returning to Pexonne, all day long we watched ambulances hurrying forward to Badonviller and Village Negre and back through Pexonne filled with wounded and gassed soldiers. A German observation balloon was high above Bremenil, watching our roads. It was a grim realization of the casualties we could expect in the future.

That day, I got up out of sick bed to go to a regimental hospital up the street where there was a dead German. He did not seem to be over 18. It was the first dead German I had seen close up. I was impressed with the futility of war and the tremendous sacrifice, even in the death of only one enemy boy. I shuddered as I thought of the many Americans who had been killed that morning.

By Decoration Day, I had recovered from the fever. On that day at sunset, an American soldier was buried in the cemetery at Pexonne. Chaplain Robb led a solemn procession from the infirmary behind a pine casket borne on the shoulders of six comrades while soldiers and civilians followed. The chaplain's services aroused our patriotism to high fervor and his closing prayer, as we stood by the open grave, was a stirring challenge to every soldier to face his duty, even if it meant death, yet be prepared for death if it should come. "Taps" sounded at sunset and slowly we made our way back to the village.

During our stay in Pexonne, I made range cards to post at each gun emplacement. These cards showed the exact range to each strategic point within range of these guns. If the Germans should come, the range would not be guessed, but accurate.

June 2nd, officers went forward on reconnaissance preparatory to making a relief and entering the lines again. Up in the area of Village Negre, where the gas attack occurred, we found all green vegetation had been killed by the heavy concentration. All the hundreds of rugged pine trees in that forest were scorched as though from the heat of fire. The needles were seared, dead, and falling off. Yet the daisies were blooming unscathed.

7. This was the so-called "Spanish influenza" which normally caused three days of high fever and then lingering weakness for some time thereafter. The influenza pandemic of 1918 killed more people worldwide than the war killed in four and a half years.

On June 3rd, we again entered the front line in the Badonviller Sector, which was immediately to the left of Village Negre and was code named "Chamois." I had charge of posts A-14 and another post immediately in front of the cemetery of Badonviller. I think it was known as A-15. June 5th, the Battle of Belleau Woods started near Chateau-Thierry.[8] Our intelligence service now reported a large body of German troops training in the rear areas immediately before us. We were cautioned to prepare for an attack which we expected any day.

I had not yet recovered from the fever I had. I was subject to violent coughing spells. Several times they were so severe that I would have to lie down on the ground until they were over. I was very weak, but did not wish to leave the Company to go to the hospital just when we were expecting a heavy attack.

In line with plans to resist the expected attack, Major Winn took me with him one day while we selected a line of reserve machine gun positions to which we could retire if driven from our forward positions. Sergeant Coover was in command of A-14. Sergeant Brenner was in command at the post in front of the cemetery, which I think was A-15. Major Winn and I selected some new positions near A-13 in a grove and at a new dugout near the stone quarry northeast of Badonviller. I had command of Sergeant Coover's section and Sergeant Brenner's section.[9] I spent most of my time at the post occupied by Sergeant Brenner.

It was about this time that Captain Lightner was relieved of the command of D Company[10] and Lieutenant Means made Company Commander.[11] One of his first acts was to remove a number of corporals and sergeants whom he considered incompetent. One of these was Sergeant Coover of my section. Corporal Howard Achey was promoted to sergeant and given sergeant Coover's section. Corporal Achey protested against promotion, preferring to remain with his squad as corporal. His squad had developed a fine *esprit de corps*. It was composed of Achey, Armstrong, Hawthorne, Lapham, Fetter, Matt, Main, and McLaughlin, and I think Humphreys also belonged to this squad. But when Achey was shown that he would be more useful as a sergeant than as a corporal, he gladly consented to step up. Of course, he would have had no recourse unless Lieutenant Means had seen fit to revise his promotion order. In subsequent engagements, Sergeant Achey had become perhaps my most reliable sergeant. I would not say that Brenner was not equally as reliable, but

8. June 5th is mistaken and should be June 6th. On orders from the French command, the Marine Brigade of the 2nd Division hurled itself into Belleau Wood which was basically one big machine gun nest covering about a square mile of thicket. Without preparatory fire by artillery, they rooted out the enemy with rifle and bayonet from June 6 through 25, 1918.

9. Since Lieutenant John F. Noxon was gassed, Lieutenant Parkinson was for the first time in command of the entire platoon composed of two sections or four squads.

10. Captain Lightner was transferred on June 16, 1918 (Means).

11. Through the remainder of the war and all of its fighting Monroe A. Means with Lieutenants William P. Andres, John H. Geiszel, and Nellis P. Parkinson were to be the core officers of D Company.

Hotchkiss Machine Gun Squad

A lieutenant commanded a machine gun platoon consisting of four squads. Each machine gun squad was led by a corporal and included eight privates.

Privates	Duties
No. 1	*Gunner* carried the M1914 Hotchkiss machine gun (52.8 lbs) into action. Fired the gun, corrected stoppages (jams), and cleaned it.
No. 2	*Assistant Loader* carried the M1915 tripod (40.7 lbs) into action. Watched for signals from corporal; passed them on to gunner.
No. 3	*Loader* carried traversing head (17.6 lbs) and one ammo box into action. Loaded the gun and assisted gunner in correcting stoppages.
No. 4	*Ammunition Carrier* carried spare parts case and one ammo box. Returned empty ammo boxes to the ammunition station.
No. 5	*Ammunition Carrier* carried two boxes (576 rounds) into action. Supplied ammunition to the loader (No. 3).
No. 6	*Ammunition Carrier* carried two boxes (576 rounds) into action. Supplied ammunition to the loader (No. 3).
No. 7	*Driver* handled the gun mule, M1907 gun cart, and equipment. (Nos. 7 and 8 were commonly known as "mule skinners.")
No. 8	*Driver* handled the ammo mule, M1907 ammo cart, and ammo. Supplied ammunition to the ammunition station. Replenished his cart from the combat train behind.

Source: *Supplement To Machine Gun Drill Regulations*

Each member of the squad was cross-trained for other duties. If the squad sustained a casualty, the number below him moved up to replace him.

Eight men seems like a lot to feed just one voracious gun. However, the Hotchkiss machine gun fired at a cyclic rate of 500 rounds per minute and was capable of sustaining 400 rounds per minute. Further, the steady mount of the tripod and mechanical control virtually eliminated aiming errors due to nerves in combat. Depending on range, a single machine gun was worth about 50 to 90 rifles in the field. That was a huge multiplier that more than compensated for the eight needed to keep a gun in action.

I seemed to understand Achey more readily and placed great confidence in him.

The dugout at A-15 was deep and large. Rats burrowed behind its board walls and lice and fleas inhabited the bunks. But 16 steps down, it formed a good bomb shelter. From one end a tunnel ran forward and a ladder mounted up to a seat in a steel tower with a small slit, like in a tank turret, for peeping. Once, while Private Dick Kerr was watching, a bullet came through the slit and struck him, but the force of the bullet had been spent getting through the crack and he was unharmed.

As we passed from Post A-15 to Badonviller, we used a large communication trench deep enough to conceal a man walking erect. One day, as I was passing a place where the parapet was low, I heard the singing of a bullet and felt the swish in the air near my face.[12] A German sniper had been watching that low place with his gun trained. It was only a yard wide, but that gave him time to draw a bead and fire. The trenches at this point were far apart. He was no doubt lying concealed in No Man's Land, waiting for his opportunity at the low spot.

It was about June 6th, one morning at "Stand To" at the post in front of the cemetery, that we heard heavy shelling in the woods to our right at Village Negre. The wind was from that direction and that ground was higher. We saw light mist hanging low, gradually moving toward us from those woods. We knew it to be gas that was settling from the higher ground carried in our direction by a light wind. We donned gas masks as soon as it came near and wore the masks for three and a half hours. We protected our dugout by nailing up my blankets as gas curtains. There were no casualties in our company at this time, but there had been some casualties in the Village Negre Sector, where the infantry had again suffered a heavy gas attack.

Our company headquarters was in the town of Badonviller and, as was the custom, all officers came in the town for meals. We had just finished our evening meal at about six o'clock on June 18th. I was in the latrine across the road when the Germans suddenly opened fire. A heavy concentration of gas and high explosives fell all around and struck the building where we had just eaten. We hurried to take shelter in the cellar of one of the buildings and wore our gas masks for about three hours.

In this dugout were Lieutenant Olson—who had been assigned to our company—Lieutenant Means, and myself, along with a large number of enlisted men. At the start of the firing, Lieutenant Andres rushed out to his platoon post. He was knocked down by a shell on the way, but was not injured. I knew that the bombardment was concentrated on the town and believed it to be only harassing fire. Lieutenant Means agreed, so I did not rush through the heavy shelling, but waited until a lull.

Then, as I hurried through the streets of Badonviller, I found the streets cluttered with debris from buildings and many unexploded shells. The town was burning in two or three places, but the fire was extinguished before much damage was done. When I reached A-13 with my mask on, I found Sergeant Achey right on the job. I went on out to Brenner's post. They had not been molested. I stayed there overnight, and next morning we had to wear gas masks again for two hours as the gas settled from the woods of Village Negre over in our direction.

12. Lieutenant Parkinson was the second tallest man in Company 22 at Fort Sheridan. Height was not necessarily an advantage in the trenches as he discovered here.

Shortly after the firing started, Captain Bunch, Regimental Surgeon, came dashing up in his motorcycle side car. He advocated taking the doctors to the wounded, rather than carrying them heavily and slowly to the rear for medical attention.[13] In campaigns that followed, he always was in the thick of the fight with the attacking waves. He seemed to be trying to get killed, but he was unscathed in every battle, only to meet his death in a taxicab accident in New York the day we landed while on his way to meet his fiancé. Likewise, Major Brewer of the 168th Infantry, 3rd Battalion, went through the war with just a wound in the arm, only to die in an automobile accident a few years after the Armistice.

On June 15th, the French General[14] commanding the 6th French Army, in which we were serving, cited the Rainbow in Order #50 for outstanding service during these three months.

On June 19th, we were preparing for the relief of our division.[15] We had been in this sector approximately three months, had our baptism of fire, and received very valuable experience. We were ordered to retire the night of June 19th.

It was quite evident by the extensive shelling which the Germans maintained throughout the day that they knew a relief was in progress.[16] We dreaded the march to the rear, because we knew that the roads were being swept by German artillery fire. But a beautiful rainbow in the western sky told us it was time for the Rainbow Division to move to larger fields to conquer.

The relief order arrived during the day. In this written order, Major Brewer called attention to the fact that the Germans were shelling the rear areas, but he promised that when the hour for relief actually arrived, our own artillery would retaliate with counter-battery fire that would smother the German fire. This gave us a good feeling to know that our artillery would be on the job while we were marching to the rear. I routed my sections through the woods to the vicinity of B-3, then diagonally to Fennviller, in the hope of avoiding the highway from Badonviller, which I expected to be heavily bombarded. While my sections were marching to the rear we did not suffer from German fire. We did not hear our own artillery firing, but we knew that their work had caused the German artillerymen to seek shelter.

After each of my sections had been started safely to the rear under command of their sergeants, I joined Lieutenant Means at Badonviller. We assisted in getting the equipment out and the relief was completed that night. During

13. It could take as many as ten men to laboriously carry a stretcher bearing just one wounded man slowly back to an aid station through shell-churned, knee-deep mud.

14. This was General Duport.

15. Relief of the 42nd Division occurred from June 16 through 26. Parkinson's platoon withdrew on the night of the 19th, but elements of Company D did not leave until the 20th.

16. Measures were taken to shroud this relief of the 42nd Division in secrecy and darkness. Yet the Germans were well aware of what was going on. By night they heavily shelled the area; by day they sent over balloons with the message, "Good Bye 42nd, Welcome 77th". This episode exemplifies both the difficulty of keeping secrets and the dry humor of psychological warfare.

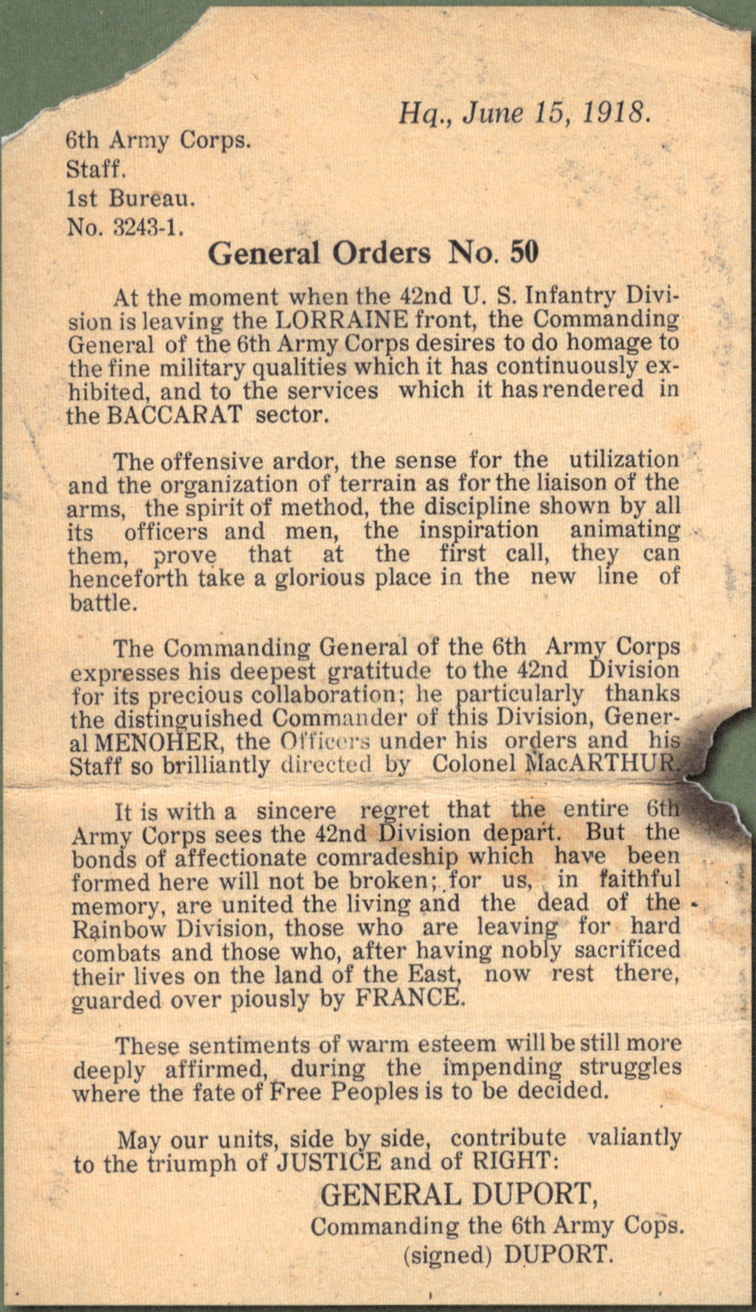

Hq., *June 15, 1918.*

6th Army Corps.
Staff.
1st Bureau.
No. 3243-1.

General Orders No. 50

At the moment when the 42nd U. S. Infantry Division is leaving the LORRAINE front, the Commanding General of the 6th Army Corps desires to do homage to the fine military qualities which it has continuously exhibited, and to the services which it has rendered in the BACCARAT sector.

The offensive ardor, the sense for the utilization and the organization of terrain as for the liaison of the arms, the spirit of method, the discipline shown by all its officers and men, the inspiration animating them, prove that at the first call, they can henceforth take a glorious place in the new line of battle.

The Commanding General of the 6th Army Corps expresses his deepest gratitude to the 42nd Division for its precious collaboration; he particularly thanks the distinguished Commander of this Division, General MENOHER, the Officers under his orders and his Staff so brilliantly directed by Colonel MacARTHUR.

It is with a sincere regret that the entire 6th Army Corps sees the 42nd Division depart. But the bonds of affectionate comradeship which have been formed here will not be broken; for us, in faithful memory, are united the living and the dead of the Rainbow Division, those who are leaving for hard combats and those who, after having nobly sacrificed their lives on the land of the East, now rest there, guarded over piously by FRANCE.

These sentiments of warm esteem will be still more deeply affirmed, during the impending struggles where the fate of Free Peoples is to be decided.

May our units, side by side, contribute valiantly to the triumph of JUSTICE and of RIGHT:

GENERAL DUPORT,
Commanding the 6th Army Cops.
(signed) DUPORT.

A Scrap of Paper. Citation of the 42nd Division from General Duport, June 15, 1918. Tattered, stained, and burnt on one edge, Lieutenant Parkinson carried this through the "hard combats" and "impending struggles" that followed. *Editor's collection.*

the day, however, our company suffered twenty casualties in the other platoons. The casualties were mostly from mustard gas, which closed the eyes of many of these men, since they stayed on duty at their posts that during the previous night had been drenched with mustard gas. It taught us how treacherous mustard gas could be. This post was later moved and men with gas masks on filled up the shell holes where the mustard gas had fallen in gas shells.

The casualties from this engagement were gas wounds, as follows: Lieutenant Means, 1st Sergeant Roy Rhodes, Sergeants Stark and Kiphorn, Corporal Pennell, and Privates Beamsderfer, Shipman, Denlinger, Downs, McGinnis, Reemsnyder, Proffit, Shay, Bishop, Derlinger, Imhoff, Beck, Foulke, Myers, Rogers, Cramblett, and Ryan.

We marched back that night to the town of Neufmaison, the first town to the rear of Pexonne. We had been relieved by a French division[17] that had been severely shot up in the German drive at Mt. Kemmel. As we marched back, we met elements of the 77th Division from New York City marching into our section, where they were brigaded with this veteran, though battle weary, French division.

After spending the night at Neufmaison, on June 21st we marched to Rambervillers. This was a hard march. Men in the trenches were not used to long marches. We all arrived very much exhausted, but saw that the men were comfortably billeted in the barracks, with a bunk for most of them. The men whose feet were most blistered were able to bathe them and rub them so that next morning, we were all ready to march to our next destination. The march, however, was not begun until dusk, and we arrived late at night at Thaon-les-Vosges, a pleasant village where civilians still lived and sold good wine and good beer.

We very much enjoyed our stay at Thaon. We knew, however, that we were going to a more lively sector. Therefore, we tried to make the most of the limited time we had in Thaon. I loaned practically all the money I had to members of my platoon, and the same was true of the other officers. After I was about broke, Private Fanus of Lieutenant Andres' platoon asked me for a loan which I had to refuse. I regretted this very much at the time, but even more so about a month later when he was killed on Hill 212 near Sergy.

On June 24th, our battalion entrained four companies on two military trains. We spent two days on this train riding through Neufchateau and Bar-le-Duc to Vitry. On the second day, another rainbow appeared in the sky to our left as our train puffed along toward Vitry. We detrained June 26th at Vitry-le-Francois. From there we marched a few kilometers to the village at St. Amand.

17. This was likely the French 61st Division.

CHAPTER 4: CHAMPAGNE

St. Amand-sur-Fion was a small village located on the Fion River, which is a tributary of the Marne. The village is located south of Chalons. It was generally understood from some source that we were to spend two weeks in this village in special training. We enjoyed the time at this village, as the inhabitants were very cordial and were thrilled at the arrival of American troops. There had been a great deal of newspaper publicity regarding the fighting by the 2nd Division in the vicinity of Chateau-Thierry.[1] We knew that we were not transported into this area for rest and understood that it would be only a question of time until we, too, would be in the area of heavy fighting.

Major Winn entertained all the officers of the battalion at a dinner on the evening of June 28th. At this dinner I became acquainted with the other officers of the battalion. These were Captain Palmer and Lieutenants Sola and Fred Walker of A Company; Captain Boyce Miller, Lieutenants Sidney Brown, Steward D. Saye, and William Cann of B Company; Captain Peacock and Lieutenants Brown, Travis, O'Keefe, Stratford, and Wingo of C Company; and also Lieutenant Howland, Battalion Adjutant, and Lieutenant Joe Turner, Battalion Supply Officer. We had a very pleasant evening and made the most of our opportunity to enjoy the evening, since our orders had been changed and we were to move toward the front the next day. We frequently had wine and champagne, but we never put on any of those drinking orgies before going into battle such as have been pictured as customary in the movies.

The night of June 29th, we marched to the village of Marson, and the following night marched to the village of Tilloy-et-Billay. On one of these marches we passed near Camp Nablette, which was a large training and rest camp that had been used by the French in this area. At Tilloy, we were just a few meters from a large French airdrome, and one night saw the French bombing planes returning from a trip over the German lines. We were interested in watching

1. In June the Marine Brigade of the Second Division had struggled bitterly to take Belleau Wood. Soon after, the Regular Army Brigade of the same division took the village of Vaux. These small gains at great cost were morale boosters for the French.

the signals from the small colored lights on the aeroplanes as they arrived over the field. They were answered from the ground by the flashing of large search lights which illuminated the landing field and enabled the planes to land safely.

At Tilloy, after a day's rest, we prepared for the rehearsal of an attack that our division was to make in conjunction with two French divisions on the German positions at the town of Olizy about July 4th. This was to be our initial attack. Our company was to be with the 3rd Battalion of the 168th Infantry, which was to pass through the 1st Battalion when it reached the first objective. We were to advance to the final objective and be prepared to withstand the inevitable counter-attacks which always came after the Germans had lost a position. The counter-attacks, in many instances, were more severe than making the original attack.

After rehearsing a few days, we were notified of a change of orders. The French General Staff had learned of a heavy concentration of German troops between Chateau-Thierry and Reims. If our attack had been attempted, it would have been at such great disadvantage and against such heavy hostile artillery that we could not have succeeded. Even if we had succeeded, we would have been overwhelmed by the German counter-attack. Our division would have been practically annihilated. We, lower down in the ranks, did not know this at the time, of course, but learned of it afterward. It illustrates the efficiency of the Intelligence Section of the French General Staff.

We were transferred July 3rd to the 4th French Army, under command of General Gouraud, and that night made a very hard march of about thirty-five kilometers to the town of Suippes, where we arrived at daylight the morning of July 4th. The road we traveled was almost straight north, but it was crowded with French and American troops, including infantry and artillery and an almost endless procession of caissons, ammunition wagons, supply wagons, machine gun carts, and rolling kitchens. We were completely exhausted on reaching our destination.

Our battalion was quartered for the day on the outskirts of Suippes, where we drew our wagons and carts up against the side of a large, long building. We all laid down for a rest and slept for a few hours. I made my bed on a stretcher which I unfolded and set up on the ground. We were all conscious that this was July 4th. We all knew that we were heading into the line to withstand a tremendous German drive. The last four drives by the Germans[2] had resulted in victories and large gains, although the Allied line was still unbroken.

2. The German "Peace" Offensives in the Spring of 1918 were meant to end the war before masses of American troops could get into action and turn momentum in favor of the Allies. The first drive was launched near Cambrai and St. Quentin penetrating some 45 miles across the Somme River to Montdidier from March 21 to April 5, 1918. (Lieutenant Parkinson's narrative probably counted the two successive phases of this Somme offensive as two distinct drives.) The next drive was along the Lys River near the Belgian border making smaller gains from April 9 to 29. The most ominous thrust was the Aisne Offensive from May 27 through June 4 which put the Germans in Chateau-Thierry and within striking distance of Paris. In spite of the small American gains at Belleau Wood and Vaux, the Germans seemed to have the upper hand. The mood in Paris was dark and expectations were that the next offensive might break the French altogether.

Chain of Command
Battle of Champagne, July 15-18, 1918

General Henri J. E. Gouraud
FOURTH FRENCH ARMY

Major General Charles T. Menoher
42nd RAINBOW DIVISION

Brigadier General Robert A. Brown
84th BRIGADE
167th Infantry Regiment
168th Infantry Regiment
151st Machine Gun Battalion (Companies Attached to Infantry)

Colonel Ernest R. Bennett
168th INFANTRY REGIMENT

Major Guy S. Brewer
THIRD BATTALION (168th Infantry)

1st Lieutenant Monroe A. Means
COMPANY D, 151st MACHINE GUN BATTALION
(Attached to Third Battalion, 168th Infantry Regiment)

2nd Lieutenant William Andres - 1st PLATOON (4 MG Squads)
2nd Lieutenant N. P. Parkinson - 2nd PLATOON (4 MG Squads)
2nd Lieutenant Earl Olson - 3rd PLATOON (4 MG Squads)
2nd Lieutenant John H. Geiszel - SUPPLY TRAIN

About noon, I walked down the road to the village of Suippes and bought two bottles of excellent wine from the French Army Canteen. This was very excellent wine and just the stimulant we needed after the long, tiring march. All day long I dreaded intensely the possibility of German aviators locating our battalion behind these buildings. The sun was not shining, but it was not raining and aviators could have come. After locating us, they could have directed artillery fire that would have caused heavy casualties. No aviators disturbed us, however, and that night at sundown we formed for another lap on our march to the front.

As our battalion moved out on the road, the sound of tremendous artillery fire was heard in the woods a short distance ahead of us. We learned afterward that the French were making a raid. At this time, however, we did not know the cause of the firing. I recall that I dreaded moving forward at that time more than I had ever yet dreaded anything I had to do since entering the army. The raid was over, however, and the artillery fire ceased before we came up even with their guns.

Our column had to move very slowly because of the congested traffic conditions, as many units like ours were moving forward to battle positions. The march was not long, but we were delayed often by traffic conditions. Lieutenant Travis of C Company suffered a broken leg when his horse fell on him. Our machine gun companies were again assigned to infantry battalions. As usual, our company was assigned to the Third Battalion, 168th Infantry under Major Brewer. At daylight, we unloaded our equipment in the scrub pine woods north of Camp 3.5 along a rock-paved highway known as the Old Roman Road, having been built by Caesar's slaves over 2,000 years previous.

After much difficulty, Lieutenant Means located Major Brewer and our company was assigned to trench positions in the sector of trenches known on the fortification maps as "Rouen." The sector of trenches immediately to our right was known as "Verdun." The trenches were well organized—one line after another. Although there had been fighting here early in the war, the lines had remained stationary for about three years. At the time of General Nivelle's offensive in 1917, the French had repeatedly hurled themselves against these German positions and been repulsed as many times, always with terrible losses.

We were approximately three kilometers behind the front line, which was occupied by two French divisions of *Chasseurs*.[3] The *Chasseurs Alpin* were a select corps of the French Army, a dashing, daring lot which had won for themselves the nickname "Blue Devils." They wore navy blue uniforms, black putties, and Sam Brown belts with a navy beret titled jauntily on one side of the head. When ex-President Roosevelt addressed us at Fort Sheridan Officers Training Camp, he gave the *Chasseurs* credit for being the finest fighting corps in existence.

We did not know it at this time, but General Gouraud's plan was to withdraw from the front lines as soon as the attacking waves of Germans approached.[4] This would be after the Germans had wasted the larger part of the barrage on the front line position. The withdrawal was to be back to the intermediate line, where the main resistance would be given after the Germans had wasted their strength against empty trenches. American troops, all of them from the 42nd Division, were in position in the line of defense, which after the evacuation of the first line would be the line of resistance.

My platoon occupied machine gun positions located in trenches manned by M Company of the 168th Infantry. Lieutenant Doocy and I had headquarters in a large dugout deep under the chalk surface of the ground. It was an excellent shelter about sixty feet below the surface. Nothing but a direct hit by an aerial bomb or a large-caliber shell could harm it. My gun positions were at the edge of this woods and located to the left in the midst of this scrub pine

3. "Chasseur" means "hunter" in French.

4. The actual plan was to withdraw from the first line *before* the preparatory barrage. Parkinson knew this as his next sentence shows, but he expressed himself unclearly here.

General Gouraud's Plan of Defense

The German build-up for a major offensive in Champagne became apparent to the Allies by early July 1918. Gouraud's plan for the defense of his sector called for:

1. Vigorous raids on enemy positions to seize prisoners. These would supply vital intelligence on the timing of the impending German attack.
2. Occupation of the first line of trenches up to the last minute. This would deceive the Germans as to Gouraud's true intentions.
3. Abandoning the first line of trenches just before the attack. The second, or intermediate line of trenches would become the Main Line of Resistance (MLR). Then Germans would waste most of their artillery fire on empty positions.
4. Sacrificial strong points behind the abandoned first line. These would break up German infantry formations, separating them from their rolling barrage. These strong points were key: Artillery would be indexed forward according to a prearranged timetable. By holding up the German infantry, those in the MLR would gain crucial time to get out of dugouts and into battle stations before the enemy was upon them. Of course, this meant that the sacrificial strong points were truly sacrificial and would be wiped out.
5. Getting the jump on artillery fire. This counter-battery fire would diminish the effectiveness of the German shelling.

All went according to Gouraud's plan and the Germans were repulsed. For the most part, the men assigned to the sacrificial strong points were either killed or spent the remainder of the war in German prison camps.

woods, where fields of fire had been cut by removing the trees so as to open lanes in two diagonal directions from each gun position, forming a "V."

Since the large dugout was crowded and was not near enough to my gun positions, I located another small dugout in front of the trenches. It was large enough to shelter two squads and deep enough to withstand a direct hit by a German 77. It had an opening at both ends, with stairways of about half a dozen steps leading to the surface. I occupied this position with Corporals Shaffer's and Roberts' squads. Corporal Humphrey and his squad occupied a dugout and gun position about 100 meters to the left in the woods, as described above. Sergeant Achey, with another gun crew under Corporal Hawthorne, was located in an open trench about 200 meters behind Corporal Humphrey and near the Old Roman Road. They had instructions, however, to take shelter in a strong dugout located nearby and occupied by a French battery of artillery in case of severe bombardment. We took these positions July 5th and 6th.

From the time we entered this sector, for about nine days I did not hear a single sound that I knew to be hostile fire. Only occasionally did aeroplanes from Germany attempt to observe us. The silence was ominous. We knew that ahead of us, the Germans were assembling men and artillery for the most gigantic attack that had yet been attempted.

We had strict instructions about exposing ourselves to observation. My dugout and gun positions were located in an "L" of the woods, just where a road came diagonally across an open field and entered the woods back to the Roman Road. This corner was under strict observation from German balloons at the edge of the woods, where our machine guns could get a good sweep at the advancing lines. It was also right at the intersection of a main trench line where a large dugout was located and many men were sheltered. Some of them inevitably exposed themselves to enemy observation.

Furthermore, our position was right along this road to the rear, which the enemy would be certain to keep covered so as to interfere with communication as much as possible. All these combined conditions made our position one on which the Germans would be certain to concentrate heavy artillery fire. Add to this, every clump of trees in this scrub pine woods sheltered French and American artillery. At this particular point it was the heaviest concentration of our artillery that I had seen at any time. Guns were literally hub to hub, concealed under trees or placed in the open and carefully camouflaged. These artillery positions were known to the Germans, because each night the French conducted raids under support of fire from these French guns. During the day we could walk about in the pine woods, but many times each day we would be overwhelmed by a sudden outburst of fire from the French artillery located at points among us.

At night, when harassing fire was being conducted or a barrage was thrown for a raid, those woods resounded and the ground shook for hours at a time from the heavy fire these Frenchmen in our midst were sending to Germany. We knew that as soon as the German attack started, a heavy hostile fire would attempt to smother these artillery positions known to the enemy. In addition to other reasons stated above, I knew we would be in for a hot time as soon as the Germans were ready to attack.

We had lots of confidence, however, in this heavy concentration of artillery, machine guns, and infantry. Although we knew that the four previous German drives had been successful, we were confident that we would break the attack here. We did not see how any person could survive the fire that was prepared from positions just within our sight. We were told that similar preparations had been made from the Argonne Forest clear over to Reims.[5]

Our confidence was further increased by an order received throughout the entire army from General Gouraud. We knew General Gouraud to be one of the most picturesque French commanders. At the outbreak of the war, he was the youngest of all French generals. He had been wounded five times in action. On one occasion, with the Gallipoli French Expedition, he was wounded in the arm. It was a nasty wound and surgeons told him it would take a long time

5. At least 2,000 Allied batteries (about 8,000 guns) were waiting along this sector.

to heal, but that they could eventually save the arm. He asked if it would heal any quicker by amputating the arm. When answered in the affirmative he ordered the arm amputated so that he could return to the front sooner.

July 7th, we received an order from him translated as follows:

July 7, 1918

To the French and American Soldiers of the Fourth Army:

We may be attacked at any moment.

You all know that a defensive battle was never engaged under more favorable conditions.

We are awake and on our guard.

We are powerfully reinforced with infantry and artillery.

You will fight on a terrain that you have transformed by your work and your perseverance into a redoubtable fortress. This invincible fortress and all its passages are well guarded.

The bombardment will be terrible. You will stand it without weakness.

The assault will be fierce, in a cloud of smoke, dust, and gas.

But your positions and your armament are formidable.

In your breasts beat the brave and strong hearts of free men.

None shall look to the rear; none shall yield a step.

Each shall have but one thought: to kill, to kill-a-plenty, until they have had their fill.

Therefore, your General says to you: You will break this assault and it will be a happy day.

(signed) Gouraud.

By authority of the Chief of Staff
PETTELAT.

This order meant that we should fight it out to the last where we stood and yield nothing. Every man in our division understood this order. It was a grim reminder that the approaching attack was the critical period of the war, but all faced it with determination and readiness to stand to the last. The spirit of General Gouraud seemed to permeate his entire command.

There were so many troops concentrated in this sector that it was impossible for all of them to sleep in dugouts. Therefore, they pitched pup tents in the pine underbrush where they were concealed from enemy observation. My platoon had pup tent shelters pitched in this manner near the gun positions.

By constant raids, the intelligence service of the French General Staff knew as early as July 10th that the German attack would come between July 13th and

French General
Henri J. E. Gouraud.
Gouraud was a rare breed—a French general who was actually respected and liked by the Americans he commanded. This profile view conceals the fact that his right arm was amputated due to a severe wound at Gallipoli. *Editor's collection.*

Colonel
Ernest R. Bennett.
Commander of the 168th Infantry Regiment. *Photo from Taber, The Story of the 168th Infantry.*

Major
Guy S. Brewer.
Commander of the Third Battalion, 168th Infantry Regiment. *Photo from Taber, The Story of the 168th Infantry.*

15th. General Gouraud's plan of defense required, if possible, that he know the exact time. Therefore, continuous raids in various parts of the French front lines were made each night and morning.

On the night of July 12th, at about 10:00, a breathless messenger came from Major Brewer's headquarters with the message that the attack was expected next morning and that the artillery preparation by the enemy would begin at midnight. With this warning I awakened all men sleeping in the pup tents and ordered them to battle positions. They responded promptly, but after waiting several hours, when no attack developed, they went grumbling back to their tents.

On the night of July 13th, which was the eve of French Independence (Bastille Day), at about 11:00 P.M., I received from Major Brewer's headquarters another warning that the attack was again expected and artillery preparation would begin about midnight. Therefore, shortly after 11:00, I aroused the sleeping men who were not already on guard duty and, with some difficulty, got them to battle positions in the shelter of the dugout. Again, after waiting for several hours, we found that the alarm had been false. There was considerable grumbling, and several of the men made the boast that they would not again leave their beds for an alarm until they knew it was real. I knew how these men felt and had great sympathy for them.

Again, on the night of July 14th[6] at 11:50 P.M.,[7] I received from another breathless messenger, Frank Cramblett, a written message from Major Brewer reading:

July 14, 1918

Word just received from Regt. Hq. that attack is expected at midnight.

Maj. Brewer.

Knowing how the men felt, I debated for a moment whether I should arouse them, but only for a moment. I went to the pup tents and aroused each man. Some of them went to the dugout shelters. Others laid down again after I had passed on. I came back to each tent and in some cases had to issue positive commands for these sleeping men to take their posts. In two or three tents some had removed their shoes. I did not permit them to wait to put them on, but ordered them through the woods in their stockings, carrying their shoes to the shelter of the dugout. In murmuring undertones I heard much grumbling about someone being scared to death of a few shells and that they could not see why the prospect of an attack should call for such a wild rush for a dugout. "They had been under shell fire before," they thought, and "they weren't afraid of a few shells."

After all the men had left the tents, I, with Corporal Shaffer, followed hurriedly to the dugout. There the men were all standing nearby on top of the ground. I ordered them down into the dugout. They obeyed with more grumbling and muttering. The last man had just entered the dugout and Corporal Shaffer and I stood outside on watch.

Suddenly, the woods rocked with tremendous explosions. It seemed that every gun opened at the same instant. Every piece of Allied artillery for miles in both directions, right and left, forward and behind, began their heaviest fire on the German lines. In a brief second or two the Germans answered fire. True to my predictions, they concentrated a tremendous fire right on our corner of the woods, where the road entered and the trenches crossed. They were endeavoring frantically to silence our many pieces of artillery.

The sky was aflame with continuous flashes from the German lines, emphasized by a contrast of red and green rockets from them. Every time a gun was discharged a tremendous bright flash resulted. As the roar was continuous, the flashes also maintained a continuous light. German shells were exploding

6. Just after dusk on that very night a French lieutenant had led a raid on German trenches and returned with prisoners. These provided exact information that the German artillery preparation would commence shortly after midnight and the infantry assault at 4:00 A.M. The French Command passed this intelligence on to the 42nd Division at 10:45 P.M. The French officer who led this last minute raid is probably the real hero of Champagne.

7. This was just ten minutes prior to the anticipated eruption of massive artillery fire which explains why Lieutenant Parkinson was so eager to get his men into the dugout without delay.

Heavy Artillery. The Germans amassed artillery for the barrage at Champagne. Here a battery of German 210mm howitzers are in action in an unknown location. The second from the left is in the recoil position. The one in the middle has the barrel lowered for loading. The second from the right is about to fire. Note the camouflaged paint, hydropneumatic recoil mechanisms, and the *Radgurtel* wheel pads for keeping the heavy guns from sinking in the mud. *Editor's collection.*

all around us. The fire became so heavy that Shaffer and I took shelter in the dugout entrance. Other men stood guard by turns in the doors of the dugout, waiting to report the minute that the German barrage should lift so that we could rush to our gun positions. We had taken in our machine guns and part of the ammunition, but had left the heavy tripods and a few boxes of ammunition in the emplacements so that we could begin firing quickly, if necessary.

In the open field in front of us, a French battery galloped into position, wheeled into line, quickly threw up some camouflage covering, and opened fire. Elsewhere in this open field we could see French artillery firing from positions camouflaged so well that even we had not suspected their location. Other French batteries were firing in the open. One of these French batteries nearby suffered a direct hit on one of their guns. Soon another one was put out of action, but they continued firing without interruption until all their guns were silenced by enemy fire. They had a task to fulfill and they did it according to General Gouraud's famous order.

Shells began falling right on top of our dugout. Three or four direct hits were made on the roof, but did no damage to us underneath, except that one of the timbers was knocked from one of the doors. These shells were mixed with gas shells. I nailed one of the gray blankets I had brought from Morehouse and Wells of Decatur at each door. These blankets, as gas curtains, prevented the gas from settling into our dugout. Several times previous I had felt that some of the men under my command begrudged my having these two extra blankets in addition to the two blankets which each man carried in his pack. Most of them had left their blankets in their tents and they were pleased to have these blankets available. Otherwise, they would have had to wear gas masks for about three hours.

A little later, I could see that shells were no longer falling right on our dugout. I sent corporals to their gun positions to inspect tripods. One tripod had suffered a direct hit and was demolished. The other was brought in. Through the heavy artillery fire, Privates Rodman and Bryson came from the Battalion Headquarters of Major Brewer to learn how we were faring. The message which Private Rodman carried back with him never reached Major Brewer. He was killed when a shell's direct hit blew his head off on the way back. Private Bryson was also killed while carrying a message.

At Corporal Humphrey's position at the outbreak of the attack, they had brought their ammunition and guns into shelter, but their tripod also was demolished. During a period of the bombardment when the fire was not at its heaviest, Corporal Humphrey sent Private Wayne McLaughlin to me with a message making this report.

> We got the gun in safely shortly after the bombardment started but before we could get the tripod in. A shell hit it and blew it and six boxes of amm. to pieces. Send ammunition with bearer. Everything else O.K.
>
> Corp. H. S. Humphrey
> (RECEIVED BY RUNNER 7:30 A.M., JULY 15, 1918)

Private McLaughlin came all the way through a trench, but was knocked down by a shell on the way. On the way back he was wounded, and when he arrived was sent to the rear. Sergeant Achey, at the other machine gun position, first sheltered his men in several open trenches, but when he saw the intensity of the German fire, they all retired to the shelter of the dugout occupied by the French battery 50 yards ahead on the trail and watched this French battery operate their pieces. They remained alert, ready to take battle positions should the enemy come within their range.

About 5:00 A.M., I received a message from Major Brewer saying that the attack had been delayed, but that it had started at 4:15 A.M. It had penetrated the first and main line positions in many places and they were rapidly advancing to our line of resistance. He cautioned us to remember the order to yield no ground and "fight it out where you are." I was pleased with the manner in which my men responded. They made ready to open up intense fire as soon as any enemy appeared. Thus far, however, we had seen none of the enemy. The intermediate positions, one kilometer ahead of us, had stood fast. We were not permitted an opportunity to fire a shot at the Germans, but we passed through five hours of the most intense artillery fire I knew either before or since.

About 7:00 in the morning, word came to us from the headquarters of Major Brewer that the German attack had been stopped. The artillery fire had slackened somewhat, but it continued to be heavy at intervals, so that we spent most of the time in shelter. Although the German drive had been stopped, throughout the day they made several further assaults on the first line ahead of us. These assaults were repulsed by our troops in conjunction with the French.

By noon, although hostile fire was still heavy at intervals, we knew that the battle had been won. During lulls between hostile fire, our men moved about through the trenches and woods to see what had been happening. There was not a pup tent in our camp that had a direct hit. Some of the men had left their canteens and mess pans in their tents. Almost every one of these had been struck directly or by fragments. One of the men who had done much of the grumbling, after viewing the destruction, exclaimed to his comrades that never again would he hesitate to take shelter when Lieutenant Parkinson told him to. This was not in my presence, but Private Patrick, one of my runners, reported it to me later. Again, I felt that I had the confidence of my men.

On other excursions through the woods, our men came in contact with the French in this section. From some hidden source these Frenchmen brought forth canteens of red wine and cognac. They greeted every American with enthusiasm and shared their drink with our troops. There was great jollification at the victory, even though shells were still falling and hostile planes were darting to and fro overhead. One large squadron of planes, numbering about forty red-nosed Fokkers, was said to be under the direct command of Baron von Richthofen, at that time the leading German ace.[8] They dived at our trenches, firing on any troops they saw. One of them, locating our machine gun emplacements, directed artillery fire of about twenty shells on us. They all fell in our midst, but miraculously, none of us were injured before we had time to take cover. A machine gun in Lieutenant Andres' platoon was blown up in the air and lodged in a tree.

About noon, I went back to Major Brewer's headquarters, where my company commander, Lieutenant Means, was also stationed. It was another strong dugout. There had been great havoc back there during the bombardment. The camp of frame huts had been practically demolished, although the one in which Lieutenant Means had been accustomed to sleep was not touched. He had not slept there that night, however, nor anywhere else. The shells continued falling heavily, not in the form of a barrage, but many German guns were still harassing our lines of communication. It required skillful dodging for me to get back to my position.

Throughout the entire days of July 15-18th, the harassing fire from artillery and from hostile planes continued, although it gradually diminished. About noon on July 18th, we were again overwhelmed by the admirations and adula-

8. Actually, Manfred von Richthofen (the Red Baron) had been shot down and killed about two months before on April 21, 1918.

tions heaped upon our troops by the nearby Frenchmen. Wine and cognac were again passed around to some of our men. Others were hugged joyfully and kissed on both cheeks by jubilant Frenchmen.

The news had just arrived of the Chateau-Thierry salient near Soissons, where the First and Second American Divisions had counter-attacked and penetrated the German lines for many prisoners and large gains. It could be seen that this last great Peace Offensive for the Germans had been stopped in its tracks. General Foch, through the aid of our fresh American divisions, had seized the offensive from the Germans, who were now retreating from the entire salient of Chateau-Thierry.

Plans taken from prisoners July 15th showed that the Germans had planned to be in Suippes by 9:00 on the morning of July 15th and in Chalons by 3:00 that afternoon. Had they succeeded it would have been impossible to save Paris, but they failed. This was truly one of the most decisive battles of the war. We were proud of our part as a division in stopping this attack, and we could tell that the French were overjoyed to know that American troops were in the fighting lines and had given an excellent account of themselves.[9]

July 19th, about noon, we had orders to be prepared for a relief. We waited expectantly all afternoon, for we suspected that the relief would occur at sundown. Definite orders did not come, however, until long after midnight. We were glad for relief, but we wanted to be able to get out and far to the rear before daylight exposed our movements to enemy observation. We had much equipment to move and many miles to go before we would be safe.

We did not receive orders until approximately 2:00 A.M. We first had to carry our reserve ammunition back to battalion headquarters on the road where our ammunition wagons could pick it up. This was a hard task and required much time. Ammunition boxes were heavy.[10] There was so much ammunition in our position, however, that it was impossible to carry it all back.[11] Enough was carried back to completely load all our wagons and the rest was left at the gun positions. We then carried our guns and tripods back to the Roman Road, where our machine gun carts were waiting.[12] We made a hurried march through breaking day back to Camp 3.5, where the stench of

9. As Major General Joseph T. Dickman, commander of the 3rd Division, would later put it, "The 42nd Division had done very well in the defense east of Reims; the 3rd Division held the Germans on the Marne; and the 1st and 2nd Divisions furnished four-fifths of the attacking infantry in the spearhead of the great drive toward Soissons" (Dickman, 128-129). The French had good reason to rejoice at the showing of the Yanks at this critical juncture.

10. An ammo box holding 12 strips of 24 rounds (288 total) weighed 28.2 lbs. Normally an ammunition carrier would lug two of these at a time. The regulation load for a platoon's eight mule carts was 88 ammo boxes, four machine guns(52.8 lbs each) with tripods (55 lbs each), and sundry tools and parts. That amounts to about 3,000 lbs of dead weight to carry.

11. Company D "had upwards of 80,000 rounds of ammunition on the line" (Means).

12. Fortunately, Lieutenant Geiszel was sent back to take charge of Company D's trains on July 18. He received the orders for relief before the rest of the company did, quickly brought the mule carts forward, and was waiting here at 2:00 A.M. Thus, much time was saved and Company D completed most of its withdrawal under cover of darkness. The other three companies of the 151st Machine Gun Battalion had to move out in daylight (Means).

dead animals was almost unbearable. There were carcasses of about 300 animals decaying in this vicinity, three days old in the hot July weather.

The animals of C Company had been picketed in this camp during the first heavy bombardment.[13] They lost every one of their twenty-four cart mules. Our other three companies were now short of animals, since we had to divide with C Company. Some of our strongest mules were pulling two carts. This made progress slow through the bad roads. By the time we reached the road leading to Suippes, it was broad daylight. Our own artillery in this vicinity was firing heavy drum fire. We waited breathlessly, expecting our road to be swept any minute with bursting shells from the enemy. Fortunately, however, no shells disturbed us. It was daylight when we reached Suippes, but our own artillery with the French had so completely smothered the German artillery that we were not disturbed. The real reason for the heavy firing by our artillery was to support a counter-attack the French were making that morning at the front to recover the ground of the first line trenches which General Gouraud had ordered evacuated in the successful strategy employed in breaking the German assault.

On the road beyond Suippes, we marched as a company to Camp Noblette, near La Cheppe, which was the assembling point of the division. This was a large French camp equipped with roughly-built cottages where troops were quartered for rest and training. Our march from our machine gun emplacements back to Suippes, after our strenuous labor moving ammunition and equipment, was made at such a rapid pace that when we had reached Suippes, we were practically exhausted. The march from Suippes to Camp Nablotte, about fifteen kilometers, was one of the hardest marches I experienced during the war.

All canteens were empty. The roads and roadsides were heavy with white chalk dust. Many infantrymen marching ahead of us had fallen out. I saw one exhausted doughboy bleeding at his nose as he fell out by the roadside. Our own men were similarly exhausted. I never saw so much straggling in any one march, but we kept moving, and late in the morning reached Camp Nablotte. Soon the kitchen was steaming, preparing hot coffee and slum,[14] which was the first hot meal we had received for some time. We had freshly cooked meals during the last few days, but they had usually been cold by the time they were carried to the front.

During this hard march between Suippes and Nablotte, we were conscious of a French aeroplane hovering high above us as our protector. Suddenly, we heard rapid machine gun fire up above. Looking up, we saw this French plane

13. The horses, mules, and carts of Company D were picketed elsewhere at Camp Nantivette (Means), just north of Suippes.

14. Apparently "slum" is short for "slumgullion", an obscure word derived from the French for "slime" and old English for "mud". It means meat stew.

and a newly-arrived German engaged in combat. After much maneuvering and diving and dipping, the German plane started falling. It must have been a distance of 6,000 feet. He fell straight down, with one wing useless. He turned over and over, but each time he made a loop he maneuvered his other wing so as to partly break the force of the fall. Eventually he landed in a nearby field uninjured, although his plane was demolished. Many of the infantrymen who had fallen out of the march now suddenly recovered and dashed through the field to where this plane had fallen in search of souvenirs.

We spent one night at Camp Nablotte resting, during which time our company officers attended a meeting of Major Brewer's officers of the 3rd Battalion. At this meeting, it was announced that we were soon to make an attack of our own. For about two hours these officers discussed tactics of open warfare, communications between units, and the matter of following up our own barrage. Although we had hoped for a long period of recreation, we knew that we were headed to a new front.

July 20th, Lieutenants Means and Geiszel went to Chalons and ordered uniforms to replace those that had been lost in the recent battle along with their other personal baggage.[15] At this camp, new corporals and sergeants were made to replace the casualties of our recent engagements. Houck and Reich were among those advanced to corporals at this time, the latter on my recommendation.

The battalion remained at Camp Nablotte until the night of July 20th. About noon on July 19th, we saw a large body of German prisoners being marched down the road from Suippes to Chalons, which passed through our camp. There was a good company of them, indicating that the attack made that morning by the French, during our withdrawal, to regain the lines formerly evacuated had been successful. All prisoners taken during the attack of the Germans July 15th had been quickly sent to the rear. However, neither the French nor the Americans were in much humor that morning to take prisoners. Very few lived long enough to get near enough our lines to surrender.

On the night of July 20th, our battalion marched to the town of Sarry, a few kilometers south of Chalons. We had orders to entrain at the nearby village of Coolus. During the day of July 21st, I was billeted in this inhabited village of Sarry in a house in the shape of a "U," one wing of which was a residence and the other two being stables. That morning, in the center of this open court, I saw a herd of half a dozen milk cows being fed and milked by the owner.

It was the custom in our company for each of the officers of the company to act as mess officer for a few days in turn. I immediately volunteered on this day and arranged with the woman for us to purchase about four liters of fresh

15. Means and Geiszel "had lost everything except what they had on their person on the night of July 17th" (Means). Just as Lieutenant Parkinson had to spend over three months' pay for his own uniform and gear upon his commission, these two lieutenants had to shell out their own money to re-equip. Uncle Sam was kind of a cheapskate with officers in this war!

milk, which was a little over a gallon in our way of measuring. For my breakfast, this lady had served me a hot bowl of milk together with toast made from French bread. It was the first fresh milk or cream I had seen in over six months. For the noon meal I arranged with another lady to fry some steaks which the Mess Sergeant furnished from a quarter of fresh beef. Also, after sufficient temptation in the form of Franc notes, she produced half a dozen eggs from which she made a delicious omelet. She also furnished some French fried potatoes and a plate of shelled beans. All of these she prepared in some miraculous way before an open fireplace with some pots and kettles that I did not understand. She seasoned them well with oil dressing and a sprinkling of garlic.

Lieutenants Means, Geiszel, Andres, Olson, and I sat down to the best meal we'd had for many months. But the greatest climax of all was when, entirely to the surprise of the other officers, this lady served the four liters of fresh milk, hot, and very slightly sweetened with sugar, with lots of toast made from American white bread. We enjoyed this meal in a way that we had not experienced for a long time. We had no wine to go with it, but it was not really missed. One of the compensations for going a long time hungry or on ill-prepared food is the fact that when you do get a good meal, you can enjoy it so much better.

Casualties of D Company in the Champagne engagement were Privates Raymond Bryson and George A. Rodman, killed; and Privates Bond, Loucks, Miller, McLaughlin, Karabetos, Bair, Rittenhouse, Earley. and Imhoff wounded.

Privates Rodman and Bryson were recommended for Distinguished Service Crosses for their service as messengers during the terrific bombardment which took their lives. But we were attached to the 168th Infantry, and the commendations were not approved by the higher officers of that organization, who naturally were more concerned with decorations for their own men.

Lieutenant Edward J. Veasey of the 168th Infantry was killed during the first volley of shell fire as he and several other billeting officers were dashing for the shelter of a dugout at Suippes. Lieutenant Elmer T. Doocy, with whom I originally shared the 60-foot deep dugout, received a shell fragment in the fleshy part of the thigh but remained on duty. In B Company, one of the gun crews was stationed in a concrete pill box. During the German bombardment, a direct hit demolished the pill box and killed or wounded those inside. Lieutenant Olson of D Company was also stationed in a concrete pill box. A large shell landed just a few feet from it and pushed it over, although it did not demolish it or cause any casualties inside. In Lieutenant Doocy's dugout, crowded with men, the air became so foul during the bombardment that all had to circulate in a line: in at one entrance, through the dugout, and with gas masks on, out the other entrance, back through the trench, and then into the dugout again. But the wounded lying inside could only gasp and struggle for air. None could be forced down to them because it was saturated with gas.

During the attack, the Germans had used tanks. A battery from the 151st Field Artillery was stationed near the front line to fire point blank on these tanks.[16] It was reputed to have made direct hits on nine enemy tanks that morning and the infantry were said to have captured five more.

Rainbow Booty. A German A7V tank captured by the 42nd Rainbow Division east of Rheims, at Champagne. The Germans produced only about 20 of these clumsy machines. *Editor's collection.*

16. The editor found no reference to this in the 151st Field Artillery's history nor in the Division histories. However, half of the 117th Trench Mortar Battery was placed in the Main Line of Resistance and they did knock out four German tanks on July 15 (Collins, 75). Evidently Parkinson confused the 151st Artillery for the 117th Trench Mortar Battery.

CHAPTER 5:
SECOND BATTLE OF THE MARNE

FORET DE BEUVARDES, FORET DE FERE, CROIX ROUGE FERME, OURCQ RIVER, HILL 212, SERGY, NESLES, CROIX BLANCHE FERME

That night, the Germans raided the nearby town of Chalons by air, dropping bombs. The anti-aircraft guns in that vicinity maintained a heavy fire for quite a while, but every few minutes we would hear a tremendous bomb explode. Some damage was done in the city, although we never learned how much. The raiders appeared two or three times that night, and on one occasion attacked the railroad station at Coolus, where Companies A and B were entraining. Bombs were dropped nearby, but there were no casualties that I know of. We knew, however, that on a following night we would entrain at the same point and dreaded the job, for fear we also might be bombed. We did not entrain until the night of the 23rd, when Companies C and D marched to Coolus. As defense, the French had mounted a few machine guns near the quay.[1] Lieutenant Means mounted eight of our own guns on a hill near the quay. While we were entraining German planes did appear,[2] but were driven off by this concentrated machine gun fire.

Many of the guns were firing tracer bullets, which were made so that the heat of the cartridge explosion caused the bullets to glow until their course could be followed in the air, one streaming after another. One of these bullets

1. The French had four machine guns positioned at the station (Means).

2. Two separate air attacks were driven off as Company D was entraining (Means).

in a gas tank would cause an explosion. Therefore, these bombers hurried away and disposed of their bombs elsewhere.

Flak. Americans using a French Hotchkiss machine gun in the anti-aircraft role. At Coolus, eight machine guns of D Company, 151st Machine Gun Battalion, drove off German bombers intent on harassing the movement of the 42nd Rainbow Division. *Editor's collection.*

Our train pulled out as soon as we were loaded, and the following morning entered a large railroad yard. As the train stopped for a few minutes, we got out and looked around and were greatly thrilled by the sight of the Eiffel Tower, which we knew was a landmark of Paris. Our maps showed us to be in the railroad yards of Noisy-le-Sec, a suburb of Paris. Some of the enlisted men thrilled at what they believed was going to be a trip to Paris and our long expected 14-day leaves.

While standing here, a long train passed us going in the other direction. It was filled with black colonial troops in the khaki uniform of the French Moroccans. These Moroccans were just returning from the front, where, on July 18th, they had attacked between the 1st and 2nd American Divisions in the American counter-attack south of Soissons. As soon as they passed, the track was clear and our train moved forward. It switched on to a circular siding and we were soon headed out, leading away from Paris. It was the nearest we came.

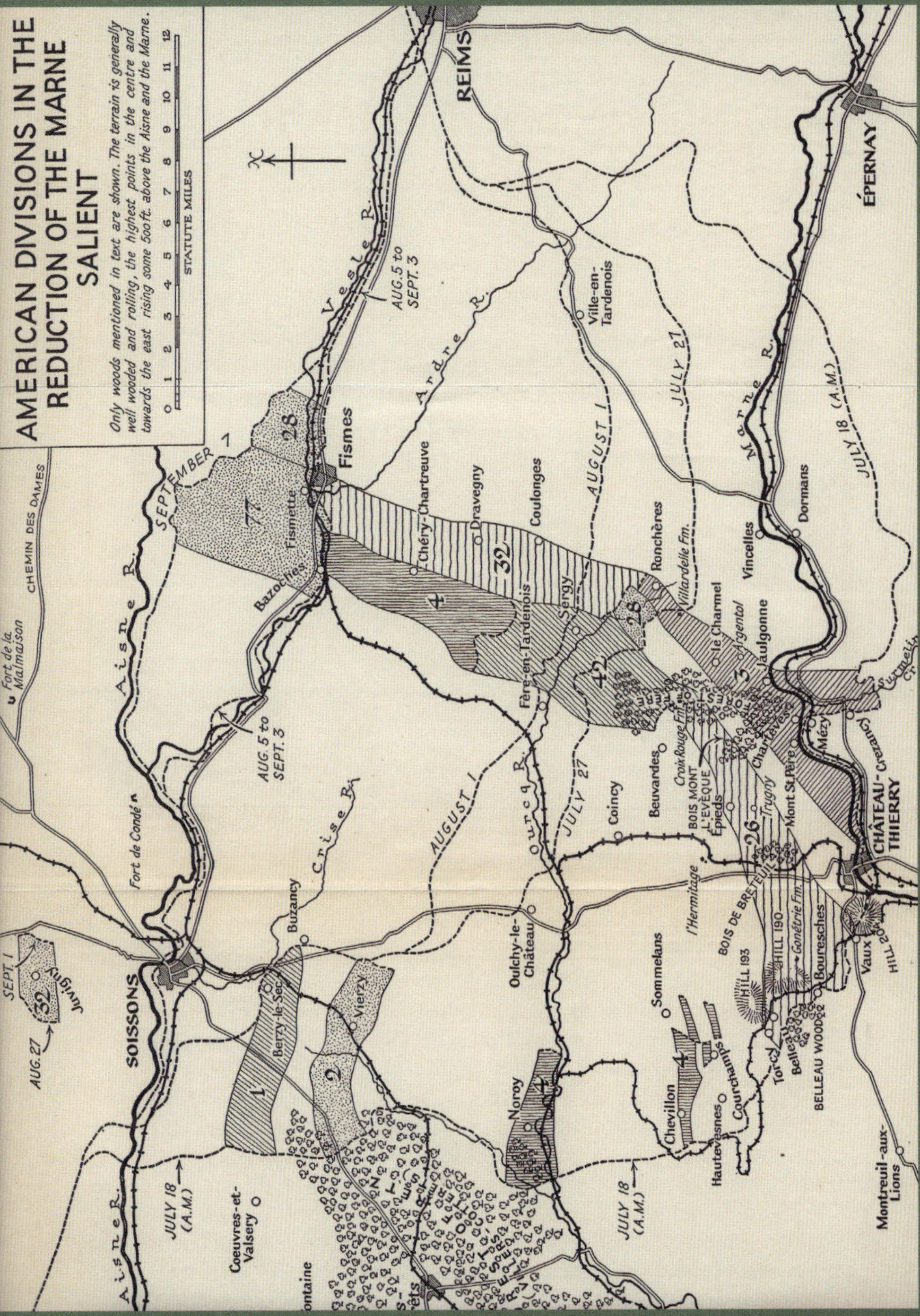

Map from Pershing, *My Experiences in the World War.*

Chain of Command
Ourcq River Crossing, July 27-August 1, 1918

Major General Hunter Liggett
I CORPS
4th US Division
26th US Division
42nd US Division
167th French Division

Major General Charles T. Menoher
42nd RAINBOW DIVISION

Brigadier General Robert A. Brown
84th BRIGADE
167th Infantry Regiment
168th Infantry Regiment
151st Machine Gun Battalion (Companies Attached to Infantry)

Colonel Ernest R. Bennett
168th INFANTRY REGIMENT

Major Guy S. Brewer
THIRD BATTALION (168th Infantry)

1st Lieutenant Monroe A. Means
COMPANY D, 151st MACHINE GUN BATTALION
(Attached to Third Battalion, 168th Infantry Regiment)

2nd Lieutenant William Andres - 1st PLATOON (4 MG Squads)
2nd Lieutenant N. P. Parkinson - 2nd PLATOON (4 MG Squads)
2nd Lieutenant Earl Olson - 3rd PLATOON (4 MG Squads)
2nd Lieutenant John H. Geiszel - SUPPLY TRAIN

Soon we found ourselves going northeast, in the direction of Meaux and Chateau-Thierry. At the stations along the way we saw numerous American troops from other divisions and headquarters organizations. We detrained at La Ferte Sur Jouarre. This was a good-sized town where some civilians still lived. The railroad station had been hit by an enemy bomb and was nearly demolished. The 3rd Battalion of the 168th Infantry had also detrained here.

On the streets near our detraining point, I again met Lieutenant Doocy from the old Company 22 at Fort Sheridan and from Wesleyan University. We told each other of the men of our old company that each of us had seen. He told me of the death in action of Lieutenant Paul Derrickson at Cantigny and I told him of the death of Lieutenant Adrian C. Edwards, who had been killed with the 26th Division at Seicheprey, as well as the death of Lieutenant Payette. These men had all been with us in the same company at Fort Sheridan. I also spoke of the death of Lieutenant Veasey, who had been killed with our division at Suippes. While waiting for our ship the previous January at New York City, Lieutenants Derrickson, Edwards, and Veasey had occupied adjoining rooms with Lieutenants Ed Carlson, Verne Rogers, and me at the McAlpin Hotel. Half of our party had already been taken, and I could not keep this fact from entering my mind repeatedly, as I knew we, too, were moving to the front.

Camions. A column of trucks transporting Americans along a road. Riding in trucks was easier on the feet. "We knew, however, that troops were hauled in camions only when they were needed badly at the front." *Editor's collection.*

After detraining, we marched a few miles to the deserted village of Jaignes. About an hour later, we received a number of replacement troops to bring our strength up to normal, replacing the casualties we lost at Badonviller and in the Champagne. This fact also meant we were moving into a big fight. At sundown, we were ordered to form immediately with gun equipment and ammunition. We waited along the main street of the village for what seemed a long time. At last, a number of trucks painted French gray-blue drove up, driven by Chinese or Annamese troops from French Indo-China. The trucks were small and covered with canvas. The only opening was the rear end. We loaded into these trucks which were called camions.[3] The number of men in

3. They loaded into these camions on July 24.

each truck, together with our packs, would about fill the truck, but in addition, we had to make room for our machine guns, tripods, and all the ammunition boxes we could possibly pile in. Our wagon train, kitchen, and carts were to follow by road.

We moved in a long column of camions in a direction that none of us could tell because the trucks were covered and only those at the rear end could see out. We knew, however, that troops were hauled in camions only when they were needed badly at the front, so we expected action the next day.

The trucks moved without lights, but maintained a sufficient speed to make the journey very rough. Our driver could speak no English, so he quietly followed the truck ahead of him. We followed along in this manner for several hours until the truck stopped and the driver came around to the rear end of the truck, asking in French for "Leutnant." He made me understand that he had lost the truck ahead of him and was off the road. I then climbed in the front seat with him. We drove up the road to a town where I inquired of a French soldier about the name. He answered, "Chateau-Thierry." The last I had heard of Chateau-Thierry, it was in possession of the Germans. I knew that we were nearing the place where we would unload and go over the top.

We drove up the street and located an American military policeman. He could give us no information as to where the rest of our trucks had gone, but headed us out on a road toward the front. After traveling some time, we overtook a column of camions like our own. All were stalled in a traffic jam. Placing one of my men in the front seat so I could hail him if the column should move on, I walked up the line and found that each of the trucks ahead was filled with troops from Company B of our battalion. This told me that I was somewhere near the right place, but Company B was attached to the 167th Infantry and I had no idea where our 168th could be found. As the column moved on, I followed in our truck after reporting to Captain Boyce Miller of B Company.

After another long ride day broke,[4] and a little later the entire column stopped on an open road. Ahead of us I could see infantrymen and machine gunners unloading from a long line of trucks. Our truck was the last in line. An American lieutenant of the transport service came along and ordered us to unload. I protested and told him my predicament. He could give me no information, other than the town just ahead was the town of Epieds. I went forward to locate his captain, who hurried back with me to find all other trucks had gone. Our men had just unloaded and our truck was turning around. Overhead there was a battle in progress between half a dozen of our planes and an equal number of Germans. All on the ground were in a hurry to get off the road before enemy planes reported our concentration to their artillery. We overtook our driver just as he had gotten turned around and was ready to head back. We loaded up again and, with directions from the captain, drove

4. This was July 25, 1918.

up the road to Epieds and turned to the right toward the town of Trugny, where the 3rd Battalion was unloading.

Between Epieds and Trugny was a line of German trenches, with many dead Germans still lying unburied. This line had been taken by the 26th Division. At the outskirts of Trugny, I was relieved to meet Lieutenant Means. At this corner of the road I noticed a large German eight-inch cannon or howitzer that the 26th Division had captured in their attack. I have later seen many photographs of this same gun captured at this particular position. We unloaded quickly and, following Lieutenant Means' lead, soon joined the rest of the company in front of Trugny. As we passed the outskirts of Trugny we saw many dead Germans there. I passed near one whose body was bloated to two or three times its normal size. We had no time to stop for sightseeing.

As soon as we overtook the rest of our company we were ordered forward. The infantry had already started forward in a long column. We followed in squad columns along the narrow road, which was nothing more than a trail. We were endeavoring to keep pace with the infantrymen, who were carrying packs and rifles. We were carrying our packs and our machine gun equipment with extra boxes of ammunition, so that each man had no less than 60 pounds and some of them 100 pounds extra equipment to carry.[5]

Soon the trail we were following led to a point where it had been obliterated by the fire of our own six-inch rifles. Great holes that would cover a wagon and team were blown all around us where our guns had, a few days previous, been firing on a German battery. We did not know where we were to go and only had orders to follow the infantry. Therefore, we could not afford to slacken our pace and maintained this killing pace along this rough trail through the forest. Our company was strung out along the road over a long space. All our men were moving, but some were now almost exhausted and moving more slowly than others. We soon crossed an open field and hurried to the next shelter of trees, finding ourselves in the midst of men of the artillery of the 28th American Division.[6] As we stopped for a minute to gain our breath the Germans began shelling heavily. They were shelling just as heavily on the road ahead of us and upon a first aid station nearby. It was at this point that Private A. H. Breitegan received wounds of which he died.

We forged on, still carrying our heavy loads, and finally the trail came to a point where it was overlapped by trees. The infantry were now out of sight, but at this point we met Captain Bunch, Chief Medical Officer of the 168th Infantry Regiment. He told us where the infantry had stopped and we moved on under his guidance, but at a more bearable pace. Captain Bunch had been

5. Major Cooper D. Winn would later complain, "It is simply not reasonable to expect that a weapon which requires for use several pieces of equipment, each weighing 40 pounds or more, can be carried by hand fast enough to keep up with infantrymen who are operating with only a nine pound rifle" (Reilly, 837). Fortunately, things would change after the Ourcq River crossing.

6. Although the Rainbow Division was relieving the 26th Division, elements of the 28th Division were also present in this area (Reilly, 317).

with the British forces prior to the Americans entering the war. He had demonstrated to us at Badonviller that he was fearless under shell fire. As we marched along the road he saw a shovel, dashed to grab it, and exclaimed in his North Carolina accent, "I may need this shovel soon. You boys get one soon as you can."

These shovels had been left behind by the Germans. Although we were already loaded down with heavy equipment, our men had enough faith in Captain Bunch that as we went down the road, almost everyone increased his burden by picking up a large shovel.

Captain Henry E. Bunch. 168th Infantry Regiment Surgeon. (Here he is shown as a Major after the war.) Bunch was highly regarded by Parkinson and others of the 151st Machine Gun Battalion. His philosophy was to bring his medical aid to the men, not *vise versa*. At Cote de Chatillon, he would promise the infantry, "If any of you men get hurt, the first aid station will be here until we take the top of the hill. Then it will be on top of the hill." *Photo from Taber, The Story of the 168th Infantry.*

We rounded the corner of a trail and turned into the woods (Foret de Beuvardes), finding ourselves in the midst of the 3rd Battalion, 168th Infantry. They too were digging in. Our company hastily assembled in a designated position and we began digging foxholes in which to lie for shelter. It was raining hard. We threw the dirt out of our holes and banked it so that the water would not run in. We covered our holes with shelter-halves and lay down inside to be sheltered from the rain. About sundown, we used part of our reserve rations. We had nothing to eat since the night before and our rolling kitchens were miles away. At dark, the Germans began a heavy shelling of our woods. At intervals all night long they bombarded the woods with shells of heavy caliber. We guessed them to be 155mm. A number of men in the infantry battalion were struck, but our own men all escaped, no doubt due to the energetic digging we had suddenly learned to do.

Our battalion was not holding the front line. Ahead of us, the First Battalion during this night had taken over the front line from the exhausted 26th Division.[7] At daylight, they went over the top.[8] The 3rd Battalion, to which we were attached, followed in support, ready to pass through them and continue the advance as the First battalion became exhausted. In order that we could carry more ammunition, we left all our packs and blankets behind and took only light packs, including our iron rations. Our machine gun company followed the Third Battalion.

7. Reflecting on the frame of mind men had when relieving spent combatants, Lieutenant John H. Geiszel of Company D later recalled, "You met the men you were relieving coming out. They were exhausted - dirty - smelling of sour sweat and fear-dazed by shell fire - frightened - inhuman animals, and you knew that if you came out alive, it would be like that!"
8. This was July 26.

The woods in which we were located was a small section of the Foret de Beuvardes, which adjoined the Foret de Fere. We moved out on the road going north near the lake east of Courpoil. Near this lake the road turned west for a few hundred yards and then back south for a distance before it again turned east. Just as our battalion started out, a volley of German shells wounded three men of the Third Platoon: Private Aaron Jenkins, who later died in the evacuation hospital; and Privates Harry R. Wright and Charles R. Wagner.

We moved on up the road, turned east, back south, and again east. The First Battalion had gone over the top ahead of us and wounded were now going to the rear along our lines. Our company was strung out along the road and trail, covering a long distance. The infantry battalion was likewise strung out in single file along the trail. They must have been standing too close together along the trail ahead. We noticed some shells were falling ahead of us. Then the order was passed back along this long line of men, "To the rear!"

The infantry moved to the rear, but Lieutenant Means had us stand fast. The command was repeated, being carried back from ahead. The infantry continued moving back in an orderly manner. We could hear the shells exploding a few hundred yards ahead in the woods and see the infantry retire while we machine gunners held our ground. We were sure that the Germans had broken through and that the machine guns were to cover the retirement of the infantry.[9] While we still waited, the command came back again, "To the rear! Double time!" Lieutenant Means had gone forward to learn what was happening and this message, "To the rear! Double time!", had been given him by an officer. We therefore started to the rear, but not at double time.

The trouble was that the infantry were too closely congested on the narrow trail ahead, and the only way they could protect themselves against heavy casualties was to take distance to the rear. The double time order was given by someone of subordinate capacity who became excited when the movement was not fast enough to suit him. No harm was intended, but only the cool action of half a dozen officers prevented a small panic. We therefore trudged back over the road for about a half a mile, carrying our heavy equipment over the same places where we had laboriously carried it before. After taking sufficient distance, the line again started forward.

When we boarded the camions several nights before, the Third Platoon, under Lieutenant Olson, had tied ammunition carts behind the camions and towed them to the unloading point. Since then, they had pulled them by hand, hauling the ammunition for their guns. As we had gone forward the first time, enemy fire on the road made a direct hit on one of these carts, killing Corporal Julius Lyons and wounding Privates Benjamin E. Keenen, Sylvester Furlow,

9. Three things were drilled into the minds of machine gunners in training: (1) They were never to abandon their posts in the face of the enemy because, (2) machine guns were ideally suited to hold ground by repelling attacks or counter-attacks and, (3) machine guns should be employed as a rear guard to cover the withdrawal of retreating infantry. Means was prudently acting according to a machine gunner's duty here.

Clifford Boden, and Henry J. Pearson. These casualties were in addition to those wounded just as we started.

As we went back in accordance with our orders to march to the rear, we passed the place where Lyons' body and the demolished carts were lying in the road. Men were beginning to carry the wounded to the rear. Owing to the need of ammunition carriers, we had orders to assign only two men to each stretcher. Dewey Clark and another man came to me carrying Clifford Boden, who had been badly wounded in the groin. Boden appealed to me to furnish two more men to help carry him to the rear, as a man on a stretcher is a very heavy load for two men. I had to refuse this request. It was one of the hardest things I ever did, but a few yards down the road the two stretcher bearers stopped for a rest. I saw two men from my platoon slip out of line and join the two already carrying the stretcher. I did not have the heart to order them back. They hurried down the road to the first aid station in the forest and all rejoined us later.

This rapid march to the rear carried us clear back along the east and west road to the lake and back on the north and south road to within a few yards of our starting point. Then the orders came to move forward again. Going forward, I was in command of the last platoon along the road and had been the leading platoon when we were marching to the rear. The 3rd Platoon was far ahead on the east and west road, where they had suffered their second bunch of casualties, including the life of Corporal Lyons. The Germans began shelling again. I dreaded passing along this heavily-shelled east and west road, so I led my men east through the heavy forest via a short cut to the place where we had arrived before the march to the rear was ordered. Wounded men were still coming back–walking cases, with a head bandaged or an arm in a sling.

It was getting dark and we moved along the trail leading eastward, thence to a main road south, and turned east again in the heavy forest. It was still raining heavily. There were old German trenches in this forest which we followed in an eastward direction till we came to a group of dugouts formerly occupied by the Germans. This was to be our station for the night. We posted guards and went to sleep inside these dugouts. They were really not dugouts, but small wooden shacks completely banked over by earth and sod.

I crowded into one of the dugouts with the men of one of my sections. There were about four bunks made from chicken wire and a small table. When the advance started in the morning, our packs had all been left behind in the woods under guard. There was not a blanket or shelter-half in the company. Two men crowded into these bunks intended for one man. Some slept on the floor and I, with another enlisted man, turned an ammunition box on end and sat, bent over a roughly-made table. This dugout was not intended for a shelter from the rain. It was only a bomb shelter. The heavy rain soaked through the roof and dripped down in rivulets in twenty places. The only place I could lay my head on my arm as I bent over the table was directly underneath one of these drips. For several hours I laid this way, trying to rest, but with water dripping in a good-sized stream striking my helmet, I could not sleep. I was resting my limbs, but the dripping water pounding on my helmet almost drove me mad.

After several hours in this manner, I was aroused by a call from the outside. I hurried out with my hand on my automatic, not knowing what to expect. I answered the call, and in turn was answered by an American voice out of the pitch black darkness and rain. "We have a wounded sergeant out here on a stretcher. We have been lost in the woods all night. Where is the first aid station?" I hurried out there, still on my guard, and found three Americans carrying a wounded soldier. The wounded man was unconscious and the men were about exhausted. I knew the location of the first aid station about three hundred yards away. I helped them carry the litter back there. Halfway there, the path we were following was swept with machine gun fire. We could not flop without dropping the wounded man. We kept on going and delivered the wounded sergeant to the surgeon at the first aid station.

About this time, a platoon of infantry from the 167th Regiment, without an officer, reported to Lieutenant Means, saying they had lost their organization. Lieutenant Means took command of them, sent them back to the woods where we had left the rest of our ammunition, and under Sergeant Roy Rhodes, they carried a large quantity of ammunition forward to us. That morning, the First Battalion had attacked Croix Rouge Ferme, a strongly fortified position with open fields of fire in all directions. They had driven the Germans from this position with heavy losses to themselves.[10] The 2nd Battalion was to lead the assault the morning of the 27th. During the night and toward morning of the 27th, we sent a detail back to try to locate our kitchens, which were supposed to be in the woods somewhere in our rear.

Meanwhile, in the morning of the 27th, we formed in the edge of the Foret de Fere woods. We formed in platoon columns, ready to advance from the edge of the forest through the open ground leading to and beyond Croix Rouge Ferme. The advance was not ordered. We stood there in the rain for several hours in formation, waiting for orders.

In the open before us, half a dozen French cavalrymen on black horses and in horizon-blue uniforms galloped toward the Croix Rouge Ferme to draw enemy fire so observers could locate the machine gunners we were to face in the advance. Up and down they rode before our lines, almost continually under fire from the enemy—a veritable sacrifice for the protection of larger bodies of troops. There had been about 25 of them in this patrol yesterday. Casualties of men and animals had reduced them to six. The next day, I saw the two survivors gallop toward a hedge occupied by the enemy until artillery and machine gun fire drove them back, but they had forced the enemy to disclose the positions of their guns.

As we stood there, we were surrounded by many dead bodies, casualties from the First Battalion attack the day before. There must have been a dressing

10. The 167th Infantry had taken Croix Rouge Ferme with the bayonet (Wolf, 32).

station located where we were, because we saw, in addition to the men lying where they had been killed, about twenty piled close together. These men were almost all partly naked, where the clothing had been removed to get at the wounds. They had evidently died while wounds were being dressed and their bodies were laid aside.

My platoon stood for over an hour waiting in this forest for orders to advance. Then we moved forward, following the Third Battalion again. This battalion was to move in single file. Our company followed them the same way. As we crossed this open space, we passed the bodies of several German machine gunners killed at their emplacements. We moved across the open space to the edge of the forest on the other side. This was the forest south of La Croix Blanche Ferme. As we turned east, we entered a long communication trench at the edge of the forest. At dark, the Germans began shelling this forest and the rain was again falling heavily. We had orders to follow "L" Company. In the darkness, the last platoon of L Company became detached from the column ahead and we marched off in the dense woods, following them as they wandered, but we did not know they were lost. Finally, Lieutenant Means learned of our predicament and that we, too, were lost by following this platoon.

We did not know where we were, nor where the Germans were. We set up machine guns, posted a line around our position, and sent out scouts to locate the Third Battalion. While we waited, we were served from the rear with a meal of cold coffee, beans, and bacon, which was the first food we had from our own kitchen since leaving Jaignes. The infantry had dug fox holes throughout this woods. Our men took shelter in these fox holes against the heavy artillery fire from the Germans that was pounding our vicinity. Large shells, which we estimated to be 155mm, threw up earth around us and exploded in trees overhead. This was a terrible strain on our men.

The rain was still falling and the fox holes were full of water. I procured two ammunition boxes and placed one under my hip and one under my shoulder to keep my body out of the mud, then laid down as comfortably as possible, trying to rest. Later, I leaned against a large tree with one of these boxes for a seat. The rain beat against the trunk of this tree. I wore a raincoat, and I thought I was comfortably settled when a large shell exploded in the tree above me, sending shell fragments and broken limbs down all around me. I heard the fragments strike the ground, but none struck me.

It was pitch dark, except for the flash of exploding shells. During a brief lull between volleys, I heard someone feeling his way around in the dark. Then I heard a slip in the mud, the sound of hobnails on a helmet, and Lieutenant Means' voice yelling, "Get your foot out of my face!" He had been lying down in a fox hole with his helmet over his face to turn the rain. This prowler had stepped on the helmet and his foot slipped off on the Lieutenant's throat. He took the situation more humorously than I would have, however.

I walked to the edge of the woods and made up my mind that if I could not sleep while waiting for the scouts to report, I would do a little scouting myself. I looked out toward the farm and saw that it was being pounded mercilessly with artillery. As I watched, it stopped raining and the moon broke through the sky. Just as I was starting toward the farm, I heard the voice of Lieutenant Means ordering the company to fall in. Sergeant Weidman, one of the scouts, had located the 3rd Battalion.

At 1:30 A.M., we marched across the open field to the forest north of the White Cross Farm.[11] At 3:00 A.M., there, in the edge of the Foret de Fere, nearest the town of Sergy, by the light of the moon, we spied a row of vacant dugouts. Into these we quartered our men. Sergeant Achey and his section found a shallow dugout in the ground covered a foot deep with loose feathers that had been emptied from some feather bed. These tired men crawled in and a dozen of them were soon asleep in those soft feathers.

I, with Lieutenant Andres, First Platoon, and Lieutenant Olson, Third Platoon, were standing together, waiting for Lieutenant Means to return. He had gone to report to Major Brewer of the 3rd Battalion. As we stood there, a messenger from Major Brewer came, ordering our company to send forward one platoon of machine guns immediately to attack at daylight with the 3rd Battalion. From the edge of the Foret de Fere, the ground sloped for about 800 yards[12] down to the Ourcq River. His battalion was down at the river and was waiting for our platoon to join him before advancing across the river and up Hill 212, which was the key to the town of Sergy. Lieutenant Means was not present. It was fast breaking daylight. I knew that if we did not go forward now, we would have to cross 800 yards of open ground after daylight under heavy German fire. Therefore, I told this messenger that my platoon would be up there as soon as possible.

I disliked very much disturbing these men so soon after they had snuggled themselves away in those feathers. They were all fast asleep and partly undressed. It is sometimes a hard job to get one man awake after he has had a good night's rest. It was a real job to get a dozen tired soldiers awake and dressed after their hard night when they had only about thirty minutes rest.

At last they were ready. With my platoon sergeant Sergeant Brenner, we started down the ravine which sloped to the Ourcq. We had covered about half the territory when shells fell in our midst. The men were not under observation. It was still too dark. We were just caught by a chance volley. Fearing a heavy barrage, I led the men down to the stream, which had steep sides, and started to march them down the bed of the stream, wading in water a foot deep. They preferred the open, however, so we got out and started overland again. We had intercepted a messenger from Major Brewer, who had been sent back, telling us to hurry with the machine guns. The first messenger had not yet reported back to Major Brewer. We hurried forward, carrying our heavy equipment with great effort, with shells falling near enough to make it uncomfortable.

11. This was July 28 which would prove to be so eventful.

12. The open distance was actually about 1,500 meters (Means).

On the slope to the left and north of us, leading down to the Ourcq in the breaking daylight, we saw a battalion of the 165th Infantry in battle formation going over the top and advancing across the Ourcq River. This was formerly the 69th New York National Guard regiment, a historic Irish Regiment dating from the Civil War days when it and another Irish regiment from New York were known as the Irish Brigade.

Our men, advancing to the Ourcq River, were breathless with their heavy loads. We had our large tripods and our parapet mounts. I ordered the four large tripods concealed in the wheat field through which we were passing. Our advance was now somewhat easier. When we were within 300 yards of the 3rd Battalion, they rose out of their fox holes and started across the river. We followed on hurriedly after them and arrived at the river, where it was crossed by a road. The bridge had been destroyed. Ordinarily, the river was about the size of Stevens Creek, near Decatur, but the heavy rains had swollen it out of its banks. The water was too deep to wade, but where the bridge had been blown out, we crossed on the debris.

The Ourcq River in 1919. It was along this stretch of the Ourcq that the Rainbow Division made its assault in late July 1918. The heights north of the river would be the bloodiest ground the 151st Machine Gun Battalion would fight for. *Editor's collection.*

As we gained the opposite side, the Germans were sweeping the entire bank with machine gun fire. I had already reported to Major Brewer. He ordered me to report to Lieutenant Lainson, who was commanding the assaulting company. I met Lieutenant Doocy, but no one could direct me to Lieutenant Lainson. Machine gun fire was growing heavier. As I ran from one place to another, trying to locate Lieutenant Lainson, my men urged me to keep down. They were all lying prone. The fire was coming mostly from an old mill to our right. I ordered Sergeant Achey to advance with one squad in this direction and see if he could silence the guns in that location. It was an impossible job, however, as I later learned. There were dozens of German machine guns in that direction, all carefully placed and concealed.

As Lieutenant Doocy's line started to swing up Hill 212, their flank was exposed. Therefore, I ordered Sergeant Dudley and Corporal Shaffer to take one gun and advance behind Lieutenant Doocy's line to protect his flank. I then started again looking for Lieutenant Lainson. I had not found him and was coming back to the place where the bridge was destroyed, where two of my squads still remained. I found him there inquiring for me and reported how I had already placed two of my squads. He approved and told me more of the plan of attack on the hill. I kept the other two guns in reserve, waiting until the line should advance. As the line moved up the hill, German machine gunners resisted stubbornly. Our lines suffered heavy casualties, but did not stop. A number of prisoners were taken and the line reached the first crest of the hill, but had not yet fully taken it.

I saw Sergeant Achey's squad creeping forward to get in contact with the machine guns on our right. As I knelt down in the open field at the foot of the hill with a messenger near me, a German machine gun opened fire on the two of us. We flattened out quickly, with our heads pointed toward the German fire to expose the narrowest possible target. We were low down, in a very slight depression, but not enough to cover us completely. The bullets zipped all around us, striking the mud. I expected any minute to be hit, but laid there perfectly still and told Patrick, the runner, not to move, but to play dead. After they stopped firing, we laid perfectly still for some time as though we had been struck. After allowing a few minutes for their attention to go elsewhere, we rose suddenly and ran to the road ahead, where a bank several feet high afforded us protection against enemy machine guns.

While I was kneeling in the open field, before the machine gun fire began on us, I was watching the advance of Sergeant Brenner, who was leading the two remaining squads of my platoon to the shelter of the same road to which Patrick and I later rushed. When I arrived there, I met Lieutenant Means. He complimented me for going forward that morning. Lieutenant Andres' platoon had followed mine under cover of darkness.[13] The 3rd Platoon, under Lieutenant Olson, had waited for Lieutenant Means' further orders. As they came across the open field they were caught in a heavy barrage: three men were killed and four or five wounded.[14] Their advance had been at the break of day.

Lieutenant Olson, with his platoon, was now back at the blown-out bridge. Lieutenant Andres, with his platoon, was up the hill along the same road. I reported the position of Sergeant Dudley with his squad and Sergeant Achey.

13. Andres actually crossed the open space south of the Ourcq at the break of daylight, but had been covered by lingering fog until he reached the river (Reilly, 428).

14. Lieutenant Olson's Third Platoon could only get two of his four Hotchkiss machine guns across the Ourcq. Later on that day of July 28 he took possession of a captured German MG08 and put it into action "reducing some back flank fire we were receiving" (Means).

At Lieutenant Means' suggestion, I ordered Achey to withdraw to this same line along the road. Although the Germans at the top of the hill had observation on our movements, the bank which this road cut in the side of the hill was the logical place to organize our defensive lines. We were about one-third of the way up the hill and had a good field of fire should the Germans attack from any direction.

The farthest line of infantry had gone about two-thirds up the hill and were stopped. I advised Lieutenant Means that I was going to see how Dudley was getting along on top of the hill. I walked up the road and across a wheat field to a small clump of bushes in direct observation, but the Germans did not fire on me. In the edge of this clump of bushes I located Dudley and his crew. Just in front, out in the open fields, infantrymen were lying in the wheat stubble.

Lieutenant Doocy, rifle in hand, was standing erect, looking toward the German lines. I walked up to him. He explained the military situation to me, showed me where the German outposts were, and pointed to a clump of bushes where a German machine gun was located. He, with about fifteen sharpshooters, was waiting for the gunner to lift his head. Lieutenant Doocy, having his eye on the exact spot, was standing up so as to tempt the gunner to raise up in a firing position, which would, of course, expose him to the rifles of this entire platoon. I realized that this was no place for a man armed only with an automatic pistol. I hastened back to the woods where Dudley and Shaffer were located with their gun crew guarding the flank. I then went on down the hill and reported to Lieutenant Means.

Lieutenant Elmer Doocy. Platoon commander in the 168th Infantry Regiment. Doocy was fearless at the Ourcq River, using himself as a decoy to draw German machine gun fire so his sharpshooters could pick off the gunner. He was later killed in action at St. Mihiel. *Photo from Robb, The Price of Our Heritage.*

The attack on Hill 212 had been made by the Third Battalion. The front lines were stopped by flanking fire from Hill 188 on our right. The First Battalion came across the open space to our rear and to our right, attacking Hill 188 about the middle of the day. They were caught in a terrible barrage as they came down the slope toward the river. As we looked back from our position on the hill, we saw their men mowed down by artillery and machine gun fire. Heavy shells landed in their midst and exploded with large geysers of dust and dirt. Several times I saw bodies lifted in the air by the force of an explosion. This was the most severe fire that I had yet seen any body of troops experience. The survivors kept on, however, coming down to the river, and took shelter behind the dike to the right of the mill along the sheltered slope of a bank formed by a canal, through which water was turned into the mill race.[15]

Later that day, or perhaps it was the next day, they attempted to advance again from the canal position up to Hill 188. Major Brewer was also furnishing a company to attack in the direction of Cierges. The attack was stopped in its tracks by tremendous machine gun fire from the top of the hill, where they were concealed in the edge of the woods. There must have been fifty machine guns up there,[16] judging from the fire that began as soon as the men left their shelters at the canal. Major Brewer ordered me, along with three machine guns, to silence these many guns that had us outnumbered and a great advantage over us. I protested mildly, but began attempting it at once.

Nemesis. Germans dug in with their MG08 machine guns. "There must have been fifty machine guns up there" on Hill 188 dueling with Lieutenant Parkinson's three machine guns. *Editor's collection.*

Although I thought the order unwise and impossible to execute, I don't criticize Major Brewer in any way. He was a gallant and competent officer and unflinching in danger. His knowledge was far superior to mine. I led the first crew under Corporal Roberts south of the mill. Gunner Sam Resh attempted to set up his gun on the bank of the canal. He was wounded by a deluge of

15. The big picture from battalion perspective: "This day's work again demonstrated the impracticability of operating machine guns in the manner that our companies were used here. For Companies A and D were never able, during the actual advance, to assist the infantry with their fire and both companies suffered heavy losses in the valley of the Ourcq and around Sergy. Remaining in these positions during the night of the 28th, these companies, closely supported by the other two companies, were able to assist the infantry a little in holding the acquired positions. But in the attack on Hill 212 and Sergy but little assistance could be rendered, although each time the infantry attacks were launched the machine guns accompanied them" (White and Peavy).

16. Parkinson's estimate is not so incredible. The 84th Brigade's Adjutant referred to the hills north of the Ourcq as "the teeth of machine gun resistance" (Wolf, 32).

machine gun fire. The other two squads were instructed to follow me at safe intervals. As the enemy saw them concentrating in the vicinity of the mill they opened up with artillery. Corporal Roberts was wounded, along with another man whom I do not remember, and the gun was put out of action. As the other two squads arrived, the artillery fire was so heavy that we could only take shelter behind the canal. Meanwhile, the infantry attack had been called off and the few that had advanced some fifty yards were withdrawn to the line along the canal.

Tables Turned. A German MG08 machine gun mounted as an anti-aircraft gun. Lieutenant Earl Olson pressed two captured MG08s into American service as anti-aircraft guns after losing a couple of his Hotchkiss machine guns crossing the Ourcq River under heavy fire. *Editor's collection.*

The line of the First Battalion was moved to the right and the Third Battalion took over this sector in the vicinity of the mill. Lieutenant Cotter was in command of this company of infantry. Under the direction of Lieutenant Means and Major Brewer, my three machine guns were permanently stationed in this location to protect our flank.[17] We dug emplacements under a hedge that traversed the canal and were fairly well protected.

One day[18] in this vicinity, the Germans started a counter-attack through the open space between Hill 188 and Hill 212. Gunner Armstrong noticed them crawling through the wheat, bringing up machine guns with them. Before they could place their guns to open fire he opened on them and drove them away.[19]

Many attacks had been made at the top of the hill on the town of Sergy at frightful cost to the men of the Second and Third battalions. It was the mission of my platoon, to which Sergeant Dudley's squad had now been returned, to protect this right flank. The First Battalion had been withdrawn from the line on the right, so we were the extreme right of our division.[20] The First battalion was used in the subsequent attacks to our left at Sergy.

17. According to his commander, Lieutenant Parkinson had "three guns ... on the right of the infantry battalion and the other on the left, all doing very good work" (Means).
18. Probably July 29.
19. According to Lieutenant Means, "Lt. Parkinson's three guns were in such a good position to stop a German counter attack" (Means in Reilly, 430).
20. The French, who were assigned the sector to the right of the 42nd Division, had not kept up with the Americans. So Lieutenant Parkinson's machine gun platoon was holding the extreme right flank of the division as it was fully exposed to the enemy (Means).

German Crawl. Germans dragging their MG08 in its collapsed position. The *Schlitten-lafette* (sledge-mount) was designed to be carried like a stretcher or dragged across the ground. Gunner Armstrong of Parkinson's platoon drove off a counter-attack between Hills 188 and 212 when he noticed Germans crawling through a wheat field like this with their MG08s. *Editor's collection.*

After several of these attacks on Sergy were unsuccessful, the entire regiment was organized for an attack which was to be assisted by a battalion of infantrymen of the 4th Division. Platoon commanders were called early on the morning of July 30th to Lieutenant Means' headquarters on Hill 212. It was explained that the attack would start at 7:00, and I was ordered to support the attack by setting up my four guns in a clump of trees which he designated on the map. The day previous, I had been scouting around in that vicinity and knew that, while these woods were once in our hands, they had been evacuated and were now about 300 yards in front of our farthest outpost infantry, and about 200 yards from the strong resistance line of the Germans in the nearby woods. I called this to his attention, but Lieutenant Means urged that I take this position.

Therefore, I started off with my four machine gun squads in open formation, crawling through the wheat fields and up the hill, towards those trees. After a long distance through the standing wheat, we came to a space where it had been cut. We crawled forward with even greater interval and distance. The Germans opened fire on us when we were about 300 yards from our destination. Their machine gun fire was so heavy that we could not hope to survive it. I ordered the men to withdraw to the cover of the line and learned that the woods toward which we were headed were almost 300 yards in front of our farthest outpost. These men in the infantry line were soon to make the attack, but they advised us against entering the woods or attempting to do so with machine guns.

I hurried down the hill and reported to Lieutenant Means; we were assigned to positions near the mill, where we threw overhead fire on the same target at a range of about 1,700 meters. After the attack started, a German aeroplane located our emplacements and directed heavy artillery fire upon us. One emplacement, of which Private Beck was gunner, was completely covered by a large limb knocked off the tree above them by shell fire. It fell directly in their emplacement and knocked their gun over, so that they had to cease firing, but they soon removed the limb and resumed fire.

On the night of July 30th, while we were sleeping under the protected slope of the road on Hill 212, we were constantly disturbed by a German battery far to the south of us near Dormans, from which position they could fire on us from our rear. They had the exact range, and threw high explosives right into the fox holes we had dug on these slopes which we thought were protected. They began at dark, and four shells would come in a volley. Every 20 minutes or half hour, these shells would arrive. We would first see a flash far to the south, then hear the report of the gun about the same time as we heard the shells on a high trajectory come singing toward us, then the heavy explosions as the four 77 shells landed along the side of the hill. Then a call for "First aid!" or "Stretcher bearer!" would be heard in the night. Almost every volley wounded someone. One of these shells penetrated the bank just behind the fox hole where Major Brewer and Lieutenant Christopher were lying. The explosion blew them both out unharmed. These regular salvos continued all night long and through the next day, until the advance of our troops in that section forced the withdrawal of these guns.

The artillery ahead of us could not reach us on the reverse slope of the hill. They fired heavily on the hill above us, but the steep bank on the side of the road gave protection. They did, however, reach us with gas, so that we had to spend much of our time each night wearing gas masks.

During the day, aeroplanes harassed us by diving toward our line with machine gun fire. Lieutenant Olson of the 3rd Platoon mounted some captured German machine guns,[21] and the next trip over by these aviators, who were making regular rounds, we gave them a machine gun reception that drove them away. As they flew on down the line, a doughboy with a Chauchat automatic rifle opened fire. One of his shots struck its mark and, as this German flier fell, his plane collided with another German plane, so that one infantryman got credit for bringing down two planes.[22]

21. By July 30, Lieutenant Olson had pressed two German MG08s into his platoon's service to replace those lost approaching the Ourcq on July 28 (Means). Olson had previously studied the MG08 and had given his men some instruction in its operation (Means in Reilly, 429). Such was the payoff for cross-training.

22. As fantastic as this sounds, this may be the same incident described by Captain Graef of the 150th Wisconsin Machine Gun Battalion: "I saw two enemy airplanes collide and fall just north of the Ourcq. One of the pilots evidently was shot by the thousands of rifle and machine gun bullets fired at him" (Reilly, 446-447).

Private Walters, one of the squad under Sergeant Dudley, was killed by shell fire while the squad was operating with Lieutenant Doocy's platoon at the top of the hill. As our company hugged the shelter of this low bank at the side of the road, Privates Davis and Fanus were killed by machine gun fire that enfiladed the road, and the next day Private John Harkcom was killed.

Communications to the rear had to be made over the open slope back to Foret de Fere. All efforts to bring food up from the kitchens during the day were unsuccessful. The German artillery fire killed or wounded everyone who tried. At night, however, beginning about July 30th, we began to receive meals carried forward from the rear. The only water supply was from the stream at the mill. Heavy rains had this stream running at a swift current about knee-deep. We had to wade this stream every time we passed from Hill 212 (Lieutenant Means' headquarters) over to my post beyond the mill.

This stream came direct from the German lines. The water seemed clear and was cool. For a while we had lime tubes to sterilize this water, but soon we had to use it without sterilization. It continued to rain almost every night and parts of some days, but the days, for the most part, were hot, and the sun beat down against the men sheltered on the Hill 212 road. At night, the rain chilled us through as we half slept. This exposure, the irregular meals, and the unsterilized water caused an epidemic of dysentery which greatly weakened our men.[23] Other infantry troops were having the same experience.

One day, when we had gone eighteen hours without food, I discovered a gunny sack lying along the roadside. At the bottom was about a peck of bread crumbs. The sack had originally contained bread for the infantry companies and had been discarded, but these crumbs had been eaten. Many of these crumbs were green with mold, but we picked through them and found a few that were safe to eat. We did not stop, however, but finished those that were moldy, too.[24]

Our troops had made repeated attacks on the strong town of Sergy on the plateau. They had driven the Germans out, but the enemy artillery fire was so heavy that our troops were driven out seven or eight times before the town was finally occupied permanently. All this time, however, we had kept the Germans out and had kept a line of patrols between the enemy lines and the town. The town was finally occupied permanently August 1st.

After this attack, I had been to Lieutenant Means on Hill 212 and started across the open ravine to the right. Every person who passed through there was under direct observation by the enemy for a distance of about 100 yards, but only on a few occasions had the enemy fired on us here. They used this place to watch our movements. As I passed through this day I was entirely

23. Water contamination was from dead Americans, Germans, and animals which had been decaying for a couple of days since the attack on the morning of July 28 (Means).

24. Whether he is talking about a pleasant dinner behind the lines or scrounging for scraps to eat in a dearth of supplies, allusions to food problems are little details Parkinson gives that are often missing from the grand accounts of generals and armchair historians.

alone, but a German 77 from the top of Hill 188 opened fire on me. Shells fell rapidly near me, so I sprinted to the shelter of the old mill. I arrived there breathless, as another battery of several guns laid down heavy fire on the lines through which I must pass to reach my platoon. It was near noon. This shelling was local. Therefore, I took shelter in the mill, where a few squads of infantry were sleeping in the cellar.

I, too, soon fell asleep. I must have slept for half an hour when I was awakened by heavy shelling which I could tell was not local. Therefore, I hurried to my platoon and took shelter with them in a hole dug under the protection of the dike of the canal. I had a good view of the long slope to our rear and saw that it was covered with advancing troops. They were advancing in splendid formation under cover of our own artillery barrage, which was what had awakened me. As they reached the Ourcq River, which was then and there shallow enough for them to wade through, the Germans opened up heavily with artillery. Many casualties occurred, so these advancing troops rushed forward to the shelter of our dike. They were from the 32nd Division, which was relieving the 28th Division, part of which was still on our right. As we were the extreme right of our division, some of their troops overlapped our lines as they moved forward to leapfrog the 28th and advance the attack.

One platoon of machine guns that reached the line 100 yards to our left suffered many heavy casualties, including their lieutenant. A section of infantry reached the dike at our position. They had lost two or three men killed and several wounded. Two of the slightly wounded men were still with the advancing troops. The heavy fire and the casualties around them had greatly excited them, although when they reached the dike, they reformed their lines, and under the leadership of their lieutenant prepared to advance. As I lay in my hole, watching their rush to our dike, I saw them all take shelter in vacant fox holes.

One boy, who did not seem to be over eighteen years of age, had no fox hole. I invited him to climb in on top of me, which he quickly did, as the German range had been shortened so that the barrage was falling right on our position. I could tell this boy was scared and I, too, was scared. We always were when under fire, but I will never forget the picture of this frightened youth of eighteen rushing through that barrage and his heavy breathing, which I not only heard, but felt, as he laid on top of me. Their lieutenant sent two men back to look after their wounded and prepared to continue the advance. With the cry, "Come on boys! You're in a war now," he led his line across the canal, which they jumped at this point in perfect formation toward the town of Cierges.

Our platoon did not know these men had relieved the 28th Division. We were completely exhausted and hungry, and rejoiced in the belief that it was our division that had been relieved. I hurried to Lieutenant Means' post of command and received the disappointing news that we were still to continue our advance.

While I was here, I saw the familiar figure of Tom Heffron. He was the man from Company 22 at Fort Sheridan with whom I had the fight. There was now no sign of ill will. I rushed down the hill and we both grasped hands warmly. As his line came up to where it passed directly over Lieutenant Means' headquarters, I shoved a cup of coffee and a bacon sandwich in his hand which had just been sent forward from our kitchen. Our troops were now eating. He emptied the canteen in a few quick droughts, but when I urged him to stay for more, he said, "No, I cannot. I've got to take my platoon up here to get some Germans," and with rifle in hand rushed on. This all had happened so quickly that he had not, at any time, fallen behind the nearest of his troops, whom he had been preceding a good distance. The next time I saw troops from the 32nd Division, I learned that Lieutenant Heffron had been killed as he continued this advance. After the battle, his platoon was taken over by Lieutenant Wallace P. Holcombe, whom I had known for years in Centralia, and who was a fraternity brother of mine at Millikin. At the outbreak of the war, he had received his commission at Fort Sheridan.

Major General Charles T. Menoher. Commander of the 42nd Rainbow Division. *Editor's collection.*

The advance of the 32nd Division overlapped the line of the 42nd only a few hundred yards. It went forward, so that the line on our right was brought up parallel with the line at the top of Hill 212 and in the vicinity of Sergy. On the night of this day, August 1st, we were ordered to prepare for a further attack on the morning of August 2nd. Our infantry troops were so completely exhausted and reduced by casualties that the 117th Engineer Regiment was ordered to assist in the attack.

Colonel Douglas MacArthur, who had seemed to be everywhere during this attack, assumed personal charge of the advance on August 2nd.[25] He was Division Chief of Staff, and without shirking his duty could have remained far in the rear at Division Headquarters. But when information was being sent to the rear at such heavy cost in lives of messengers, he had, during these trying days, come forward himself and visited all positions on the division front so as to take first-hand information back to General Menoher, our Division Commander.

25. MacArthur had surmised that the enemy was then withdrawing quickly. He concluded that to press the Germans immediately would prevent them from digging in and preparing tough defensive positions. So he personally went up and down the 42nd Division's line and ordered an aggressive advance. The Germans later established their lines across the Vesle River, but MacArthur's actions had gained the Americans much ground and spared many lives from being wasted had an advance been delayed.

It would have been impossible, I believe, for our machine gun battalion to have advanced farther if it had been necessary to carry our equipment. Lieutenant Means ordered forward a few machine gun carts, and on the morning of August 2nd, in broad daylight, we went over the top with our machine guns mounted on carts, ready for action and being pulled by mules.

Only desultory resistance was encountered. The Germans were attempting to withdraw to the Vesle River. Their artillery and machine gun fire fell nearby, but we suffered no casualties. We moved forward to the fortified town of Nesles. There we saw the historic tower of Nesles, built high in the air at the time of the Prussian War of 1870. The Germans had used this tower as an observation point from which they had directed accurate artillery fire on our positions at Hill 212 and the surrounding territory. The ground surrounding this tower had been plowed and replowed by explosions from our own six-inch rifles that had been firing at long range. We sheltered our animals in this town and took position in the outskirts beyond, expecting suffer heavy fire at any time. Rain was still falling. The only shelter we had was in these big shell holes, which were sticky with mud and partly filled with water. I took shelter in a shell hole that had been blown at the foot of a large manure pile and soon had several men in it with me, as we all attempted to absorb the warmth from this pile. We all lay in this position until night, when we received orders, official this time, that we would be relieved during the night. About 11:30 P.M., we were relieved by a regiment from the 4th Division and started for the rear.[26]

All the carts had not participated in the advance that morning. But the rest had been ordered forward and carried our equipment back for us through the town of Sergy on the road back through White Cross Farm to the Foret de Fere. This was a hard march, as the men were completely exhausted, but none fell out. We were going back, away from the battle. We camped at our field kitchen in the forest, not far from the town Fere-en-Tardenois. Sergeant Troop had a good meal ready for us when we arrived about 2:00 A.M. We laid down and slept till long after daylight.

Next morning, we looked through this part of the woods and found that we were in the midst of a German ammunition base. The woods were filled with large piles of German gas shells which they had left behind in their retreat. There were many such piles throughout the woods, each of which contained several American boxcar loads of these shells. These shells were marked with red, blue, or yellow crosses to indicate that they were loaded with chlorine, phosgene, or mustard gas. We placed gas sentinels to warn immediately in event of any leak in these shells.

The following day, with Lieutenants Olson, Andres, and Saye, I was examined by a medical officer to determine whether my physical condition would warrant promotion. Our company furnished details to police portions of the battlefields, bury the dead that had not already been buried, and salvage

26. This relief was on August 2 (Means).

Another Maxim Maxim.

"Machine guns form a valuable support for infantry."

Cartoon by Captain Bruce Bairnsfather. Obviously, "support" for infantry was a play on words. Conventional wisdom called for machine gunners to accompany attacking infantry. This meant machine guns were out of action while advancing, gun crews were shot down while setting them up, and resupply of ammunition was dicey. Major Cooper D. Winn concluded that what infantry really needed was not accompanying machine guns, but accompanying machine gun fire. He convinced Douglas MacArthur of this while they watched the fight for the Ourcq River. The shift in tactics would pay off nicely at St. Mihiel and Cote de Chatillon. *Cartoon from Bruce Bairnsfather, Fragments From France, 1917.*

equipment. This detail was under Sergeant Roy Rhodes, who had now been made First Sergeant to succeed First Sergeant Dudley, who had been gassed.

This same day, Major Winn led officers of the battalion back to the field where we had most of the fighting. On horseback, we rode from one position to another and studied the tactical situation so that we could benefit by our knowledge in future engagements.

As we rode through this entire field, we saw details everywhere burying dead. The losses had been heavy on the slope of Hill 212 and the vicinity of Sergy. In almost every case, these boys had died with their faces toward the enemy. The face of a man killed in action first turns white and pale from loss of blood, but these bodies had been lying so long that the faces were now black and their joints stiff. It was a tragic sight, seeing these men rolled in blankets and lowered into shallow graves. After a brief service by a chaplain, several of whom were now in the field, the grave would be closed and a rifle stuck in the ground at the head with an identification disk or a name written on a board to identify the body.

The casualties of our company during this engagement included: Corporal Moore; and Privates White, Cover, Davis, Fanus, Walters, and Harkcom. Wounded: Corporals Shaffer, Roberts, and Westerhoff; Sergeants Weidman and Frey; and Privates Litner, Miller, Lapham, Clark, Myers, Ryan, Hall, Smith, Musser, Kiscaddin, Fawber, Resh, Meekins, McCullom, Gatchell, Winnerling, Fishel, Stiffell, Houck, Brown, Leaman, Gruver, Sidwell, Meither, Kilpatrick, Kissinger, Nixdorf, and Mechanic Roth.

For the Distinguished Service Cross, we recommended 1st Sergeant Rhodes, Sergeants Demuth, Deetz, and Weidman, Corporals Stumpf, Keagy, and Shaffer, and Private Gatchell. But again, the recommendations were not approved by the infantry officers under whom we served, so no decorations were awarded our men.[27] These officers were more concerned with honors for men permanently under their command.[28] However, after the Armistice, Sergeant Robert E. Deetz was awarded the Cross of the Belgian Order of Leopold. That was the only decoration awarded in our entire Battalion. That no more were received by our men was due, at least in part, to the fact that always before a battle, our battalion was broken up, and each company attached to an infantry battalion whose commanders recommended few awards to those not permanently under their commands.

Back in the forest, our Iowa Regiment of infantry was greatly thrilled at this time by a delegation of congressmen from the state of Iowa, who visited the regiment and brought greetings and messages from home.

27. A total of 36 men of the 151st Machine Gun Battalion were recommended for the DSC during the war. Only one decoration was ever awarded by GHQ (White & Peavy).

28. To be fair, the 168th Infantry had its own dissatisfaction with medals received: "D.S.C.'s were being ladled out by the bushel to the Regular Army divisions, and only a few strays dribbled in to us" (Taber, II:269). So it was understandable to ration the meager supply of decorations among their own men. Yet that does not change the fact that heros of the 151st Machine Gun Battalion largely went unsung by commanders who were not their own.

Brigadier General Douglas MacArthur. Until July, 1918, MacArthur was Chief-of-Staff for the 42nd Rainbow Division. Thereafter he was commander of the 84th Brigade including the 151st Machine Gun Battalion. One of his first orders was to assemble the 151st Machine Gun Battalion under its own command and no longer attach its companies to infantry battalions. The shift, prompted by Major Cooper D. Winn, would later pay off with great dividends. *Editor's collection.*

On the morning of August 10th, our battalion formed after much cleaning and policing of clothes, animals, and equipment. We were to be inspected by our new Brigade Commander,[29] Douglas MacArthur, who had been promoted to Brigadier General for his distinguished work in the battle.[30] He succeeded Brigadier General Brown who, being near retirement age, was ordered to service elsewhere. He had done good work as commander in this brigade, but the needs of this war were for young men, and General MacArthur, age 37, assumed command of our brigade. We almost worshiped this man because of his excellent combat record. As Colonel and Division Chief of Staff, he had personally insisted on participating in the first raid of the Division at Badonviller and had returned with a wound and a German Lieutenant prisoner.[31] In this battle, he had spent most of the time in the very front lines with the doughboys. Generals of his kind quickly catch the imagination of the doughboy and the morale of our brigade was quickly back to normal as we learned about our new fighting general.

On the afternoon of the 10th, with the lines forward being established, our division, which was still in reserve, was relieved and ordered back. We marched back through the towns of Beuvardes, Trugny, Epieds, and others, all bearing evidence of the heavy artillery fire about us on all sides. At Trugny, I jerked down a German sign from above the entrance of a dugout. It read, "Unterstand Fur 70 Mann," meaning shelter or billets for seventy men. I mailed it home as a souvenir.

29. MacArthur received this command on August 6, 1918.
30. Actually, MacArthur had already been promoted the previous June.
31. On March 1, 1918, MacArthur accompanied Company F of the 168th Infantry in its raid on German lines in front of Badonviller (Reilly 152-153). "It turned out to be the first time Americans ever fought their way into German trenches" (MacArthur in Reilly, 191).

In one other town along the road I noticed the division canteen. This was the first time I had seen it, and I knew our own troops had no recent opportunity to buy anything. We had been well fed the last few days on vegetables, meat, and coffee, but it had been months since any of them had purchased any sweets. Against strict orders not to leave the column while marching, I slipped out of the line as we passed through this town and hurried back to the store, where I purchased six one-pound cans of chocolates. This was all they would sell me. I hurried back and overtook our column.

I gave one to my platoon, where each man had about a bite. I gave Lieutenant Andres, Lieutenant Olson, and Lieutenant Means each a can, who in turn shared them with their men. I was holding the other two boxes in reserve to be distributed later. It was all my own money that I had spent, so I opened one of these boxes and ate a good part of it myself. We marched back to the town of La Charite, a suburb of Chateau-Thierry. The remaining box of candy was stolen from me that night, much to my disappointment, as I fully intended to pass it out to my platoon, but I could not censure the man who stole it had I discovered him. I would have done the same thing myself if I had the opportunity.

Unerstand Fur 70 Mann. (Dugout for 70 men.) This wooden sign, measuring 5" by 14", was taken by Lieutenant Parkinson from a German trench at Trugny after the fight for the heights of the Ourcq River. His habit was to collect souvenirs *after* fighting was over and mail them home. *World War History & Art Museum (WWHAM) collection, Alliance, Ohio.*

When the ration cart came to us that night, it brought a sack of mail. I had half a dozen letters from home. As we were bivouacked along the roadside, without lights or fires, I climbed into a combat wagon and lit a candle, where I read and reread the letters from home.

On our march back to La Charite we, as usual, passed many French troops. I recognized one French officer in black uniform with red trimmings as belonging to the division to which I had been attached in Nancy and Hoeville. I inquired about my friend, former interpreter and guide Lieutenant Eugene Etienne, as well as the other officers of that battalion. He had not seen them recently, but knew them to be in this vicinity.

On the morning of August 11th, we saw long lines of camions loaded with infantry of the 77th Division driving forward. They all were anxious to get to the front. We sympathized with them secretly, but outwardly ridiculed them as being raw troops. We knew, however, that they would soon have abundant

Fig Leaf. Lieutenant N. P. Parkinson's helmet. This was the helmet he wore when he played dead, head forward, in an open field at the foot of Hill 212. An American helmet did not offer much protection. It was especially meager cover from the German machine gun fire directed at Parkinson and his messenger. *World War History & Art Museum (WWHAM) collection, Alliance, Ohio.*

experience.[32] Lieutenant Andres and I walked into the town of Chateau-Thierry, down to the river, where the bridge had been blown out. This was the historic bridge where the machine gunners of the 3rd Division had stopped the last German attack.[33] This town had been terribly punished by shell fire. All the civilians had gone.

That night we resumed the march as a battalion through the towns of Chateau-Thierry and Vaux to the outskirts of Bouresches. We were to be billeted in Bouresches. We waited along the road outside of town while billeting officers went forward to arrange assignments of billet. Then I saw an asparagus bed in a field nearby. The tops had grown to maturity, but after a careful search I found one solitary sprout, six inches long. This I gathered, and searched high and low for more. I had my teeth all set for a mess of asparagus. Although I found no more, I cooked this solitary stalk and had two good bites of unseasoned asparagus that night.[34]

We spent two days in the town of Bouresches, which is within just a few yards of Belleau Woods. Many of our men visited this wood and brought back tales of evidence of the hard fighting the previous June by the Second Division. Officers of our company were quartered in a large building on the main court of the town. All these buildings were ruined by shell fire, but in certain corners we found shelter against rain. In the yard of this building, three men of the Second Division were buried. They were Army soldiers, not Marines. The attack at Belleau Woods had included severe action at Bouresches.

Along with a medical officer (Lieutenant Williams or Erskine), on August 12th, I took an ambulance to Chateau-Thierry supplied with money, hoping to be able to buy some dainties for the battalion. This proved impossible, however. On August 12th, we saw coming into the street of Bouresches an old

32. Starting on September 26, the 77th Division would get its real fighting "experience" clearing out the Argonne Forest. Therein the so-called "Lost Battalion" was surrounded for several days and held its own in spite of no food, repeated attacks by the Germans, heavy casualties, and a misguided artillery barrage upon them from their own division.

33. This valiant effort by machine gunners of the 3rd Division stopped the German Aisne Offensive (May 27 to June 4) in its tracks.

34. This story is famous (or perhaps infamous) in the Parkinson family. The elder Parkinson told it often and asparagus came to be the family's "official" vegetable. Few of his grandchildren liked asparagus or ate it. However, asparagus was prominently served and Nellis and Florence Parkinson's 50th wedding anniversary dinner in 1970. For two bites in 1918 asparagus had merited a kind of figurehead status, but was not fit for general consumption.

man pushing a cart bearing a few belongings, including bedding, as well as a woman and two children. They located their former home, now in a mass of ruins, in the town of Bouresches. With very little demonstration they immediately began clearing away debris, coming back to the place they called home. Men of our company volunteered, and soon the remaining portions of the stone walls were covered by a rough shelter built out of scrap lumber by our men and these French civilians. The next day, they were cutting the wheat in their field that had remained unharvested during all the recent fighting.

At noon on August 13th, we left Bouresches and marched to the town of Champigny, on the Marne River. This town was soon filled with troops of our battalion. We marched on about one kilometer to the Chateau of Tanqueux. I was billeted in a room in this large chateau. The owner was still living there. The man was a native American, but since his marriage he had lived 30 years in France and was now a French subject. He and his wife were hospitable to me and I enjoyed the stay there. On the night of August 14th, the Germans raided the nearby town of La Ferte. The hum of motors and the firing overhead awakened me, but I did not trouble to get out of bed.

German M1916 Helmet. Lieutenant Parkinson picked up this helmet in Bouresches, at the edge of Belleau Wood. Two months prior this was the site of bitter and prolonged fighting by Marines of the 2nd Division. *World War History & Art Museum (WWHAM) collection, Alliance, Ohio.*

On August 15th, orders came permitting 48 hours leave to Paris. All the officers of our battalion went and a large number of our men. I loaned all the money I had to men of our platoon who were permitted to join this party. It was necessary, however, for one officer to remain with the battalion. I, being junior officer, received that assignment.

During that day, I took the battalion to the delousing station set up on the Marne River bank. Our clothes were steamed and thoroughly cleansed while we all took a swim in the Marne. The infantry regiment was doing likewise farther down the river. I learned later that one of the men of this regiment, who had risked his life in several valorous exploits in the last battle and came out unharmed, had drowned while swimming. I heard "Taps" and the rifle salute at his grave the next day.

On August 16th, I made requisition for complete supplies to replenish machine gun parts and other equipment lost in the battle. On this day, as I was still in command of this battalion, the man at Chateau Tanqueux came excitedly to my headquarters and led me to his front yard. In a corner there was a mule half buried. The hole had not been dug deep enough and two of the hoofs and almost one entire hind quarter were now exposed above the ground since the rains. Hoof brands showed the mule belonged to the 26th Division. I refused to exhume it and bury it deeper, but did have a detail of men cover it up completely by heaping a high mound of earth over it.

The men from our company were expected back from Paris at suppertime on this day. I had plenty of time, and on instructions from Captain Means, who had been a captain since orders dated July 10th,[35] prepared a fine meal for the five officers of our battalion[36] to be set at five o'clock. I located some fine port wine, a bottle of Champagne, a dozen eggs, some fresh hulled butter beans, and got some nice steaks from the mess sergeant, together with potatoes and carrots. A French lady prepared these in a most excellent fashion with proper French seasoning.

At five o'clock the men had not returned. I waited until six, then sat down to the meal alone. It had not suffered by being kept warm. This French lady knew how to do that. I took liberal helpings of food, including the wine. At 7:30 the officers had not yet showed up, so I continued eating and finished one bottle of wine. Slowly, but surely, I kept on eating, mixing food with wine and coffee. Before I realized it, all twelve eggs were gone and I had eaten several plates of beans, two steaks, and many other things so that, except for the meat and some of the wine, there was practically nothing left for the rest of the officers.

I do not see how it could be possible for one man to eat as I ate that evening. I cannot account for it, except by the fact that for months we had been in trenches, and only on rare occasions had we really been fed to our complete satisfaction. We had plenty of food the last few days, but none to compare with these well seasoned dishes cooked by this French lady. With the wine and Champagne, everything went down easily and I suffered not the least discomfort.

At 8:30, with Sergeant Zeiders of the stables, I rode down the road toward La Ferte. I was now expecting the officers to return at 8:30. I met them on the way, walking back. They mounted the horses which we were taking to them.

On Saturday, August 17th, A and B Companies entrained at La Ferte. We of D Company went to town to shop. I bought several vases and mailed them home. I also mailed home a number of souvenirs, among them: a German helmet that I had picked up at Bouresches, handfuls of buttons I took from German uniforms of various kinds, and the base of a six-inch German shell in brass which I had picked up in Foret de Fere. In La Ferte, we found some partially ripe bananas and some small hard oranges which we ate greedily. I also bought a pair of pajamas, and from that day became the object of the envy of all the officers in my battalion.

Sunday we entrained at La Ferte in 43 minutes. The train moved up the Marne Valley through Chateau-Thierry, Dormans, Epernay, Chalons, Vitry-

35. According to Means, his promotion to captain was effective as of July 31 and he learned of it on August 9 (Means).

36. Parkinson meant "company" not "battalion" here. Company D had 5 officers while the battalion had the officers of four companies plus those of HQ.

le-Francois, Chaumont, and Langres, and we detrained at Bourmont. We were served dinner on the quay and marched to the nearby village of Sauville.

The French village of Sauville, well behind the battle area, received our battalion most cordially. Old men, women, and children all joined in a general opening up of the village that made us feel that our stay with them would be pleasant. Hardly a family, however, had not lost a father or a son in the French Army. In the home where I was billeted a peasant woman, apparently in her thirties with three small children, had been left a widow at Verdun. She was valiantly trying to operate the small acreage that her husband had tilled before the war. This was typical of almost every home in this village. Yet we heard no complaint, and the entire citizen population seemed to bear their sorrow in silence and made every effort to treat us as guests.

After a day of rest, we were issued sufficient new uniforms and new equipment to give our battalion a passable appearance. By day, we participated in open order drill and battle maneuvers. In conjunction with the infantry battalion from a nearby area, we rehearsed several hypothetical attacks on nearby wooded hills.

The 151st Machine Gun Battalion during maneuvers at Bourmont, France, late August, 1918. Precious few photos were taken of the 151st Machine Gun Battalion between March and November, 1918. This photo was taken during a lull just before they were thrown into the St. Mihiel Offensive. Lieutenants Andres, Geiszel, and Parkinson were not photographed until they were in Luxembourg after the Armistice.
Editor's collection.

Major Winn had lost his watch in the last battle. I had a wristwatch given to me by friends at the Conservatory at Decatur and also had an open-faced watch which I had formerly carried in my pocket. At this time, I loaned Major Winn my pocket watch. He used it to time the barrage fire in the battle of St.

Mihiel and part of the Argonne, then returned it to me as soon as he had opportunity to buy a new one. Every few days a wagon would come to this village, issuing a beef ration to the civilians. The French had meat in limited quantities, but it was carefully husbanded and shared.

On August 21st, I had ridden Captain Means' horse to the town of Vittel and had measurements taken for a new uniform. I visited hospitals there and saw many wounded from our division, including Lieutenant Baumet, who had been wounded by machine gun fire at Foret de Fere and Red Cross Farm. I had secretly hoped that I might by chance find my good friend Major Jesse T. McDavid, who had entered the medical corps from Decatur. For months before the war he, Chester,[37] and I had discussed the possibility of America entering the war and had, at that time, discussed our respective plans for entering the service. I knew he was commanding a base hospital, but did not know which one.

On August 25th, I received orders to take a detachment of one squad from each company to a divisional Signal Corps School at Bourmont. That Sunday evening, we went by truck and were billeted in St. Thiebauld, with orders to report for school the next morning. My quarters were in #14, on what we would call Main Street. From a small shop in this town I bought a handmade silk apron which I sent home to Florence[38] as a souvenir.

The school was conducted in the nearby village of St. Thiebauld, adjoining Bourmont. Monday morning we attended lecture. In the afternoon we assembled for field maneuvers, but immediately on assembly Major Garret, in command, announced that we were all ordered back to our units, as the division was to move to the front. I assembled my detachment at the appointed time and waited for the truck to take us back. Just as I loaded them in, I met John Leas of Decatur on the road. He knew the truck driver, climbed on the seat to ride part way with us, and we had a good visit. This truck had some other detachments besides our own. We delivered them at other villages along the way. In passing through one of these villages, I waived at Lieutenant Doocy as he stood in the street. It was the last time I saw him.

Tuesday, August 28th, and Wednesday, August 29th, we prepared for the movement forward. We had long been hearing rumors of a tremendous Allied drive to extend from Belgium to Switzerland. That evening, as the rain continued to fall, we saw another beautiful rainbow in the sky, and a rainbow means only one thing to the Rainbow Division: a battle.

I was ordered to report to Lieutenant William Cann of B Company. Captain Brown of that company had been sent to Machine Gun School. I was assigned Andy Perrion as orderly and messenger, and was also assigned Captain Brown's big black horse, which seemed to be the best mount in the battalion.

37. Dr. Chester B. Parkinson.

38. Florence North who later married Parkinson.

CHAPTER 6: ST. MIHIEL

FORET DE LA REINE, BOIS DU JURY, FLIREY, SONNARD WOODS, ESSEY, PANNES, BENEY, CHATEAU ST. BENOIT, HAUMONT, MARIMBOIS FERME, NONSARD WOODS, MONT SEC.

The night of August 30th,[1] our battalion marched to Bulgnéville. It was raining as usual. We arrived at daybreak, and the troops were bivouacked in a field nearby. Lieutenant Cann and I, by invitation of Captain Palmer of A Company, joined their company officers' mess. Lieutenants Olson and Nichols were the other officers of his company. During the day, I rode my black horse to Vittel and got my uniform. That evening for dinner, Major Winn invited Lieutenant Cann and me to be his guests, where he and his staff were billeted in an excellent French home. The table was covered with rare linens, and we were served from solid silver and beautiful china. It was quite a treat, and the first time I had the use of a napkin since leaving the steamship *St. Louis* eight months before.

From Bulgnéville, we marched that night to Gironcourt. I was billeted in the same building with Lieutenant Andres of D Company. Lieutenant Geiszel and Captain Means were across the street. Lieutenant Cann was further up the street. Next morning, we received 49 replacements for B Company and 51 for D Company. These were to bring our strength to normal, since the casualties suffered in the last action. Other companies received similar numbers.

On Sunday morning, September 1st, Lieutenant Andres and I attended the village church. The services were Roman Catholic, which was Lieutenant

1. As of August 30, 1918, the 42nd Rainbow Division was assigned to the IVth Corps commanded by Major General Joseph T. Dickman (Reilly, 532).

Andres's faith. I was a Presbyterian,[2] but we worshiped side by side in the same pew. Each found comfort in his own faith, but had a sacred respect for the faith of the other. We never did discuss this question, nor even speak of it. We didn't need to. We just knew. We found that out cowering before the same exploding shells at Sergy, Hill 212, and Champagne, we were sending unvoiced prayers to the same God. The best prayers of a soldier are unspoken, and I doubt if ever a soldier waited out a real barrage knocking dirt over him and sending death through the air without trying to pray.

We stayed at Gironcourt until September 4th, rehearsing field problems with the infantry by day, and each evening the 168th Infantry Band gave a concert.

At this village, a passing truck struck a mule and injured it, so it had to be killed. In a few minutes word spread throughout the village. Frenchmen gathered round, and soon both hindquarters had been converted into mule steaks, which the civilians eagerly took home to their tables. September 4th, at night, we marched to the village of Battigny. Our billets for officers were in a barracks of a frame building of hasty construction which the French were using as a Y.M.C.A. I spread my bed on one of the mattresses and went for a walk about the village, as I was not yet sleepy. When I came back at bedtime, Major Ross, Regimental Adjutant of the 168th Infantry, had ranked me out of my mattress, so I slept on the floor.

Next morning, at a nearby French canteen, I bought a few French cigars which were very poor in quality, but the only kind available in France, except, of course, those we occasionally received from our own organizations. I also bought two small pocket-sized tins filled with menthol candy with a gum base. These small pieces of candy were valuable to me for several weeks thereafter. Each time I became hungry, one of those dissolved in my mouth would tide me over. I also bought three or four flat cans of French sardines. Since they fit in the pocket easily, I had made it a rule, when possible, to keep a supply of these on hand, in addition to my regular emergency ration of corned beef.

From Battigny, we moved that night to Thuilley. At dusk, we passed a camp of German prisoners enclosed in barbed wire. On these marches at night, I was constantly entertained by the humor and wise cracks of the boys of this company, who were from Macon, Georgia. Several of them were especially humorous, and their drawl southern accent was interesting for me to hear. The veteran troops had much fun at the expense of the replacements who had not yet been under fire by greatly emphasizing the dangers of battle and the chances of becoming a casualty. The march from Battigny to Thuilley was tiring and slow. Two or three times I went to sleep on my horse. I got off to walk, hoping to keep awake, but twice went to sleep walking. At Thuilley the next day, Captain Lightner returned to our battalion, but was attached to Battalion headquarters, so Captain Means retained command of D Company.

2. Parkinson descended from French Huguenots and Scottish Covenanters who were forerunners of Presbyterians.

Chain of Command St. Mihiel Offensive, September 12-16, 1918

Major General Joseph T. Dickman
IV CORPS
1st US Division
42nd US Division
89th US Division
3rd US Division (Reserve)

Major General Charles T. Menoher
42nd RAINBOW DIVISION

Brigadier General Douglas MacArthur
84th BRIGADE
167th Infantry Regiment
168th Infantry Regiment
151st Machine Gun Battalion

Major Cooper D. Winn
151st MACHINE GUN BATTALION

1st Lieutenant William Cann
COMPANY B, 151st MACHINE GUN BATTALION
2nd Lieutenant N. P. Parkinson (Second in Command)

Sergeant - 1st PLATOON (4 MG Squads)
Sergeant - 2nd PLATOON (4 MG Squads)
Sergeant - 3rd PLATOON (4 MG Squads)
SUPPLY TRAIN

Also, a beautiful rainbow in the afternoon sky told us we were again scheduled for action at the front.

On the night of September 7th, the battalion marched through the pouring rain in the direction of Toul. Roads were congested with traffic. Progress was slow. We spent more time standing idle in the rain, waiting for traffic to clear ahead, than we did marching. After many hours of this, we suddenly turned completely around in the road and retraced our steps. Someone had gotten us on the wrong road, and we had gone several laborious kilometers from our course and spent hours waiting in the rain to get to go in the wrong direction. At daybreak, we reached our destination and bivouacked in a field four kilometers south of Toul. On the night of the eighth we made another hard march, likewise delayed by congested traffic, and in the morning bivouacked in the woods near Sanzey.

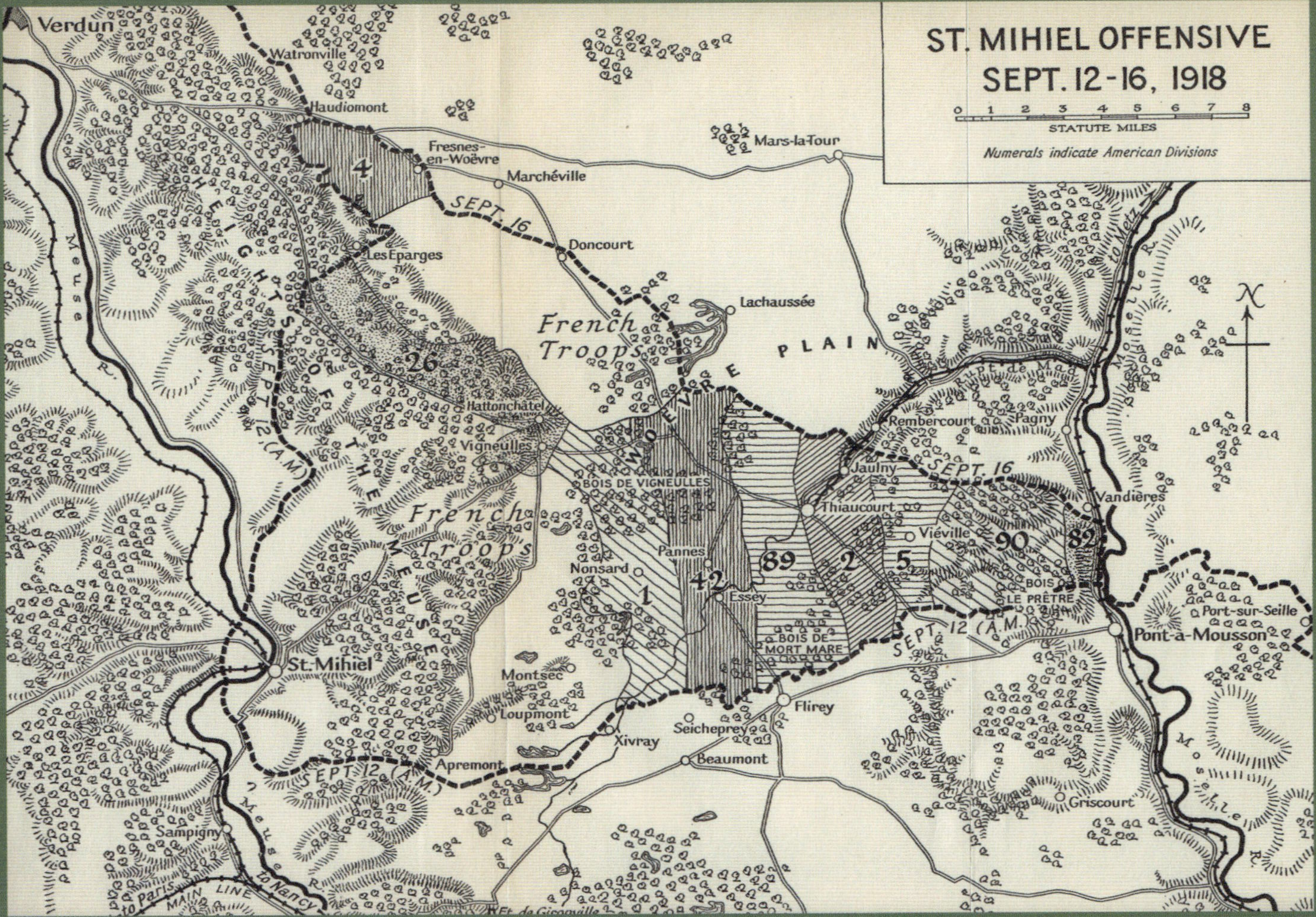

Map from Pershing, *My Experiences in the World War.*

On the night of the ninth, a short march took us to another woods a little nearer the front lines called Foret de la Reine. It continued raining heavily most of the time. The ground was soggy and muddy, so that we could not keep dry, even in pup tents. Our troops, however, collected rough limbs and broke them up in lengths to give them solid foundations on which to spread their blankets. This was not a soft bed, but it was a dry bottom, and pup tents kept off the falling rain. As our wagon train was still with us, I set up my cot each night, rolled up in my blankets, spread a shelter-half over me as a top cover, and slept comfortably even in the hardest rain.

All through these woods shells were being hauled forward and piled in rows. Shells of all calibers were piled in pre-designated places, ready for the artillery to come in at the last minute and start firing. We could see this was going to be no small raid, but truly a great American offensive.[3]

Several nights before, a mule had got loose from our picket line and strayed. Of course, he was probably taken in by one of the other organizations crowded in these woods. They were all short of animals. Since there was one less animal to care for, one of our mule skinners was transferred from the stable detail to a machine gun squad as ammunition carrier.[4] He did not like the change, particularly on the eve of battle, because mule skinners usually stayed in the rear with the stock. As we marched along the road in the woods, other men in the company were teasing him because of the change they knew was so unwelcome to him. As usual, it was raining and pitch dark as we halted for a rest period in the woods. Off in the darkness to our left we heard a mule bray. This ex-mule skinner was on his feet in an instant. "There's my old mule now!" he shouted, and dashed off in the darkness in the direction of the sound. Sure enough, in a few minutes he came back leading the mule he had lost. The mule had scented our other mules as they passed, recognized the scent, and brayed. His former master recognized his bray in the dark, went right to where he was tied, and in spite of protests of the men guarding the picket line of that company, untied him and brought him back to his own. Both man and beast were again assigned to their former duties.

On the afternoon of September 9th, an artillery battery took position across the road from us. In a few minutes Lieutenant O'Keefe of C Company recognized his brother among the officers in charge.

On September 10th, our battalion received the order covering the attack, although we did not know the exact date.[5] On that day, the four company

3. For all intents and purposes, St. Mihiel was the first American-led offensive of WWI. Before that, Americans had been operating in conjunction with and under the command of the French and British.

4. This mule skinner typified what happened to most of the replacements the 151st Machine Gun Battalion received. New men were transferred to the Battalion to bring it up to authorized strength just before heading off to a fight. Usually these green troops were relegated to being ammunition carriers. Seasoned veterans did the shooting; newcomers did menial labor.

5. The Germans anticipated that an attack was coming at St. Mihiel. However, they were taken by surprise by its timing. They had expected it to come later than September 12.

commanders went forward to reconnoiter. It poured rain all day. When they returned, I had opportunity to read the order for the attack. We were a part of General Dickman's IV Corps. With the First and 89th Divisions, our 42nd was to advance to drive in a wedge on the south side of the salient.[6] The order stated, "The 42nd Division will deliver the main blow." We had the position of honor in the plan of attack, but from previous experience we knew what that honor would cost. None of us would shirk, but we had an extreme dread of what we might be coming into. We knew that many a French division had hurled itself against the fortifications in this sector and had been thrown back with heavy and staggering losses.

We had heard how Mont Sec dominated the entire region. We felt that when we endeavored to envelop this mountain we would run into a situation perhaps more difficult than Hill 212 and Sergy had been. We knew some would be killed and wounded, but always expected it would be someone else. Someone else! That's the spark that kept up our spirits. "Someone was doomed today, but I will be among those spared, at least for today. If I must go, it will be later on, but today I am to be lucky." You would watch the man at your side. "Poor fellow. This may be his day to go, but not mine!" Thus, we hoped so intensely that we almost made ourselves believe that way–yes, almost!

On the afternoon of September 11th, we were told that the zero hour would be next morning. At five P.M., we formed on a trail in the woods in the gathering twilight to march to the trenches from which we were to launch the attack. Captain Charles Travis, who had been injured by a fall from his horse sixty days previous near Suippes, suddenly appeared for duty just in time to take command of C Company. Lieutenant Cann and I were the only officers in B Company. He was in command.

Eastern Slope of Mont Sec. This was the stronghold that gave the Germans such a commanding view of the St. Mihiel Salient. The axis of attack for the 42nd Rainbow Division was to the right. In the foreground is a captured German 150mm gun. *Editor's collection.*

As the column moved down the road toward Mandres, we could see the outlines of Mont Sec, a dull grey mass looming on the horizon north of us. It was my first view of this mountain, and as I saw how it dominated the plains in every direction, my misgivings based on previous reports were in no sense diminished.

6. The 3rd Division rounded out the IVth Corps and was held in reserve.

Where the road forked at Mandres, we turned to the right and continued toward Bois du Jury. It was from trenches on the east edge of these woods that we were to jump off next morning. Captain Means and Lieutenant Cann were marching their companies together, as they were to depart adjoining positions.[7] As we reached the place where we left the highway and started through the field to the woods, the Germans began pounding the highway with tremendous artillery fire, using both high explosives and gas. In this fire we unloaded our carts to go the rest of the way on foot.

We had to carry our heavy equipment in the dark through thick lines of barbed wire, which we could not see. We could not tell where an opening was, except by following the wire until we felt a passage. After half an hour of slowly and laboriously picking our way through the night, wire, and exploding shells, we reached an open field at the east edge of the Jury woods and then made more rapid progress still on top of the ground. It was pitch dark and raining. We had to cross several trenches, the bottoms of which were deep in mud and water. With our heavy equipment we could not jump across the trenches.[8] As I had very little equipment compared to what other men were carrying, I jumped in the trench and allowed the company to step on my shoulder in order to cross the trench in two long steps.

Flooded Trench Near Flirey. It was in a trench like this that Lieutenant Parkinson stood, making himself a stepping stone for the rest of B Company as men crossed in two long steps. *Editor's collection.*

At last, we descended into a narrow communication trench leading to the front line trenches. It was so narrow that with packs and equipment two men could not pass. At this point, after we were all in the trench, we met a platoon of infantry from the 89th Division moving out of this same trench. Our division was taking over half of the area occupied by the 89th Division, which was to attack in the morning at our right, on the other half. This platoon had a long journey to the rear, then to our

7. For the first time in the war, the 151st Machine Gun Battalion was operating as a unit under Major Winn's command instead of having its companies attached to the 167th and 168th Infantry Regiments (Reilly, 551, 570).

8. Each gunner carried the 52.8 lb weapon and each assistant loader the 55 lb tripod. Loaders and ammunition carriers lugged two ammo boxes weighing a total of 56.4 lbs. This was all in addition to their personal gear. So these Yanks were neither nimble nor quick.

right, and back to their jumping off place. As we were almost to our destination, we retraced our steps, heavily, to where we could get out of the trench and let them pass. We could not use the top of the ground here because it was impassable with barbed wire entanglements.

Finally, we reached our destination after great effort in the muddy trench, and about 12:30 stationed the men in the front line trench at the point from which we were to jump off.[9] There was no shelter from rain, nor from artillery. In some places these trenches were floored with duck boards, which gave dry footing, but we could not sit down or lean against the sides, except to sink in soft mud. It was still very dark, and we did not know what our surroundings were or how close to the Germans we were. We spoke only in tense whispers, and then only when absolutely necessary. The men showed excellent spirit under these hardships and wished for the time to come when they could start doing something. The 49 replacements who had not been under fire knew even less what to expect, but they had great confidence in the remainder of the company, because they knew that they were among veterans.

Communication Trench Near Flirey. One way streets like this meant for frequent backtracking when faced by troops coming from the other direction. *Editor's collection.*

After the men were stationed, I explored the trenches nearby, but could find no shelter for them. I found one small dugout in the side of a trench where Captain Palmer of A Company and two or three other officers were crowded in as headquarters. It had begun to rain harder and, at their invitation, I took shelter in this dugout, which was crowded holding three men. We had six inside now. The roof was made out of about six inches of dirt over corrugated iron. It would withstand shell fragments, but not a direct hit. At my position in the dugout, the rain soon seeped through the rusted iron above and dripped on my helmet. This pounding so annoyed me that I stepped outside to stand in the rain.

It was now 1:00, and promptly the large concentration of guns in our areas opened fire. For four hours they sent a great rain of shells into Mont Sec and all the surrounding territory. We heard the explosions of these guns behind us and the swish of thousands of shells sailing over our heads to the enemy.

9. This first day of the attack at St. Mihiel was September 12.

The enemy replied, although not severely. Enough shells fell near us to keep us constantly under tension, but we suffered no casualties in our immediate organization.

Around the trench to our left, which was outside the sector of our company, I heard the report of a rifle and soon afterward saw an American soldier limping toward the rear, shot through the foot. He was one of the 89th Division. Ordinarily I would have learned his identity and caused his arrest, as it was quite clear it was a self-inflicted wound.[10] But I had other things on my mind. In all the war, this was the only incident of this kind I knew about.

I took station with my men about ten minutes after one and stayed with them throughout the bombardment. Rain continued to pour and the sides of the trenches became very slippery. At five o'clock it was breaking day, although not yet light. We discovered a place in the trench where we could climb to the surface on the forward side. Lieutenant Cann mounted first, stood on top, and gave me a hand as I followed. I gave each man in the platoon a hand to help him up this place. I dreaded standing erect, but must confess that my nerve was greatly strengthened by the manner in which Lieutenant Cann walked around. After the war Private Wing, one of the replacements just arrived, told me how he admired my courage to stand there on top of the trench. I never told him how terribly "scared" I was.

As I helped each man up, Lieutenant Cann directed them a few yards forward where, kneeling low, the line formed and started forward. The artillery fire began falling near us and machine gun bullets hissed over our heads. The Germans were firing high. It was not yet light enough for us to be seen at a distance, but the Germans knew that this was one of the places where we would be leaving the trenches. The fire display ahead was caused in some measure by our own rolling barrage, which started rolling forward.[11] We followed as closely as was safe and passed through the front line trenches which had been abandoned by the Germans as we approached.[12] They fell back to the Sonnard Woods, which was a heavily fortified position.

The infantry suffered many casualties passing through these woods.[13] I learned later that it was here that Lieutenant Doocy was killed and Major Brewer was wounded. This wood also cost the life of Lieutenant Currie, patrol leader, and Lieutenant Smith of the Regimental Machine Gun Company, who had relieved me on my first hitch in the trenches at A-14 at Badonviller.

10. This soldier was probably AWOL as well since the 89th Division had been relieved from this sector. No doubt he lagged behind his outfit to avoid being seen by witnesses who knew him.

11. A rolling barrage was systematically indexed forward over enemy positions as infantry followed closely behind. Normally the barrage was advanced about 100 meters every three minutes or about a third of a soldier's regular pace at a march (Reilly, 147).

12. The four companies of the 151st Machine Gun Battalion were advancing between the first and second waves of attacking infantry, ready to render fire support when and where needed (Means; White and Peavy).

13. "The 3rd Battalion, 168th Infantry, most determinedly led, slashed into this resistance to the accompaniment of heavy machine gunnery, and with splendid *elan*, drove straight into the woods and seized its near edges with all their defenders" (Wolf, 41).

Our company escaped casualties in this wood because the enemy were firing high in our sector, but Company D lost Private G. J. Reemsnyder and Corporal Frank Cramblett, both killed by machine gun fire, and Lieutenant Geiszel and Privates Patrick, Taylor, Dixon, Gleason, Herr, and Madlem were wounded.[14]

No Man's Land Near Flirey. This ground was typical of where the 42nd Rainbow Division jumped off September 12, 1918. *Editor's collection.*

Lieutenant Cann then ordered me to the rear to bring up the ammunition carts and the company rolling kitchen. I did not wait for a second command, but with my orderly, Andy Perrion, ran the entire distance back to our jumping off place. We then walked hurriedly to the rear. As we reached the town of Mandres, we saw many batteries of artillery along the road still firing the rolling barrage. Prisoners were now being taken to the rear. Past Mandres, we hurried on and at the echelon ordered the machine gun carts to fall in line and the kitchen to follow. Lieutenant Joe Turner, in charge of the battalion supply train, asked me to help him lead the battalion train forward, but I had special orders for my company carts and kitchen and had to refuse.

Just as we started forward, Sergeant Troop of D Company called to me and handed me a pan of hot doughnuts they had just made. These lasted only an instant. In this brief pause, mule drivers of the entire battalion gathered around, asking for news from the front. They cheered loudly and profanely as I told them of the success we had. It was one of the few occasions where I heard cheering from the troops at the front, although sometimes, in a sudden rush forward, they would yell and whoop.

It was no longer raining. Riding my big black horse, I led the gun carts and our kitchen team at a trot up the road through Mandres, turned to the right, and saw our artillery batteries moving forward so they could again be in range. On this road I met Sergeant Harry Gruger of D Company who gave me first word of Lieutenant Geiszel being wounded.[15] Gruger had just taken him to

14. Reemsnyder was shot through the temple while mounting his machine gun on its tripod. Other guns of Company D were soon in action suppressing enemy machine gun fire from the Bois de Sonnard. "In a very few minutes the infantrymen were able to advance without any more trouble" (Means). Cramblett was killed and the others wounded beyond the woods toward Essey.

15. At this point Sergeant Gruger took command of the 3rd Platoon (Means).

the dressing station. I tried to go directly through the Jury Woods with the carts, but in what had been No Man's Land in the front of these woods, I found it would be impossible to get these carts across the trenches.

No Man's Land Near Flirey. Another view of typical ground that the 151st Machine Gun Battalion attacked across at St. Mihiel. *Editor's collection.*

There were many wounded men being cared for by hospital detachments. There were many dead Americans and some dead Germans. I will never forget one poor doughboy who lay in a shell hole dead. A shell fragment of steel about three inches long and an inch wide had struck him on its flat side and lay embedded its own thickness in his temple, a perfect inlay. There was not a drop of blood on his face. Nearby, a wounded German was looking wistfully toward us. He could not speak and had not yet had any attention, but with ammunition for the front lines, I could not stop. I called to a hospital detachment nearby to care for him as soon as possible.

As I stood on the edge of Jury Woods, facing Mont Sec in the distance, I saw before me a panorama of a battle greater than any Civil War general ever saw. Bursts and clouds of smoke and geysers of dirt several miles ahead showed where our barrage was falling. Mont Sec and the heights of the Woevre were being pounded by our artillery fire. Rows of trenches stood out before us leading to the horizon, both to the right and left. Before them were matted entanglements of barbed wire. Through these masses of wire were often seen the path of a Whippet Tank,[16] many of which were still maneuvering on the plain before me, and others, which were out of action, dotted about the fields, where they had become casualties. We turned the train about and retraced our steps clear to the Mandres road, which we followed parallel to the front lines, toward the town of Flirey.

At the outskirts of Flirey, we passed under a large railroad bridge that had been blown up years before. At Flirey, we again turned on a road leading out toward No Man's Land and found ourselves in a heavy congestion of traffic, ambulances, ammunition wagons, caissons, kitchens, and supply wagons. All were endeavoring to move forward. In four years of fighting this road had been destroyed where it crossed No Man's Land. Engineers were picking up stones

16. Along with tanks plowing through wire, St. Mihiel saw the first use of Bangalore torpedoes of WWII fame in clearing wire (Dooly, 69).

Silent Gun. German 105mm artillery captured in the St. Mihiel Salient on the first day of the attack. *Editor's collection.*

from nearby fields, trying to make the road passable. After long effort I got my train forward to this point. At an especially bad hole, a Colonel of Engineers had taken charge. Every large vehicle that had tried to pass through had gotten stuck and delayed the entire line. He ordered no more to go through until the hole was repaired, but that was awfully slow work. We could not take to the fields because they were blocked by trenches and wire.

Recollection. Americans moving into the St. Mihiel Salient with Mont Sec faintly looming in the distance. On the first morning of the attack Lieutenant John H. Geiszel of D Company was wounded by a shell fragment in the back of his neck. He did not return to duty until after the Armistice and he had a nasty scar to show for it. Nearly fifty years later Geiszel recognized this Signal Corps photograph in a book and scribbled a telling note beneath it: "I think it was a shell from this mountain (hill) that wounded me." *Editor's collection.*

As we stood in this congestion it started raining, and again a beautiful rainbow formed in the sky. Our men were cheered at its sight. We were from the Rainbow Division, but were in the sector of the 89th.

Traffic Jam. Column held up by an ammunition wagon stuck in the mud in the St. Mihiel Salient. Under similar circumstances Lieutenant Parkinson disobeyed the direct orders of a colonel and pushed his field kitchen through a muddy hole in the road. They barely made it and Parkinson avoided being court-martialed. *Editor's collection.*

I was impatient with the delay and, while the colonel was up the road and before the hole was repaired, I asked the driver of our kitchen if his team would be able to make it through. He was pretty sure they would. Therefore, with as many men pushing as could possibly lay hands on the big rolling kitchen, I ordered him through in defiance of the Colonel's positive orders. I held my breath as the team strained through that mud, but they made it by a hair's breadth and the road ahead was much easier. It was easier for the light carts to get through. So all my train moved forward, where I soon passed the Colonel of the Engineers. I would have been court-martialed if the kitchen had got stuck, but I took the chance and won. Few battles are won without taking many such risks, staking all on your own judgment.

On the road ahead we met large detachments of German prisoners returning. One group of about fifty, led by one American rifleman and followed by another, marched down the road. By their side was a French corporal, kicking the prisoners in the pants every time he suspected one was getting slow. He was calling them the vilest names and having a fine time in his way of getting even. He was doing no real harm and, since he had been in this war longer

Scapegoats. German prisoners taken in the St. Mihiel Offensive. Lieutenant Parkinson saw one such column of prisoners led by an American rifleman and followed by another. A French corporal kicked Germans in the pants and called them vile names as they passed by. *Editor's collection.*

than we had, no Americans interfered, allowing him to go ahead with his own entertainment. He was a member of a French artillery battery in that vicinity.

After crossing No Man's Land, the road leading to Essey became a first class rock road, such as is common in France. We moved as rapidly as possible. Three American tanks that had been put out of action were standing by this road. In one, the lifeless American driver lay still. It was now growing dark. At the outskirts of Essey we turned off the road behind the sheltered slope of a steep hill and I ordered a meal cooked. I went forward to find the exact location of Lieutenant Cann and the Company. They were bivouacked on the road beyond Essey. It was still raining. I returned and loaded the cans of beans, hamburgers, and coffee on a machine gun cart and brought the men at the front a hot meal. They had not had any hard fighting since I had left them and had suffered no casualties. They were to advance next morning, again at daylight. We had no more rations, so we could give them nothing more to eat, but Lieutenant Cann ordered me to follow the advance next morning as closely as possible with ammunition carts.

Next day,[17] the advance went beyond Pannes and we followed along the road with twelve ammunition carts,[18] stopping in the town of Beney. I had lost

17. This was September 13, the second day of the battle.

18. Lieutenant Parkinson left the company's twelve machine gun carts and the rolling kitchen in echelon at Pannes.

contact and turned to the right at this town, but soon found that I was in the 89th Division sector. The Germans were shelling this town as we retraced our steps. In Beney, we saw a large caliber gun, about eight inches, which had been left behind in the retreat. We turned left at the fork of the road and passed over open country across the railroad toward St. Benoit. From this point the road was concealed by camouflage built along the sides and top. As I led the train of twelve ammunition carts through Beney at a trot, I noticed that all but five had turned off and gone back to Pannes, but I proceeded with these five. I had no idea how badly our company might be needing ammunition. Seeing men lying in the field to our right, I rode out to them and inquired how far the lines had advanced ahead. They indicated a position to me far ahead. It later proved that the lines had never reached that point.

We rode across this open field to the edge of the Bois de Dampvitoux and skirted the west edge of this timber in the direction of Louiseville Farm. As I neared the edge, still with the woods between me and the enemy, I tied my horse to a sapling and concealed the carts in the edge of the woods. Then I went on foot across the open field. A few hundred yards ahead were men lying in the open. I intended to inquire further about the lines, but was pleased to find this was my own company. In a minute or two I had reported to Lieutenant Cann.

We were preparing to set up some machine guns to aid the infantry in driving the enemy out of Louiseville Farm. No enemy fire was falling near us, but out of a clear sky four shells came over in one salvo and landed in the woods where my carts were concealed. Two of the carts were struck with direct hits. Two mules were killed instantly and two more were wounded, so that they had to be shot. Two drivers were killed and two more wounded. My horse was not touched. I hurried back there, and with the help of Corporal Collier loaded the wounded men on the carts and sent them to the rear after unloading the ammunition.

The infantry line, including our company, then moved forward to the road to the right of Chateau St. Benoit. This road was the final objective of our division. When this first line of doughboys arrived, General MacArthur was there waiting for us. He had been out scouting in front with some patrols. This was our final objective.

On one of the carts was a meal for the company. We took it back to a deserted German camp in the Bois de Dampvitoux and brought it back hot. They had only one meal each day of this battle, but from many squads men came to me and spoke of my good work. In the last battle they had been in they had gone for days at a time with no food from their kitchen. I was pleased to know that the men approved of what I had done. I am sure that I did not have difficulties to encounter that their mess sergeant had in the fighting on the Ourcq River.

While these lines were being consolidated by men digging in, our company located and dug emplacements. Our lines were now under heavy fire from the

Finish Line. Men of the 167th Infantry in foxholes near St. Benoit. The road shown at the right was the final objective of the 42nd Rainbow Division on the second day of St. Mihiel. St. Benoit is over the ridge, while Louiseville Farm is behind the photographer. Along here, Parkinson and machine gunners of B Company, 151st Machine Gun Battalion, dug in with the infantry to consolidate a fixed line of defense, "the St. Mihiel Salient, now being a thing of the past." *Editor's collection.*

enemy artillery. They had many Austrian 88s which, when fired, always reached the target ahead of any warning whine. I spent part of each day with the company in the lines and at night slept with the echelon in Pannes, where I visited frequently with men in the echelon of Company D. They were bursting with pride at having captured four horses during the battle: three from the Germans and one from some American outfit. Our boys just picked it up while it was loose. It was not much of a horse, but became my mount for the rest of the war after I was returned to D Company. One of those taken from the Germans was a large draft animal, much needed by us. The other two were good mounts, one coal black and the other snow white.

One day at St. Benoit, I saw an enemy observation balloon burst into flames. A few seconds afterwards, just ahead of us, we heard machine gun fire in the air and saw one American aviator, who had just set the balloon on fire, fighting five red-nosed German Fokkers. They had him surrounded and cut off from the American lines. By a most spectacular series of dives, side slips, and loops, he maneuvered his plane so that he escaped safely to our lines where our own artillery drove the enemy planes back.

September 13th, while at Chateau St. Benoit, I started back on foot to the echelon at Pannes. Coming over the open road at the railroad crossing, I saw the entire battalion echelon on the road moving forward and led by Captain Lightner. He did not know where the front line was, but he wanted to get the echelon forward. I knew there was no shelter for them on the front line. Therefore, I persuaded him to turn them back. I went on to Pannes and was returning to the front on horseback when I saw that the entire echelon had stopped at Beney for the night. I knew that the enemy had pounded this village mercilessly with artillery every night so far and again persuaded Captain Lightner to take his train back to Pannes. I ordered the train of our company to go at once, which they did, but Captain Lightner decided to let the others cook supper where they were.

At that moment we heard machine gun fire overhead and, directly above us, saw at least sixty aeroplanes darting in all directions in combat.[19] I do not know what portion of them was ours, but they moved up the line. Even as we were watching them, the Germans opened up with severe artillery fire on our positions at Beney. Therefore, Captain Lightner wisely decided to move out before supper. I did not wait for them, as my company had already gone. I galloped up the camouflaged road to the Chateau.

Ammunition Train. German narrow gauge railway in woods of the St. Mihiel Salient. This was used to shuttle ammunition and supplies within the German interior lines. Company B of the 151st Machine Gun Battalion bivouacked along a railway like this in the Bois de Beney. *Editor's collection.*

About September 16th, the Third Battalion of the 168th Infantry was relieved from the front lines and moved back to bivouac in Bois de Beney. Our company bivouacked with them along a narrow gauge railway. On this railway were two German locomotives which our division had captured. I took the locomotive bell from one of them for a souvenir. It was about the size of a pint cup. I later mailed it home. In moving I misplaced my blanket, so I slept in a ration cart filled with hay.

One day, on the way back to camp, I saw a German plane dive from the sky to burn one of our observation balloons. The balloon was hauled in quickly, but the plane came so close that the observer jumped out in a parachute. During that day he had

19. Supposedly Billy Mitchell had 1,481 airplanes at his disposal for St. Mihiel. However, Lieutenant John H. Geiszel of Company D noted that on the first day, "we only saw (at St. Mihiel) 5 American planes and they were being chased by 1 German plane." Perhaps the heavy rain that morning had kept many of them grounded before Geiszel was wounded.

to make three or four jumps, but the enemy did not succeed in destroying his balloon.

On September 16th, with the St. Mihiel Salient now being a thing of the past, the division prepared to occupy the sector and consolidate it as a permanent line of defense. This sector, from this date, became known as the St. Benoit Sector. The 84th Brigade took over the entire divisional front and permitted the 83rd Brigade to retire for a few days in the rear area.

General Douglas MacArthur established Brigade headquarters in the Chateau St. Benoit, which formed a part of the first line of defense. When he sent a message to his regimental commanders, he had to send runners to the rear. Most generals would have been far behind their regimental commanders. Our general wanted to know more about conditions at the front than could be told by telephone. General MacArthur, of course, wanted to take advantage of fine quarters in the large chateau. But in doing so he expressed to his doughboys his unlimited faith in their ability to prevent the enemy from swooping down to capture him in this exposed position. The Germans undoubtedly would have attempted this had they known that a brigadier general was living so near the first line outposts.

The positions of B Company were consolidated in the line along the road between St. Benoit Chateau and Louiseville Farm. Company headquarters, where Lieutenant Cann and I slept, was in a small culvert along this road. Our men were shy of blankets, and some of the company in the chilly September nights protected themselves with German blankets that they found in rear areas, and in some cases with German overcoats. Our men had not yet been issued their own overcoats, and each carried only an extremely lightweight raincoat which was of practically no aid in keeping warm and of questionable value in turning rain any heavier than light showers. Some nights I slept in the front lines; others I spent with the echelon at Pannes. I do not remember how I alternated.

Our company kitchen was located close to the church in Pannes. The church steeple was a target of the enemy every time they fired on the village. This harassing fire of enemy artillery increased daily. It was evident the Germans were greatly reinforcing the line ahead of us. They could not imagine the Americans attacking in the difficult Argonne region and must have suspected that all the American activities in this sector were directed toward Metz. Therefore, their artillery attempted to prevent concentration of our troops at night for attack. On the night of September 16th, the 168th Infantry raided Marimbois Farm and the 167th raided the village of Haumont. Both returned with prisoners that verified the above information.

A detail led by Sergeant Sloan and myself on about September 15th had gone forward to the vicinity of Louiseville Farm and buried the bodies of Privates Cook and Ware, who had been killed on the morning of the 13th when their machine gun carts were struck. Ordinarily pioneer detachments from the infantry buried the dead of our organization. We attempted to find material from which to make them coffins, but were unsuccessful. Therefore, we rolled them in blankets and marked their graves in the open field south of Louiseville Farm.[20] Afterward, the detail heaped mounds of earth over the carcasses of the mules that had been killed at this place to check the stench of their decaying bodies.

During the days between September 15th and 21st, a squadron of small Whippet tanks maneuvered along the roads of this sector in broad daylight in plain view of the enemy. There were also a number of large French Schneider tanks. These were to make demonstrations in this vicinity. We could not understand at the time why they were exposing themselves, but of course learned later that it was the intention of our General Staff to lead the Germans to expect an attack in this vicinity and thereby draw reinforcements from other parts of the line.

These ruses were successful,[21] and the artillery fire from the enemy increased daily. They attempted a few raids on our lines to take prisoners. No raid by them was successful. Their casualties were heavy, and in several instances the raid, intended by the Germans to obtain information from us, resulted in our infantry taking prisoners who gave valuable information to us. After repeatedly and deliberately exposing themselves to enemy observation, the tank squadrons withdrew one night and started toward a front, unknown to us, where a new battle was said to be pending. It proved to be the Argonne.

At Pannes, one squadron of big French Schneiders was moving out at dusk. Each tank towed a high two-wheeled cart behind for hauling equipment and materials. The Frenchmen of this squadron were still celebrating the St. Mihiel victory of the previous week and were making merry with a plenteous supply of liquor. (Like aviators, the Tank Corps of the French were a privileged class of combatants because of the hazardous nature of their duties.) Therefore, cognac abounded and all were happy. As the last tank of this squadron fell into column on the highway, two happy Frenchmen rode in the flat bed of the trailer, sitting erect on folding stools. They faced the rear to throw kisses and wave us many hilarious goodbyes with their canteens. But they were suddenly interrupted, as the mischievous driver swerved the tank from the road and headed straight for the standing stone wall of a ruined building, dragging the trailer behind. He passed right through the wall, nosed down into the

20. The British and French had learned the hard way that details burying their fallen comrades darkened morale badly. Seeing a buddy shot down while adrenaline was flowing was one thing; shoveling dirt over his lifeless body under more reflective circumstances was quite another. Yet the American newcomers still often had combat units bury their own dead. Lieutenant John H. Geiszel of Company D lamented, "To do this and clean up a battlefield after your outfit had won it always seemed particularly odious, particularly when the dead started to ROT" (emphasis his).

21. Tactical deception is usually most effective when it supports the preconceived notions of the enemy. A classic example came later in WWII when the Allies took great effort to reinforce the German expectation that the colossal D-Day invasion would be at Calais rather than in Normandy. Along the St. Benoit Sector, these demonstrations by tanks and ruses by raiding parties did just that: they falsely confirmed what the Germans already suspected.

French Schneider Tank. Lieutenant Parkinson was amused by a squadron of Schneider tanks moving out from Pannes. *Editor's collecton.*

cellar, and caterpillared up the opposite side. The tank pushed over another wall as it headed out on the road again, bouncing this trailer and two passengers through the walls and over debris in the roughest journey I ever saw a vehicle make. The two Frenchmen succeeded in holding on and came through untouched by falling stones to wave again as they reached the highway once more.

In order to continue our demonstration, raids were planned on the day of September 21st for the following morning. The 168th Infantry raided Marimbois Ferme and was supported by the artillery and guns of D Company. The 167th Infantry raided the village of Haumont. In addition to several batteries of 75s and 150s,[22] some of which were in the front line trenches and fired on the town point blank, the 167th Infantry raid was to be supported by the machine guns of Company B.

During the morning of the 21st, Lieutenant Cann and I reconnoitered the entire front of this regiment, looking for places in which we could set up our machine guns for overhead fire to cover the raid. Almost all places of advantage had already been taken by the artillery. We finally decided, about 11:00 A.M., on a place in the open along one of the trails where we had a clear field of fire. This exposed us to aerial observation during the day. Suspecting an attack, German aeroplanes were hovering constantly over our lines. Lieutenant Cann and I had figured the data for the overhead firing and waited several hours for the planes to move away so we could set up stakes as a guide to our firing at

22. Parkinson probably meant the 155mm guns of the 150th Field Artillery.

night, when we would have no other means of laying our guns accurately. We did not dare do this work under observation of the planes, because we knew they would radio the information to their artillery, who would wait until we opened fire, then put our guns out of action with concentrated fire on our positions.

We waited in the nearby underbrush until almost sundown, but the planes gave us no opportunity. We could lay these firing stakes only while it was yet light, and finally near the close of the day we were compelled to set up these stakes under direct observation of the planes above us. Immediately when it was dark, the gun crews were brought forward and began digging gun emplacements and shelter trenches as the only means of defense against the heavy artillery fire we knew would come. We stationed our guns in line on both sides of this trail. By 11:00 all had dug in deeply and, posting guards, we attempted to sleep.

True to our expectations, at 2:00 A.M., the Germans began shelling this position. For forty-five minutes they pounded our positions with one of the most intense concentrations of fire I had yet passed through. At 4:00, we began firing as per schedule and immediately the barrage of the enemy came down on us again. One of the guns was put out of action, but the remainder were dug in deeply and continued firing until 4:30. Our mission was then accomplished and, by platoons, the company retired to the rear along this road, the shells still falling.

After three platoons had started running back with their equipment, Lieutenant Cann and I, with orderlies and a man from the hospital detachment, started running after them. As we ran, the seven in our party became closely grouped. I was the last of the seven and called to those ahead to scatter out. I stopped to give them opportunity to move ahead. They had not gone more than five paces when a shell landed under the last one of them and exploded forward. Private Collier, under whom the shell landed, was badly wounded in the groin. Corporal Blassingame and Sergeant McClelland were also slightly wounded. The rest of the party, not knowing anyone had been wounded, continued on. Those of us behind were able to walk, with the exception of Collier, who was badly wounded. The man from the hospital detachment returned, bringing his stretcher. He, Corporal Blassingame, Sergeant McClelland, and I lifted Collier on the stretcher and started carrying him to the rear.

The other three men bearing the stretcher were small in stature, all at least six or eight inches shorter than I. As we carried this stretcher on our shoulders, it was necessary for me to keep in a stooped position to keep the stretcher level. We could no longer run. In addition to our other burdens of equipment, the wounded man weighed approximately 200 pounds. Shells continued to fall around us as the Germans kept harassing this road, expecting to find troops moving along it one way or another. It is much comfort to men under shell fire to be permitted to flop on the ground occasionally, but with this wounded man we could only march slowly to the rear. He had begged us at first to leave him behind. He now became delirious and at each shell burst begged us not to drop him.

We put forth our best effort in the direction of a railroad farther on which did not seem to be under fire. As we arrived there, almost exhausted, the Germans increased their range, and although not firing so rapidly, followed us for a mile down this railroad, dropping shells continuously about fifty yards behind us. They were increasing their range just enough to keep pace with our steps. As the shells burst around us, their fragments were thrown forward and whizzed all about us. Fate seemed to be with us, however, for we finally reached the dressing station in a dugout along this railroad in the edge of Dampvitoux Woods and gave Collier into the care of the surgeons, who were dressing other wounded men. In this action, Private Thomas G. Whitaker was killed and about seven men wounded of B Company.

It was now breaking dawn in the east. The battle smoke in the light of the approaching sun gave vivid color in the direction of the front we had just left. We proceeded back to Pannes. As we passed the town of Beney, we saw two planes in combat above us. The German plane was forced to land nearby, but we were not interested enough to go over there. The raid had been highly successful. The infantry had taken many prisoners, and from them obtained valuable information.[23] Due to the excellent overhead fire by our artillery and machine guns, our infantry suffered few casualties, but inflicted heavy casualties on the enemy.

Lieutenant Cann arrived at Pannes after having his wounded heel dressed. As it was not a severe wound, he attempted to stay with the company, but by night the pain became so intense that he did not protest when Major Winn ordered him to the rear. This left me in command of the company with no other officer. The following day, however, I received notice that 1st Sergeant Sloan had been commissioned 2nd Lieutenant.

The night of September 25th, Major Winn called me to headquarters in Pannes[24] to give orders for a demonstration we were to make on the morning of September 26th. He greeted me with these words:

> The American Army is to attack in the region of Verdun tomorrow morning, opening a battle which will mean the end of the German Army. Our Intelligence Section knows that the enemy reserves are almost exhausted. The Allies still have plenty of reserves. Therefore, this battle will be continued until all the German divisions are exhausted.

23. Among this "valuable information" was disclosure that the Germans were bringing up a large gun with the Chateau St. Benoit as the intended target (Amerine, 181). General MacArthur and his staff soon evacuated their HQ before it was leveled (Amerine, 182).

24. Major Winn's HQ for the 151st MG Battalion had been in the Chateau St. Benoit with MacArthur's brigade HQ before prisoners divulged that it was soon to be the target of a large caliber German gun.

Chateau Whole. German prisoners in front of Chateau St. Benoit. These POWs were taken in a raid by the 167th Infantry on September 22, 1918. Company B's machine guns covered the attack with overhead fire. MacArthur was confident that Brigade Headquarters, located in the chateau, would be well protected by his men from ground attack. However, interrogation of these prisoners disclosed that the chateau was the intended target of a big German railroad gun being brought up. Immediately a German 77mm shell fell in the courtyard in seeming confirmation. MacArthur and his staff evacuated their ritzy HQ shortly before it was demolished by 280mm or 310mm shells (accounts conflict on the caliber). *Photo courtesy of US Army Military History Institute.*

Chateau Shattered. Chateau St. Benoit after direct hits by nine German shells. It is shown here in 1919 just after the war. *Editor's collection.*

About Face. Side and rear of Chateau St. Benoit after it was pounded by German artillery. *Editor's collection.*

I could not believe what he had to say and stared at him in amazement to think that the war was nearing its end.

This time our company was not to engage in fire, but was to take position between Beney and St. Benoit to be available in the event of a counter-attack by the Germans. With 1st Sergeant Powers and Lieutenant Sloan, I searched through this region and selected a position of shelter under the quay at the railroad crossing on the Beney-St. Benoit Road. When I returned to Pannes shortly before dark, I was delighted to find that Captain Brown and Lieutenant Saye had returned from school. They now assumed command of the company. This night, we experienced a heavy exchange of fire between our lines and the enemy. The enemy seemed to be expecting an attack in this region, and the ruse of our General Staff had succeeded in drawing attention from the main American blow, which opened the morning of September 26th in the Meuse-Argonne region.

Betreten der Wiese Verboten. (Entering the Field Forbidden.) This German placard, measuring 6" by 13", was jerked from the edge of the Nonsard Woods in the St. Mihiel Salient by Lieutenant Parkinson. The field was previously subject to Allied artillery observation and sniper fire. Signs like these, "abounded here and every place the German army occupied." Most wound up in bonfires and ash heaps after the war. *World War History & Art Museum (WWHAM) collection, Alliance, Ohio.*

On September 28th, our brigade was relieved by the 83rd Brigade of our division. We retired to the shelter of Nonsard Woods, to the rear and left of Essey. In these woods, the Germans had built about 40 rough timber cottages resembling a rustic German beer garden.[25] Most of these cottages were equipped with stoves and we spent the next two days cleaning up, resting, and soaking up heat. From a tree at the edge of the woods, I jerked off one of the "Verboten" signs that abounded here and every place the German Army had occupied. I sent it home as a souvenir and today value it highly.

Besides the casualties already mentioned in D Company, Corporal Gochnauer and Privates Harmon, Werner, and Munyan were wounded.[26] Also, when the enemy destroyed the Chateau St. Benoit, Sergeants Haire and White[27] of Battalion Headquarters were wounded.

25. The St. Mihiel Salient had been static for nearly four years. Here in the Bois de Nonsard Germans led cozy lives behind the lines. In addition to the cottages, they had built tennis courts, bath houses, and theaters. They cultivated vegetables in their gardens and even raised children, some of whom were now three years of age (Dickman, 137).

26. The first three of these men were gassed on September 15; Munyon was wounded on September 22 (Means).

27. Presumably this was Miller G. White, Jr., one of the authors of the 151st Machine Gun Battalion's History. He was originally from Company B as was Arthur H. Peavy.

CHAPTER 7: THE MEUSE-ARGONNE OFFENSIVE

Bois de Montfaucon, Eclisfontaine, Exermont, Hill 263, Bois de Romagne, Hill 288, Hill 242, Landres-et-St. Georges, Cote de Chatillon.

September 30th, I was ordered back to D Company just as the battalion formed to march out. We knew by this movement that we were headed toward the Meuse-Argonne Drive, which was now in full swing.

As the battalion was forming in the evening, a bright rainbow again formed over us. As I passed my former comrades in B Company, Sergeant Dozier called to me: "Lieutenant, look at the rainbow! I'll bet the Boches are rolling their packs. They know the Rainbow Division is coming after them." Sergeant Powers of B Company headed a group of three or four non-coms who came to me and expressed regret that I was leaving their company. They recalled the manner in which they had been fed during the St. Mihiel advance and wanted to give me credit.

We marched through the town of Apremont and passed close to Mont Sec, which was now in our lines, then bivouacked along the road on the other side of Apremont. While here, we received newspapers that told us that Bulgaria had made a separate peace with the Allies. This pleased us all, although we dared not hope that the Germans would make peace very soon. That night at dusk, a long line of covered trucks drove up and stopped where we camped. A solemn yellow-skinned Buddhist[1] sat at each wheel. They were Annamese-Colonial troops from the French Province of Indo-China. Suddenly they all dismounted and began jabbering and gesticulating while we loaded in our equipment and climbed in afterward. None of us had any doubt as to our destination. Troops ride in camions only when going into battle.

Edge of Apremont. The town was leveled by artillery fire before and during the fight for St. Mihiel. *Editor's collection.*

The column headed north and passed through several darkened villages. One of these we identified as the town of Souilly. The column of trucks passed on and our battalion was unloaded at the village of Seraucourt,[2] from which all inhabitants had departed. The officers of the battalion were billeted in two adjoining buildings. Lieutenant Brown of C Company had gone to sleep near the exhaust of one of the trucks during the trip and was almost overcome by monoxide gas. During the following day, we explored the surrounding fields and came upon a French 380 millimeter gun that had just been firing at long range into the German lines. We stayed at Seraucourt two days.

On the night of October 3rd, we marched to the town of Brabant. On the road I fell out of line as we passed through a village where there was a French

1. It is doubtful that Buddhists, who are pacifistic by conviction, would serve as military truck drivers. Americans of the early 20th Century tended to lump oriental peoples together as Chinese and Buddhists regardless of their actual ethnic origin or religious practice.
2. Spelling for this village varies widely in accounts: "Saracourt" (Parkinson), "Seraycourt" (Means), "Serancourt" (White & Peavy).

canteen. Here I bought a bottle of red wine. We had no opportunity to spend money for thirty days, so I had over two months' pay on hand. It did not look like we would need much cash during the coming months, and I hesitated to go into battle with much money on my person. Therefore, I used my surplus Francs to send a money order home. Next day at Brabant, 1st Sergeant Roy G. Rhodes became ill with the flu and was sent to a hospital in the rear. Captain Charles Travis of C Company was also threatened with the flu, but when I shared the bottle of port wine with several of the officers—and gave him a double portion—he seemed to be greatly benefitted.

The Road Through Apremont. The 151st Machine Gun Battalion passed through here on its way to the Meuse-Argonne fight. *Editor's collection.*

At Brabant we were in Army reserve. Next day, we resumed the march toward the front. Along the road there was the usual congestion of traffic going to and from the front. Looking forward, we could see many American observation balloons and later came to the positions that since the battle of Verdun had been the Allied first line trenches. It was from these trenches that the attack had been launched September 26th. The 79th Division had occupied this particular sector.

Hill 304 at Malancourt. These German machine gunners were watching ground that would be taken by the 79th Division on September 26, 1918. The 151st Machine Gun Battalion marched past this former No Man's Land on their way to join the Meuse-Argonne Offensive. *Editor's collection.*

By the roadside we noticed several newly-made graves. We saw where the road had been newly rebuilt of crushed rock leading to the place where the town of Avocourt had been. This town was now completely demolished. Not even a wall was left standing. It had been pounded to pieces, and every fragment of stone seemed to have been pulverized by artillery fire. It was from the ruins of these buildings that the engineers had obtained the stone to rebuild the road over which we had passed.

Leaving Avocourt, we passed over No Man's Land. Here were many swamps and bogs. Several places the road was built for several hundred yards from planks laid on heavy timbers. As we proceeded across No Man's Land, we saw where the road had been cut through unlimited mazes of barbed wire. We next entered what had been Bois de Montfaucon. Great trees two feet through had been shattered by shell fire and only their stumps remained. The ground, through three years of fighting, had been plowed by shell fire and was one great swamp or bog where the rain had seeped into the shell holes.

We were again in another tremendous jam of trucks, ambulances, artillery pieces, caissons, supply wagons, machine gun carts, and tanks moving toward and from the front. We could only advance a few steps at a time on the bottomless roads, then had to wait a long time standing in the mud for the congestion to clear. There was no place to sit down. The sides of the road were worse than the road.

After struggling many hours and making only a short advance along the northern road, we turned into a dirt road running east and a little later camped among the stumps and sprouts which our maps showed to be a dense forest under the name Bois de Montfaucon. The difficulty of crossing this terrain during the first days of the attack had prevented the American army from making a much greater advance during that stage. The infantry had fought through, but could go only so far until the artillery and supplies moved up behind them to support them.

In this woods south of the city of Montfaucon, along with the infantry troops, our battalion bivouacked in pup tents. Captain Means pitched a tarpaulin from one of the combat wagons over a leaning stump and used this as company headquarters. Lieutenant Andres, Captain Means, and I were the only officers of the company at this time. At night, we slept under this tarpaulin. Mail had come and many of the men had received newspapers from home. I, too, had received a roll of *Centralia Sentinels*. I collected some that had been discarded by others and spread them out in many thicknesses as a bed underneath the tarpaulin. They seemed to keep the chill of the wet ground from our bodies.

We stayed in this wood several days and had opportunity to explore the nearby regions. "Dead Man's Hill," the famous fortified hill north of Verdun, was visible nearby. In the open field toward Montfaucon, I saw four or five big shell holes so large they would have concealed a caboose. We could see the outlines of various trenches, but they had been practically obliterated by shell

Avocourt In Ruins. Rubble of the town of Avocourt, France. *Editor's collection.*

Rocky Road. Another view of devastated Avocourt. Lieutenant Parkinson said the town "had been pounded to pieces and every fragment of stone seemed to have been pulverized by artillery fire." Resourceful American engineers used the rubble from Avocourt to pave roads in the Meuse-Argonne Offensive. *Editor's collection.*

Cannon Fodder. Stockpile of artillery projectiles ready for the Meuse-Argonne Campaign. *Editor's collection.*

Barometer. Stacks of artillery ammunition for the Meuse-Argonne Drive. Lieutenant Parkinson learned to gauge the caliber of impending attacks by the size of artillery ammo dumps he passed along roads leading to the front. *Editor's collection.*

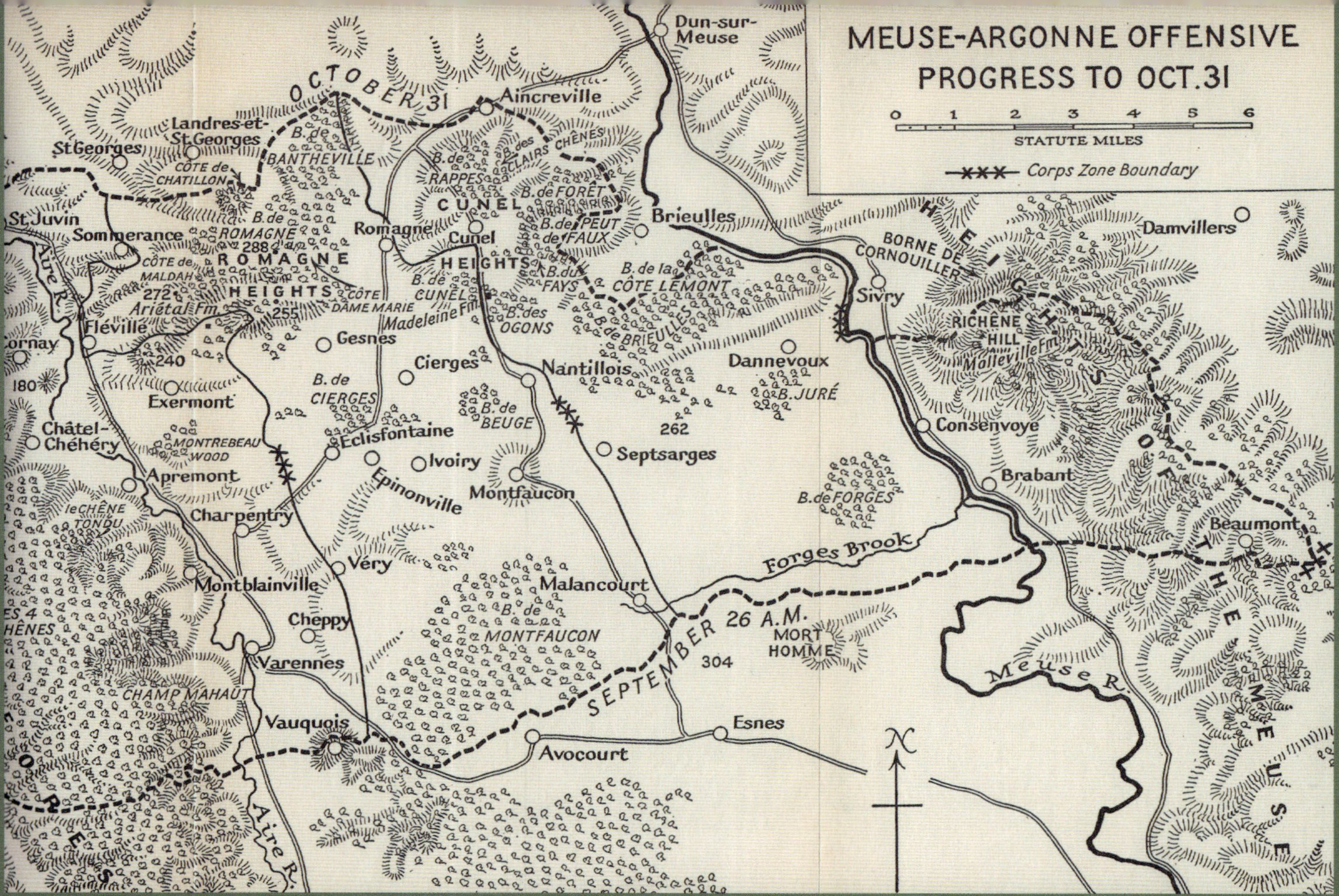

Map from Pershing, *My Experiences in the World War.*

fire. I saw concrete dugouts and machine gun pill boxes which had been built by the Germans. I remember distinctly seeing a great deep hole, eight or more inches in diameter, driven down into the soft ground at an angle of about 45 degrees, where a shell from our lines had penetrated deep into the earth but had not exploded. Had it exploded, it would have demolished a German pill box that was immediately above it. About the field over which our troops had advanced, we saw where men had been buried. Scattered over the field were many different articles of discarded equipment. One of these was a new Browning machine gun of the lightweight type. We had heard much of this great machine gun for many months, but this was our first sight of it. Our battalion was equipped with the French air-cooled Hotchkiss.

Better Late Than Never. An M1917 Browning machine gun in action. This model of machine gun was adopted by the US Army seven weeks after war had been declared on Germany in April of 1917. Pershing was so impressed with the Browning machine gun that he withheld early deliveries, fearing one might fall into copy-catting German hands. It was not issued to combat troops until the Meuse-Argonne Offensive. The 151st Machine Gun Battalion got their first glimpse of a Browning machine gun in early October, 1918. They were eventually equipped with Brownings, but not until the new year after the Armistice. *Editor's collection.*

Looking northward to the city of Montfaucon, which was in ruins, we saw one large building still standing. It was in this building, we learned afterwards, that the German Crown Prince had built a deep dugout underground with periscopes leading to the tower on the roof so that he could view the battle of Verdun safely. The enemy shelled the town of Montfaucon, but were not disturbing us in this wood. The wood did not give concealment because the trees had been mostly shot away, but every time aeroplanes came near thousands of American troops hid themselves under bushes and behind stumps like baby quails in the brush.

On this line running east and west were many American observation balloons. Sometimes as many as twenty could be counted from our right to our left. Many times we saw these balloons hauled in rapidly to avoid enemy planes.

The Prince's Lair. Infantry of the 42nd Rainbow Division advancing through St. Baussant in the Meuse-Argonne Offensive. The German Crown Prince's deep dugout was previously under the building on the left. Using periscopes he watched the Battle of Verdun in 1916 in relative safety. *Editor's collection.*

Several times we saw balloons shot down. On one occasion, after shooting down an American balloon, the aviator turned his machine gun on the observer, who was descending in a parachute, and when the parachute landed the observer had been pierced by many bullets.

Frequently at sundown, we could see groups of ten or twelve planes pass over us from our rear toward Germany, flying in a "V" formation like a flock of wild geese or ducks. We knew these squadrons to be composed mostly of bombing planes, with a few combat planes along for protection. One evening, about October 6th, we saw two or three of these squadrons pass over with many more squadrons still appearing behind them. We began counting, and counted 140 planes in sight at once, with more coming. Lieutenant Andres and I had just spoken to each other and verified the number when we heard machine gun fire in the direction of the second observation balloon to our left. We looked up to see it in flames and the observer jumping in his parachute. Instead of turning directly home, and in spite of the 140 Allied planes in the air, the German aviator who had shot it down headed straight east. Before it could be drawn in by our men at the windlass on the ground he had also set fire to the observation balloon nearest us. He was then just above the treetops, or rather, where the treetops had been before they were shot away.

French St. Chamond Tank. The French tanks mounting 75mm guns that Lieutenant Parkinson shared the road with on October 10, 1918, were St. Chamonds. *Editor's collection.*

In heading back north toward his own lines, he passed directly over us. Hundreds of doughboys seized their rifles and opened fire from the ground. He was so near some fired with pistols. As he passed over we saw him leaning over the side, taking photographs. All this happened with 140 Allied planes in the air at the same time. As our troops saw him making his safe getaway, even those who had been firing at him joined in shouts of admiration for this plucky exploit. Only a few of the 140 planes above us were combat planes. They had the job of protecting the bombing planes. They did not dare leave the bombing planes to chase this one enemy plane because he might be trying to draw them away so that other enemy planes concealed in the clouds could fall upon the slow moving bombers. Although the German aviator passed over us unscathed, he was intercepted a few seconds later by two Allied planes nearer the front, and forced to land within our lines.

The Division Headquarters of the 32nd Division was across the road to our north. We heard reports daily of the advance made by the 32nd, 1st, and 91st Divisions, but all reports of advances also bore the news of frightful casualties. We knew that any morning we might be finding ourselves going over the top somewhere in this wooded, hilly Argonne region.

On Thursday, October 10th, at 10:00 A.M., we formed on the east and west road, ready to head out on the north road. Along the road with us was a squadron of French tanks mounting 75s. For six hours we stood on this road with the animals hitched to the wagons, stamping restlessly in the mud, waiting for the word to go but without advancing a yard.

We had orders to relieve the First Division. We had heard that in nine days they had suffered 11,000 casualties. Never before had our battalion gone into the line without first seeing a rainbow. The sun was shining now and the sky clear. There was no prospect of a rainbow. This caused much speculation and foreboding of evil among the men, because no rainbow had been seen. Repeatedly I heard men say, "Where is our rainbow?" or, "I'd feel a damn sight better if I could see a rainbow." The other rainbows had always been so bright and timely that their absence at this time became emphasized. While few of us admitted to being superstitious, there was not one who felt any better because the rainbow had not appeared. We had nothing else to think about as we stood waiting to go into battle.

As we waited that afternoon on the road at a point just opposite the division headquarters of the 32nd Division, we saw an aeroplane return from the front, drop a message, and circle in a perfect arc just above the treetops. The air was perfectly still, and the exhaust from the motor hung in the air where the plane had passed. Suddenly a mule skinner from Georgia called excitedly, "There's our rainbow!" We looked where he was pointing and saw that the exhaust left by this aeroplane had formed a perfectly colored rainbow immediately over our heads. Cheers came from the entire column and the men began shouting, "Let's go now! Now we are ready!"

We had stood on this road from 10:00 A.M. until 4:00 P.M. or later without moving forward a step. It was hard on men and animals, but the phenomenal appearance of this rainbow put us all in excellent spirits. Finally, the column moved out on the main road. We officers all shook hands with Lieutenant O'Keefe, who that night was going to the rear under orders to return to America. We all envied his orders and all dreaded this front to which we were going. Each time I entered battle I had dreaded it more than ever before, but although it was terrible after getting into these battles, none was as bad as I had feared beforehand. This was no exception. I knew it would be a hard fight and wished I did not have to go up. My comrades felt the same way, but when the order came all responded willingly and cheerfully.

The column moved out on the main road and immediately passed an entire German artillery battalion moving to the rear. It had been captured by the rapid advance of American troops. We soon passed by the Montfaucon tower.

At Montfaucon, we turned west along the road toward Eclisfontaine. None of our company knew where we were headed. We were following along behind the infantry column. We stopped every 50 minutes for ten minutes rest. I had learned to go to sleep instantly and soon practically all were fast asleep, lying on the wet turf beside the road. At the call "Fall in!" we were all up and moving before we were fairly awake. I was leading my horse, as I did not care to ride. No one else seemed to want to ride. That night everyone seemed to be perfectly willing to walk. We had done no marching for a week.

A few hundred yards up the road we were startled from our silent trudging through the mud by the whine of a shell high in the air. It descended in our midst with a flop, but did not explode. Three or four more fell about us with a long whine beforehand and a flop or thud as they struck the ground, either on the soft dirt or hard road surface. So many duds got the men laughing and joking, but it was not long until one did explode on the road nearby. Some big pieces of artillery in the road ahead of us had again congested traffic, so we could only crouch by the roadside and listen to the shells fall.

I was still leading my horse. Nobody wants to sit high on a horse while shells are falling. Neither did I want to pass the buck to my orderly while in danger. I could only take shelter in the small ditch by the roadside, which was as far as my beast could follow. I felt sorry for my horse, as he stood there on the road while shells filled the air with scattering shrapnel. He was untouched, however, and I do not believe he made a single unnecessary move. He was thoroughly broke to shell fire. About half the shells falling were high explosive, which exploded on striking the ground, and the others were shrapnel, which were timed to burst over our heads and shower down hundreds of balls the size of marbles.

The line moved forward gradually in short jerks of fifty to one hundred yards, and finally we were within sight of the Eclisfontaine crossroads. The infantrymen along this road with us suffered heavy casualties from shrapnel, but our company seemed immune. Not a man nor beast was touched.

In early morning, we reached the buildings at the crossroads and the men bivouacked in the fields behind the shelter of some of these buildings while the animals were picketed up the road behind a hedge. The medical officers of our battalion were kept busy far into the night, aiding in dressing wounds of the men of the 168th Infantry who had been struck. I afterwards learned that fifty-four casualties were suffered by Companies A and B of the 168th just in passing through Eclisfontaine. That was more than they had lost in the entire St. Mihiel Battle. Our battalion was simply lucky. With shells bursting on all sides of us and over us, no other word can account for our escape.

Lieutenant Andres and I spread our blankets on the south side of one of the buildings of stone and slept till daylight, then awoke and started rolling up our blankets. It was necessary for us to throw one blanket away because it had been spread out on several piles of dung.

Along the hedge near the picket line, the cooks were preparing a meal at the kitchen. It was raining again. As we stood about waiting for the mess call, one of the men discovered the body of a soldier of the 91st Division in the hedge. Apparently, he had crawled in to take cover and had been dead five or six days. He was so far in the hedge that passersby had not seen him. We arranged for his burial. After the meal was served, the company moved south of the town under cover of the trees of an orchard. This ground had been conquered by the 35th Division. Machine gun emplacements occupied by the Germans had been dug in several places in this orchard. Several Germans were still unburied. Quite a few had been buried, and there were many American graves in fence corners and along the fence rows of this region.

On Friday evening, October 11th, we formed as a battalion in single file, moving up the ravine by a narrow trail toward Exermont. During the day, our officers had called at the headquarters of the 1st Division and asked to be shown the positions they would take over that night. They were told it would not be necessary to go forward to the positions,[3] but that guides would be furnished that night. As the head of the column now waited at the appointed place for the guides, we were in the rear, in single file on the trail leading through the ravine. As usual, shells began falling. Most of them broke on the bank above us and only a few came dangerously near, but as we heard the whine of each shell, all were so near us that we could not tell which ones to dodge and which ones to ignore. Most of the men stood upright, but I laid flat all the time. All were impatient to get going. After dark, in the rain, the line did start. Later our guns and ammunition were unloaded from the carts and we started across the country.

As we climbed one ridge by a slippery path carrying our heavy loads, we suddenly came to a ridge almost perpendicular. It was pitch dark. We could not see any way around, but we did see that the path led upward. The ground was so muddy and so slick one man could not go up alone. It was only by boosting one man after another upward that we formed a human chain that assisted the rest of the company forward. We passed through muddy ravines amid harassing shell fire and through a valley drenched with gas. At this point the guide informed us he was lost.

Lost! Of all times to be lost! Pitch dark, in the Argonne Forest, slipping into shell holes knee deep in water and floundering out, only to sink deep in the mud again. Deadly mustard gas was hanging low next to the ground and more and more was coming in every minute as the enemy sent high explosive shells and gas shells to explode in the valley and the ridge ahead of us.[4] It

3. The 1st Division had attached its machine gun companies to infantry battalions just as the 42nd Division had done through the Ourcq River crossing. Since the 151st Machine Gun Battalion was now operating as a unit, the exact machine gun positions would not be taken up by the incoming machine gunners. Instead, officers of the 151st Machine Gun Battalion later made their own reconnaissance and selected positions on Hill 263 in the line of relief (White and Peavy).

4. This relief, "was made under the worst possible conditions ... the night was very black, the valleys and woods were full of gas, and the mud ~ enough said" (Means, emphasis his).

would have been bad enough had we known where to go, but with our guide lost we knew not which way to turn for fear of walking right into the enemy.

Captain Means was preparing to send out scouts when he heard a familiar voice at the top of the next ridge. He hurried forward, and from Major Stanley of the 168th Infantry learned our location and was directed to our destination. Struggling along, making very slow progress in the mud, we finally reached the top of Hill 263, north of the village of Exermont. This was a high hill, and at its peak there was an abrupt cliff about forty feet high. It was behind this cliff and its sloping sides that our company was posted in fox holes that had been dug by men of the 1st Division. The top of the hill was ours, but the forward slope was partly still in the hands of the enemy.

It was October 12th when we took over this position. During that day, Lieutenant Andres' platoon was sent to Hill 269 to our right, where a large opening had been left in the line by the interchange of troops the night before. As the rest of the company huddled under the shelter of this cliff on Hill 263, we scouted around in front of us. Here I found, for the first time, one of the German anti-tank guns,[5] a great rifle fired from the shoulder, firing a steel-piercing bullet the size of a large cigar. It had been left behind by retreating Germans.

On this day, men of the infantry passed by carrying a wounded German they had found in the underbrush. He had been left behind after his wound had been dressed by comrades. When the Americans came, he lay concealed until hunger, thirst, and pain forced him to call for help. He was not unhappy now, however, because as they carried him by us on a stretcher he sat upright, sipping a cup of coffee and smoking a cigarette while waving to us. Another German found in the underbrush was not so fortunate. A bullet from the side had blinded both eyes and gone through the bridge of his nose. He was still living and feared he would not die.

This concentration of troops behind the cliff was known to the Germans, but they could not reach us as long as we stayed close behind the cliff. But at unexpected intervals they laid heavy fire on the cliff above us. Some shells passed over and fell behind, but a few yards to our right, where the cliff was much lower, the infantry suffered several casualties. One boy from Alabama had both legs shot off by a shell that landed directly in his fox hole.

Our mess cans had just been carried up from the rear with a meal of slum,[6] rice, and coffee. As our men formed to eat, a lieutenant of the 167th Infantry, 37mm platoon, asked to attach his platoon to my company for rations. Since we were having only one meal a day, and had drawn rations for only our actual number of men, I had to refuse this request. His platoon had drawn rations through their own regiment. However, I did offer to share my mess kit and canteen with him. He accepted, and we sat on the edge of my fox hole while

5. These were Mauser pattern rifles, 13mm in caliber.
6. Presumably "slum" is short for "slumgullion", meaning meat stew.

we ate. The mess detail had also brought mail, including four or five letters for me. He noticed that one letter was from Decatur, Illinois. "Do you know anybody in Decatur?" he asked. "That's where I live," I replied. "I live in Decatur, too," he answered. On further questioning, I found that he lived on the 1400 block of West Wood Street. I lived on the 1300 block. I had known his parents, but he had been away from home several years. His name was Howard Travis. We saw each other in Decatur often after the war.

On Sunday, October 13th, the other two platoons of our company marched to Hill 269 to reinforce Lieutenant Andres. There was no road. The trail through the forest was stopped and blocked by deep shell holes and by fallen trees. As we laboriously made our way through, the Germans drenched this valley with gas. As we neared Hill 269, many shells of heavy caliber fell in our midst. It was pitch dark when we arrived and raining steadily. We merely flopped at whatever place we could find among the men of the First Platoon who were already there.

I sat on a chunk of board and leaned against the side of a trench. I wrapped in a blanket underneath my raincoat and the helmet turned the rain from my head as it trickled down the sides of the trench upon me from the ground above. When dawn first broke, I straightened my cramped legs and stood up to shake off the chill. Right at my head I saw a pile of dead men. Eight dead Germans were lying in a row like cordwood, and the water from their bodies had been trickling down over my head and shoulders all night. There were five or six graves with wooden crosses and helmets where Americans had been buried.

On the forward slope of this hill were three more dead Germans, who had evidently been killed in a charge up the hill. One was a lieutenant, wearing a very fine pair of boots. Sergeant Humphrey's own shoes were in tatters. He measured and found that the officer's boots would fit him. He tried to pull them off, but the joints were stiff. He dragged the body around in the mud for some distance to where a sapling forked as it left the ground. Throwing arms and shoulders of the corpse through this fork, he pulled again. He was assisted by Private Olds, who held the body down in this fork. After hard struggling, however, they made no progress and the boots had to be abandoned.

During the day, shells from our own rear fell on this hill and all around. They were 150mm caliber.[7] We complained by sending runners to the rear, but were advised a few hours later that all the ranges had been checked and that it was German shells falling on us. We sure liked having some officer three miles to the rear tell us we didn't know the difference between shells

7. Parkinson probably meant the 155mm guns of the 150th Field Artillery located directly behind them near Exermont. (They used French Schneider medium guns while the 149th and 151st were both equipped with French 75mm field guns.) On the night of May 14-15 the 155mm guns of the 150th Field Artillery had dropped friendly fire on the positions of the 168th Infantry in front of Badonviller. Several men were killed when a shell made a direct hit in their dugout's entrance from behind. This was now at least the second time the Rainbow Division was apparently shelled by its own 150th Artillery.

coming from our own rear and shells from the enemy in front of us after dodging big 150mm shells all day. Nevertheless, the shells continued to fall directly from our rear. They would come in salvos of three or four every fifteen minutes and came so close that all of us ducked. We complained again, but the shells kept falling. The range was probably figured correctly, but the gun barrels probably were worn with overuse, so as to make the firing data inaccurate.[8]

That night, we moved over the difficult trail back to Hill 263 to its forward slope, where we took position in a small gravel pit. After arriving there with the carts, I volunteered to go back with some of the carts to bring up ammunition. Captain Means usually took this hard detail himself, but I had an easy day and I knew that Captain Means was almost exhausted. We had only covered half the distance back when a careless driver of the leading cart allowed a telephone wire to become wrapped around the axle of his wheel. The cart blocked the trail for all behind it. I dared not go ahead for fear of breaking the wire. I did not want to break or cut the wire, because I knew it was a telephone wire which would be of great importance when the attack started as planned for the following morning. Therefore, we unloaded the carts, left this one standing till morning, sent the mules and other carts to the rear, and carried the ammunition forward by hand.

The gravel pit where our company took position was at the side of a trail that led around Hill 263, turned to the right at the pit, and led into the Sommerance-Romagne road. This road continued to the right and slightly forward over Hill 288, which was in possession of the Germans. The east and west road from Sommerance to Romagne was just a few yards in front of us at a considerably lower elevation. Around this gravel pit was an undergrowth of young oak trees and plum thickets. The gravel pit was open on the east, but on the other three sides afforded a steep bank ranging in height from four to ten feet.

Under protection of this bank, our company dug fox holes. Machine gun positions were prepared on the surface above in concealment of the thicket. This road in front of us was built of crushed stone, worn down to a smooth, solid surface. All night long the Germans kept pounding the road in front with rapid harassing shell fire. Each shell explosion shook our position, even though the shells did not fall dangerously near. Before the vibrations of one shell ceased, another would explode. Many shells skimmed over our heads and fell on the ravine behind. Others passed overhead and to our left to land on top of the hill in the vicinity of the cliff we had left.

Every night we were alerted several times for gas. We all learned to sleep with our masks on and frequently did so. The bottom of my fox hole was damp, although not very muddy. Ever since coming into this sector, I had carried a

8. This was a natural conclusion coming from a machine gun officer. Regulations called for removing machine gun barrels from service in overhead barrages after firing 14,000 rounds (*Manual of Equipment*, 59). Worn barrels could result in bullets falling dangerously short.

half-inch board about five inches wide and three feet long. This I used under my shoulder and hip each night to keep me out of the mud. My helmet and shoes supported the extremities of my body. I carried this board on my pack each time we moved.

In our immediate foreground was the Cote de Chatillon, a steep wooded knoll heavily fortified by the enemy, who were still in possession of it. A well organized trench system extended from Landres-et-St. Georges over Cote de Chatillon and on over the crest of Hill 288. Beyond and between Cote de Chatillon and Hill 288 was Hill 242 and Tuilerie Farm, all heavily fortified. This system of enemy trenches was known as the "Kriemhilde Stellung," being part of the famous Hindenburg Line. About forty kilometers beyond was the railroad center of Sedan, through which a railroad passed supplying the entire German front in the northwest of France and Belgium. If this railroad traffic should be interrupted by the fire of the Allied guns, the German armies farther west would be cut off from supplies. This was the main objective of the entire American drive in the Argonne. The Germans were ordered to defend the Kriemhilde Stellung to the last, because as soon as we passed through this position the way was open to the town of Buzancy, from where our long range guns could dominate the Sedan railroad.

These hills were covered with a dense forest filled with undergrowth and thickets. There were no north and south roads, only a few unimproved trails which had been cut up into almost a bottomless mire by the traffic of thousands of men, animals, and vehicles. There was no way for us to take these positions except to fight through the wire entanglements and thickets and over the trenches. From the top of these hills the enemy had direct observation. Many *minenwerfer* fired down constantly on our position in the gravel pit at short range. At least one German 77 fired on us point blank from the top of Cote de Chatillon. Machine guns and *minenwerfer* on the top of Hill 288 had direct enfilade fire right in our gravel pit. Snipers fired every time a head showed above the bank. It was this sector that the Rainbow Division had to conquer. Before us were stationed the best troops in the German Army with orders to fight to the last.

Major General Charles P. Summerall had been in command of the First Division while they were in this sector before us. When his division was relieved, he was promoted to the command of the Fifth Army Corps, of which we were a part with the 32nd Division.[9] During the Boxer Rebellion in China in 1900, he had served as lieutenant in Captain Reilly's Battery. Despite much intentional interference by their jealous Russian and German allies, they dragged an artillery piece to the gates of Peking. There, under heavy fire from the top of the wall, Lieutenant Summerall dashed directly up to the gate and marked the location of the cross bars with chalk. A few well-placed shells fired point

9. General Summerall's elevation to Corps Commander and the 42nd Division's transfer to his Vth Corps each had occurred on the night of October 12-13, 1918.

Chain of Command
Cote de Chatillon, October 14-16, 1918

Major General Charles P. Summerall
V CORPS
32nd US Division
42nd US Division
89th US Division

Major General Charles T. Menoher
42nd RAINBOW DIVISION

Brigadier General Douglas MacArthur
84th BRIGADE
167th Infantry Regiment
168th Infantry Regiment
151st Machine Gun Battalion

Major Cooper D. Winn
151st MACHINE GUN BATTALION

Captain Monroe A. Means
COMPANY D, 151st MACHINE GUN BATTALION

1st Lieutenant William Andres - 1st PLATOON (4 MG Squads)
1st Sergeant Roy G. Rhodes - 2nd PLATOON (4 MG Squds)
1st Lieutenant N. P. Parkinson - 3rd PLATOON (4 MG Squads)
Sergeant - SUPPLY TRAIN

blank at these chalk marks tore down the gate and allowed our troops to enter. Captain Reilly was killed that day in Peking, but 18 years later his son, Colonel Henry J. Reilly, as Colonel of the 149th Field Artillery in the Rainbow Division, was serving under Major General Summerall.

On October 14th, we were ordered to advance: the 167th Infantry against Cote de Chatillon and the 168th against Hill 288. The other two regiments were to attack Cote de Maldah. The 48 machine guns of our battalion were now all stationed along the forward slope of Hill 263 for overhead fire on Hill 288 and Cote de Chatillon. We were no longer attached to the infantry battalions, but operated as a machine gun battalion under Major Winn, who was about this time promoted to Lieutenant Colonel. We were of much more benefit to the infantry under this plan than advancing with them.

On the morning of October 14th, our entire battalion placed a heavy machine gun barrage on Cote de Chatillon, Musarde Farm, and Hill 242. The Alabama Infantry advanced to the forward edge of the Romagne Woods in front of us and, under cover of our barrage, reached the wire at the foot of Cote de

Chatillon. It was impenetrable at this point, so their attacks stopped after gaining that portion of the Cote not enclosed by the wire.

The 168th Infantry, Iowa Regiment, assaulted Hill 288. With tremendous losses and many deeds of valor they reached the crest of the hill and occupied most of the slope of the north side, but the farthest edge still remained in possession of the enemy. These advances had been made after the most sanguinary hand-to-hand struggles, in which twenty-five to fifty men at the point of bayonet would take one machine gun position, only to find the survivors must rush another machine gun nest in order to prevent annihilation. The Germans echeloned their machine guns in depth, so that each new hill we captured was instantly enfiladed by their fire from two or three surrounding knolls.

During the initial stages of the attack our machine guns were of assistance, with a barrage placed on Tuilerie Farm and Hill 242. At the same time, other portions of the battalion were firing on Cote de Chatillon. We could help only in the initial stages because of the dense woods. From our position we could not tell how far the infantry lines had advanced. We could only assume that they had advanced according to the time as scheduled, and when time came for them to be in our zone of fire we would have to lift the range.[10]

While firing this barrage, we were subject to a tremendous artillery fire on our gun positions on the forward slope of Hill 263. A German aviator flying overhead reported our position to the enemy and a heavy concentration of gas and high explosive shells was upon us in a few minutes. Sergeant Cliff Dudley was wounded and one of his guns knocked down by this fire. I was lying in the same fox hole with Sergeant Achey, observing the action from this position. During a very brief lull in the firing, I moved along the line to the position of another of my guns and took shelter in another shell hole to observe the work of this gun crew. Corporal Hawthorne came after me in just a couple minutes with the news that Sergeant Achey had been struck. Private Churchill had also been wounded. As I came into the gravel pit, I saw that they were preparing to carry these two men in using a large board as a stretcher. I recalled seeing a stretcher on the side of the hill above and hurriedly obtained it.

There were several other casualties in our company this morning. The extra men in the company not actually required in the gun positions were sheltered in the gravel pit behind the steep bank. Their duties were to keep ammunition carried forward and to replace casualties in the gun crews.

After we had sent Achey and Churchill to the rear, Private Beck pointed to a place where the bank had been knocked down into the quarry by a shell bursting on the edge above. He and Private Victor had occupied the same fox hole. A shell bursting above them on the bank had knocked the bank down

10. Throughout the assaults on the Kriemhilde Stellung, the 151st Machine Gun Battalion was operating on "Parkinson Time". Major Winn had lost his watch sometime during the Ourcq and Sergy attacks. Since St. Mihiel, he had been timing battalion machine gun barrages using an extra timepiece that Lieutenant Parkinson had loaned to him.

on them and buried them with dirt. He had struggled free and was just now really coming to himself. We started digging hurriedly and after some time uncovered Private Victor. His helmet had fallen over his face so as to give him a little bit of air. Men were tramping over this loose dirt above him, running to and from the gun positions and carrying the wounded back. At first, he had heard and felt their steps, but he was practically unconscious when he was finally released. Although he attempted to stay with the company, the shock was so severe that he was sent to the rear.

While firing this barrage along the line to our left, German shells began falling in the underbrush on a steep slope in front of the platoon of Lieutenant Andres. At the first salvo, his men heard something rushing through the thicket and suddenly, for a brief instant, they saw a wild boar dash in their midst and disappear beyond before they could make any effort to shoot him.

On the evening of October 14th, I was sent to join the advance with the First Battalion of the 168th Infantry, who were to continue the attack under command of Major Ross. Lieutenant Woodall of C Company and I, along with the several runners, reported to Major Ross. Our job was to move forward with the infantry and direct overhead fire of our machine guns on the points of resistance which the infantry could not reduce by rifle fire. Major Bunch, the medical officer, was at the battalion headquarters of Major Ross. He announced to the men assembled, "If any of you men get hurt, the first aid station will be here until we take the top of the hill. Then it will be on top of the hill." The men were encouraged by the spirit of Major Bunch, who believed in taking the medical attention to the wounded in the line, rather than have them carried to the rear to him.

The advance started, and in the thicket on the downward slope of Hill 288, we encountered concealed entanglements of wire. As we attempted to cut our way through, the enemy opened up with withering machine gun fire and a tremendous concentration of artillery fire. It was impossible to advance and suicide to stay there. Major Ross called off the attack and we retired to the cover of the woods, bringing the dead and wounded with us. The enemy continued to pound our position with high explosives. Several men were wounded even while in their fox holes, and a German prisoner was also wounded while on his way to the rear under guard. Lieutenant Woodall and I returned to our companies on Hill 263, where all night long the woods resounded and the ground trembled from the roar of shells bursting on the road ahead of us and in the woods and ravines around us. The attack was to be resumed the next day.

On the morning of October 15th, we again threw a barrage on Hill 242, Cote de Chatillon, Tuilerie Farm, and Musarde Farm. During the day, the artillery again pounded our positions, but not so severely. A 77 on top of Cote de Chatillon gave us the most trouble. The Alabama Infantry were unable to make any progress this day through the wire of Cote de Chatillon, but the 168th Iowa, after an entire day of sanguinary hand-to-hand fighting, short rushes, and stealthy stalking of enemy positions, found themselves by evening in possession of Hill 242 and Tuilerie Farm. But Cote de Chatillon still held out against us. It was the key to the whole front of this sector and must be taken so other divisions on our right and left could advance. But it could not be taken until Cote de Maldah was captured, and the enemy must be driven from the trenches before Landres-et-St. Georges. These two later positions were in the sector of the 83rd Brigade.

At midnight, General Summerall, Corps Commander, visited the headquarters of the 83rd Brigade and relieved the brigade commander, Brigadier General Lenihan. He transferred Brigadier General James J. Reilly,[11] son of his Boxer War Captain, from the artillery brigade for his successor. He also relieved the colonel of the 165th (New York) Infantry of that brigade. Next, he called at our brigade headquarters of Brigadier General MacArthur. After partaking hurriedly of a midnight lunch, with hardly a spoken word he left with the verbal order to General MacArthur: "You will give us Cote de Chatillon tomorrow or report 5,000 casualties. Military necessity requires few words." General MacArthur, with a salute, replied, "Sir, I will give you the Hill tomorrow, or report no brigade." This word was handed on down to the companies and the platoons as we prepared for the opening of battle on the 16th.

Major General Charles P. Summerall. Newly elevated from command of the 1st Divison to command of 5th Corps, Summerall faced the challenge of breaking the Kriemhilde Stellung. Several attempts had failed when he called on Douglas MacArthur at his 84th Brigade HQ. Summerall's order: "You will give us Cote de Chatillon tomorrow or report 5,000 casualties." MacArthur's reply: "Sir, I will give you the Hill tomorrow, or report no brigade." *Photo from Pershing, My Experiences in the World War.*

This hill had to be taken regardless of the cost. For two weeks it had been withstanding the assaults of the 1st, 32nd, and 42nd Divisions. Prisoners we had captured showed that the Germans were sending in new troops from their finest divisions each night with orders to hold till the last. The wire in front of the 167th Infantry had stopped every attack. The 168th must attack through a greatly exposed field.

The men of this battalion already had three days of hand-to-hand struggle. During this 72 hours, they had constantly seen their comrades killed and wounded at their side. They knew that on the morrow, a large number of them would also fall. It was a rare tribute to the spirit and morale of this regiment to see the way in which they prepared for the advance on the morning of the 16th. They had been so long under these withering fires and had seen the

11. Parkinson probably meant Colonel Henry J. Reilly.

What Did He Say?

Accounts vary as to how Douglas MacArthur replied to Summerall's grim order.

1. MacArthur's version, as recorded in 1936 was, "If this brigade does not capture Chatillon you can publish a casualty list of the entire brigade with the brigade commander's name at the top" (Reilly, 660). Many of MacArthur's biographers repeat this wording.
2. In his memoirs, published in 1964, MacArthur recalled saying, "All right General. We'll take it, or my name will head the list" (*Reminiscences*, 66). Some historians follow this account.
3. Lieutenant Parkinson, of the 151st Machine Gun Battalion, remembered it in 1930 as, "Sir, I will give you the hill tomorrow, or report no brigade." This was not firsthand from the midnight meeting, but it was firsthand from the grape vine within the 84th Brigade on the morning of the attack.

The first version supplied by MacArthur to Reilly is probably correct, or close to correct. Apparently, MacArthur omitted reference to "the entire brigade" in his subsequent memoirs which concerned his own career. (Egos often display selective amnesia.) Parkinson's version "was handed on down to the companies." Naturally, the men of the 84th Brigade were mainly concerned with their own lives, so their sacrifice or survival was the element preserved by word of mouth within the ranks. At any rate, what really mattered on the morning of October 16, 1918, was not what was said the previous night in MacArthur's HQ, but what the men heard the next morning. "Sir, I will give you the Hill tomorrow, *or report no brigade*" is what resonated in their heads as they assaulted Cote de Chatillon. They knew that the mission before them was do or die.

strength of their companies gradually shot away. From 250 men, some now numbered only 85 or 100. On the morrow, these same companies would lose more. It seemed to these men that they would never be relieved and that it was only a question of how many days they could hold out before the final and inevitable time when they, too, should fall. But with a great devotion to duty, they responded to the appeals of their officers and prepared to take this hill and, if necessary, to be one of the 5,000 casualties which must be experienced before admitting failure. They knew they could not fail and resolved to take this hill in a grand sweep forward, the cost be what it may.[12]

Our machine guns were concentrated against Musarde Farm and the Cote de Chatillon. At the given time, the men of the 168th rushed forward. In one company they were to rush forward, one man at a time from each squad, to a given line. This was the manner in which they endeavored to pass over the open fields before reaching the edge of the woods. When the signal was given,

12. This is a prime example of the "Cromwellian austerity" (Wolf, 18) which characterized the fighting of the 168th Infantry.

one man from each squad rushed forward while their comrades covered their advance with rifle fire. Every man of the rushing party was swept down by machine gun fire. Realizing this plan would not work, the entire company, led by the captain, dashed forward, headed at all cost for the trench at the edge of the woods. Only 25 men reached it. Eight were killed and over twenty wounded, including the captain. This was similar to what the other companies experienced, but they all went forward, regardless of cost. When they had advanced halfway up the hill, the 167th Infantry, still stopped by the wire in front of them, moved over to the right and crossed the trenches behind the 168th. When inside the enemy wire they moved back to their front again, and at a given signal, with a few isolated squads from the 168th, they carried the hill with the bayonet and Cote de Chatillon was ours.

Our company and battalion maintained an overhead machine gun fire together with the artillery.[13] Although we could not silence the enemy fire, we greatly diminished its effectiveness and prevented our casualties from being heavier. For many months afterward, each time one of the doughboys would see us they would almost invariably hail us in the most complimentary tone for the barrage we gave them this day. They liked to hear the crack of machine gun bullets as they passed overhead. This day, we had 48 guns[14] rapidly firing while the Alabama 167th was maneuvering to get inside the wire. When they made their final rush, of course, we had to cease firing.

Since we did not advance our casualties were not as heavy as the infantry. During the first three days we lost the following men from our company: Sergeants Howard Achey and Cliff Dudley; and Privates Carpenter, Seiders, Dennis, Victor, Churchill, and Matt, all wounded.

The capture of Cote de Chatillon straightened out the line in this vicinity and stopped the flanking fire which had been delaying them for many days, so that the 84th Brigade was now able to take a section of trenches in front of the town of Landres-et-St. Georges.

Our divisional Machine Gun Officer, Lieutenant Colonel Dravo, had been made regimental commander of the 165th Infantry in the general shake up on the night of October 15th. Major Winn was now promoted to be Division Machine Gun Officer.[15]

Under direction of Major Winn, acting as Divisional Machine Gun Officer, our Company D, still located in the gravel pit of Hill 263, was assigned several

13. The 84th Brigade Adjutant described the assault as, "Splendidly supported by the machine guns of the brigade, handled as a unit" and "supported by a most vigorous massed machine gun fire from the 151st Machine Gun Battalion and the brilliantly controlled artillery fire of the 151st Field Artillery" (Wolf, 48; see also Amerine, 196).

14. Major Winn also employed 12 spare Hotchkiss machine guns for this barrage. So actually the 151st Machine Gun Battalion had 60 guns in action. Winn estimated that the battalion poured nearly one million rounds into Cote de Chatillon in 45 minutes (Winn in Reilly, 713).

15. Soon after, Major General Summerall called a conference of all the commanders of machine gun battalions in the Vth Corps so Major Winn could instruct them in the tactics he had used at Cote de Chatillon (White and Peavy).

defensive sectors to cover with a machine gun barrage in event of an attack by the enemy. Lieutenant Andres and I figured out the proper ranges and gun elevations and made range charts to be posted at each gun emplacement.

The newspapers had been carrying the news of requests of the Germans for an armistice. We were very tired of fighting, and we were hoping that an armistice could soon be effected. The men of our command, however, were not so anxious for an armistice that they would want it at the expense of our security against further aggressions by Germany.

Contrary to the general belief that the rank and file of an army does not know the cause of the war, I was decidedly conscious and aware of the fact that the men of my company knew what they were fighting for. They were tired from the campaigns and hardships they had been through, without enough rest at any one time to permit them to completely recuperate. They were especially tired from the campaigns of the last ten days and were looking forward to the time when the division would be relieved. But they also knew that the German divisions were having even greater hardships, and that there were no rested German divisions in reserve to give them relief. We could see, therefore, that a little extra hardship at this particular time might make it possible to end the war. This was the hope that kept up the spirit of all men in our company and stimulated us to withstand the exhausting hardships and exposure we were suffering, sleeping on the wet ground in the cold October rains in positions so exposed that they could never build fires for heat. Thus far, no overcoats had been issued and the men had been sleeping at night on the wet ground between two blankets and during the day had only the warmth of their flimsy leaky slickers as coats.

During the next few days, the Y.M.C.A. sent supplies of cakes and cigarettes forward to our position. The Captain had a small dugout built in this gravel pit which he used as company headquarters during the day and as officers' sleeping quarters during the night. Our men also had been in this location long enough that they were finding some comfortable positions. Major Winn took me with him one day over to Hill 288, where Company C was in position. Lieutenants Brown and Stratford were complaining of illness and dysentery at this particular moment.

Every night, the enemy continued to bombard the road in front of us and the hill above us, so that shells were exploding below or screaming overhead to the ravine behind. They would frequently lay down a heavy drum fire on the road in front and cause the hill to tremble and vibrate constantly with explosions. This fire was usually mixed with a number of gas shells, so that we were alerted for gas several times each night. During the day, owing to the fact that our position was stationary, we had plenty of food and some smokes.

The church steeple at Landres-et-St. Georges had been used through all this fighting as an enemy observation post. The Americans had hesitated to shoot it down, but the harassing fire of the Germans now became so destructive to us that General Reilly,[16] new commander of the 83rd Brigade, gave orders to have this observation post destroyed. One of the artillery batteries was assigned the task. The first shell passed on one side. The angle was corrected and another shell passed on the other side. The two angles were divided. A shell then made a direct hit on the steeple and destroyed it as an observation post.

German planes came over on several different days, each time dropping small hand bills of propaganda urging the Americans to come over the top and surrender. Orders from General Headquarters were issued that officers would collect all such propaganda. It was out of the question for us to collect it, and it was furthermore unnecessary, because the wording was so awkward that it was humorous to the men of the ranks. This propaganda really had just the opposite effect to what the Germans intended. I collected two or three samples of each and sent them home as souvenirs.

October 17th and 18th, Lieutenant Andres and I went forward to the hedge north of the Romagne Woods and west of Cote de Chatillon. Raids were being planned by the infantry against Landres-et-St. Georges, so we selected machine gun positions along this hedge from where we could fire a covering barrage during the raid. We passed down Sommerance-Romagne Road to the west end of Bois de Romagne and turned north. Just as we turned, we found an abandoned German *minenwerfer*. I took off the sight leaf as a souvenir. At the same time, I noticed a saw-toothed German bayonet and laid it aside, expecting to pick it up on my way back. I did not get back that way that day, and when I did return the bayonet was gone.

Turning north along the edge of the woods, I saw a caisson of the 149th Field Artillery that had suffered a direct hit from enemy shells. Six dead horses were lying where they had fallen in their tracks. On the front edge of the woods, the engineers were laying out trenches, which were to be dug as a defensive position. There was a small stream running east and west at the lowest point between Hill 263's slope and the rising slope of Cote de Chatillon. There were many shell holes just where a trail crossed this stream. The heavy rains had flooded this small stream, and it had been made a heavy bog by the traffic of men and animals and the explosion of shells. On the bank of this small brook I came across a bare human foot that had been severed from the body at the ankle. The shoe and sock had been removed. There was not a corpse in sight, just this naked foot with long untrimmed toe nails lying in the cold and rain. Very likely, the wound did not completely sever the foot at first. The shoe and sock had probably been removed while attempting to dress the wound and the few remaining shreds of flesh had been broken. It was as gruesome a sight as I saw during the entire war.

Lieutenant Andres and I selected gun positions for each of our platoons. These were along the hedge in front of the Romagne Woods and along the ridge running west from Cote de Chatillon. That night, we returned with gun

16. It appears that Henry J. Reilly was still Colonel at this time, but he was promoted to Brigadier General later.

crews and dug an emplacement for each gun. On the ridge north of this stream I picked up some more pieces of artillery shells exploded here. I mailed them home for souvenirs.

About October 19th, we were issued woolen overcoats. They had a very decided influence for a better feeling and spirit in our company. It was easier to keep warm and we were all being well fed.

About October 22nd, possibly the 24th, we had orders stating that we would be relieved at 5:00 P.M. No organization was to take over our exact positions. Therefore, promptly at five o'clock we began moving to the rear. The men were elated at the idea of getting far enough back where they could build fires. Our machine gun carts came forward, the equipment was loaded, and we started the march back. The only possible path to the rear was over an unimproved trail cut through the forest, poorly drained, and with no paving or stone whatsoever. Supplies for thousands of men had been hauled forward over this trail during the past two weeks of heavy rains. Heavy artillery pieces and caissons had been dragged through the mud by sheer force and ammunition wagons hauling heavy shells had cut down deep.

The rain of the last day made these roads almost impassable. There were many holes so deep that it was out of the question for a mule to pull a cart through. Some were so deep that even after the mules were unhitched there was a question whether they would not flounder in the bog. Through two miles of this continuous mire we struggled back with our heavily loaded machine gun carts and ammunition carts where shell holes had made heavy mires in the road. The mules frequently had to be unhitched and the carts drawn through by men with long ropes, and with others at the wheels hip deep in mud. We made this hard march back to Exermont by nightfall and had about a quarter of a mile of good macadamized road before we turned off on another trail which, if anything, was worse than the one we had been on. In one of these bogs on this trail one mule did flounder. It was impossible to drive around, and the whole train of carts had to wait until the mule could be unhitched, the cart dragged back off of him, and enough of the mud dug away so that he could rise. It was a terribly hard march, but we were going to the rear, so the men did not complain.

Our destination was a farm house south of Exermont. This farm house was in sight. Through the darkness, we saw the approaching form of the familiar white horse ridden by the messenger of Major Winn. At the rear of the column, he inquired for Captain Means in a voice that was heard by all and that told us all was not well. He was directed forward and there delivered his message to the Captain, who called all officers and non-commissioned officers to him. "There has been a mistake somewhere," he said. "We were not relieved. It's been a terrible job coming out, but we will have to go back. Although it is going to be a hard march, I know we will all make it without complaining. We have never failed yet."

We all returned and explained to our men. The column turned about and again struggled through the mud. I did not hear one complaint the entire trip back. We reached Exermont in less time than it had taken us to make the journey the other way. At Exermont, however, we received a welcome order permitting us to stay there overnight, with instructions to return to our posts early next morning. We quartered the men partly in some ruined buildings and partly on the reverse slope of a ridge where they bivouacked.

Meanwhile, in this town Captain Means discovered headquarters of the 149th Machine Gun Battalion. Company D had at one time been a part of that battalion, so that the officers were intimately acquainted. They invited us to sleep in the room with them, where they had a fire built in a fireplace. All but Lieutenant Andres and I had cots. We spread our blankets before the fire and soaked up heat all night long. It was the first heat we'd had for three weeks since leaving the cottages in Nonsard Woods.

After spending the night at Exermont, we marched back to our gravel pit on Hill 263 the next morning. The line of march was along a trail between two ravines running diagonally toward the northeast. On one of these reverse slopes, several batteries of large caliber howitzers were firing on the enemy. As we stood directly behind the guns, we could see the large projectiles leave the muzzles and we could follow their course for some distance.

We returned to the gravel pit with less difficulty than we had experienced coming out. We had been in the mud so much that we had learned the easiest way to pull the carts through.

In the field at the side of the trail, we passed the ruins of an American aeroplane. Its blood-stained cockpit told us the story of a fatal crash.

On October 26th, General Summerall cited the 84th Infantry Brigade under General MacArthur in corps orders for distinguished service. In this phase of the battle he also cited the 67th Artillery Brigade, but the other brigade of our division (the 83rd Infantry Brigade) was conspicuous in its omission. The citation order follows on the next page.

HEADQUARTERSFIFTHARMYCORPS
American Expeditionary Forces

France, 26 October 1918.
From: Commanding General, V Army Corps
To: Commanding General, 42nd Division U.S.

Subject: Service of 42nd Division with V Army Corps

1. Upon the termination of the service of the 42nd Division with the V Army Corps, I desire to express my appreciation of the manner in which portions of the Division had performed the missions assigned to them. In particular I wish to commend the following units:

The 84th Infantry Brigade:
This Brigade, under the command of Brigadier General Douglas MacArthur, has manifested the highest soldierly qualities and has rendered service of the greatest value during the present operations. With a dash, courage, and a fighting spirit worthy of the best traditions of the American Army, this Brigade carried by assault the strongly fortified Hill 288 on the Kriemhilde Stellung and unceasingly pressed its advance until it had captured the Tuilerie Farm and the Cote de Chatillon, thus placing itself at least a kilometer beyond the enemy's strong line of resistance. During this advance the enemy fought with unusual determination with a first class division and in many cases resorted to hand-to-hand fighting when our troops approached his rear. The conduct of this Brigade has reflected honor upon the Division, the Army and the States from which the Regiments came.

The 67th F. A. Brigade.
This Brigade has remained continually in action since the entrance of the Division into lines, and by self-sacrificing devotion of duty and the high skill of its officers and men it has contributed greatly to the success of all operations.

CHARLES P. SUMMERALL,
Major General Commanding.
Headquarters 1st Army Corps,

October 28, 1918.

From: Commanding General, 1st Army Corps, Am. E. F.
To: Commanding General, 42nd Division, Am. E. F.

Subject: Congratulations.

1. The return of the 42nd Division to the 1st Army Corps was a matter of self-congratulation for the Corps Commander, not only because of previous relations with the Division, but also because of the crisis which existed at the time of its arrival.

2. The standard of efficient performance of duty which is demanded by the commander-in-chief, Am. E. F., is a high one, involving as it does on an occasion such as the present, complete self-sacrifice on the part of the entire personnel, and a willingness to accept cheerfully every demand even to the limit of endurance of the individual for the sake of the cause for which we are in France.

3. The taking over the front of the 1st Army Corps under the conditions of relief and advance, together with the attendant difficulties incident to widening the front was in itself no small undertaking, and there is added to this your advance in the face of the enemy to a depth of five or more kilometers all under the cover of darkness, to the objective laid down by higher authority to be attained, which objective you are holding, regardless of the efforts of the enemy to dislodge you. The corps commander is pleased to inform you that the 42nd Division has fully measured up to the high standard above referred to , and he reiterates his self-congratulations that you and your organization are again a part of the 1st Army Corps, Am. E. F.

(Signed) H. Liggett
Major General, U.S.A.

CHAPTER 8:
THE RACE FOR SEDAN

LANDRES-ET-ST. GEORGES, FLÉVILLE, IMÉCOURT, VERPEL, BUZANCY, OCHES, STONNE, RAUCOURT, HARAUCOURT, BULSON, THELONNE, SEDAN, GRANDES ARMOISES, THE ARMISTICE, GERMONT, ALLIEPONT, BRANDEVILLE.

All units now made preparations to participate in a general advance all along the line. We felt that we should be relieved and not be called on to advance in this next phase, but preparations indicated that we would be in the attacking waves. The positions Lieutenant Andres and I selected on the ridge west of Cote de Chatillon were chosen as the jumping off line for the machine gunners on the advance. We did not know the exact time set for the advance, but understood that it would be the latter part of the month, and that it would extend from the Meuse River clear to the Channel. All front line divisions were to attack at the same time. We prepared to fire overhead barrages and advance with the infantry.

October 31st, two officers from the Machine Gun Companies of the Marine Brigade reported to Captain Means. They wished to reconnoiter the front lines and select positions for a line of departure, stating they had orders to pass through our division in the approaching attack. This was good news to us, as it indicated we would be relieved.

I guided these officers forward and showed them the positions we had selected. They chose some of our positions and some others a little further to the right on the ridge in the open. While we were going forward to examine these positions, we were under enemy observation. A shell from Germany broke above the treetops just a little to our right. A few seconds afterward, another one broke a little to our left. They probably were not registering on just two men, but we made it a point to leave that vicinity rapidly. I returned to the dugout and found that our battalion had received orders for relief. The attack was to be November 1st. The Second Division was to leapfrog ours, and our guns were to fire until the enemy was driven out of range. We were to fire from the positions already occupied by us on Hill 263.

That day, we were visited by two lieutenants from the Tank Corps. They requested guides through the lines in front of us so that they could select positions for launching their tanks in attack. I led them forward and pointed out our extreme outpost line. I also suggested to them positions in the Bois de Romagne, where they could conceal their tanks until time for the attack to start. These lieutenants were decidedly pessimistic as to their chances of surviving this attack. If I remember figures correctly, they claimed that out of a squadron of 24 tanks that started September 26th, only six were left. They did not see how they could avoid ultimate annihilation, since they were being put in the front waves of every attack. They faced their duty bravely, however, and when the attack finally started the next morning, we heard the rumbling of their tanks as their caterpillars started moving out of Bois de Romagne.

On October 26th, Sergeant Christopher Demuth of our company was surprised to see his brother walk into our gravel pit. He was a lieutenant in a machine gun company of the 6th Division. This division had not yet been in battle, and this lieutenant had been sent forward to be attached to our company as observer during the coming attack. It was purely coincidence that he was attached to the company in which his brother was Sergeant. We relieved Sergeant Demuth from other duty and assigned him to guide his brother while with us.

Aeroplane activity was increasing. The enemy suspected an attack in this region and was sending planes over to see what was going on. We had some planes in the air, but the enemy still had mastery in this section. On Thursday, October 31st, we were all prepared for the attack, which was set for 5:00 A.M. November 1st.

Major Winn was now acting as Corps Machine Gun Officer. He coordinated the work of all machine guns in the Corps for the barrage the morning of November 1st.[1] Captain Means was Battalion Commander and Lieutenant Andres was Company Commander. We had orders that as soon as the enemy got out of range of our guns we would be relieved and could retire to the rear. We had twenty-one days of severe duty in this difficult sector. In the preparatory barrage, our company was to cover the road leading east from Landres-et-St. Georges, beginning at the eastern edge of the city and extending several

1. As of November 1, the 42nd Rainbow Division was transferred to the 1st Corps under command of Major General Joseph T. Dickman (Means; Reilly, 775).

Chain of Command
The Race For Sedan, November 1-8, 1918

Major General Joseph T. Dickman
I CORPS
42nd US Division
77th US Division
78th US Division
80th US Division

Major General Charles T. Menoher
42nd RAINBOW DIVISION

Brigadier General Douglas MacArthur
84th BRIGADE
167th Infantry Regiment
168th Infantry Regiment
151st Machine Gun Battalion

Major Cooper D. Winn
151st MACHINE GUN BATTALION

Captain Monroe A. Means
COMPANY D, 151st MACHINE GUN BATTALION

1st Lieutenant William Andres - 1st PLATOON (4 MG Squads)
1st Sergeant Roy G. Rhodes - 2nd PLATOON (4 MG Squds)
1st Lieutenant N. P. Parkinson - 3rd PLATOON (4 MG Squads)
Sergeant- SUPPLY TRAIN

hundred yards east along the road to harass the movement of troops. The artillery on all sides of us started at 11:00 P.M. Batteries of 155mm guns were firing from front line positions. Every reverse slope was dotted with the flash of firing cannon. The largest concentration of guns in a given sector any time during the war was firing from our sector that night, but the guns immediately near our company were not so thick as during the Champagne Battle. It was thrilling to hear the roar of artillery on both sides, in front and behind, all firing steadily.[2]

2. This was an example of the so-called "Summerall Barrage." As an artillery officer and then as division commander, Summerall learned to concentrate all available firepower in front of one infantry brigade. After that brigade had broken through enemy lines, fire was shifted to support another brigade. The effect was to shatter one narrow sector at a time instead of spreading fire along the entire assaulted front. Here Summerall focused all the artillery in his Corps to support attacks by the 2nd and 89th Divisions (Reilly, 750-751).

Map from Pershing, *My Experiences in the World War.*

At 2:00 A.M., our machine guns opened with intermittent fire. At 4:00 A.M., we began a heavier fire which we continued until 5:00, when the infantry went over the top. It was breaking daylight, but we could see no great distance ahead. The smoke of the firing had settled in the ravines around us and our artillery had been dropping smoke bombs in front of the advancing infantry to conceal them. Nevertheless, we saw the flashes through the smoke and heard the reports. We knew that we were not to advance, and as we continued our fire, we could feel free to watch what was going on. At first, the enemy answered our fire and some shells fell near us, but it was not long until most of his batteries were completely smothered. The enemy could see that it was a general attack and no doubt began withdrawing his artillery pieces to avoid capture. As the infantry schedule of advance caused us to raise our range, we were finally firing at a range of about 4,500 meters to 4,800 meters. This was our limit for overhead fire without danger to our own advancing troops.

At 7:00, the advance passed beyond the positions over which we could fire with safety, so we began a leisurely return to Exermont. The carts had been brought forward and the company was sent back by platoons under their sergeants, all of whom were now thoroughly familiar with the country back to Exermont. After all platoons had been safely started back, Lieutenant Andres and I remained to watch the battle for a few minutes. While firing our guns, before 7:00, we saw a few prisoners returning along the trail along Hill 263. Just as they passed our position enemy shells began falling near them. They were carrying one of their wounded, and as the shells came closer they called to each other, "*Machen sie schnell! Machen sie schnell!*"[3] It did us a lot of good to see the enemy running from his own fire. He was getting some of the medicine we had been taking for the last nine months.

About 8:00, Lieutenant Andres and I began a leisurely trip to the rear. As we crossed one ridge we came upon a column of about 200 German prisoners that was being marched to the rear by four doughboys. They had stopped a few minutes to rest. Lieutenant Andres spoke German perfectly and I had known enough in school so that I could understand. The enlisted men were glad and eager to converse with us, but the two or three officers in the group held themselves aloof. The enlisted men asked if we thought peace would be here in a week. Finally one officer, a captain, came to inquire from what part of America we came. He wanted to know what chance there was for a "magistrate" to make good in New York City. We did not know what the duties for a magistrate would be, but we painted the opportunities of New York City to this German in the brightest terms. We could imagine what kind of a reception a German would receive in America under the high tensions of wartime prejudice, but we gave this man no inkling of it and told him to come on over to our wonderful country.

3. "Make haste! Make haste!" or "Hurry up! Hurry up!"

Practically all of these prisoners had their packs rolled,[4] indicating that when the barrage started they were preparing to move either to their rear in retreat, or to our rear as prisoners.

Lieutenant Andres and I continued on to Exermont. Here, in a vacant lot south of the church, several hundred prisoners were concentrated at the headquarters of the Marine Brigade. They were being questioned by the Marine Intelligence Section and, although we had always been under orders not to fraternize with German prisoners, no objection was made when Lieutenants Olson, Andres, and I engaged them in conversation.

One German lieutenant expressed his extreme disgust at being taken prisoner. His statements translated would be something as follows: "Think of it! I have been in this war for over four years. I have fought and killed French, British, Belgians, Russians, Italians, Serbians, and Rumanians. I never was wounded and have always been on the winning side. Last night, about ten o'clock, we relieved a division at Landres-et-St. Georges and before I saw the light of the next day I had been made a prisoner by Americans. You Americans don't know how to fight! You are an unmilitary people. It is ridiculous to think of me, after all my campaigns, having to surrender to an untrained crowd of Americans who come over the top smoking." He was of the most overbearing Prussian type—a member of a Prussian Guard Division.

Lieutenant Olson laughed in his face when he spoke of having to surrender to an untrained crowd of Americans and said, "Well, you didn't have to surrender, did you?" The officer then replied in broken English, "What would you do? Your artillery barrage fell on us so heavy that we had to stay in our dugouts for three hours. When the barrage lifted, and we rushed to our positions, American tanks were on both sides of us and closing in behind. The American infantry was coming over in four or five waves in front of us. What could we do?" Then, turning pointedly to Lieutenant Olson, he said, "What would you have done?"

Lieutenant Olson winked at us and then answered, "I sure as hell would not have surrendered. I'd have fought it out to the last. I would not have suffered the disgrace of surrender. I might have been killed, but I would have taken a lot of you Germans with me before going." Lieutenant Olson spoke in a spirited tone and with clenched fist made emphasizing gestures. The German lieutenant believed every word of Lieutenant Olson's bragging and answered meekly, "Yes, I know the Americans are brave, even if they can't fight!" Other German prisoners who were not officers were standing by and Lieutenant Andres translated. Although they dared not give vent to much pleasure, we could see that inwardly they seemed to enjoy his discomfiture. Lieutenant Olson, of course, was making these wild statements purely to impress this proud German with the bravery of the Americans. We knew, and

4. This belatedly fulfilled the forecast by Sergeant Dozier of Company B that the rainbow seen at the outset of the Argonne Offensive would send the Boches packing because they knew the Rainbow Division was coming after them.

he quickly volunteered to us on the side, that under the circumstances described by this German officer he probably would have surrendered just as soon.

He understood English, but spoke mostly German. We understood some German, but spoke mostly in English.

Because of their extreme youth, our attention was called to three boys in the enclosure. We engaged them in conversation and learned that they were school boys from Hamburg, sixteen years of age, just called to the colors. After a few weeks training, they were rushed to the front as replacements in one of the divisions before us. They arrived at the front after dark the night before. When the barrage opened they were under fire for the first time. From their description, they certainly had a real baptism of fire. For three or four hours they cowered in an open trench. They had no dugout for cover. Shells were breaking all around them. Several of their comrades were wounded and dirt was thrown over them several times, but miraculously they escaped injury. They did not know they were experiencing one of the heaviest bombardments in the four years of the war. They thought the front lines were like this every night and humorously told how they knelt and prayed for deliverance. When morning came, they had no fight left in them and welcomed a chance to surrender when the first American wave came toward them. Like the German officer, they had come into a new sector after dark and were prisoners before daylight. Their attitude, however, was just exactly opposite of the officer. Although they regretted being captured, they saw the humorous side of it and did not hesitate to joke about it. They were happy at having passed through that heavy artillery fire unscathed.

We visited with a few other groups of prisoners, most of whom seemed to be neither greatly elated nor greatly disappointed that they were prisoners. They had already had a sample American meal of corned beef, good coffee, and white bread. All of these were delicacies in their own army. They were sure that they were going to be well fed and all predicted peace in the near future. In this group of German prisoners we could see that, although most of them were relieved to be temporarily out of the conflict, they were at heart patriotic and loyal to their Fatherland.

We continued back to where the kitchen and echelon were located south of the city. During the afternoon, the company formed to divide some commissary supplies that had been obtained. There were some chocolates, cigarettes, and cigars. There was one box of 15-cent Robert Burns cigars that few of the enlisted men wanted to buy. Therefore, after the company had an opportunity and none had bought them, I bought the entire box. These were a blessing to me in the days that followed, and I made it a practice to distribute a few of these at some of the most trying moments to some of the men whom I knew greatly enjoyed smoking a good cigar.

That night, Lieutenant Andres and I slept in a stone building. We set up our cots in this building in the late afternoon. When we came back after supper, another lieutenant from a supply company had also set up his cot and started a fire in the fireplace. We spent a pleasant evening toasting ourselves before this fire.

We stayed in Exermont until the morning of about November 3rd, when we started moving forward again. We were Corps Reserve, and it looked like we would be in the front wave again any day. The march was slow. We were merely following up the advance of the front lines. Just before we had entered Landres-et-St. Georges, we saw where an American flame-throwing unit had been operating their equipment in the attack November 1st. We also saw where some of our trench mortar batteries had done excellent work.

A little further along the line we saw where an army ration truck had become stuck in the mire. It could not be moved forward, backward, or to either side, but since it was blocking traffic, it was simply dumped on its side and rolled down an embankment. This was a common occurrence. Many a truck was destroyed merely to prevent it from blocking the traffic that always followed in the wake of an advancing army. This truck had been unloaded and a few raw potatoes were still lying in a rut. Part of a loaf of bread was in the ditch at the side of the road. Our men scrambled after these potatoes and this loaf of bread. Several of them got two or three potatoes each and a hand full of bread pinched out of this loaf. When we next halted, they built a fire and cooked them in their mess kits.

Beyond the town of Landres-et-St. Georges, the fields literally had been plowed and re-plowed by the artillery fire of our guns on the morning of November 1st. For an area of several acres it would have been impossible for any human being to have remained in one place during the bombardment and live. There did not seem to be a square foot of earth that had not been upturned by shell fire. Nightfall on Sunday, November 3rd, found us in the vicinity of Fléville. It was raining hard. We slept on a hill west of Fléville and north of Exermont. It was the protected side of a very steep ridge. We selected it because fox holes had already been dug and it was easy for our men to bivouac here. It rained all night, however, and if we so much as stood up outside our fox holes, the side of the hill had become so slippery from men passing to and fro in the rain that we had difficulty going where we wanted to. We were just as likely to slide on down the hill and land with our feet on top of someone in a fox hole.

The morning of November 4th, we started forward, still following up the front line divisions as they were advancing. When we passed through the town of Fléville, headquarters of the 80th Division had a notice posted on the bulletin board to the effect that peace had been signed. We had heard many rumors of peace, but this notice was actually on the bulletin board of an army division. We accepted it as authentic and all inwardly rejoiced, but few openly, in the fact that the war had ended.

As we passed beyond Imécourt, in the direction of Verpel, we came to a line of German machine gun emplacements where dead Germans were still lying at their posts. From this ridge we could count eight or ten machine gun pits with perhaps a dozen or more dead Germans. Some had fallen over their guns, indicating they had been operating to the last. Others were a few steps behind their pits, indicating that they had been shot by rifle fire as they started to run. Many of them bore bayonet marks.

Almost in sight of Verpel, we stopped by the side of the road to await further orders. We had no rations, but on the side of the road there was a field of probably 20 acres of full grown cabbage heads. The Germans surely knew how to grow cabbages. We found many cabbage fields during the next few days. Though we had nothing to season it with, the mess sergeant started cooking a big kettle of cabbage. In the meantime, each of us had devoured one or two heads raw. They were crisp and solid. Although unseasoned raw cabbage is not the kind of diet one would select, we relished this as our noon day meal.

Ruins of Buzancy. The French town of Buzancy was one of many stepping stones for the 151st Machine Gun Battalion on their drive to Sedan. *Editor's collection.*

We were still inwardly rejoicing in the news of peace. Being in Corps Reserve, we were behind the line of combat and had not heard any shell fire for several hours. Out of a clear sky, however, half a dozen shells suddenly came over and fell on the town of Verpel, about a kilometer up the road. That shattered all our dreams of peace. Before the cabbage was cooked enough to eat we were ordered to move on. We passed through Verpel and Buzancy toward Haraucourt. We turned to the right, and at sundown stopped along the road near St. Pierremont. The road ahead was being shelled mercilessly by the enemy. Beyond we saw a motorcycle rider with bandaged head approaching. He must pass through the shelled area. As he neared the barrage of the falling shells he opened at full speed to run the gauntlet. For an instant he was lost in the clouds of smoke and geysers of dirt, but emerged on our side still riding. He stopped, however, at our camp on the roadside because he had been wounded again in the arm. We bandaged it and put it in a sling for him. He then resumed his journey, guiding with one hand.

The kitchen had drawn rations and was now attempting to complete cooking the evening meal. We had orders to continue the march forward that night to St. Pierremont, expecting to go over the top the next morning.

A detachment of an officer from each company was ordered forward, without waiting for supper, to reconnoiter the positions we were to occupy. I went for our company with Lieutenants Wingo, Saye, and Lowe to report to the Brigade Adjutant. We rode forward at a trot for about a kilometer. We dreaded our job of reconnaissance, especially on an empty stomach. Since we were going into the line next morning, we also knew that it would mean no sleep that night while we were moving into position.

After we had cantered about a kilometer down the road, we met an officer from Brigade Headquarters who informed us that the orders were changed. We would bivouac for the night where we were. We wheeled instantly and turned back to our camp. After the first few leaps it became a horse race. Lieutenant Saye of B Company, on the black horse I had ridden during the St. Mihiel Drive, won the race, and I finished last on the stove-up bay plug I had ridden. It was one of the four taken by D Company in the battle of St. Mihiel. Three of them were captured from the Germans and this one I rode was just picked up loose, apparently having been abandoned by its former owner as worthless. However, he carried me a good many miles. In some way, we had obtained the impression that he had formerly been used by an American M.P. The only name we ever had for him in our company was "M.P." I did not mind being the last in the race a bit, because I knew we were going back to this bivouac to have a good night's rest. All told, I used eight different horses during the war. Four were really assigned to me and four others belonged to other officers. None of my horses were shot, but two were worn out and I was out-ranked twice.

We had no food since morning, with the exception of the raw cabbage we had eaten along the way. The cabbage that the mess sergeant had tried to cook at noon was not done and the rations did not come up until late. When they did come, the cooks began preparing supper. After cooking bacon they had no place to carry the grease rendered, so they poured it on the ground. It ran into an impression that had been made about two inches deep by a horse's hoof. While it was still hot, I dipped a head of raw cabbage in this grease and lunched on it. About 20 minutes later a good hot meal of slum[5] and coffee was served.

A heavy wind was blowing from the northeast. The tarpaulin that Captain Means had pitched as company headquarters threatened to collapse any time. We officers crowded our cots into the shelter of this tarpaulin and slept comfortably in spite of the slapping canvas and some aeroplane bombs that the enemy dropped on some infantry troops in the woods to our west.

Early on the morning of Tuesday, November 5th, we started forward again. We passed near St. Pierremont and on through the town of Oches. The roads were jammed with traffic. We were following the 78th Division with orders to leapfrog them and go over the top. At the town of Oches a bridge had been blown out, so that the carts and wagons could not cross a deep stream. We

5. Apparently "slum" is short for "slumgullion" or meat stew.

sent scouts in both directions to find a crossing place and one returned and reported a stone dam down the stream. Water was running over it in places, but it was just a few inches wider than the tread of our carts, so that by careful driving the machine gun carts passed over. The larger wagon train was not attempting to follow us, as it was hopelessly tied up in the traffic congestion.

West of the town of Oches, we reached the position to which we had been directed as having been occupied by the 78th Division, but there were no troops anywhere in sight. The entire battalion, therefore, deployed in platoon columns[6] and scouts were sent ahead. We moved forward in lines of platoon columns until we reached a line about one kilometer south of Stonne. We were to the left of the Stonne-Oches Road. Here we spent several hours while Major Winn established liaison with the other units of our division. We were here in the front line with our mules and machine gun carts, which would have made excellent targets had the enemy seen us. We knew, however, that we were due for a long advance and preferred taking a chance with our mules and carts, rather than undertake to carry our heavy equipment the long distances that were in store for us.[7]

The conversations among all officers of other units we met indicated that Sedan was our objective. Our division was the extreme left of the American line. To our left was the 4th French Army under General Gouraud. The regimental officers were speculating as to how soon we could reach Sedan. It was in Sedan that the French suffered their greatest defeat at the hands of the Germans in 1870. We thought it would be quite an accomplishment for our division to recapture this historic town.

As we waited in line while liaison was being established with the other units of our division, a solitary shell whined over our heads and fell on the slope several hundred yards behind us. As we watched the place where it exploded, we noticed that American infantry were coming over the top in squad columns. We had brought our machine gun carts and mules far ahead of our own infantry lines! Soon the infantry passed through our line, however, and went on to the left of Stonne.

While waiting here one man, whose name I don't remember, was sitting on a stump. When our line started forward, half a dozen shells came near us. One made a direct hit and demolished the stump our man had just vacated. Another burst in front of the First Platoon and wounded Private Earl Ryan's little finger. It was his third wound of the war. Although this one was only a flesh wound in the little finger, he was sent to the rear for an anti-tetanus serum injection. He rejoined us later.

All this time we were waiting, the road south of Stonne was under continuous drum fire from German artillery, so that it was practically impassable. At the same time, the town of Stonne was being shelled mercilessly by the

6. This meant "each squad followed by its gun and ammunition cart" (Means).

7. Captain Means said on this day they "met with practically no resistance and the advance consisted more of a pursuit than an attack" (Means).

enemy. French civilians were fleeing from Stonne into our lines. Until the last few days this region had been safe behind the line of combat, but our rapid advance had brought it into the fighting zone. These aged French inhabitants carried their belongings on hand carts and baby buggies and left their homes behind to the ravages of war. As they passed near us they cheered us with "Vive la Amerique!" I never saw people desert their homes in better spirits. They evidently felt that it would only be temporary, because they could see that the Germans were moving out quickly.

At sundown, it was decided to spend the night in bivouac west of the town of Stonne. We selected an advantageous spot where the mules could be picketed and our carts concealed if a German aeroplane should pass over the next day. We were not worrying very much about aeroplanes, though, because it was raining hard. Several of us commented on the fact that this was election day in the U.S.A.

Lieutenant Andres and I decided to make our bed together on a small grass-covered bank. This sod was soaking wet, but we first put down one shelter half and then two blankets. We then sat down on this bed and two other blankets were put over us, and on top of that another shelter half which we drew up over our heads and tucked in below the one on the bottom. We both wore our overcoats covered by our raincoats, kept our gas masks at our chests, and our side arms and belts were not removed. We leaned back against the bank and soon fell asleep. The shelter half turned the rain and we slept dry all night long. We did not dare change our position. The gas mask, web belt, and pistol each of us wore made it almost impossible for us to move without getting out from under the shelter. But we slept warm and dry, even though we were cramped. When morning came, we debated which one would make the first move. We knew the shelter half had cupped a pool of water immediately above us. He insisted that I move first and I insisted that he move first. Finally, I yielded and got out safe. When he then started to get out, about a quart of water was dumped on his face and throat.

We had gone to bed the night before on empty stomachs, having had no food since about noon. The mules were ravenously hungry. We had a few oats for them each day, but there was no hay. They were continuously gnawing at trees, shrubs, and dead grass at every opportunity. We could not tie them to trees because they would girdle the tree in a few minutes time. In a few minutes we passed through a field of sugar beets. They were not a palatable vegetable, but we ate some raw. The mules refused them. A little later we passed a small turnip patch. There was about one for each man in the company and the patch was soon "exterminated."

We started forward the morning of November 6th at 7:00 without any breakfast. The road through Stonne made a sharp hairpin curve and a bridge on the curve had been blown out, leaving an impassable chasm. Scouts were sent in all directions to discover another way around. Captain Means found an old French man who had not left Stonne, and this Frenchman guided us to a point west of the village where there was a steep decent on a narrow trail. It had not been used for years. It was grown up with sprouts, but was passable. We locked the wheels of our carts and slid them down with men holding them back using ropes from behind. Otherwise, they would have overrun the mules hitched to them. In other places, it was necessary to lift carts over terraces that were too steep to be taken by the mules and the mules were unhitched and led up.

We reached a good road again. Two companies of our battalion were on this road under command of Captain Means and Captain Travis, and the two other companies were sent forward on another road to our left.[8] We came to another place where a bridge had been blown out and the stream was too muddy and deep to ford. While we waited, however, we carried rocks from the blown out stone bridge and practically paved the bottom of the stream, so that it was possible to drive our carts over the stream in water about knee deep to the mules. The infantry lines were marched across the fields and our two companies along the roads.

While the infantry was being delayed by machine gun fire and was waiting for our artillery to drive them out, we stopped at a farmhouse between Stonne and Raucourt. We were there perhaps an hour. The lady of the house was still there. It had been used as headquarters for a German Division which had hastily withdrawn the day before. They had left some supplies behind. The men of our company scrambled to the kitchen, where a line was formed, and some were fortunate enough to obtain a few bites of food. I slipped into a room where Major Bunch, a medical officer of the 168th Infantry, and a few infantry officers had found some food. It was pickled rabbit, bread, and honey. I had a few good bites from a rabbit's back, a slice of bread, and honey and a snort of cognac. I did not like cognac and never used it, but I felt the need of a stimulant after having been without food and very little in sight.

We soon heard sounds of artillery driving the enemy machine gunners from their positions. Liaison had been established with our lines on both sides and a general advance began again. We kept to the road with our machine gun carts. Captain Means and Captain Travis, with half a dozen enlisted men, formed the point. While we stayed out of observation between two hills, they would go to the brow of the next hill and signal for us to bring the column forward. This plan would be repeated at the next elevation. The halts of the column were all made on low ground while the way was scouted ahead for us.

While Lieutenant Andres and I were watching from the brow of one of these hills for a signal from the next hill, we saw the infantry battalion halted in a field to our left. They had been stopped by a machine gun and had sent a patrol forward to drive it out. We heard a few grenades exploding, and looking in that direction saw two Germans running for their lives back toward Germany. There seemed to be about a half mile of level ground. They ran desperately,

8. "Cap. M. A. Means with C and D Cos. covered the right flank of the Brigade as well as the division; Major Winn with the other two Cos. covered the left of the Brigade" (Means).

with a number of American riflemen shooting after them. Apparently they escaped harm, however, as they finally disappeared over a hill on the horizon.

Another time, while waiting for a signal from the top of the next ridge, our company was waiting on the road between ridges. Over the ridge behind us and down the road came General MacArthur and one orderly carrying the General's gas mask and helmet. I saluted. "Are there any of our troops in front?" he asked me. "Just a scouting party of six men," I answered. He returned my salute and kept on going right on out in front. As he passed out of ear shot one of our mule skinners drew his breath and exclaimed, "Man! What a General we've got! Right out with the scouts! No war by telephone for him!"

As our line moved forward, the road took a sharp curve to the right. With our carts and animals we followed this road, though it took us some distance away from the infantry battalion we were to support. We had orders to proceed to the town of Haraucourt and wait for further orders. As the road took a great curve around the hill the infantry went over, we came to the town of Raucourt.[9] It was built on a plan characteristic of many French villages. It was one winding street about three kilometers long with houses on both sides and no other streets.

As we entered the outskirts of this village, the French inhabitants came into the streets and hailed us. The Germans had been gone only a few minutes. Before leaving, they had told the inhabitants the Americans would probably be there in about a week. This town had been a quartermaster depot for a German Army Corps and many supplies had to be abandoned when the army left so hastily. The French inhabitants, during these fifteen minutes, had already overrun the quartermaster depot and were carrying the supplies to their homes. These supplies consisted mostly of black potato bread and jam.

As we marched along the street, an old French woman shoved a loaf of bread in my hand. A few steps farther, a French woman had a bucket of jam opened and held it invitingly toward me. I dipped this loaf of bread deep into the jam and came out with the loaf completely covered. A dozen men following me were treated in the same manner. This was about 4:00 in the afternoon. Except for a few raw sugar beets that I had eaten that morning, and the piece of bread and pickled rabbit at noon, it was the only food I had. We marched through this town without stopping, and soon, without even a break in the houses, found ourselves in the village of Haraucourt.

We had orders to wait at this point for further orders from Major Winn, so our carts were drawn off the street against the side of a building to be as difficult to observe as possible if an enemy plane should come over. While we

9. The 77th Division History claims that the town of Raucourt was liberated by them amidst great jubilation by the citizens (Adler, 95). What the men of the 77th Division did not know (or would not admit to in print) was that Companies C and D of the 151st Machine Gun Battalion had already passed through on their way to Haraucourt. These machine gunners did not stop long enough to join in the local festivities which were later lavished upon the 307th Infantry of the 77th Division as they marched into town and paused for the party.

waited the inhabitants came forth, rejoicing at their deliverance. They had been under enemy occupation for four years. All men of military age had been taken to the rear as prisoners of war. The women had been made to work in the fields for four seasons at one franc a day and the Germans took the crops. They were overjoyed at our coming.

Out of Sight. A Hotchkiss machine gun crew of the 77th Division overlooks Raucourt, France, in early November, 1918. The 77th Division claimed to have liberated Raucourt from the Germans. However, Companies C and D of the 151st Machine Gun Battalion had reached Raucourt ahead of them and had already passed through without stopping. Captain Means and his men were already ahead in Haraucourt getting kissed by the liberated women and feeding German newspapers to their hungry mules. *Editor's collection.*

It was not safe to speak to them unless you were ready to be kissed on both cheeks. One old woman, who must have been 70 years of age, must have kissed twenty-five or thirty of the Americans. She would slip up behind a boy and grab him and kiss him. None of the rest of the troops would give warning. It was considered a good joke on anyone whom this old woman could kiss. Finally this woman found Jerry Peltier, one of our enlisted men from Michigan, who spoke French fluently. Jerry engaged her in conversation, and before long we were feasting on black bread and steaming black chicory. We relished this hot coffee, even though it was of very poor quality.

There seemed to be an abundance of black potato bread. It was not brown bread, but almost totally black. It was made from potatoes, probably without yeast, and was heavy and soggy. It would do if a person were starving. We knew our mules were hungry and, since there was plenty of it, each of our mules had a loaf of bread. That day, while waiting at the farmhouse, the mules had been gnawing ravenously at the dead grass and anything they could bite. One mule skinner came out of an old building with an arm full of old German newspapers. Someone yelled, "What are you going to do with those papers?" "I am going to feed them to my mule," and he did. While his mule was eating other mule skinners begged him to divide, but he refused and his mule ate every scrap.

Shortly after halting on this main street, one of the mule skinners had sneaked away, looking into cellars, hoping to find something to eat. In one he came face to face with a crouching German who immediately surrendered. The mule skinner, whose name I do not recall, led his prisoner out and reported to Captain Means, who assigned him to the care of the men of headquarters section. This prisoner had been left behind to be sacrificed on a machine gun when his regiment retreated. As soon as his officers were far enough gone to make it safe, he deserted his post and hid in the cellar until he found a chance to surrender. He refused to die when the rest were running. He was overjoyed when he found he was to be treated kindly.

The retreating Germans had told the inhabitants that they would refrain from shelling the town for 24 hours so as to give them opportunity to leave. We knew then that we were safe, as we had over 23 hours more. The shells were falling ahead of us outside the town, where our infantry patrols were encountering resistance, but not falling in the village. We were right at the church, and usually the village church steeple was the central target.

To our rear, a patrol of American infantrymen entered the village in street fighting formation. They advanced from one place of shelter to another. Our boys yelled for them to "Come on! We won't hurt you!" They were from the 77th Division and were followed by several platoons who marched through the town and entered the fighting on the hill in front. Others followed in close formation, and soon there was a large number of troops of the 77th Division in town in addition to our own two companies. A lieutenant of that division came to where the officers of our company and C Company were standing in a group and said, "The General orders all officers to assemble at the church." We did not recognize the general's name, so Captain Means told this lieutenant we were from the 42nd Division, and no doubt the general was not wanting to see us. The lieutenant said he would let us know and went on.

A few minutes later a brigadier general[10] came galloping down the pavement and drew up in front of us. "Who is in command of this outfit?" he inquired. We all came to attention. Captain Means saluted and answered, "Captain Means, Sir, of the 151st Machine Gun Battalion." "What are you doing here? You are out of your sector." "We are here under written orders," Captain

10. This must have been Brigadier General Harrison J. Price. He was in command of the 154th Brigade advancing on the left of the 77th Division (Adler, 160).

Means answered. "Where are they?" the general demanded. Captain Means produced the orders, which clearly stated that our battalion would go to the town of Haraucourt and wait for orders from Major Winn. "Those orders were changed last night. You have no business here. You can't have credit for capturing this town. Our brigade gets the credit. Get your companies out of here!" Captain Means answered, "General, my commanding officer has given me written orders to wait here for instructions from him." Then the general roared, "Well, get in touch with him and keep out of my way!" Captain Means then sent another runner to Major Winn, who ordered us to march to the town of Bulson, a short distance to our left. We made this march after dark.[11]

Bulson was built around a public square, in the midst of which was the village church. The men were housed in a hayloft on the northeast corner of the square and the kitchen was set up under the trees in the church yard.

The German prisoner had been sent to the Brigade Intelligence officer. We thought we were rid of him, but soon he came back to us under guard and we had to feed him and let him sleep in the hayloft with the men of our company. German prisoners in our division were considered a liability. We had tried to get rid of him several times, but he always seemed to come back. We did not want to spare a man to escort him to the rear, and neither did any other outfit in our division. We could not give him away. We regretted that we did not give our prisoner to the Brigadier General of the 77th Division, who was so anxious for his brigade to have credit for everything captured. We had really captured the town, but his brigade got the official credit because the revised orders had made that his sector.[12]

On many occasions during the war, I had noticed that the officers of our National Guard regiments were not interested in making any particular record as to prisoners captured. Particularly at St. Mihiel, many prisoners were taken by our first wave troops, but all disliked to spare the men necessary to escort them to the rear. So they gave them away to other outfits at first chance. It was different, however, with such divisions as the First and Second, who were officered by Regular Army officers anxious to make reputations. At St. Mihiel, the Second Division had credit for taking the largest number of prisoners, but many of them were prisoners that the 42nd and 89th Divisions had really captured. In sending them to the rear, we were glad to turn them over to the Second Division troops, who were trained to hold on to them and take full

11. The modest and concise Captain Means recorded only this about his liberation of Haraucourt: "Our Cos. had in fact advanced more rapidly than the Infantry. For C and D Cos., following a road that took them slightly out of the divisional sector then swinging back again, entered the town of HARAUCOURT in advance of our own front line Infantry. Thus they were the first American troops to enter this place. The last of the enemy had left the town a short 15 minutes before" (Means). The 151st Battalion history acknowledges that Companies C and D were "the first American troops to reach the town of Haraucourt" (White & Peavy).

12. The 77th Division History makes no mention of these two companies from the 151st Machine Gun Battalion beating them into Haraucourt. To read their account, they were the initial and lone liberators of this small town (Adler, 95-97). Not everything read in history books is complete and accurate!

credit for their division. The men in our brigade were interested in winning the war and did not care who got credit for the prisoners captured.

We had entered Bulson after dark. Lieutenant Olson of A Company and Lieutenant Andres and I were assigned billets in a building on the south side of the square. The Germans were not observing any 24-hour armistice in Bulson. They fired on this church repeatedly during the night. We were directly south of the church and in the center of the cone of fire. Shells burst around us, but we were too tired to move. We just laid low and trusted our good luck.

Shortly after dark the ration cart had come up with us. The kitchen then began preparing a meal. We relished what we had to eat, but the rapid advance had made rations short. We had been underfed for several days, and again all went to bed hungry after a scant meal.

On the southeast corner of the square, in a stone building, several officers of our battalion and a few from the 167th Infantry gathered around a fire for the evening. Soon we heard the sound of marching troops. We went outside and found the streets filled with infantrymen with full packs from the First Division. General Parker[13] of that Division had interpreted an order given the previous day to mean that there would be no divisional boundary lines.[14] We realized that this was the same order that caused the brigadier general of the 77th Division to order us out of Haraucourt and claim credit for capturing the town.

General Parker, in an effort to win glory for his division, had withdrawn one brigade from the line so that in his real sector he was advancing in half strength. The other brigade had been marched across the rear of the 77th Division and, I believe, the Second Division,[15] at right angles to our line of advance with the intention of getting into the 42nd Division area and race our division for the honor of capturing Sedan. This march across the rear of adjoining units was contrary to all military tactics. It confused the lines of communication. That was why our artillery and our wagon trains had been unable to keep pace with us. The roads had been congested by this ambitious maneuver. This sector was overmanned, while the sector that properly belonged to the First Division was only half-manned. In his book on the war, our Corps Com-

13. Brigadier General Frank Parker.

14. Lieutenant General Hunter Liggett was in command of the First Army. On the evening of November 5 he had issued orders to Dickman (1st Corps) and Summerall (5th Corps) concerning the advance to Sedan. He ended it by stating, "Boundaries will not be considered binding" (Reilly, 775-776). He clearly meant for some flexibility for the most expedient advance forward over roads and terrain. Liggett certainly did not mean whole sectors should be disregarded in long maneuvers sideways! Pershing even said that the order only applied to the boundary between the American 1st Corps and the French on its left "assisted on its right by the V Corps" (Pershing, II, 381). This clause in the order clearly implied the 5th Corps (including the 1st Division) was not to take the lead in the drive on Sedan!

15. The First Division was just to the right of the 77th Division. Therefore, the First Division crossed the sectors of the 77th and 42nd Divisions, but not the Second Division (Dickman, 183).

mander, Major General Dickman, severely censured General Parker for this maneuver.[16]

The troops that we now saw in the town of Bulson had marched 30 kilometers that day and were still marching. They were an exhausted bunch of doughboys, and we certainly gave thanks that our superior officers were not trying to build reputations at our expense. This particular regiment was under the command of Lieutenant Colonel Theodore Roosevelt, Jr. He was not, however, responsible for this movement. He was following orders of superiors and did so in true Rooseveltian fashion.

As was the invariable custom, our boys bantered these troops as they marched forward and cautioned them not to get hurt, because the Germans were in that direction. These 1st Division troops, however, were able to take care of themselves in reply. They marched steadily on. They sent out patrols north of Bulson, and one of these patrols "captured" a patrol of the 165th Infantry of our division, including General Douglas MacArthur, who was out in front with this patrol.[17] When this fact became generally known among the men of our brigade, we had lots of fun at the expense of the 1st Division troops we met. While their generals were ordering them on long marches for the honor of capturing a town, our general was going over the top with us. After marching 30 kilometers, they had advanced only to the point where they could "capture" our general.[18] We were proud of our General MacArthur because we saw him so frequently in the front outposts.

Next morning, Thursday, November 7th, after a scanty breakfast, the entire battalion marched from Bulson on the road leading to Thelonne. Machine guns were mounted on the carts hauled by mules. We still preferred taking a chance with our mules rather than work so hard carrying our equipment. Shortly outside of Bulson, the column came to a halt where the road passed behind a small ridge. The infantry in front of us had been stopped by heavy artillery and machine gun fire. Major Winn went forward on reconnaissance to work out some plan whereby our machine guns could be of assistance.

While we waited along this road, an American photographer in a Signal Corps uniform passed by, going toward the front. He acted like he was taking

16. See Dickman, pages 184-193. He concluded by saying, "The Commander of the First Army, General Liggett, characterized the movement of the 1st Division, November 6-7, 1918, as the worst tactical atrocity that had ever come to his knowledge" (Dickman, 193). Pershing had "leniency" on the 1st Division only because of its splendid prior record and the approaching end of hostilities (Pershing, 381). If any real fighting had been left to do, General Parker surely would have been disciplined for his glory-grabbing blunder.

17. Learning of the proximity of 1st Division troops in his sector, MacArthur had gone out that night to warn his brigade. He wanted to avoid a repeat of Chancellorsville where Confederate pickets mistakenly shot Stonewall Jackson who was returning to his own lines after scouting Union positions. Although men of the 1st Division briefly mistook him as a German, MacArthur asserted, "The stories which have long been going around about my being taken and held prisoner are founded on this incident and, of course, are greatly exaggerated" (MacArthur in Reilly, 801).

18. The historical lesson from this episode: Definite sector boundaries between combat units matter. Without boundaries the situation quickly becomes congested, confused, and dangerous.

photographs of us, although I believe he was only pretending. He was in a jovial mood and went on forward to where the shells were falling on the next ridge. The word was passed down the line from someone that he was a representative of *Colliers Magazine* and that his name was Lieutenant Ralph Estep. We subsequently learned that when he reached the top of the hill, he joined a patrol of infantrymen that was being heavily shelled and was killed by shell fire after obtaining some close-up photographs of exploding shells.

A detachment of infantrymen from the 1st Division came down this same road, going to the front. They inquired how far the front line was. We told them it was at the top of the next ridge and that they had better be careful, unless they wanted to get hurt. They yelled back "Horsefeathers!" and kept on going. It wasn't exactly "feathers" that they said, either. They, too, were bent on capturing Sedan. In a few minutes four of them came back, each with his head or arm bandaged. They had been surprised by enemy machine gun fire and suffered heavy casualties.

The sky was cloudy, making aeroplane observation for the enemy impossible. So we were safe from the sky, but we could not understand why shells were not falling in our ravine. They were pounding the hill ahead mercilessly. About sunset, Major Winn returned. He had taken Captain Travis forward with him on reconnaissance through almost one continuous barrage of shell fire. Captain Travis reported that he was ready to turn back long before the Major would consent, and his drawl Georgia accent lent humor to the way he told the story. On Major Winn's return, the battalion moved forward at sundown to the town of Thelonne, where we were to pass the night. The last mile of the road to Thelonne was covered by our battalion through almost a continuous barrage. Shells were falling on both sides of the road. They sent fragments whining through the air and showered dirt on us. I cannot understand how it was possible, but this entire battalion of about 600 men and 200 animals marched through this continuous shell fire without suffering one casualty. On reaching Thelonne, we found ourselves in comparative safety. The retiring Germans had told the inhabitants that they also would be spared from shelling for 24 hours. We looked forward to a peaceful night of rest.

On the southeast edge of Thelonne, outside the town, was an old barracks which the Germans had at one time used as a Russian prison camp. They believed we would occupy it for shelter, so they kept it continuously under fire. We decided to fool them and did not occupy the barracks. Our company was to park its machine gun carts in a barn lot at the edge of the village. I was arranging the carts in a line before unhitching. Shells were still falling on the road we had just passed over and also on the old Russian prisoner barracks.

Suddenly, the range was shortened and shells began falling near us. I heard a thud at my feet and looked down to find that a shell had fallen on the manure pile on which I was standing. If the shell had been a foot to the right, it would have cut off my legs. If it had been a foot to the left, it would have made a direct hit on the machine gun cart and exploded, which, of course, would have afforded me no chance. It seemed a miracle that this shell had come at the exact spot and angle to miss anything that would cause it to explode. The rain-soaked manure was so soft that the fuse did not detonate. The hole where it entered the ground was less than two feet from me, and from its angle, the projectile must have passed within three or four inches of my knees. A few seconds later, another shell struck this soft manure pile. It did explode, but due to the softness of the manure, it had penetrated so deeply that we were not harmed. We were just "inconvenienced" by flying, rain-soaked manure. If either of these shells had fallen so close on hard ground, it would have meant my finish.[19]

We found that most of the houses in Thelonne were inhabited. Except for the men of military age, all the inhabitants were still there. This made it hard for us to find suitable places to billet the men of our battalion. Places were finally found along the southwest edge of the town, and a number of the officers of the battalion were billeted in the first building on the right hand side of the road entering the town of Thelonne from Bulson. In this group were Lieutenant Olson of A Company; Lieutenant Wingo of C Company; Lieutenant Turner, Battalion Supply Officer; Lieutenant Andres; and myself. Also Lieutenant Erskine, the doctor of the battalion, was with us. Across the street north, Captain Means and Lieutenant Rhodes[20] were billeted in another stone building.

As usual, our first act on finding a stopping place for the night was to search for something to eat. The lady occupying the first floor of the house where we were billeted produced some honey, cherry preserves, and brown bread. By the time we divided it equally there were only a few bites, but it staved off our appetites until the mess sergeant had supper ready.

Shells were still falling around the town, but had not come close enough to the town to be dangerous. The Germans were evidently observing the 24-hour armistice promised to the inhabitants of this village. We therefore counted on a night of rest in dry beds. At bedtime, six men in our building undressed and went to bed. In my bed roll was a pair of sheets Mother had urged me to take when I left home, and on occasions like this I brought them forth. Lieutenant Andres and I slept together in a double iron post bed on springs and mattress, between sheets and under blankets. We were tired and soon fell asleep.

We were awakened shortly afterward by a shell striking the building we were in. I heard Lieutenant Olson's voice from the bed adjoining us. "Are you going Wingo?" he asked. "Well it's plain damn foolishness to stay here," Wingo answered. I had already hit the floor and was fumbling in the darkness for my

19. Parkinson's grandson (the editor) has many fond memories of hearing his grandad tell war stories. This manure pile mishap is hands down his favorite. The close call lends urgency to it; the flying dung adds twisted humor. Parkinson always told the story with his broad grin, betraying his great satisfaction in surviving the episode and amusing his posterity.

20. Roy G. Rhodes had been promoted from First Sergeant to Second Lieutenant on October 18, 1918 (Means).

hobnails. We were all out of bed and dressing in an instant while the shells kept falling and striking the buildings nearby. The one that had struck our building had gone through the roof and exploded in an adjoining room, where the lady of the house and a six year old boy were sleeping. The lady was uninjured, but some fragments of flying stone cut a deep gash in the boy's cheek. We all hurried to the cellar as soon as we were dressed sufficiently and found the cellar packed with civilians and soldiers while the shelling kept up outside. Several more shells struck the upper story of the building, but exploded before penetrating the building to the basement.

In the midst of the heaviest shelling, an enlisted man came from the quarters where our men were sleeping and called for Dr. Erskine. Some of the men had been hit. He hurried out to their assistance. Several men of the other companies had been wounded and Private Ralph W. Olds of our company had been struck in the head by a large shell fragment and died a few minutes afterward.[21] This was on the night of November 8th, perhaps the early morning of November 9th. We slept most of the night in this cellar, but during the lulls in the shelling of the town we visited the men's quarters. No other inhabitants were injured here. Our location was very near the edge of the town. No shells fell on the main part of town. The Germans were merely trying to shave the edge of the town too closely and some of the shells did not clear the roofs of the houses near the edge. Next morning, Lieutenant Andres read a service when Private Ralph W. Olds was buried in the yard, which was enclosed by a brick wall on the right hand side of the road just as we entered the village of Thelonne.

Where Captain Means and Lieutenant Rhodes were billeted, the aged Frenchman showed us a sample of the tobacco the Germans had furnished him for the last four years. It was nothing more than dried clover and smart weed blossoms.

In my building, I picked up a sheet printed in German. It was an appeal to the German Army by Von Hindenburg, calling on them to stand fast and preserve their fighting morale until assured of satisfactory peace terms. On the abdication of the Kaiser and Ludendorff's retirement as head of the Army, Hindenburg assumed command and stood by the Army in the face of impending defeat. He thus won the confidence and gratitude of his people that later made him the first president of the German Republic.

Major Winn, who had been made a Lieutenant Colonel about this time, or perhaps a little earlier, was in touch with Brigade Headquarters. The officers of our battalion, along with some non-coms, reconnoitered the hills outside of Thelonne and selected positions from which to operate the machine guns if it should be necessary for us to go into action. From one of the hills we had a perfect view into the streets of Sedan. The night preceding, an American patrol from the 165th Infantry had entered the outskirts of Sedan. Only the Meuse River was between our infantry and the city proper.

21. Private Olds was the last casualty suffered by Company D (Means).

The Americans could no doubt have taken Sedan had they continued their advance another day. However, they were ordered by Marshall Foch to defer their attack until our division could be relieved and a French Division could participate in the actual entry of Sedan. This was planned as a matter of sentiment to the French to compensate them in some measure for the humiliation of the defeat suffered in this town in 1870, when a large army under Napoleon III was surrounded by the Germans and captured. Our division was therefore ordered to retire.

On the afternoon of Saturday, November 9th, I was sent as billeting officer to our battalion to meet the billeting officers of other units at regimental headquarters of the 168th Infantry, located in the town of Haraucourt. As I entered Haraucourt, I noticed the regimental colors of the 168th Infantry unfurled, standing in front of headquarters. It was the first time I had seen the colors of a combat unit unfurled since leaving Fort Sheridan in the U.S.A. It gave me a patriotic thrill to salute it as I passed by. I entered the room where the billeting officers were to meet. Few had arrived. We were to be under the guidance of Lieutenant Benz, a French officer attached to the 168th Infantry as interpreter and liaison agent with the French. He was a handsome man of good military bearing and neatly uniformed.

While we were waiting for other American officers to report, the door opened and a French artillery captain entered. This man, too, was of striking physique, probably 35 years of age and of splendid appearance. As these two officers of the French Army saluted each other and exchanged words, I was eyewitness to the most impressive example of military courtesy I had ever experienced. "Bonjour mon Capitaine." "Bonjour mon Lieutenant." They greeted each other in modulated tones with beautiful inflections of voice, timed with graceful military salutes, and heels together and shoulders back in an easily poised position of attention. It was all so natural, no effort to either of them.

After the formal exchange of courtesies, which we American officers also extended to the best of our ability, the French artillery captain inquired how far the lines had advanced. He was living in Sedan when he joined the colors at the outbreak of the war, but his family had not been able to leave the city before it was overrun by the Germans. He had not seen his family since and had only slight news. Hearing that the Americans were nearing Sedan, he had received permission to leave his command about 75 kilometers away and was trying to get into the town with the nearest Allied troops. He was much disappointed when he found that the line had not yet entered, but was pleased to know that only the river remained to be crossed, and that it would probably be no more than a day or two until the French would really occupy the city.

This French officer brought us the news of the surrender of Austria. When discussing the terms of the armistice to which Austria agreed, he made the gesture of having picked up something hot and suddenly dropped it. We could not understand all he said in French about the terms of the agreement, but his gesture was enough to show us that it meant complete surrender by Austria.

The following day, we received a two-page issue of the Paris edition of the *Chicago Tribune*. It was two days old, but gave us particulars of this Austrian peace. Thus far, Bulgaria, Turkey, and Austria had sued for peace, leaving only Germany yet at war against us.

It was arranged by our billeting detail for our battalion to march from Thelonne to a deserted chateau west of the town of Haraucourt. The men slept the night of November 9th in this chateau. We slept in Haraucourt. Since we were marching to the rear and the Austrian peace had become known to us, the rumor was current that the 42nd Division, with a few other experienced American divisions, was to sail for Italy and invade Germany from the south by passing through Austria. This made a fine story, and the men really became enthusiastic over the possibility of traveling a few days, rather than having to fight so much at this time. It was only a rumor, of course, as no such plan was ever intended. Many times during the war rumors, though false, had been the means of keeping our men in the best of spirits.

On leaving this chateau, the name of which I do not remember, we marched on Sunday, November 10th, toward the rear. We knew that the terms of the Armistice had been submitted to Germany, but there were few of us that entertained whether Germany would accept the terms. We had heard so many false rumors of the Armistice that we were skeptical about all. The march to the rear was not begun until late in the day. We took our time. The town of Grandes Armoises was our destination. We passed through Maisoncelle and several towns the names of which I do not remember.

One place along the road the bridge was blown out. We found a place where the machine gun carts could ford the stream, but the heavy wagons had to take a longer route. In order to save several miles, however, all the machine gun carts of the battalion were marched along an unimproved trail through a field leading to this ford. The stream was not wide, but it was rather deep. A tree had been felled across the stream and it was hewn flat on top so that a man could walk across. The opposite bank was so steep that a mule could not climb it if hitched to a cart. Therefore, the carts were pulled through by hand, and each mule skinner walked across the log and led his mule through the water. It was quite a scramble for the mules to ascend the opposite bank, especially after a few had crossed and it had become wet. The water was cold, and after about half a dozen of our mules had crossed in this manner one mule did an unexpected thing. With his nose he pushed the mule skinner off in the water and the mule walked across on the log instead. After this incident several of the mules were persuaded to cross on the log, although some of them preferred to take the water.

The men were tired of marching, and the road from this point to Grandes Armoises led back in the opposite direction. There was much grumbling among the men, because it seemed to them that we were unnecessarily doubling our tracks. We reached Grandes Armoises after dark. Lieutenant Andres and I were billeted in one place where a middle-aged couple still lived, having remained in their home during the battle that had gone on around them. Our heavy wagons, including the kitchen, had to take a more circuitous route, so they did not arrive until several hours after we did. Therefore, our supper was again delayed. This couple, however, treated Lieutenant Andres and me to a liberal spread of bread and honey and a can of Eagle Brand condensed milk of American make. We wondered how this delicacy had reached them and were advised that it had been furnished by the Red Cross, and that the German soldiers very seldom ventured to appropriate any of the Red Cross supplies for fear they would be withdrawn and the burden of feeding the population would be thrown on their rapidly diminishing supplies.

The next day, I walked to the north end of this village and noticed that several trees nearby were heavily overgrown with mistletoe. They were too high to climb and the mistletoe always hung far out on the limbs. I did manage, however, by throwing clubs, to break off a few branches of mistletoe. I enclosed a few sprigs in each of several letters which I wrote home that night.

At dark, French soldiers began marching through the town toward the front. They were from one of the most honored regiments of the entire Fourth French Army under General Gouraud. They were marching forward, preparing for the entry into Sedan. It was a thrilling sight to see these French soldiers marching through in long columns of horizon blue. I had seen French soldiers many times in formation, but it gave me an extra thrill, because I knew these men were marching to retake the town of Sedan, which meant so much to their national pride. As they marched by, one company after another, we called to them, "Vive la France," also, "On to Sedan." They answered, "Vive la Amerique. Sedan? Oui! Oui! Certainement!"

Our kitchens came up later at night and, if I recall correctly, it was about 10:00 when we had a supper of warmed corned beef and coffee.

The morning of Monday, November 11th, our battalion was on the march early. We knew that the German representatives had been scheduled to meet Marshall Foch about daylight, but we had not heard anything about the outcome. We were marching back toward the town of Germont. Much of the way we marched on unpaved roads. Our underfed mules found great difficulty in pulling the carts through the mud. Our men were sinking in mud almost to their ankles at each step. Attached to our battalion was a French sergeant as interpreter and liaison officer whom we called "Chief." Somewhere along the march he learned of the location of a French artillery battery. He rode over there on horseback to find out the news.

While we were plodding along in the mud, we heard the sound of a galloping horse behind us and saw this French sergeant, who was of tremendous size, mounted on a little horse, riding toward us with his knees high in the air and his elbows flapping. He was shouting, "De Armisteece is signed! De Armisteece is signed!" As he galloped past the column, his horse splashed water and mud on our men. He had no doubt expected to be received with hurrahs and cheers. But instead, when the men were splashed with water and mud he was greeted with, "To hell with your Armistice. Get that G___ d____ horse away from here or we'll bump you off." Another doughboy yelled, "The war may be over for the Germans, but we will start in on you if you don't quit splashing mud on us." About this time, one of the mules fell in the mud and was too exhausted to rise. The men gathered around, pulled the cart off of him, and forgot all about the Armistice trying to get him up and the cart under way again.

I had often imagined how joyfully we would receive the final news of peace, but I must confess that there was very little change of expression in our column. We had the thrill spoiled by so many false rumors, and when we did have reason to believe it true, we were too busy combating hardships to take much notice and too tired to be joyful about anything.

We passed through a wooded country, and along the road I noticed many dead horses. They were still unburied. Several of these horses had steaks cut from their hindquarters. We reached the town of Germont about 11:00 A.M. It was devoid of inhabitants, so we found many good billets, although many of the buildings were complete ruins from the ravages of war. We had not yet had official verification of the signing of the Armistice. We felt pretty sure, but were not positive. About noon, the rations came forward and the kitchens served us a meal.

Shortly afterward, General MacArthur drove up in his automobile and inquired for headquarters of Colonel Winn. While his car was stopped, one of the enlisted men called to him, "General, is it true that the Armistice is signed?" General MacArthur then gave to us the official statement that the Armistice had been signed and had become effective at 11:00. It was not often that the enlisted men heard General MacArthur in actual conversation. They accepted his statement regarding the Armistice as final. It was hard to believe, but all the men of our battalion were soon wearing a smile and rejoicing that the war was over.

Our spirits were further improved when the clerk began distributing a bag of mail that had come up with the ration cart. Immediately on hearing the news of the Armistice, I wrote a letter home to my father and mother to let them know at the earliest possible time that I had reached the end of the war in safety. It took nine days for this letter to reach them and about six days for their letter to reach me in reply. At supper time that evening, Captain Means urged every man in the company who had not already done so to write his home folks and report his safety. In the mail that I received was a package containing five pounds of lemon drops and five pounds of chocolate almonds. They were somewhat stale, but for several days I was the most popular officer in the battalion. Five pounds did not go very far, however, divided among all the men, so I did not distribute them except to the officers, and only when some of them might call on our company headquarters. Candy was a rare delicacy in the A.E.F.

The clothing I had been wearing was almost alive with cooties. In the building where the officers of our company were billeted there was an old fashioned cook stove. We built a fire, and I found a water can from a German machine gun that had been discarded. This was a rectangular steel can about five inches by nine inches and about eighteen inches long with a handle on one edge. It served as a means of carrying water for cooling German machine guns. After taking a bath and changing clothing, I heated this steel can on the stove until it was hot enough to press the clothes I had been wearing. In this way I killed the eggs as well as the living cooties.

The officers of A and B companies invited us that evening to join them in a poker game. Captains Brown and Palmer and Lieutenants Olson, Saye, and Sloan usually arranged a poker game as soon as their pay checks came. They were excellent fellows from the vicinity of Macon, Georgia, but too good with their bets for us northern boys. We wanted to celebrate in some way, however, so Lieutenants Andres, Rhodes, Captain Means, and I had a penny ante game after supper with lemon drops as refreshments.

It was common knowledge now that we were to form a part of the Army of Occupation. We felt honored that our division would be one of the two National Guard Divisions so selected.[22] The Army of Occupation consisted of the First, Second, Third, Fourth, Fifth, and Sixth Regular Army Divisions, the 42nd and 32nd National Guard Divisions, and the 89th and 77th National Army Divisions. Later on, the 33rd National Guard, 90th National Army, and a few others were added to the Army of Occupation.

On Tuesday, November 12th, we marched from Germont to Alliepont. The line of march led through the town of Imécourt. In this town traffic was heavily congested at the main crossroads from supplies going forward and our division moving in the opposite direction. Alliepont consisted of just two or three houses and a large barn a short distance from Imécourt. There was not a shingle left on the barn, and although on the maps it looked to be large enough to billet the men of our battalion, there was no shelter whatever. The men found shelter in other partly ruined buildings and pup tents.

Here we were thrilled with the privilege of building fires in the open and lighting candles without attempting to hide the light. One group of enlisted men had gathered fire wood and built a fire in a shell hole out of the sweeping wind. As they huddled around this fire there was a sudden explosion and one of the men was badly wounded. They had built their fire directly over a buried German grenade which was exploded by the heat of their fire. It seemed tragic that anyone should have to be wounded in this manner after going through the entire war unharmed.

At this place, Lieutenant Wienges reported to our battalion and was assigned to C Company. He also was from Georgia, but had been a member of

22. According to the commander of the Army of Occupation, "The divisions designated were those which had rendered the most conspicuous service during the war; the selection was a reward for valor and hard fighting" (Dickman, 199).

the 31st National Guard Division and came to us as a replacement. He was very sensitive to the fact that he was with a company of seasoned troops and that he had never been under fire. It was a difficult situation for him, but he soon won the confidence of all his men and other officers. A few weeks later no one would have known but that he had always been with the battalion.

On Wednesday, November 13th, we marched to the town of Landres-et-St. Georges. It was the same town that we had faced so long ago stationed on Hill 263 in the Battle of the Argonne. We looked south and saw the old hill standing out on the skyline and could see what an outstanding target it was for German artillery at the time we had been there. All buildings in the town of Landres-et-St. Georges were completely in ruins. It was hard for a company to find places to sleep. Therefore, the battalion marched out on the road leading to the east toward Bantheville.

It was here that Lieutenant Geiszel, who had been wounded at St. Mihiel, returned to us.[23] We were delighted to see him and to know that he was getting along well. He had an ugly scar, however, on the back of his neck where he had been hit by a shell fragment.

Just outside of Landres-et-St. Georges we set up our pup tents by the side of the road. There was a strong wind blowing here which almost swept our tents away. It was a continuous struggle to keep the flaps staked down, but it was necessary, because the wind chilled us through as it swept along the hillside. The road along which our pup tents were pitched extended parallel to the ridge and was just halfway down. At the foot of the hill below us was a long line of mules and horses picketed and their wagons and carts. The men of the 168th Infantry were bivouacked in pup tents on the hillside above us.

About dark, one of the infantrymen at the top of the hill decided to celebrate the end of the war. It is a part of an infantry platoon's equipment that they have a supply of rockets of various colors–red, yellow, green, and blue–each discharging various numbers of stars. Codes were agreed upon so the infantry, by shooting these rockets, could communicate with artillery in the rear. Since the war was over, these doughboys got tired of carrying rockets. Someone now fired a rocket high in the air. It arched over us and lit among the animals at the foot of the hill. It caused a commotion among the animals, so someone else repeated it. When two or three had landed among the animals, the mule skinners began cursing back. The infantrymen answered with more rockets and, instead of arching, shot them directly at the mule skinners below. Then someone from the foot of the hill located a supply of rockets and fired some of them toward the top.

Soon we were between two fires, as these two outfits of American soldiers fired rockets at each other. One of our tents was set on fire with sparks and we had to hug the ground for ten or fifteen minutes as closely as we had for

23. Geiszel returned to duty on November 14 (Means). For the first time since before St. Mihiel, Company D had recovered to its normal contingent of five officers: Captain Means, First Lieutenants Andres, Geiszel and Parkinson, and Second Lieutenant Rhodes.

an artillery barrage while these American rockets passed low over our heads, going both ways. The officers at the top of the hill tried to stop the fireworks, but it had no more than stopped when someone from below fired into them again and it was resumed. For about twenty minutes we were in a maelstrom of sizzling rockets of all colors. We were glad when the supply was exhausted. It was bed time and we thought the fireworks were about over, when some doughboy located a large supply of rockets which the Germans had left behind in Landres-et-St. Georges. He appeared about this time and all began shooting rockets of new hues and colors. We had to hide in the small ditch at the side of the road until these rockets were also exhausted. Fortunately, there were no casualties among the men, but several of the mules were burned by being hit by rockets. One mule was so severely injured it had to be killed.[24]

Fireworks! French signal rockets in a trench at Champagne, July, 1918. On the night of November 13, 1918, men of the 168th Infantry grew weary of carrying signal rockets and decided to celebrate the war's end by firing them off. As rockets landed among the 151st Machine Gun Battalion some of the machine gunners answered in kind. For about 20 minutes the two units fired, "a maelstrom of sizzling rockets of all colors" at each other. Officers tried to stop the intentional friendly fire, but the storm only passed when the supply of rockets was exhausted. *Editor's collection.*

24. The reader will be hard pressed to find reference to this small-scale "civil war" in the division or regimental accounts. The 168th Infantry history records only that men celebrated by firing off pyrotechnics and that, "No one stopped them, or wanted to" (Taber, II, 235). In fact, much of what happened following the Armistice and the circumstances of the Occupation are glossed over in most histories. This is another example of the detail Parkinson preserved.

Next morning, with Lieutenants Saye, Walker, Sloan, and Turner, I rode horseback on a billeting detail for our battalion to the town of Brandeville. We passed through the towns of Bantheville and Dun-sur-Meuse, then entered Brandeville. The strong sweeping wind was still at our backs during the ride. I was still riding the stove up M.P. horse and had difficulty keeping up with the other four, who were well mounted. At Brandeville, the five of us arranged billets and a short time later, when our companies marched in behind us, we guided them to the billets we had selected. In this town the Germans had left behind a large number of Sibley stoves which we set up so that most of the men had heated quarters in the partially ruined buildings.

About noon, on the road leading from Germany, we saw a ragged group of men walking toward us. They proved to be some Russian prisoners that the Germans had released under the terms of the Armistice and were coming into the Allied lines at this point. They were hungry and tired and asked for food. We intended to let them join us as soon as our dinner was ready, but before it was ready the road was dotted with others following. They were of practically all nationalities: Russian, British, and French predominated. Their uniforms were worn and practically gone. Some were dressed in German equipment. All were dirty and unshaven. There were a few African French Colonial Negroes. This influx of prisoners continued all that day and the next. There must have been 1,000 of these released prisoners. They begged us for food, but we could not begin to feed them. Military police gathered them together and marched them on back to a place where they were fed.

Here our men were all equipped with wool-lined leather sleeveless coats. Worn under our overcoats, these were helpful in keeping out the chill of the November wind. During the afternoon, some of the men were prowling around the various buildings. They entered one large building which the Germans had been using as a warehouse. It was filled with hundreds of barrels of sauerkraut. Many were broken open, and we ate more sauerkraut that day than most of us had seen for several years previous. By chance, one barrel was broken open and it proved to be heads of cauliflower, pickled in the same way that cabbage is pickled for kraut. This was tempting food. We ate it cold, and for several hours you could see doughboys walking the streets, munching on a head of pickled cauliflower stuck on the end of a bayonet.[25] This lasted only for a few hours, however, because the MPs soon took charge of this warehouse and kept all prowlers out. We stayed at Brandeville for three days, drawing new equipment to replace that lost in the campaigns and resting until we should begin the march to Germany as part of the Army of Occupation.

During the closing days of the war our Division Commander, Major General Charles E. Menoher, was elevated to the command of an Army Corps. Briga-

25. The picturesque scene of doughboys eating plundered pickled cauliflower stuck on the ends of their bayonets is priceless. Parkinson's narrative is loaded with these singular anecdotes.

dier General Douglas MacArthur was Division Commander during our drive toward Sedan.[26] He had been recommended for a promotion to Major General, and it was expected that he would become regular Division Commander. When the Armistice was signed, however, all recommendations for promotion were canceled. General MacArthur came back to his old brigade and Major General Flagler took command of the division. He had not been in any of the campaigns. The men of our division resented having a man like MacArthur denied promotion and a combat division like the Rainbow given to the command of an inexperienced general.

General Flagler promptly made himself unpopular with our men by issuing orders the first day stating that, now that the war was over, we would have to exercise the greatest discipline and make our division a first class military organization. We all had expected to do that and no comment would have resulted had his orders stopped there, but he closed with a paragraph stating that if the officers were unable to instill a strict discipline into their men, that there were many good officers in the rear areas that would be glad to take over our places. This we considered very untactful and unfair. The officers of our division had made it one of the two or three best combat divisions. All looked forward to going home with the division, and we felt that this threat was an excuse being held over our heads so some of the officers from the rear areas who had not had combat experience could take our places when the danger was over and have the honor of leading our troops home. We also felt that the threat by General Flagler was unnecessary. We had demonstrated our willingness to do the right thing and to do what was best for the military service and did not feel that threats were called for. This order by General Flagler was sent to all units of the division and was not confined to any certain unit. To use the vernacular of that date, he just started in the first day "cranking us off."

26. MacArthur was 42nd Division Commander for two days: November 10-11, 1918.

CHAPTER 9: MARCH TO THE RHINE

THE MARCH TO THE RHINE, IRE-LE-PRES, VIRTON, BELGIUM, SIMMERN, LUXEMBOURG, ROSPORT, THE GERMAN BORDER, EISENOCH, BOOS, MAYEN, WALDORF.

November 20, 1918, our division, as part of the Army of Occupation, started moving toward the Rhine.[1] We were the reserve division in our corps. Two others preceded us. It was a general order from General Pershing that all units should advance in formation so they could take battle formation quickly in the event of hostilities. Each unit of the division was to march first with a "point" composed of half a dozen scouts in front, followed two or three hundred yards behind by an "advance party" or "support." Two or three hundred yards behind the "advance party" would be the unit in regular formation. Our machine guns were mounted on carts, ready to go into action quickly if needed, and the battalion marched each day preceded by an advance party and a point.

1. Most histories of World War I virtually end with the Armistice. Little attention is paid to the conditions and events of the March To the Rhine or the Army of Occupation in Germany. Parkinson's narrative is a valuable exception to this tendency. He gives us a rare glimpse into this epilog to the Great War. The histories of Company D, the 151st Machine Gun Battalion, and the 42nd Rainbow Division add little to Parkinson's account. Another noteworthy account of the Occupation is that by the Third Army's Commander, Major General Joseph T. Dickman (see Dickman, 195ff). While Parkinson covers some of the minutia experienced by the men, Dickman tells of some of the broader military and political issues.

It is much easier to march at the head of the column than at the rear. Those at the rear are required to stop and start frequently and move at an irregular pace, even though the advance elements move at a steady gait. For this reason, our four companies and headquarters section alternated each day. When one company worked forward to the lead, the next day it would take formation in the rear of the column and each day move one position forward, thus working to the head of the column again.

During the first day's march, our battalion left Brandeville, marched north through the town of Ire-le-Sec, and billeted at night at the town of Ire-Le-Pres. These were small villages a few kilometers south of Montmédy.

November 21st, we crossed the French boundary and entered Belgium in the southeast corner, near the town of Virton. Our billets for the night were in the village of Virton. The march was resumed the next day through the towns of Basse, Signeulx, Musson, and Halanzy to Guelff. As our column entered each village along the way, we were greeted with church bells ringing. The inhabitants came into the streets and cheered as we passed. In one village, the name of which I do not remember, a brass band made up of old bearded men above military age, led by the mayor of the village, played patriotic airs as we marched through at attention. In many of these places, committees were prepared to welcome us as part of the delivering army, but as our orders were to proceed, we could not delay, even at a celebration in our honor.

At the town of Guelff, we billeted for the night. We had arrived in the afternoon, and a short time before dark the ration cart came up with a quarter of frozen beef. While the cooks were preparing this beef for cooking, the word quickly spread among the inhabitants. They had not even seen any fresh beef for months and months. Men, women, and children gathered around our kitchen wagon. We felt selfish not dividing with them, but our rations were short. We were having only two meals a day, and we were under orders not to attempt to give food to the inhabitants. The cook had cut away the shank bone. He threw it on the fire to burn, as had always been the custom, but the inhabitants standing by plunged onto the fire to rescue the bone. The mess sergeant, realizing its value, sawed it up in small pieces for the children.

In this town, I was billeted with a Belgian family who spoke both German and French. This was my first opportunity to try out the German I had learned in school. Although it had been years since I had studied, many of the words came back to me and I could carry on a conversation and understand them if they did not speak too rapidly. In each succeeding town, we always found that the inhabitants spoke German, some of them in preference to French. I became rather proficient after a few days. Lieutenant Andres had spoken German at home since boyhood and there were several enlisted men who knew German, so we had a much easier means of conversing than we had with the French.

November 23rd, we marched from Guelff through Hoberger, Udange, Weyler, Waldkonig, and Eischen to the town of Septfontaines, in the country

Chain of Command
The March to the Rhine, November 13, 1918

Major General Joseph T. Dickman
THIRD ARMY
III Corps (2nd, 32nd, 42nd Divisions)
IV Corps (1st, 3rd, 4th Divisions)
VII Corps (5th, 89th, 90th Divisions

Major General J. L. Hines
III CORPS
2nd Division (Gen. J. A. Lejune)
32nd Division (Gen. Wm. Lassiter)
42nd Division (Gen. C. A. Flagler)

Major General Clement A. Flagler
42nd RAINBOW DIVISION

Brigadier General Douglas MacArthur
84th BRIGADE
167th Infantry Regiment
168th Infantry Regiment
151st Machine Gun Battalion

Lieutenant Colonel Cooper D. Winn
151st MACHINE GUN BATTALION

Captain Monroe A. Means
COMPANY D, 151st MACHINE GUN BATTALION
1st Lieutenant William Andres - 1st PLATOON (4 MG Squads)
2nd Lieutenant Roy G. Rhodes - 2nd PLATOON (4 MG Squds)
1st Lieutenant N. P. Parkinson - 3rd PLATOON (4 MG Squads)
1st Lieutenant John H. Geiszel - SUPPLY TRAIN

of Luxembourg. Septfontaines was the name shown on the French maps, but the more common name used here was the German name, Simmern.

The schedule of advance called for a halt along the entire line on this date. All units were to stop and reorganize for the next phase. We were notified that we would be in this town until December 1st. Therefore, we prepared to make ourselves comfortable. We found the best billets available for both men and officers and proceeded to recuperate and prepare for the long marches still before us.

The Germans had, of course, occupied this country during the four years of the war, so food was scarce. Although German Marks were rapidly falling in value, the inhabitants would accept no French money except at exchange values based on par. This meant that for five French Francs we received only four German Marks. The actual value of the Mark on this date on the exchange was about fifty or sixty percent. It did not make a lot of difference, however, because there was very little to buy, except stationery and trinkets. Food and wine were practically all used up. Some men in Germany, however, did pool their Francs and persuaded one man to sell a young pig. They paid some outlandish price and arranged to have it on Thanksgiving Day. A few of the enlisted men and non-coms who were in on the deal had it cooked for their own private party.

For the officers' mess Thanksgiving Day, November 28th, the five officers of D Company purchased a goose. It cost 55 French Francs, or the equivalent of $11.00, and the woman in whose house we had officers' table roasted it for us. We each had a small helping at noon and planned to save the rest for supper that night. When supper time came, the family had eaten up the rest. They claimed that they thought it was only scraps.

Arrival of American Troops in Luxembourg. The first Americans entered Luxembourg on November 21, 1918. The 151st Machine Gun Battalion followed close behind. *Editor's collection.*

The town of Simmern was located at the foot of a small mountain. At the top were the ruins of an old castle. On two or three occasions we climbed to the summit and explored these ruins. They gave us a vivid picture of the early feudal days, when the lord of the castle had lived with the homes of his subjects nestled in the village at the foot of the mountain under his protection. The man in whose home we had officers' mess was a collector of rare coins and antiques. He had a number of coins which he claimed to have found in the ruins of the castle on the hill. One of these he gave to me as a souvenir. It indistinctly bears the date "1765" and was struck by the XII Heller Reichs, Stadt Achen.

While stopping in this village, several of the officers of the company received permission to travel to the city of Luxembourg a few miles to the south. We rode horseback to the railway station, which I believe was named Klein Bettingen. We left our horses in charge of some American troops stationed there and rode on the train to Luxembourg.

Arrival of American Troops in Luxembourg. *Editor's collection.*

This was a beautiful old city located in a beautiful valley where the river flowed between two high cliffs a mile apart. In this village, Lieutenants Saye, Andres, Brown, Geiszel, and I passed by the Royal Palace and saw the Luxembourg Standing Army of 250 men "standing around" in brilliant uniforms. Luxembourg was really an independent country, perhaps the smallest in the world at that time. It had been over-run by the Germans during the war, but outside of that, all nations recognized it as an independent country ruled over by a Queen and Parliament.

The five of us traveled down the middle of the streets with our hobnails beating the cobblestone pavement. Suddenly, Lieutenant Saye, whom we affectionately called "Strawberry," stopped and pointed to a sign in a window. The sign read, "American Ice Cream." We almost stampeded the place to get in and order a dish. It was made largely of cornstarch and condensed milk, but nevertheless, it was frozen and good. We ate one large dish each and then re-ordered.

We passed by a café where we agreed to meet for our noon-day lunch. We then separated and each went his own way. At an attractive shop I bought a beaded bag which I sent home to Florence. The merchant claimed that it had been hand made in Austria. A few minutes later I met Lieutenant Geiszel on the street. He had found a place to have his picture taken. Lieutenant Andres and I then followed him to a photograph gallery and had photographs taken. We came back a few hours later. I sent them home, but they must have been misplaced. I have never seen them since.

We visited the cathedral and other interesting points before time for our train late in the afternoon. We returned to Klein Bettingen by train and by horseback to Simmern. I think the date that we were in Luxembourg was Saturday, November 30th. Captain Means had a leave of a few days previously and had gone through the town of Mersch on his way to Luxembourg.

Sunday, December 1st, the schedule of German retirement and our follow-up schedule called for us to resume the advance. We marched from Simmern through the villages of Boose, Donneklange, and Miespal to Heisdorf. Monday, December 2nd, we marched from Heisdorf through Helmjange, Niederanven, Axe, Roodt-sur-Sy, Berg, Hagedorf, and Wecker to the town of Manternach, where we were billeted for the night.

From Manternach, on December 3rd, we marched through Leilig, Herbarn, Dockweiler, and Rosport. At the town of Rosport we marched across the Saur River bridge. This river was the German boundary. Immediately across this river was a great high mountain. Fog and clouds were hovering around it, and we could not help but imagine what would have happened if this mountain had been manned by enemy machine gunners like some of the hills we had encountered in the Argonne Forest before the Armistice. We marched through the town of Mindes to Eisenoch. Battalion headquarters and Companies C and D billeted in Eisenoch, but the town was not large enough, and Companies A and B marched on to Menningen for billets. After arriving in Eisenoch, we saw a German funeral procession marching from the church to the cemetery. The casket was borne on the shoulders of the men in a procession led by the priest and the mourners followed chanting a funeral dirge.

Wednesday, December 4th, we made a short march to Idesheim. Thursday, December 5th, we marched through Idesheim, Sulm, Rohl, Ruttinger, and Metterich to Gindorf.

From Gindorf, we marched through Oberkail and Eisenschmitt to Bettenfeld. This was a hard march. Men were always exhausted when we arrived at our destination.[2] Each morning we had breakfast of beans and bacon or beef stew, and occasionally some oatmeal, rice, or raisins. All rations were short, and we always started the march hungry. There was no food for a noon-

2. The original timetable called for the Americans to leave one day's march as a buffer between themselves and the withdrawing Germans. As looting began to take place in the intervening vacuum, the Germans asked the Americans to pick up the pace and close the gap (Reilly, 859). This simply compounded the exhaustion among the troops.

Entering Germany. Men of the 18th Infantry Regiment, First Division crossing the Moselle River into Germany. *Editor's collection.*

day meal and no time to stop to cook. We could only march all day until we arrived at our destination for the night. Then our ration cart would have to go back several miles to the ration dump to draw rations and return to our village before the cooks could even begin preparing supper. Many a day, we had breakfast at 6:00 and nothing more to eat until supper at 9:00 or 10:00 P.M.

It was out of the question to buy food along the way, except that at one place in Belgium we found a man selling fresh sausage made of horse meat. There was such a scramble to buy it that the owner of the place had closed up until more could be cooked. When I came into the place he recognized me as an officer and sold his entire supply to me still warm. I took a small portion for myself and the other officers of the company, and the rest I turned over to Sergeant Brenner, with instructions to divide it with our men and the men of the other units waiting in line.

During these days, when we marched all day hungry, the men learned to hold back a piece of bread and bacon for noon-day lunch. But we were always hungry and never had enough at breakfast, so it did not matter whether we ate our food all at breakfast or saved a little for noon. We had trouble with some of the men stealing rations at night. Of course, we kept a guard posted at the kitchen so that civilians did not disturb our supplies, but it finally got to the point where it was necessary to check every bit of food and hold the guard responsible. Our own men were trying to get on guard so they could swipe a bit of bread. We always received some nice white bread.

At the town of Bettenfeld, one German ex-soldier who had been discharged and returned home since the Armistice noticed our white bread. "If we Germans had bread like that to eat, you confounded Americans would never have beaten us." He had no chance to say anything more. Half a dozen Americans were on him in a minute in a mock dispute as to who should have the honor of giving him a good pounding. They had no intention of harming him, but gave him a good scare. A sergeant appeared and quickly got the situation under control. He played his part by ordering the German turned free. The German was scared, nevertheless.

The main roads on which we marched were for the most part macadamized, but the entire German Army had retreated over them and the Americans were now advancing over them before repairs could be made. Thousands of men, animals, and wheels had ground down the surface of the roads until, in many places after a rain, they were ankle deep in slush which resembled newly-poured cement. As we marched on the right side of the road, trucks passing on the left splashed a stream of slush all down the column. We learned to stand in close to the passing vehicles so as to be splashed below the knees, rather than on the neck or face if farther away.

A loaf of bread had fallen unnoticed from some ration cart far ahead of us. Traffic following had rolled it around in the slush until its crust was completely covered. It looked just like a stone in the road to those who passed ahead of us, but as we came by, a passing truck wheel broke it partly in two so that underneath the hard-baked crust, clean white bread shown forth. Men scrambled from line to pick it up, cut away the muddy crust, and divided the soft white loaf remaining.

Saturday, December 7th, we marched from Bettenfeld through Bleckhausen to Waldkonigen. From Waldkonigen on Sunday, December 8th, we marched to Boxberg, where two companies stayed. One went on to Beinhausen and the other to Neichen. I think that D Company was at Beinhausen.[3]

Monday, December 9th, we marched from Boxberg to Boos. The schedule of German withdrawal required us to wait here until Saturday, December 14th. At this place, we made a special effort to obtain shoes for the men. Our campaigns and long marches had worn through the shoes of almost every man. The shoes of the animals were also worn through. It required lots of manipulating and scheming for us to obtain the shoes needed for the animals. We finally obtained an issue of shoes for the men, but they were all extremely large sizes. A few days later, we were able to exchange them for smaller sizes. We also obtained an issue of clean underwear and some of the men had their worn out clothing replaced.

3. Captain Means says that Company D was billeted in Boxberg with Company C (Means).

At Boos, two men from B Company were court-martialed for being AWOL three months. The night we left Sauville (August 30th) they slipped away, and during three months they wandered over France, bumming food from other outfits and always claiming to be moving toward their company at the front. As soon as the Armistice was signed and the danger was over, they returned to B Company for a regular boarding place. One of them asked me to defend him. I have forgotten his name. I did my best for him, but he got 90 days in the guardhouse. At that he got off easy, considering his guilt.

Each day, General Flagler drove along the road inspecting the discipline of all units as they marched. Day after day he sent orders calling for stricter discipline. He seemed to expect every unit to march in perfect formation as if on parade. Many a unit commander was surprised on marching through some village to have the General show up suddenly and reprimand him for slight infractions of marching discipline. Perhaps the distance between carts would be too great or too small, or not even. Or instead of leading the mules with reins, some of the men drove them with lines.

The roads were steep, the mules were underfed, and many of them were so exhausted that never a day went by that some mule had to pull in two carts, and usually it was necessary to double back a few miles to bring in a wagon or cart where the draft animal would be exhausted. Often a shoe would wear out on the rock pavement and the animal would have to limp along the rest of the way while any minute we feared General Flagler might step out from some building with a reprimand for allowing lame animals to straggle.

Saturday, December 14th, we marched to the town of Bell. Here the officers were billeted overnight in a pleasant German home. A girl of about 18 was especially hospitable at the place where we were billeted. She took special pains to see that our meals were well cooked, and in the evenings she sang and danced with us. In an army of two million men, it is pleasant to be in the atmosphere of a nice woman in a nice home.

Sunday, December 15th, we marched to the town of Waldorf. While we stopped on the hill overlooking the village, Lieutenant Andres remarked that the town looked familiar. The billeting detail had gone ahead and later returned with orders for us to march in and take over the billets assigned. As we entered the town, we crossed a bridge over a small stream. Lieutenant Andres remarked, "I know this is the place. When I was nine years old my father and mother brought us back to their old home town on a visit." As soon as we were assigned to billets, he began inquiring about relatives and located several cousins. He made himself known and the old village burgermeister told us the story of how when Bill, years before at the age of nine, had come to visit his cousins, he had insisted on teaching them all how to box. Although he was younger than most of them, he knew what it was all about and had passed black eyes and bloody noses liberally among the boys of the village.

Waldorf was to be our permanent place in the Army of Occupation, but it wasn't large enough to give all men comfortable billets. My room was in the home of one of the Andres relatives, so I was well treated. In fact, all the men were well treated in this place.

We had reached the town of Waldorf by marching from Bell through Mayen, which was the largest German town we had passed through.

Friday, December 20th, we took up the march again. General MacArthur had arranged larger billets for us at Kripp-am-Rhine. We marched through the town of Franken and on to Sinzig, where we crossed the bridge of the Ahr River and turned to our right to Kripp, on the bank of the Rhine.

CHAPTER 10: ARMY OF OCCUPATION

KRIPP-AM-RHINE, THE RHINE, SINZIG, REMAGEN, BARON VON NEGRE, COUNT TA VEGGE, THE GREBES, A FOURTEEN DAY LEAVE, COBLENZ, METZ, TOUL, PARIS, LYON, ORLEANS, GENERAL PERSHING, BREST, THE MINNESOTA, NEW YORK CITY, HOME.

The town of Kripp-am-Rhine, on the south and west bank of the Rhine, was in a level flat valley. On the opposite side of the river, however, were steep cliffs and mountains. We were not permitted to cross the river. At this point, the Rhine was the boundary line between the zone of the Army of Occupation and the line of the German withdrawal. Several of the men did slip across the river to the town of Linz, though.

At Kripp, 90 men of the company were billeted at some sort of community house or school called "The Hetlau." Since we were to be here for several months,[1] we insisted that every man have a bed to himself and this was arranged. My billet was a room in the home of Baron von Negre. He was a man in his late 50s. The neighborhood gossip said he spent his early life in the German

1. The Armistice was technically just a temporary truce until the Peace Treaty could be negotiated and signed. It had to be renewed on December 17, 1918, and again on January 18, February 17, and March 16, 1919. In the meantime, hostilities could theoretically resume if the peace talks collapsed. The Army of Occupation was held in place along the Rhine for just such an eventuality. Of course, the disarmament terms of the Armistice were so exacting on Germany's military might that there was little threat of any real resumption of war.

Army and had reached the rank of captain when challenged to a duel by some other German officer. He declined to fight and was therefore forced from the army. He had a small income. It was not enough to live on, but enough to exist on. He was too proud to work, so he just barely lived.

He had one room fixed up as a museum, where the walls and tables were covered with trophies of his hunting and military service in German Africa. The first night I was in his home, he greeted me with great hospitality and invited me in to his museum, where he explained his trophies and souvenirs. We discussed many things, or as many as my knowledge of German would permit.

He brought out some wine, which we enjoyed, and then he became enthusiastic. He went to the cellar and brought out a rare flask, the contents of which he explained as follows. It had been a tradition in his family centuries before that each generation should make cognac and seal it up to be kept for a century. Before filling a small glass from this flask, he told me that his great grandfather had made this cognac at the time of Napoleon. His grandfather had been an officer under Blucher, the Prussian General who aided in defeating Napoleon at Waterloo. It was the family tradition that each time an old barrel was opened, another one should be made to replace it and set aside, not to be opened under any circumstances until it had attained the same age as the one just opened. I expected to have a rare glass of liquor. I suppose it was rare, but I could not tell. It was like any other cognac to me. I did not like strong liquor anyway. I took this drink as an acceptance of his hospitality and declined a second, although he insisted that I partake with him.

Home Away From Home. Kripp-am-Rhine, Germany, viewed from the north bank of the river. The 151st Machine Gun Battalion was quartered in this small town during the Occupation. Circled from left to right are (1) the residence of Count Ta Vegge, Battalion HQ and billet for Lieutenant Colonel Cooper D. Winn, (2) the home of Baron von Negre, Lieutenant Parkinson's billet, and (3) the Grebe household which was D Company HQ and the billet for Captain Means and Lieutenant Geiszel. *World War History & Art Museum (WWHAM) collection, Alliance, Ohio.*

Chain of Command
Army of Occupation, December 17, 1918

Major General Joseph T. Dickman
THIRD ARMY
III Corps (1st, 2nd, 32nd Divisions)
IV Corps (3rd, 4th, 42nd Divisions)
VII Corps (89th, 90th Divisions)

Major General C. H. Muir
IV CORPS
3rd US Division
4th US Division
42nd US Division

Major General Clement A. Flagler
42nd RAINBOW DIVISION

Brigadier General Douglas MacArthur
84th BRIGADE
167th Infantry Regiment
168th Infantry Regiment
151st Machine Gun Battalion

Lieutenant Colonel Cooper D. Winn
151st MACHINE GUN BATTALION

Captain Monroe A. Means
COMPANY D, 151st MACHINE GUN BATTALION
1st Lieutenant William Andres - 1st PLATOON (4 MG Squads)
2nd Lieutenant Roy G. Rhodes - 2nd PLATOON (4 MG Squds)
1st Lieutenant N. P. Parkinson - 3rd PLATOON (4 MG Squads)
1st Lieutenant John H. Geiszel - SUPPLY TRAIN

Captain Means was billeted across the street at the family of Herr Fritz Grebe. This man had no title, but he was wealthy. He had made a fortune during the war in a marmalade factory. Neighborhood gossip had it that when sugar became scarce, he would draw sugar from the German government to be used in the marmalade, but sell a large portion of the sugar for his own profit and finish the marmalade with saccharine. At any rate, his home was splendidly furnished inside with oriental rugs, hard wood floors, overstuffed furniture, tapestries on the walls, and a grand piano with a player roll attachment. Lieutenant Geiszel and Captain Means roomed here, and company officers' mess was to be in this place. We furnished beef, bacon, coffee, sugar, canned milk, butter, and white bread. They furnished green vegetables, cabbage, potatoes, and wine. Mrs. Grebe and her family of four ate at our table. We ate as one big family.

One day, Mrs. Grebe served us an excellent salad made from a raw green plant similar to lettuce. It was excellently seasoned. We had so few fresh green vegetables that we all complimented her highly on the salad and asked that she have a double portion next meal. She told us she had obtained this salad from a neighbor in exchange for second-hand coffee grounds and agreed to try to obtain a double portion next day. We furnished some money and told her to buy it if necessary.

In France and Germany, no part of any fertilizer was wasted. Every stable drains to a pool, pond, or barrel, where the water is kept and hauled out to spread on the fields. The manure is also piled outside and hauled away. When rain falls on the manure piles, it is drained off and collected in barrels. Every peasant has, as one of his necessary articles of equipment, a large tank on a two-wheeled cart so that he can haul water out to his fields and spread it as fertilizer. The next day after we had urged Mrs. Grebe to buy extra lettuce, about 9:00 in the morning, I passed the garden where this neighbor's lettuce was growing. A large two-wheeled cart had backed in and was fertilizing the lettuce bed. I kept my eyes on the garden during the morning, and half an hour later the woman came out to gather the lettuce that was to be served us at dinner. Mrs. Grebe prepared the salad in a double portion, but never understood why none of us touched it.

The Grebe family had two sons: Hans, age nine, and Fritz Herbert, age six. These boys were excellent youngsters and we enjoyed playing with them. The Grebe house faced the Rhine River, about five hundred yards away. Next to the Grebe house was the Castle of Count Ta Vegge. He was an Italian subject and owned a leather factory in this village. When Italy entered the war he was interned as an alien, but the civilians treated him kindly. His wife was an American girl and had gone to New York City at the outbreak of the war.

Colonel Winn and Lieutenant Turner had billets in his modern castle where battalion headquarters were established. This count brought out an American flag and proceeded to make us at home. He entertained all the officers of the battalion at a dinner in the evening and made the contents of his rare wine cellar available to us without stint. There were at least twenty-five kinds of wines, cordials, and liqueurs. I did not know anything about them and did not care or dare to attempt to find out much. I enjoyed greatly some of the Moselle wine and confined my refreshments to several glasses of that during the evening.

Early during our stay at Kripp, it was necessary to punish a German ex-soldier. At a place where some men from one of the Georgia companies were billeted in a German home, they always brought their food from the mess line into the kitchen table and ate it together indoors. Once the lady of the house came into the kitchen after they had finished and found a dirty mess kit lying on the table. In anger, she hurled it far out through the window. It fell at the feet of her husband, who was working in the yard with a pick, which he now drove through the mess kit. The American soldier reported to Colonel Winn, who felt this ex-soldier should be told in no uncertain terms that anything bearing the stamp "U.S.A." should be treated with respect.

The German was therefore arrested, tried, and assessed a small fine. He refused to pay and so was committed to the guard house. His relatives offered to pay the fine, but he refused to permit them and declared he would lay it out in jail. That night, however, the mischievous Corporal of the Guard brought blankets from the bed of one of the men who was always lousy. The German prisoner curled up for a night's rest in this vermin-infested bedding, but in half an hour's time his anger had cooled to such an extent that he sent word to his relatives to come and bail him out. It was too cold to sleep without blankets and too lousy to sleep with them. He was released about 11:00 P.M., after his relatives had paid his small fine. Of course, the news of the punishment of this man spread among the other inhabitants rapidly. It made such an impression that in our entire three months at Kripp, we had no other incidents of disrespect to the U.S.A.[2]

On Christmas Eve, Mr. and Mrs. Grebe entertained at a *Weihnacht* party. Hot punch was served in a flowing bowl. The Christmas tree was decorated and all had an excellent evening, singing Christmas carols in German and in English. The two children gave it the added touch of Christmas. At Sinzig, two miles away, a family by the name of Brache were intimate friends of the Grebes. On this Christmas Eve, they were invited down to celebrate with us. The family consisted of one brother probably 35 years of age, and two sisters still in their late 20s. They were good dancers, and with the player piano going we spent many winter evenings dancing on the hardwood floors of the Grebes' parlor. The brother had been a lieutenant in the German artillery. We learned from him that he had been in the German artillery battery that fired on Chateau St. Benoit while we were occupying the St. Mihiel Sector, where Sergeants Haire and White were wounded.

Christmas Day, the entire battalion was treated to the delicacy of fresh pork for Christmas dinner. In the evening, the men of our company assembled at the Hetlau and we had a Christmas program, during which I gave two readings, including, "That Old Sweetheart of Mine."

The residence of Herr Schmidt was a big white house on the corner of the main street as it intersected the Rhine River. The officers of B Company were billeted there. He also claimed to have an American wife and said she was living in New York City. He posed as an ex-secret service agent of the German government. He invited the officers of the entire battalion to his home one evening during the Christmas holidays. Champagne flowed like water. He would set out a glass for each officer, fill them, and all would drink to the health of America. Then he would break the stem of every glass and throw

2. This case of "Georgia justice" exemplifies both the sense of humor and practical aims of men in the 151st Machine Gun Battalion.

them into the street, stating, "My American guests are too honored to use a glass the second time. In Captain Schmidt's house, we furnish a new glass for every drink." So many glasses kept going out of the window that there seemed to be a constant sound of breaking glass on the pavement. Captain Schmidt was aided as host by another typically Prussian-type young man. The Baron von Negre, the man with whom I was billeted, was there also.

Some of the men of the other companies thought it would be a good joke to get this old Dutchman drunk. They therefore made it up that in turn each of about four of them would drink to the health of this old Baron, always ending with, "Bottoms up!" In this way, they hoped to get him "under the table" without any of them having to drink too much. They started out on glasses of Champagne, one at a time. The old Baron knew that the Champagne was costing him nothing and stood right up to the buffet and emptied each glass. He went a step further, and each time a man came up to drink with him he would insist on filling the glass again. The American soldiers could not phase him. He drank double each time, with each one of the four in turn, and soon the four found that they were getting more than was good for them and had to quit. The old Baron was still sailing along on an even keel drinking all four of them down.

Colonel Winn attended this party, but the next day he notified us that there would be no more such parties. It was quite apparent that Captain Schmidt was not spending his own money. We were convinced that he was still in the employ of the German secret service and his lavish spending of money was an attempt to gain the good will of the men of our army. They realized that President Wilson was going to have an important part in the Peace Conference and that the good will of the American Army would be something worth buying.

However, there was no order not to fraternize with our allies. Count Ta Vegge, the Italian subject interned in this village, was every bit as elaborate a host and much more gracious and pleasant in his attitude. He entertained the officers of our battalion purely as a matter of good will and hospitality. On the evening of December 31st, he gave us a New Year's party. General MacArthur came for the evening, and the Count also arranged for two American girls from the Y.M.C.A. Entertainment Bureau at Coblenz to spend the evening with us. They were excellent singers and dancers and we had a pleasant party. One had sung with the Minneapolis Symphony Orchestra. About 11:30, General MacArthur and his staff from Brigade Headquarters drove away and the girls went also.

Before the Armistice, our soldiers were constantly expressing their desire to "Get the Kaiser," "Go to Berlin," or "Get a Heinie." Another perhaps equally-voiced ambition was to heap the utmost of insult upon the Germans by urinating in their sacred Rhine River. (However, they never used that word. They had one more expressive of indignity.) On this last night of the old year, after General MacArthur and his party had gone, one of our captains[3] suggested that the closing moments of the old year would be the appropriate time for us officers to form in single file, march to the bank of the Rhine, "Column Left! Halt! Right Face! Fire at Will!" and thus pay our inverse respects to this historic river of the Germans. It was so agreed, but before we got started something delayed us until the old year was gone and it was then too late.

While at Kripp, I was requested by a private in B Company to defend him at Court Martial. He was charged with disobedience by one of his sergeants. Captains Brown and Means and Major Peacock were the court. The defendant was found guilty and fined 30 days pay. Although the sentence was very light for the charge, I felt that the man should have been cleared on the merits of the evidence.

Another day, I was named by Colonel Winn on a Board of Inquiry, along with Lieutenants Walker and Saye, to investigate the shooting of a man in A Company. While Sergeant of the Guard, Sergeant McClelland of B Company had entered a cafe where many Americans were drinking and arrested one man who was causing trouble. A friend of the man arrested threatened the sergeant, who drew his automatic. Then another friend pushed a bystander against the sergeant's gun. We found that the man shot was an innocent bystander in the line of duty, and neither he nor McClelland were held. The injured man recovered.

After New Year's, the company had plenty of time to rest, so we went into a period of close order drill and a study of the new Browning Machine Guns. Our old Hotchkiss equipment was turned in and we were equipped for the first time with the new Browning.[4] We did lots of range work in a gravel pit north of Kripp. This gravel pit had been dug out of the level plain about 40 feet deep and over a quarter of a mile square. When we descended in this pit, it made a perfect range for the entire battalion to fire at ranges as high as 400 meters.

About January 20th, I received a two-day leave to go to the town of Coblenz, which was the largest town in the American area. There the sight that stood out most in my mind was the Stars and Stripes floating above the famous German fort Ehrenbreitstein. Because of its prominence, location, and strength, this fort had, by tradition, become symbolic of German militarism. I also visited the famous monument to Kaiser Wilhelm I located at the junction of the Rhine and Moselle Rivers. It was a monument to the conquests of the first Kaiser of Prussian war fame in 1870, the last word in Imperialism. But now all was changed. Both were now being over-run and trampled under foot by men of a Republic from the other side of the Atlantic.

3. This must have been either Captain James H. Palmer (A Company), Algernon S. Brown (B Company), Ernest F. Travis (C Company), or Monroe A. Means (D Company). General George S. Patton, Jr., would fulfill the plan to take a leak in the Rhine River a generation later in World War II.

4. Several American divisions were equipped with French Hotchkiss machine guns in World War I. As they were traded in for Browning machine guns and the U.S. divisions headed for home, the Hotchkiss guns were given to the French government.

I spent two days and one night at Coblenz and, after attending a Y.M.C.A. show that evening in the "Festhuas," I went to the station to board a train back to Remagen. I followed instructions as I understood them from an American railway officer, went inside a coach standing there and, while waiting for the train to start, fell asleep. I was conscious sometime later of the train starting, but did not arouse myself.

What So Proudly We Hailed. Ehrenbreitstein at Coblenz, Germany, 1919. The American flag flying over this mighty fortress along the Rhine was proof positive to men in the Army of Occupation of Allied supremacy over Germany. *Editor's collection.*

A few hours later, I looked out of the window at a station we were passing and saw that it was a strange station. Instead of American soldiers, French soldiers were on guard. I got off at the next stop and found that I had been going in the opposite direction and was in the town of Bingen. The famous old Mouse Tower was there on the island in the river. This "fortunate" mistake was accounted for by the fact that all trains in this region were operated by the Allies as military trains. Soldiers were not charged for transportation. They need only show their leaves of absence at the station and could go where they pleased. I had no authority to be in Bingen, so could not get out of the station. Therefore, I took the next train back, and by breaking day I came down the beautiful Rhine Valley.

Thus, by accident I was able to see not only the tower at Bingen, but De Lorelei, the Blucher Monument, Der Kratz, the picturesque ruins at Falkenberg, Rheinstein, Reichenberg, Rheinfels, Sternberg, and Liebenstein, and the modern castles at Sonneck, Pfatz, St. Goar, Konigsberg, and Stolzenfels, the latter being one of the homes of the Kaiser. There were also many of the scenic cliffs which rose abruptly on both banks of the river with villages nestled below them and chapels located at secluded spots among them. One of the famous chapel ruins was those at Bachrach.

The conductor on this train was especially inclined to talk and explained many of these historical points as we passed through this most famous part of the Rhine Valley. He accused me of being German born and gave his reason as the pure Berlin German which I spoke, free from the low dialects to which he was accustomed. I denied the allegation.

I arrived at Kripp the morning of the 24th. Mail had come in the meantime and a card was waiting from my brother, Hugh. It told he was stationed at Coblenz in one of the famous old forts (Asterstein, just next to the famous Ehrenbreitstein). I showed the card to Colonel Winn and he immediately included me in a group that was going to Coblenz the next day, January 26th, which was my birthday. I had known that Hugh had sailed for France, but had no idea where he was until I received this card. He was equally surprised when he was called into the office of his commanding officer of his hospital unit. We had my birthday together and spent the afternoon and night in the city, went to a show put on by the American Entertainment Bureau, slept together in a soft bed at a hotel, and the next day had our photographs taken together.

He was a truck driver in the hospital unit. Eggs had always been a delicacy in the A.E.F.[5] I had none since we had been in Kripp. He knew they were a delicacy and asked me if I would like to take some home with me. He left me for a few minutes and came back with both overcoat pockets filled with eggs that he had slipped out of a crate where he had known plentiful supplies were kept for the men in the hospital, as well as the nurses and officers of the medical corps. I packed these in a box, and that night Hugh went back to Kripp with me for a visit. We took about two dozen back. The officers of D Company and the Grebes, of course, were delighted to be able to share these eggs. They decided to throw another big party that night in honor of my brother.[6] There were 66 empty liter wine bottles in the basement the next morning.

These two leaves that I had from the company were in our own divisional area. All of us coveted an opportunity for a regular 14-day leave back into France. We had heard of them for years, but none had ever had them. My opportunity came early in February. I had several hundred Francs and borrowed some more from Bill Andres. Then I boarded a military train back toward France. The train went down the Rhine Valley toward Coblenz and then down the Moselle to Metz. I spent a day in Metz sightseeing, then took the train on to Commercy, which I knew was the 35th Divisional Area. After much persuasion, I was able to engage a motorcycle with side car. A corporal drove me to

5. During their watch on the Rhine, a railroad car loaded with eggs was sent to the 42nd Division. The 167th Alabama Infantry Regiment happily switched it off at Sinzig and took possession of the entire load for themselves. They claimed it as compensation for a carload of tobacco their homefolk had sent them earlier, but never reached them (Reilly, 871). Eggs were prized indeed within the A.E.F.

6. It was quite unusual for officers - who normally did not fraternize socially with enlisted men - to throw a party in honor of a truck driver. This just goes to show how much men accustomed to field rations prepared in mass on rolling kitchens valued good food.

Paris Guns. Captured German artillery and mortars in Place de la Concorde, Paris, April 1919. The French were keen to show off their trophies of war to the public. *Editor's collection.*

More Paris Guns. Lieutenant Parkinson saw this collection of war booty when he was on leave in Paris. *Editor's collection.*

German A7V Tank. One of the centerpieces of the war booty on display in Place de la Concorde, Paris, April 1919. *Editor's collection.*

Birds of Prey. A row of captured and surrendered German aircraft adorn Place de La Concorde, Paris, April 1919. Lieutenant Parkinson grew so accustomed to German fighters that he did not even mention seeing these in Paris. *Editor's collection.*

the village, where Calvin E. Sutherd, one of my Kappa Delt friends, was billeted with the 130th Field Artillery. I walked in on him unannounced and we spent 24 hours together. I traveled all the next day through several villages in this area, trying to obtain permission for Sutherd to go back to Paris with me, but had to give it up.

My pass permitted me to go through Paris only for changing trains. We were not allowed more than 12 hours in Paris at any one time. I reached there early in the morning, spent the day there sightseeing, and when my time was up, took the train down to Lyon. After spending a few hours sightseeing in Lyon, I took the train back to Paris and again spent 12 hours there between trains.

I made headquarters at the Louvre Hotel, which had been taken over by the Y.M.C.A. In the lobby of this hotel I met Aviation Lieutenant Harold McNabb of Decatur. We took a sightseeing trip in a taxi through Paris. We visited Notre Dame Cathedral and Des Invalides, the famous French museum; we saw many relics of Napoleonic Wars, as well as relics of the World War. We also visited Napoleon's Tomb and saw the great panoramic painting, "Pantheon les Guerre." We saw many other sights, including the Bastille Monument,

Welcome to Pontanezen! The entrance and billeting office for Camp Pontanezen outside of Brest, France. Most American troops going to and from France in World War I passed through this camp. *Editor's collection.*

Arc de Triomphe, Champs Elysees, and L'Opera. That night we attended a show at the Follies Bergere, the famous theater of Paris. When my 12 hours time was up again I took a train out for Orleans, the city made famous by Joan de Arc. I bought a few souvenirs in this place and mailed them home. Again, I returned to Paris and had 12 hours more between trains. My money was running short, so I took the train back to Kripp and arrived a few days before my leave was up.

I found the battalion hurriedly making preparations to return to the U.S.A. Animals were being groomed to be turned in and new equipment and clothing were being drawn where necessary. About March 23rd, our division assembled in a plain near Remagen and was inspected by General Pershing.[7] It was the first glimpse I had of him. Immediately afterward, all animals were turned in and we began final preparations for the return trip home.

Camp Pontanezen Tents. The 151st Machine Gun Battalion endured several inspections, delousings, and labor details here before heading home. *Editor's collection.*

We had orders to entrain at Sinzig April 3rd. The night of April 2nd, the town of Kripp was in an uproar all night. Fires were burning in many places where old equipment, rubbish, and trash had been assembled during the last day's clean up. In one cafe, where during our three months in this region the men had been buying their beer, the proprietor had been very overbearing and had become unpopular, even though he sold good beer. Against orders, he had also bootlegged some schnapps and cognac. On this night, some of the men who had come to dislike him greatly took over his place to drink up the remaining supply of wine and liquor. They handed it over promiscuously without charge. When he protested, he got only a wine bottle over the head, which laid him out for the rest of the night. This, of course, was without the knowledge of any of the officers. It all happened in a few minutes, but it was the only incident of unfairness to Germans that I had known in the entire three months.

The next morning, at 6:00, the battalion formed, marched through the main streets of Kripp and headed for Sinzig. As we passed through the streets, the German population greeted us and cheered us. They had enjoyed our stay, not only because they enjoyed the Americans, but because the Americans had spent lots of money in this village, more than at any other time in their history. We marched to Sinzig and boarded the military train of American box cars. Division headquarters was on this train, and with them our battalion was the first train out of the Army of Occupation. We rode down the Rhine Valley and Moselle Valley through Metz, Toul, Verdun, and toward Paris. When we reached Paris, we could see the train was taking a belt line around.

7. Other primary sources demonstrate that Pershing's inspection was on March 16 (Means; Reilly, 864; White & Peavy; Wolf, 55).

Captain Means was wearing a new overseas cap that he had bought to wear home. He and I were leaning out the same window, taking a last view of the Eiffel Tower. By accident I knocked this new cap from his head while the train was going about thirty miles an hour. It was pure awkwardness on my part and made Captain Means very angry. I got the worst cussing that I had the whole time I had been in the army. Just a few minutes later the train stopped at a station where we were to stop forty minutes for dinner. As soon as the train stopped, I started running back down the track to recover Captain Means' cap. I planned to go down the track for twenty minutes, or until I found the cap. At the end of the twenty minutes, if I had not found the cap, I would turn around and return to the train before it started. I had only been gone twenty minutes when I heard the bugle sound. The men climbed on and the train pulled out. The orders had been changed and I was left stranded a few miles from Paris.

I recovered Captain Means' cap and took a train to Paris. I did not have a pass, but by making friends with a Frenchman I slipped by the guard at the station. I spent the afternoon and evening in Paris, and at 10:00 that night boarded a train for Brest, which I knew to be the destination of our military train. I traveled in a French sleeping car while the men of our train were traveling in box cars. By inquiring along the way, I learned that during the night my train had passed the troop train. I unloaded at St. Brieuc, and when the troop train came along rejoined Captain Means and delivered his cap. He apologized for swearing at me, but I thanked him that he had done so, because he gave me an excuse for another day in Paris.

Our train arrived in Brest April 6th. We detrained and marched out to Camp Pontanezen, where we were quartered in tents. After several inspections,

USS Minnesota. This battleship transported Lieutenant Parkinson and the 151st Machine Gun Battalion across the Atlantic back to the States. *Editor's collection.*

Company D, 151st Machine Gun Battalion. This photograph was taken at Camp Merritt, New Jersey, upon the Company's return from France. Lieutenant John H. Geiszel is seated in the front row to the right of the man holding the fox. To the right of Geiszel is Captain Monroe A. Means, Company Commander. Most of the enlisted men were replacements since so many original members had become casualties. Absent is Lieutenant N. P. Parkinson. He blew off the photo so he could link up with Florence North, whom he had been courting by mail during the war. *World War History & Art Museum (WWHAM) collection, Alliance, Ohio.*

Eye To Eye. N. P. Parkinson survived the war and lived to the age of 88. He is shown here on Christmas, 1961, about a month before his 72nd birthday. Seated beside him on the couch is his wife, Florence, whom be began courting long distance from France. The little guy is Parkinson's youngest grandson, Joel Parkinson (the editor), at two years of age. In later years, Grandad Parkinson easily held Joel's attention with war stories instead of a flimsy cardboard tube. *Photo courtesy of Marilyn Parkinson.*

delousings, and many labor details, we formed about noon on April 14th and marched down to the dock. A ferry took us out into the harbor and pulled alongside the Battleship *Minnesota.*[8] This was to be our transport home. The second in command of this ship was Lieutenant Commander John Saxer who, as a boy in high school, had lived just one block from my home in Centralia, Illinois. We stayed all night aboard this ship, weighed anchor the next day about 3:30 P.M., sailed out the harbor, and after eleven days on the water landed in New York City April 26th.

In college, Florence and I had sometimes taken birthday dinner together since we were both born January 26th. But that date in 1918 found me on the water sailing for France, so I wrote her a letter. That was the beginning of a correspondence which lasted through the war. Therefore, on Sunday, April 27th, I telephoned her in Washington, D.C., where she was employed at the War Risk Insurance Bureau. She took the train for New York City that night, and early the next morning, Monday, April 28th, we met at Pennsylvania Station. A year later we were married.

While I was in New York with Florence, the company at Camp Merritt posed for the photographer. That accounts for my not being included in this group.

After several days in Camp Merritt, New Jersey, our battalion was broken up into detachments. I had command of a detachment composed of all men from our battalion that were sent to Camp Custer, near Battle Creek, Michigan. There were also many other men from the division on this train. I was train commander and reported in due time with this detachment at Camp Custer, where the men were mustered out of service and given mileage to their respective residences. I was given two weeks leave of absence to visit home and returned to Camp Custer to be discharged May 26, 1919.

8. The *USS Minnesota* was damaged by a German mine on September 29, 1918. When she returned to service in March of 1919 the *Minnesota's* mission was to carry troops home.

APPENDIX A:

NARRATIVE OF THE ACTIVITIES OF D COMPANY, 151ST MACHINE GUN BATTALION, 42ND RAINBOW DIVISION, IN THE AMERICAN EXPEDITIONARY FORCES

BY CAPTAIN MONROE A. MEANS, COMMANDING

On the formation of the 42nd or RAINBOW Division, Companies I, K, L, and M, 4th Pennsylvania Infantry, were on August 13th, 1917, transferred to same as the 149th Machine Gun Battalion (Divisional).

The division was made up of selected National Guard units from 26 different states.

At the time of transfer, K Company was commanded by Captain James N. Lightner. The other officers were 1st Lieutenant —— Charles[1] and 2nd Lieutenant John H. Geiszel. Lieutenant Charles was detached from the Company and the following officers assigned to same: 1st Lieutenant Guy P. Brown (formerly a battalion adjutant in the 4th Pennsylvania Infantry), 1st Lieutenant Monroe A. Means, formerly of the 16th Pennsylvania Infantry Machine Gun Company, 2nd Lieutenant Charles C. Smith, and 2nd Lieutenant Leroy A. Peters, formerly with the 8th Pennsylvania Infantry. A number of men were also transferred at this time to give the Company full war strength of 172 men. The Company at the time of transfer was in the Federal service, having responded to the call of the President of July 15, 1917, but were still at the home armory at Lancaster, Pennsylvania, drilling and getting equipment in shape.

On August 24, 1917, the Company, along with the other units of the battalion, entrained for CAMP MILLS, LONG ISLAND, arriving there on the

1. Captain Means could not remember the first name of Lieutenant Charles.

25th. This was the mobilization camp of the division. Every effort was made to prepare the organization for overseas service. New equipment was drawn and the new organization completed. The designation of the companies were changed to A, B, C, and D, with K Company becoming B Company under the change. The organization started on a period of training directed chiefly at the physical development of the men for the hard service which it was anticipated they must endure in foreign service. Two months of this sort of training was completed. The only events of importance during this period were reviews: one held for the Secretary of War,[2] and one for Vice President Marshall.[3] The officers of the Company were increased to seven by the addition of 2nd Lieutenant William P. Andres, who was assigned to the Company September 19th. About the first of October, Lieutenant Guy P. Brown was detached from the Company and sent to NEWPORT NEWS in charge of a detail to take animals across for the battalion and the division. He never rejoined the Company.

The battalion embarked at HOBOKEN October 18, 1917, entraining at GARDEN CITY, LONG ISLAND, proceeding by train and ferry to HOBOKEN. The Company embarked with six officers and 168 enlisted men on the *USS PRESIDENT GRANT*, recently taken over from the Germans. Still, as it turned out, it was not in a good state of repair. After being out four days we were compelled to turn back on account of leaky boiler tubes. The vessel could not steam fast enough to keep up with the rest of the convoy. It took six days to limp back to port. We disembarked in a terrific downpour of rain, were loaded on a decrepit old ferry boat, and were towed to FORT TOTTEN, Long Island. The wind was blowing a gale, and along with the rain we expected every minute the old tub would sink.

Here at FORT TOTTEN we had more close order drills and hikes, but finally, November 14th, embarkation orders were again received. Being transferred by ferry to NEW YORK, we embarked on the WHITE STAR liner *CEDRIC*. The convoy was made up in HALIFAX harbor. The trip was uneventful, until we sighted the Scottish coast and the north headlands of Ireland. When subs were sighted the convoy was ordered to make for BELFAST harbor, which was finally done. We stayed there two days. Then, with plenty of destroyers as guard, we crossed the IRISH SEA, landing at LIVERPOOL. From there, we went by train to CAMP WINNAL DOWNS, WINCHESTER. Here we had our first contact with the English soldier. Everyone had a chance to see the historic old town of WINCHESTER and the wonderful old cathedral. We stayed here ten days, which to most of the boys was nine days too long, as we were living on English rations.

We went by train to SOUTHAMPTON, where we embarked on the *PRINCE GEORGE* for the trip across the Channel. This trip was a nightmare. There

2. Newton D. Baker was also the conceptual father of the 42nd Rainbow Division. It was his idea to build the 42nd Division with National Guard units drawn from multiple states.
3. Thomas R. Marshall was Vice President from 1913-1921.

was hardly a man who was not seasick. We landed at LE HAVRE, marching to Rest Camp No. 2—"rest camp" in name only. We stayed here about 36 hours. From here, we loaded on 2nd and 3rd class French coaches with practically no rations. The weather was very cold and there was no way of having a fire on the train. After an exceedingly cold three-day trip, we detrained at the little village of PREX LE FOUCH, marching from there to LEFFOL LE PETITE, where we had our first contact with the French people, as well as the French billets. Here the toughening process for the men was continued. At this time it was very cold, with considerable snow on the ground, which made outdoor work sort of a hardship. But there was very little complaint from anyone, as everyone knew this work had to be done to get the battalion in shape for active campaigning.

Orders came December 24th to move, by marching, to the 7th Training Area, movement to begin on December 26th. So after a very good Christmas dinner, with chicken as the main item brought from the Company Mess fund, along with a lot of other things, orders were given to pack up. No transportation had as yet been issued to the battalion. The men's shoes were in a terrible condition and there was no chance to get others. In fact, the battalion was short of a good many items of clothing, etc., besides a good deal of other equipment, although requisition after requisition had been turned in for same. A few trucks were furnished to carry the heavy baggage, but two trips had to be made. They had all kinds of trouble, as there was a good eight to ten inches of snow on the ground, with a fierce blizzard raging. The men's packs, all extra heavy, got soaking wet from the snow melting, making them doubly heavy and thus making it extra hard marching.

The first billet after a 30-kilometer march was at MILLIERES. Of course there was nothing but barns, etc., for the men to sleep in and no way of drying shoes or clothing, but there were no complaints. The next billet was at THIVET, no better than the preceding night. Of course, if the weather had been mild it would not have been so bad. On the 28th, we arrived at CHANCY after marching a good 60 kilometers. There was no room here for the whole battalion, so Companies A and B, along with the battalion headquarters, were billeted here. The other two companies went about five kilometers further to BEAUCHIM.

January 3rd, Captain James N. Lightner and 2nd Lieutenant William P. Andres, along with Captain Kestner of A Company, were ordered to the Machine Gun School at GROUNDERCOURT. At this time, the 42nd Division School of Fire was organized at BEAUCHIM, with Major Q. O. Reitzel in command of same, thus causing the battalion headquarters to move to BEAUCHIM. This left 1st Lieutenant M. A. Means in command of the town.[4] During this period, the Hotchkiss machine guns, carts, and equipment were issued, the carts being drawn by hand, with all equipment, from LANGRES, about eight kilometers. The next few weeks, the entire time was devoted to the nomenclature of the gun and the firing of same.

4. Captain Means was still at (and now in command of) Chancy.

January 25, 1918, an order was received detaching B Company from the 149th Machine Gun Battalion and attaching same to the 151st Machine Gun Battalion. Lieutenant M. A. Means reported in person to the Commanding Officer of the same January 26th and made arrangements for animals to haul carts and equipment, as no stock as yet had been received. B Company was ordered to take station at LEFFONDS, which they did by marching January 27, 1918. Battalion Headquarters, along with the rest of the battalion, were at this time stationed at VILLERS SUR SUIZE. January 28th, 1st Lieutenant M. A. Means went to the Divisional School of Fire, which had been removed to CHANOY. Second Lieutenant C. C. Smith was left in command of the Company. Lieutenant Means returned to the Company February 5th. February 8th, the 151st Machine Gun Battalion was concentrated at VILLERS SUR SUIZE, with B Company going into some new barracks there that had just been completed. February 11th, Captain James N. Lightner and 2nd Lieutenant William P. Andres rejoined the Company from school.

February 19th, we marched to and entrained at ROLAMPONT, for our first trip to the line. The battalion moved in two sections. C Company[5] detrained at MOYEN and marched to GURVILLERS on the 20th. February 22nd, an order was received attaching B Company to the Third Battalion, 168th Infantry, which was then stationed at BADMENIL. The Company reported there the same date by marching 28 kilometers and found we were part of the divisional reserve, about ten kilometers in the rear of the line in the LUNEVILLE SECTOR. The advance units of the division were at this time on the line. While at this station, 2nd Lieutenant C. C. Smith and 2nd Lieutenant Leroy A. Peters received orders detaching them from the Company and sending them back to the States. Later we moved up to the support positions at NEUFMAISONS. From here the officers, as well as most of the non-commissioned officers, made a 48-hour trip to the line for observation.

March 16th, the Company took over the front line machine gun positions in the C. R. CHAMOIS SECTOR. As we were short of officers at this time, 1st Lieutenant Ernest Travis of C Company was attached to the Company for a few days. We were in this sector only six days, but during that time a sad incident happened. Private Sylvester Sullivan was accidentally killed. Private Cecil Edgar was sitting at the entrance of his dugout, cleaning his pistol, when same was accidentally discharged, striking Sullivan back of the ear and killing him instantly. He was buried in a little cemetery at PEXONNE, the Chaplain of the 168th Infantry, Captain Robb,[6] officiating. This was the first death in the Company. Although by accident, it brought the realization of war near to all.

March 23rd, the division was relieved by the French. D Company marched back to NEUFMAISONS and from there the battalion was concentrated at RAMBERVILLERS. The only event of importance here was getting our

5. Captain Means probably meant "B Company", although he says "C Co." in the manuscript.
6. Captain Winfred E. Robb was chaplain of th 168th Infantry.

Christmas mail, over two months past due. The Company got 32 sacks of mail, and oh, what a jollification! We expected to go farther back, but higher authorities said otherwise, for on March 28th, we were ordered to take over our same old sectors, this time a divisional sector, where before there was a battalion of French, then a battalion of Americans. This same date, March 28th, orders were received changing B Company to D Company, 151st Machine Gun Battalion.

We marched to, and again went into reserve, at BADMENIL, then a couple days later took over the 1-B, or support positions. It was at this time that 2nd Lieutenant Nellis P. Parkinson and 2nd Lieutenant John F. Noxon, Jr., were assigned to the Company March 31, 1918.

April 14th, we again took over our old positions in the C. R. CHAMOIS SECTOR. We put in 21 days during this tour of front line duty, then back to the 1-B line for eight days. May 10th, we were ordered to take over the machine gun positions in the VILLAGE NEGRE SECTOR, to the right of the C. R. CHAMOIS SECTOR. The positions here were not well sited and new ones were ordered constructed. Thus, part of the work of the Company during this time was building new positions and new dugouts. During our 16 days in this sector there was considerable activity, but no casualties in D Company In fact, as soon as the Americans went into the sector the first time things began to liven up.

On the night of our relief by the 168th Regimental Machine Gun Company, we were very lucky; our last man got out a few minutes after midnight and a few minutes after 1:00 A.M., the enemy put over a very heavy projector gas and gas shell attack. The Company that relieved us lost their captain, who died before they got him to the hospital. Their second in command and a number of their men were badly gassed. Company D, although on the 1-B line, had considerable trouble, as they were shelling the rear areas, searching out batteries and support positions. D Company suffered three casualties as follows: 2nd Lieutenant John F. Noxon, 1st Sergeant Russel H. Dudley, and Private Charles W. Anderson, slightly wounded.

It was about this time that 1st Lieutenant Baumet and 2nd Lieutenant Ackley were attached to the Company, but were not with it long; they were soon assigned to the 168th Machine Gun Company. The headquarters. of the Company, while on the 1-B line, was at PEXONNE, and the men, although much scattered in their positions on this line, were fairly comfortable.

After completing an eight-day period on the 1-B line, we again took over our old positions in the C. R. CHAMOIS SECTOR. It was at this time that 1st Lieutenant[7] Earl Olsen[8] was transferred from Company A, same battalion, and assigned to D Company for duty. June 16th, Captain James N. Lightner,

7. Actually, Earl Olsen was still a 2nd Lieutenant at this time. He had his physical examination prior to promotion on August 9, 1918 (Parkinson; Orders from Turner).

8. Means consistently spelled this lieutenant's last name as "Olsen" while Parkinson has it as "Olson". The editor retained the spellings as given in each source.

acting under a Corps order, was transferred to duty in the Services of Supply, leaving 1st Lieutenant M. A. Means in command of the Company.

June 18th, about 7 P.M., the enemy suddenly threw over a very heavy gas shell and gas projector attack on the shell-torn town of BADONVILLER, where Company headquarters were, and on the front line and support trenches (some of the trenches running into the town). Gas masks had to be worn for over four hours and should have been worn much longer, as a number of the men were gassed from slight concentration later. It takes mustard gas some time to get out of the ground, especially in wet weather, as it was then. D Company suffered 21 casualties in this attack, as follows:

Acting 1st Sergeant Roy G. Rhoads[9]
Sergeant George L. Stark
Privates Earl J. Ryan
Charles Beamsderfer
Robert Shipmen
Jacob L. Denlinger
Frank M. Downs
Jay H. B. McGinnis
Charles J. Reemsnyder
Ramond Proffitt
Sergeant John J. Kipphorn

Corporal Walter R. Pennell
Clarence Denlinger
Leverette E. Bishop
Burnell Imhoff
David W. Beck
Rowan F. Foulke
Frank Myers
Ernest Cramblet
Irl Rogers
John W. Shay

Some of these men were very badly gassed, but most of them got back to the Company later in the game.

The night of June 20th, we were relieved by the French and portions of the 77th American Division. It was very dangerous getting to the rear, as the enemy was shelling considerably, but by good luck D Company escaped without any more casualties.

Everyone was very tired of trench warfare and very glad to be relieved. The life there was very monotonous. The only thing to vary the monotony would be harassing fire by indirect methods on cross roads and roads in rear of the enemy's lines. Very little sleep was had while on front line duty, with a "stand-to" or "alert" every evening and morning from about 4:30 A.M. until break of day, at which times every man would have to be at his post. Then, of course, some guns were posted for anti-aircraft work. Hardly a day passed but they had some work to do. Then, of course, there were a great many false alarms. A number of heavy raids were staged by the enemy, but never while D Company was holding a front line position. But no matter how strong the raiding parties were, nor how heavy the preliminary artillery barrage was, they never crossed the front line trench in the divisional area. A great many times his dead were picked from our barb wire and out of No Man's Land.

9. Means consistently spelled this man's last name as "Rhoads" while Parkinson usually rendered it as "Rhodes". As with the case of Lieutenant Olsen (Olson), the editor retained the spellings as given in each source.

Our field and combat trains during this period were kept at what was called the INDIAN VILLAGE, about five kilometers in the rear of the line, but it was always possible to have our field kitchens within a kilometer or so of the front line trench. From that point, ration details carried the rations to the different posts on the line.

The night of June 20th, the Company was billeted in NEUFMAISONS. The night of June 21st, the Company marched to RAMBERVILLERS, and from there to THAON-LES-VOSGES, a very pretty, clean town, where we got two good nights' rest. At this point, we entrained C and D Companies on one section with the commander of D Company as train commander. We headed north and detrained at VITRY-LE-FRANCOIS, then marched to ST. AMAND, where the battalion did range work and had a general clean-up.

June 29th, moving orders came once more. That night, the battalion marched to MARSON and thence on the 30th to TILLOY-ET-BELLAY, where it again took station for the practice of, and attack formation preparatory to, minor offensive operations which it was then intended the 42nd Division, assisted by two French divisions, should carry out on the CHAMPAGNE front. Orders of battle again necessitated a change in orders upon request of the French General staff for American reinforcements on the CHAMPAGNE front. In anticipation of a new German offensive in that sector, the 42nd U.S. Division was placed at the disposal of General Gouraud, commanding the Fourth French Army.

July 4th, acting under orders of General GOURAUD,[10] the 151st Machine Gun Battalion was sent to SUIPPES, where it arrived on the morning of July 4th after marching a good 30 kilometers and went to bivouac for the day under such shelter as the terrain afforded. That night, the companies were once more attached to infantry battalions, with D Company being attached to the 3rd Battalion of the 168th Infantry for orders. The only information he had of his whereabouts was that his headquarters was in a large piece of woods shown on the map. The roads were a mass of troops and transportation, but luckily the Germans were not shelling. Colonel Bennett[11] could not be found, but the 2nd Battalion Commander was finally roused out of a shack in the woods and we found out what we were to do. After considerable delay, a guide was finally found that guided the Company until we got in touch with Major Brewer,[12] in command of the 3rd Battalion, 168th Infantry, already on the line. The carts and all animals were sent back to CAMP NANTIVETTE.

In the morning, the sector was thoroughly reconnoitered. The trenches and everything were found to be in bad condition. The enemy seemed to be unusually quiet, so Company headquarters was established in a little shack in the woods. There was very little shelter for the men in case of a heavy bombardment. All time possible was put in getting shelter, repairing emplacements,

10. General Henri Joseph Eugene Gouraud.
11. Colonel Ernest R. Bennett commanded the 168th Infantry Regiment.
12. Major Guy S. Brewer.

and cleaning out trenches. Also time was spent in familiarizing officers and men with the plan of defense of the section, the nature of the terrain ahead, and the prospective duties in the event of an enemy attack.

The French troops, holding the first line positions ahead of our own line, continually carried out successful night and day raids on the enemy lines, capturing many prisoners and gaining much information which was to prove valuable to the defending troops later on. After having received two warnings of an impending enemy attack which failed to materialize, the night of July 14th, shortly before midnight, information was given out by the French Headquarters that the long expected German offensive was scheduled to commence at midnight.

Anticipating the enemy's preparatory barrage, the American and French artillery commenced a heavy barrage fire on the German front at midnight. Almost before our men could seek shelter in the few available dugouts near their positions, the enemy's barrage commenced. The artillery action was terrific, a barrage such as our men had never witnessed, being placed blanket-like over the whole of the Allied front in that sector. That was just one steady roar. The barrage lasted all that night and the next day. The infantry attack started at 4 A.M., but did not quite reach our positions. The attack reached some sections of the divisional sector, but never a trench manned by Americans.

Two men were recommended for DSC: Private Raymond Bryson from Lancaster, Pennsylvania, and Private George A. Rodman from Modeso, California.[13] They were runners attached to Company Headquarters. It was necessary to send word out to some of the machine gun positions during the worst of the bombardment. These two went without a word. The following men were wounded: Privates Robert Bond, H. E. Loucks, Chas. L. Miller, Wayne McLaughlin, G. Karabetos, G. W. Rittenhouse, Edward W. Bair, Joseph A. Earley, and William Imhoff.

The little shack where Company headquarters had been established had not been touched. In Major Brewer's shack, a shell came in the room where he slept. One machine gun got a direct hit. The barrel was wound around the limb of a tree. On another the tripod was smashed. A shell very nearly tipped out one of the pill boxes with Lieutenant Olsen and gun crew inside. Lieutenant Andres, with one of his sections, was cramped in a narrow trench with about six inches of dirt overhead; shells hit all around, but fortunately no direct hits were made. Lieutenant Parkinson had a small dugout for some of his men, but it would not have stopped anything larger than a 77. Heavy shelling continued on the 16th, 17th, and 18th.

The night of the 18th, or morning of the 19th, orders were received to move out with everything, guns and all ammunition. D Company had upwards of 80,000 rounds of ammunition on the line. The echelon had been forced to move from CAMP NANTIVETTE to positions in the woods directly back of SUIPPES, so it was some ten kilometers in rear of the line. Lieutenant John

13. According to Lieutenant Parkinson both were killed by shell fire.

H. Geiszel had been sent back during the day of the 18th to get in touch with same, and fortunate it was for the Company that such an efficient officer was back there on the job. He got the different orders there a short time before they were received on the line. He brought everything—guns and ammunition carts, including combat wagons—up in less than two hours, reaching the lines, or place where the equipment was carried to, before 2:00 A.M. Everything was moved out before bright daylight, although the roads were in a horrible condition and there was considerable shelling. D Company was the only one in the battalion to remove all their equipment that night.

The battalion marched back by companies to CAMP NOBLOTTE, a large French troop camp, and from there to a small town SARRY, close to CHALONS. Here the men had a chance to get into the city for a day and Lieutenants Means and Geiszel had a chance to buy some much-needed equipment, as they had lost everything except what they had on their person the night of July 17th.

The battalion marched to and entrained at COOLUS, A and B Companies leaving one night and C and D the next. The enemy bombing planes were very active here, but the train commander, 1st Lieutenant M. A. Means, had caused eight of the old reliable Hotchkiss guns to be mounted on the quay in addition to the four French guns already in position. Sure enough, the bombing planes came over. In fact, they made two attacks, but without success, as the machine gun barrage drove them off.

This time everyone seemed to know where we were going, namely into the CHATEAU THIERRY fight. We skirted the edge of the 3rd Battalion, 168th Infantry. Here a message was received stating that Harry White, who had been sent to the hospital sick, had died of pneumonia. A number of replacements were also received here.

The night of July 24th, the entire battalion, with their respective infantry battalions, were loaded onto camions (trucks). After an all-night ride, during which the men had no chance to sleep owing to rough roads and the crowded condition of the trucks, arrived and unloaded at EPIEDS with their equipment and machine guns, including ammunition. The field and combat trains, together with all mule carts, had been left behind to make the trip up by road. The division immediately moved up and relieved the worn out 26th Division. D Company, along with the infantry battalion they were operating with, were placed in close support in the BOIS DE FERE, just south of the CROIX ROUGE FARM. The movement into the support positions was a very trying one. The men, as well as the officers, had to carry guns and ammunition a good four kilometers over roads and trails. They simply dropped in their tracks they were so nearly played out, but on a check of the Company being made, only one man was missing: A. H. Breitigan, who later turned out to be a casualty. He was hit by a piece of shell and died in the hospital a few days later. That night, July 25th, the enemy shelled the woods very hard, but there were no casualties in D Company. Although shells landed among and all around, every man had dug a fox hole and luckily no direct hits were made.

On the 26th, with the roads, woods, and trails under heavy shell fire, we started forward to take over from the front line battalions. Just as we started, three of D Company were wounded: Harry R. Wright, Aaron Jenkins, who later died in evacuation hospital, and Charles R. Wagner. A few minutes later one was killed (Julius M. Lyons) and four others wounded: Benj. E. Keenen, Sylvester Furlow, Clifford Boden, and Henry J. Pearson. The shells were bursting all around us.

Finally a halt was called. It was time, for it was so dark we could hardly see. The Company commander went forward and found we were to stay there for the night. It happened that we were near some old German dugouts. They were a Godsend, for it was raining hard; they also gave protection against shell fire. Here Sergeant Christopher H. Demuth found us, bringing rations. Our train had come forward overland and Lieutenant Geiszel, who was in charge, was doing everything possible to get rations up to us.

The next afternoon we took up the advance. The enemy had been driven out of the CROIX ROUGE FARM and the woods in our immediate front, so we took up the advance, skirting the edge of another part of BOIS DE FERE, all in single file. Here, the infantry company ahead of us got lost from the rest of the battalion, thus causing us to be lost. Late that night we established liaison. This was due to Sergeant Isaac Weidman, who went through the worst kind of shell fire to get in touch with the infantry battalion commander and later guided the Company to the position designated. (He was seriously wounded the next morning.) Before moving, Sergeant Demuth again got rations to us; not much, but every little bit helped at that time. He also, under the direction of the Company commander, brought ammunition forward and established an ammunition dump in the edge of the BOIS DE FERE as far forward as it could be brought. There was only one casualty this day: John C. Kiehl, wounded. He was attached to the infantry battalion headquarters as a runner.

At 5:30 A.M., July 28th, orders were received to send one platoon to support the first infantry wave (Lieutenant Parkinson's platoon was sent) and to follow closely with the rest of the Company for the jump-off across the OURCQ River and the heights beyond. There were a good 1-1/2 kilometers of open ground gradually sloping down to the stream, with direct machine gun and artillery fire covering same. The heights, including HILL 212, were taken, with machine gun fire from our guns of D Company, under Lieutenant Andres, assisting materially in clearing the Germans out of the wheat on top of HILL 212. At this time, three guns of Lieutenant Parkinson's platoon were on the right of the infantry battalion and the other gun on the left, all doing very good work. Lieutenant Olsen's platoon was held under cover as a reserve. The casualties in his platoon had been heavy in crossing the open ground. Before crossing the stream, he was compelled to leave two of his guns behind, but got nearly all his ammunition forward. Lieutenant Olsen used a captured German gun this day to good advantage in reducing some back flank fire we were receiving. As the French on our right were not on a line with us, it left our flank exposed, as we were the extreme right of the division. It was our duty to protect the flank, which was being done by Lieutenant Parkinson's platoon. All day the enemy fire was exceedingly heavy.

The little town of SERGY, in our immediate front, was taken and retaken three different times, finally remaining in the hands of the Americans. All guns of D Company assisted all possible in this work with both overhead and direct fire, and also assisted materially in repulsing a number of strong counterattacks. Ammunition ran very short. It was almost impossible to get back to the ammunition depot on account of the heavy fire, but under cover of darkness the supply was replenished.

On the 29th, an effort was made to drive the enemy out of the woods on our right front. Lieutenants Andres' and Olsen's platoons did some very good work here, Lieutenant Olsen using some captured German guns in addition to his own. Finally, on August 2nd, after the French on our right had been relieved by the 32nd American Division, the enemy again started to retreat. The pursuit was immediately taken up, but contact could not be maintained, as everyone was too nearly played out.

From the night of July 27th until this time the Company had two very scant meals. Dysentery was prevalent, as the only water to be had for drinking came from the OURCQ River, with a number of dead Germans and animals as well as dead Americans in same. Finally, on the night of August 2nd, we were relieved by the Fourth American Division. We could not have gone much farther. At that time we were in the FORET DE NESLES, north of the town of NESLES. The advance units of the division were relieved about two kilometers south of he VESLE River. We marched back to the BOIS DE FERE and went into bivouac. Our casualties from July 28th were as follows:

WOUNDED	WOUNDED	KILLED
Lester L. Litner	H. A. McCullom	Corporal M. L. Moore
John R. Miller	Corporal Fred Roberts	Fred E. White
James W. Lapham	Samuel Gatchell	Martins S. Cover
Dewey Clark	William J. Winnerling	David T. Davis
Joseph H. Myers	Edward A. Nixdorf	Carrol Fanus
Earl H. Ryan	Corporal J. H. Westerhoff	John G. Walter
John F. Hall	Elwood Y. Fishel	John Harkcom
Sergeant I. G. Weidman	John Stiffel	
George Smith	Charles W. Houck	
MecLeon B. Messer	Walter W. Brown	
Charles Kiscaddin	Lester Leaman	
Sergeant Warren B. Frey	Wilbur A. Gruver	
H. M. Fawber	George W. Sidwell	
Corporal Benj. Shaffer	Joseph L. Meither	
Samuel Resh	Jospeh Kilpatrick	
Walter Meekins	Mechanic Ernest F. Roth	
P. D. Kissinger		

The following men were recommended for DSC for valorous services during this engagement and advance.

Corporal Benjamin L. Shaffer, for handling his gun squad in a superior manner while detached from his platoon commander and continuing to direct same after being badly wounded.

Sergeant Robert E. Deetz, for sticking to the guns of his section after the infantry had fallen back and left them exposed and keeping the guns in action, thus assisting materially in repulsing a strong counterattack and greatly assisting the infantry in their forced retirement of a few hundred yards.

Sergeant Isaac G. Weidman, for establishing liaison with the infantry, later guiding the Company commander to the infantry battalion commander, and in addition the Company to its new location, all under the heaviest kind of shell fire.

Sergeant Christopher H. Demuth, for the bringing of rations and ammunition under the fiercest kind of shell fire. Sergeant Demuth was a big help to his Company commander in every way, always ready and willing to do whatever was required of him, no matter what the situation was.

Samuel Gatchel, Private, repeatedly went through the heaviest kind of shell fire to deliver important messages.

Corporal Charles E. Stumpf, while acting as a runner, repeatedly went through the heaviest kind of shell fire to deliver important messages, always returning promptly and ready for more work. He was also recommended for the same reason while the Company was in the CHAMPAGNE region. Sergeant Stumpf was absolutely fearless and a big help to his Company commander in every way.

Corporal Charles M. Keagy, for sticking with his platoon Sergeant when his section was in a very exposed position after the infantry had fallen back, working one of the guns in his section, helping materially in repulsing a strong counter-attack.

1st Sergeant Roy G. Rhoads was recommended for a commission for his work during this advance. Sergeant Rhoads was ready and willing at all times to do any work required of him, acting as a section leader and bringing rations and ammunition to the line. He was invaluable to his Company commander. In October, while the battalion was in the Argonne, Sergeant Rhoads got notice of his promotion.

The battalion remained in bivouac in the BOIS DE FERE north of BEUVARDES until August 10th. The main work here was getting cleaned up, replacing lost equipment, getting the men deloused, and giving everyone a chance to get a few square meals and regain some strength.

August 9th, 1918, 1st Lieutenant Monroe A. Means received an order promoting him to the rank of Captain under date of July 31st.

August 10th, under orders from Division Headquarters, the entire battalion marched to LA CHARITE, close to CHATEAU THIERRY, where they bivouacked that night. August 11th the march was resumed, reaching BOURE-

SCHES that afternoon, where a halt of two days was made. On the 14th, the battalion marched to TANQUEAUX a couple of kilometers further, but the officers were billeted in CHAMIGNY, except one officer with each Company who stayed in TANQUEAUX. At this point, the first leaves that had ever been granted the battalion were permitted, 10 percent being granted 48 hours leave in PARIS.

August 18th, the Company marched to and entrained with C Company at LA FERTE-SOUS-JOUARRE. Captain M. A. Means was the train Commander, arriving and detraining at BOURMONT on the 20th and marching to and joining the rest of the battalion at SAUVILLE the same day.

In this area, the battalion settled down to more or less permanent billets, with orders to carry out a five-week training schedule. A few days were allowed to get men deloused, clean up their clothes, and draw new equipment where needed.

Then training was taken up. The battalion commenced a series of attack maneuvers of attack formation in support of an infantry battalion. But this training was brought to a sudden close, for on the 28th of August orders were received to move that night. After hurried preparations, the battalion cleared SAUVILLE at 9 P.M. in pouring rain, arriving on the morning of August 30th at BULGNEVILLE, where it remained that day in bivouac, moving again at sundown to GIRONCOURT. At GIRONCOURT, orders were received suspending the movement of the organization. Replacements were received here.

September 4th, the march was again resumed. We bivouacked at BATTIGNY on the 5th and moved again that night to THUILLY AUX GROISELLES, where billets were secured and the battalion remained until the night of the 7th. Marching that night carried the battalion to bivouac four kilometers south of TOUL, where it remained during the 8th and marched that night in a terrific rain through TOUL to bivouac in the woods near SANZEY. A short move, again the night of the 9th, over almost impassable roads placed the battalion in concealment in the woods in the rear of the lines back of SEICHEPREY. It was at this place the orders covering the ST. MIHIEL offensive were received.

According to the orders received, the 151st Machine Gun Battalion was to attack in support of the 84th Infantry Brigade on the right of the Division's sector. On the 10th, the battalion commander, along with his Company commanders, went to the prospective positions for attack to reconnoiter the ground, select such emplacements as were possible, and prepare the necessary fire data.

On the evening of the 11th, the battalion moved to and took over its position in the jump-off trench. The battalion was in position before midnight, relieving sections of the 89th American Division. This was an exceedingly hard relief. The rain was coming down in torrents and it was almost impossible to get through the soft sticky mud.

D Company was on the left of the battalion in the edge of the BOIS DE JURY to cover the advance of the 2nd Battalion of the 167th Infantry. The field and combat trains were under cover near MANDRES.

In this offensive, the battalion was able to act, for the first time, as an individual organization under its own commander, and not placed under the command of the infantry battalion commanders.

The attack started with a terrific artillery barrage by our massed artillery at 1:00 A.M. The first wave of the attacking infantry went over at 5:00 A.M. under cover of an overhead barrage from our machine guns. The machine gun companies took up the advance close after the first waves of infantry, holding themselves in readiness to support or protect any portions of the line that might be held up.

The first three hours of this advance were rather warm. After that it was more like a Sunday walk across the mountains.

D Company, at this time, was short of officers. 1st Lieutenant Earl Olsen had been transferred back to A Company and 1st Lieutenant Nellis P. Parkinson[14] had been transferred to B Company. 2nd Lieutenant John H. Geiszel, instead of being in charge of the train, was commanding the Third Platoon. 1st Sergeant Roy G. Rhoads was in command of the 2nd Platoon and 2nd Lieutenant William P. Andres was in command of the 1st Platoon. Mess Sergeant Hiram Troop and Stable Sergeant George W. Zeiders were in charge of the echelon.

D Company had a couple of rather tight places. In one place just south of the SONNARD WOODS, a German machine gun nest was holding up the advance. The Company commander crawled forward through the mud with a couple runners and discovered a slight haze coming from the edge of the woods where the Germans were concealed. He had one of his runners crawl back (the crest that they had come over was being swept by machine gun fire) with orders to have two guns dragged forward. This was done. Lieutenant Geiszel crawled forward with them. The man (Private C. J. Reemsnyder) who attempted to put the first gun on the tripod was shot through the temple and killed instantly. But the guns, under cover of a shallow trench, were soon put in action, and as it turned out had direct fire on the German guns. The range was not over 250 yards. In a few minutes the infantry were able to advance without any more trouble.

A little further on we ran into heavy machine gun fire coming from our right front. The only way men could advance was by crawling or running from shell hole to shell hole. The Company Signal Corporal, Frank A. Cramblet, was killed and one of his runners, James E. Patrick, wounded within six feet of the Company commander as they were diving for the same shell hole. A few minutes later Lieutenant John H. Geiszel, Private Wm. Taylor, another runner, Wm. Dixon, Charles Gleason, Jacob P. Herr, and Leon M. Madlem were wounded. This was close to the town of ESSEY. That night we dug in just north of PANNES, close to the town BENEY, and prepared to resist any

14. Both Olsen and Parkinson were still 2nd lieutenants at this time. Parkinson and Andres were both promoted to 1st lieutenant a few days later on September 19, 1918 (GHQ Special Orders 262).

counter-attacks that might develop, but none came. The next morning, the advance was resumed and the final objectives were reached without further casualties.

We were ordered to dig in and organize the sector. C and B Companies were sent back in support; A and D Companies remained in the line. The CHATEAU OF ST. BENOIT was being organized as a strong point on the line until the Germans ran up a railroad gun, a 310mm, and blew same up. At least what wasn't blown up burned down. The 3rd Platoon of D Company, under Sergeant Walter Gruger, who had been in command of same after Lieutenant Geiszel was wounded, was seeking shelter along with a good many infantrymen in the cellars of same at the time, but fortunately none of the men were injured. We started to dig dugouts, reinforcing same with German elephant iron and timbers. Emplacements were dug and occupied by Captain James Palmer of A Company and Captain M. A. Means, D Company. A barrage was fired here that was a very big help to our infantry in raiding the town of HAUMONT. All the time, the enemy continued to lay an intermittent harassing artillery fire over the entire front, but the work of organizing the sector was never seriously hindered.

On the 15th, three more casualties had occurred: Corporal Gerald H. Gochnauer and Privates Paul H. Harmon and Carl Werner, all gassed. On the 22nd, Private V. A. Munyon was wounded. The two battalion Sergeant Majors were both wounded during this period. Battalion headquarters was in the old CHATEAU when same was blown up.

The occupation of the ESSEY-PANNES Sector came to an end September 27th, when the battalion was relieved and marched to MARBOTTE Barracks, near APREMONT, after spending two nights (September 28th and 29th) at NONSARD.

At MARBOTTE Barracks, the battalion loaded on camions (trucks) and after an all-night ride unloaded at SERAYCOURT, which the battalion reached the morning of October 1st. There they remained in billets until October 4th, when they marched to BRABANT, reaching there the afternoon of the 5th, and marched from there to bivouac in the BOIS DE MONTFAUCON on the 6th. From October 6th until the 10th, the battalion remained in this bivouac with rain. Most of the time the mud was ankle deep and it rained practically all the time. We were also subjected to occasional harassing fire from the enemy batteries and also had a few visits from their bombing planes. During this period the division was part of the Army Reserve.

October 10th, orders were received for the battalion to move into position in rear of a portion of the line held by the 1st Division near EXERMONT.

The 42nd Division had been placed in the 5th Corps and was to take up the advance through the ARGONNE which had been carried to that point by other divisions of that Corps.

Accordingly, on October 10th, the entire battalion moved to ECLISFONTAINE. The roads were under considerable shell fire during this move, and in the bivouac that night shells were falling all around. On the 11th, the battalion and company commanders reported as per orders to the headquarters of the 2nd Infantry Brigade, 1st Division, but there was no time for reconnoitering, as the relief had to be made that night. Guides were promised. That night, the relief was made under the worst possible conditions, with B and D Companies on the line and the rest in reserve. Guides failed to show up, thus causing delay while under shell fire with considerable gas, but finally guides were secured. The night was very black, the valleys and woods were full of gas, *and the mud*—enough said. The guides caused D Company to become lost twice, but at last, under heavy shell fire, the relief was completed and it seemed like a miracle that it was without any casualties.

We found ourselves on top of HILL 263. The field and combat trains remained at ECLISFONTAINE, with the exception of the rolling kitchens, which moved up to a point under cover where the reserve was located. Scarcely had we gotten into position when orders were received to deliver a protective barrage in support of an infantry attack. The 84th Brigade, in liaison with the 32nd American Division on the right, was to reduce a portion of the BOIS DE ROMAGNE, including HILLS 288 and 242, in an effort to break the German line of defense known as the KRIEMHILDE STELLUNG, the attack working in the general direction of LANDRES-ET-ST. GEORGES. Accordingly, on the 13th careful reconnaissance was made by all officers of the battalion and positions for all guns were selected on the forward slope of HILL 263. This position gave our guns a commanding view of the terrain over which the infantry was to advance and furnished a clear field of fire over the enemy's trenches and as far back as LANDRES-ET-ST. GEORGES. Positions were prepared, each company digging in as much as possible to protect them from the enemy shell fire to which they were exposed. From these positions the battalion fired a terrific overhead barrage, which was very successful. The KRIEMHILDE STELLUNG line, the last organized position of the Germans, was broken.

Later, from the same positions, the battalion fired overhead barrages at the taking of MUSARDE FARM, TUILIERIE FARM, and the COTE DE CHATILLON. Every gun of the battalion was employed. The terrain was exceedingly well adapted to the work in hand, and every foot of the enemy's trenches was covered. This so perfectly that the attacking troops were able to advance almost to their objective without being subjected to a heavy fire.

October 20th, we were ordered back, bivouacking that night at EXERMONT. The enemy was very active, with bombing planes as well as considerable shelling this night. The next day, D Company was ordered back to its same old positions, the rest of the battalion remaining in reserve. October 31st, all companies of the battalion returned to their old positions. That night, the 2nd American Division passed through us, relieving the infantry of the 42nd Division.

The morning of November 1st, all the machine gun battalions were in position and fired a continuous two and a half hour barrage over the heads of the 2nd Division infantry before the attack commenced. An overhead moving barrage, after the infantry attack debauched, continued this latter fire as long as safe clearance over the infantry could be had. When the 2nd Division advance waves had gotten within the danger zone of our guns, the battalion was automatically relieved and returned to EXERMONT, remaining in bivouac there during the day and night of November 1st.

During all the operations of the MEUSE-ARGONNE fighting, the liaison between the field and combat trains had been perfectly maintained in spite of every difficulty of impassable roads and incessant shell fire. Men in the front lines were fed, almost without exception, twice a day, and the ammunition supply was never in doubt, though both food and ammunition had to be brought to the lines through a valley subjected at all times to heavy shell fire from the enemy's batteries and through the worst kind of sticky mud. Our casualties in D Company were as follows. (We were in fact very lucky, for no one had been killed and not many wounded.): Sergeants Clifford W. Dudley and Howard P. Achey, and Privates Blake Carpenter, Herbert Churchill, Frank Seiders, Paul B. Herr, Raymond E. Dennis, Lewis J. Matt, and Chester H. Victor.

Upon its relief by the 2nd Division, the 42nd Division was placed under command of the Commanding General 1st Corps,[15] and under orders this battalion was moved the morning of November 2nd toward SOMMERANCE. Due to the crowded and impassable traffic conditions, the order was changed after the movement had commenced and the battalion went in to bivouac that night on a hillside south of SOMMERANCE in a pouring down rain.

New orders on November 3rd moved the battalion to bivouac just north of IMECOURT, and on the 4th to bivouac along the HARAUCOURT-FONTENCY Road, just north of BUZANCY, where orders were received for the division to again enter the front line on the 5th, the lines then resting just north of ST. PEIRREMONT.

Pursuant to these new orders for attack, the battalion moved forward on the 5th. The line companies took up their positions with the infantry north of ST. PIERREMONT, while the field and combat trains moved up to ST. PIERREMONT and went into billets there. The advance commenced almost as soon as our troops reached the line, the enemy having retreated so rapidly after the attack of November 1st that the line this day met with practically no resistance and the advance consisted more of a pursuit than an attack. Our companies, in order to keep up with the rapidly advancing infantry, carried their machine gun carts with them. The entire battalion moved in line of squad column, each squad followed by its gun and ammunition cart.

The work on this advance presented its chief difficulty in the movement itself. The terrain was very rough, so it was with difficulty that these carts and

15. Major General Joseph Theodore Dickman.

mules were brought forward, but by hard work same was accomplished. In places mules had to be unhooked and carts taken by hand over terraces and steep banks; it was as hard on the men as on the animals. The night of November 5th found the advancing lines in the vicinity of STONNE, where they dug in for the night. The weather this night could not have been much worse: hard, very cold rain all night, and in the morning, when the advance was resumed, the fog was so thick a man could not see a person five feet from him.

This was an exceedingly hard day. The infantry was advancing in raid pursuit. Captain M. A. Means, with C and D Companies, covered the right flank of the brigade, as well as the division; Major Winn,[16] with the other two Companies, covered the left of the brigade. The orders were to keep in touch with the front line infantry and be ready to give support, or be ready at any time to go into position to help resist a counter-attack. The orders were to keep on the roads as much as possible, but this was found to be almost as hard as going across country, for the Germans had made every effort to destroy same.

In one place, the whole side of the mountain had been blown out where the road had been undermined. A large two-story house could have been put in same. At this point, C and D Companies came near being held up, but finally an old trail was found going down over the mountains and connecting up again with the road in the valley. The trail did not look as though it had been used for fifty years or more, but the companies went down, the animals sliding part way on all fours. This was a very trying pursuit on animals as well as men. Carts were lifted over terraces and the mules led up. A little later a bridge had to be built. It was often necessary for the men to lift and shove the carts forward, assisting the animals.

During this work, perfect liaison was maintained with the infantry, for the dense fog in the morning, dense woods, and the difficulty of maintaining liaison with the units on the right and left had caused delays enough so that we were in close touch with them. Our Companies had in fact advanced more rapidly than the infantry, for C and D Companies, following a road that took them slightly out of the division sector, then swinging back again, entered the town of HARAUCOURT in advance of our own front line infantry. Thus, they were the first American troops to enter this place. The last of the enemy had left the town a short 15 minutes before.[17] The people were overjoyed; they hugged and kissed everyone, and brought out pots and pails of hot coffee and loaves of bread and jars of jam.

The night of November 6th, the battalion was assembled in the vicinity of BULSON. That night, our infantry patrols entered the outskirts of SEDAN. On the 7th, the advance of the battalion was carried forward to THELONNE,

16. Major Copper D. Winn commanded the 151st Machine Gun Battalion.

17. The 77th Division claimed to have liberated Haraucourt first (Adler, 95-97). However, these two companies under Captain Means of the 151st Machine Gun Battalion actually beat them to it.

about five kilometers from SEDAN and about a kilometer from the MEUSE River. That night, the battalion was billeted in THELONNE, where they suffered from a heavy artillery fire coming from across the MEUSE River. During this shelling D Company had its last casualty: Private Ralph W. Olds was killed early on the morning of the 8th. Private Earl Ryans was wounded November 5th.

On the 8th, the battalion was relieved for what turned out to be the last time, retiring to reserve bivouac on the BULSON-HARAUCOURT Road. The French had relieved the 42nd Division at this time so that they could have the honor of entering SEDAN in memory of 1870. The 42nd Division during this last advance was the extreme left of the 1st American Army.

During this advance from ST. PIERREMONT to THELONNE, the difficulties of supplying the front line companies of the battalion had been even greater than those endured by the battalion itself. The field and combat trains endeavoring to follow the line of advance met with every imaginable obstacle. Roads deep in mud from weeks of rain, plowed by shell fire, and in places entirely wiped out by mines, were crowded and jammed with the troops, trains, and artillery of three divisions.[18] November 6th, the field kitchens and ration carts, having been on the road all the previous night and all that day, finally made the town of STONNE shortly after midnight, from which point rations were sent forward to the line in small carts. The combat train had been jammed along the road by crowded traffic. Escort wagons endeavoring to reach forage and ration dumps were held for hours without moving, and it was only by continual efforts of officers and men in charge of these trains that even a portion of them finally reached the hill just south of BULSON the night of November 7th. But in spite of these difficulties, the men in the front line had at least one meal a day during this drive. A portion of the train had been compelled to remain at ST. PIERREMONT, as higher authorities, in endeavoring to clear the road of unnecessary traffic, had ordered all vehicles other than those carrying food and ammunition off the roads.

November 9th, the battalion was finally relieved from the line and marched back to LES GRANDES ARMOISES. Thus, the MEUSE-ARGONNE OFFENSIVE came to an end for this battalion after more than a month of grueling work, hard fighting, and exposure to every kind of weather and enemy fire.

November 11th, the battalion moved to GERMONT. It was during this movement that the first word of signing the ARMISTICE was received. The battalion stayed at GERMONT until the 13th, when they marched to ALLIEPONT.

On the 14th, the battalion moved to and bivouacked in the vicinity of LANDRES-ET-ST. GEORGES. While here, Lieutenant John H. Geiszel rejoined the Company from the hospital. Lieutenant Nellis P. Parkinson had also been

18. These three divisions were the 1st, 42nd, and 77th Divisions. The 42nd and 77th Divisions were advancing to Sedan on the left and right of the First Corps, respectively. A brigade of the 1st Division was moving laterally across the sector for the First Corps in an attempt to reach Sedan first (Dickman, 183). Clogged roads and confusion briefly reigned due to the 1st Division.

reassigned to the Company and had gone through the MEUSE-ARGONNE offensive with same. Lieutenant Geiszel, Lieutenant Andres, and Lieutenant Parkinson were now 1st Lieutenants, having received their promotion some few weeks previously. 1st Sergeant Roy G. Rhoads' promotion to 2nd Lieutenant had come through October 18th, so there were five officers with the Company at this time.

On the 16th, the battalion marched to BRANDEVILLE. It was at this place on the 17th that the 42nd Division was officially announced as part of the ARMY OF OCCUPATION. The following three days were spent in hurried preparation for the march into Germany. Partial new equipment was drawn, new clothes were issued as far as possible, animals were drawn to fill out the full complement of the battalion, and November 20th, the movement to the RHINE commenced.

The first day's march, that of November 20th, carried the battalion to IRES LES PREX, near MONTMEDY, from which station the march was resumed on the 21st, passing out of France and into Belgium and billeting that night at VIEUX VIRTON. Movement again on the 23rd[19] placed the battalion at GUELFF, near ARLON, and on the 23rd, the battalion marched into the Province[20] of Luxembourg, where the battalion got comfortable billets in the town of SIMMERN (SEPTFONTAINES). Here we had our Thanksgiving dinner and remained at rest for a week.

The second and hardest stage of the March to the Rhine commenced December 1st, with a long hike to HEISDORF and thence on the 2nd to MANTERNACH. On the 3rd the battalion passed out of Luxembourg, beginning six days of very hard and long marches, billeting in the successive towns of IDESHEIM, GINDORF, BETTENFELD, WALDKONIGEN, BOXBERG (wherein the battalion was divided, Headquarters and C and D at BOXBERG, one company at BEINHAUSEN, and one company at NEICHEN), and ending at BOOS.

This ten-day continuous marching from Simmern, Luxembourg, was one of the hardest on both men and animals that the battalion had ever experienced. At the end of every day's march wagons had to be unloaded and sent from five to fifteen kilometers for rations and forage. Greatly overworked, a great many animals gave out on the steep slippery hills. On nearly every day's march, it was necessary to double back the teams to get the train to its destination. Animals' shoes, as well as the men's wore out. No new ones were obtainable, and when shoes were received they were hardly ever the sizes ordered. But through it all the men displayed the same ability to go the limit, to endure any hardship, and to carry out the orders of whatever nature that carried them so successfully through nine months of almost continuous work on the front.

After remaining at BOOS for a short rest, on December 14th we again took up the march, proceeding that day to BELL and on the 15th to WALDORF.

19. This should be November 22.
20. Luxembourg was and is an independent state, not a province.

This town was intended as the final station for the battalion, but the town was small and accommodations for men and animals were insufficient. So after an inspection by the Commanding General, 84th Infantry Brigade (Brigadier Gen. Douglas MacArthur), the battalion was ordered to move to KRIPP on the RHINE, to which place movement was completed December 20th.

At KRIPP, splendid billets were secured for officers and men. D Company had one billet holding 97 men and the Company office, every man in a bed. The rest of the Company was well provided for in smaller billets.

New clothes and equipment were drawn, the Hotchkiss machine guns were turned in, and the Browning drawn. The men were drilled in close order drill and military courtesy. A great deal of time was devoted to the Browning gun nomenclature and firings, and passes (one and three days, and those long-delayed 14-day leaves) were at last granted.

2nd Lieutenant Roy G. Rhoads was sent back to France to Machine Gun School for the January course. On his return, Captain M. A. Means and 1st Lieutenant John H. Geiszel went back and attended the February course. 1st Lieutenant William P. Andres commanded the Company during the absence of the Captain. During February, 2nd Lieutenant William M. Johnson, Jr., was assigned to the Company.

The battalion remained here throughout the months of January, February, and March. Nearly everyone had a chance to get into COLOGNE, BONN, and COBLENZ, as well as the numerous smaller towns in the American area.

March 16th, the battalion was reviewed by General Pershing, Commander-in-Chief of the American Expeditionary Forces. Captain M. A. Means was in command of the battalion during the inspection, as the Major, now a Lt. Colonel, was in command of the three machine gun battalions[21] of the division formed as a regiment.

Finally, on April 5th, after turning in everything but mobile and personal equipment, the battalion marched to SINZIG and entrained for their long ride to BREST, France. We rode American box cars this time with kitchen cars, which permitted the serving of hot meals en route.

April 8th, the battalion detrained, marched to CAMP PONTANEZEN, and went under canvas for preparations for the embarkation.

After a thorough delousing, a few days of hard work, and numerous inspections, the battalion was pronounced ready for embarkation.

April 14th, acting under orders #173 Hdqrs. Base Section No. 5 S. O. S., the battalion embarked on the Battleship *USS MINNESOTA*. April 15th, the battalion said farewell to France. At 3:35 P.M., the ship weighed anchor and sailed for the good old U.S.A.

After a quiet voyage, during which only a few days of bad weather were encountered, the battalion disembarked at HOBOKEN and took a train from there to CAMP MERRITT. After another thorough delousing and new clothes

21. These were the 149th (Pennsylvania), 150th (Wisconsin), and 151st (Georgia) Machine Gun Battalions.

were issued where needed, the battalion was broken up and scattered to different camps throughout the country for discharge.

The Captain, 1st Sergeant, Supply Sergeant, and Company Clerk of D Company were sent to CAMP GORDON, GEORGIA, for a final checking of papers with the Battalion Headquarters before discharge.

During its service of over 18 months with the American Expeditionary Force, the 151st Machine Gun Battalion, or elements thereof, were in actual contact with the enemy under battle conditions for 174 days, were in range of the enemy's artillery for 206 days, established headquarters in 77 different localities, moved by rail on French trains five times and by rail on an American train once, by camion twice, and marched approximately 1,300 kilometers. It participated in four major engagements and is credited with having served in 11 different and separate engagements, including various occupations of quiet sectors. It served as a unit in the American Army of Occupation 145 days.

In casualties the battalion lost, from the time of going on the line to November 11th, 47 killed in action, 10 died of wounds, one missing in action and never accounted for, and 395 wounded in action, making the total battle casualties in killed, wounded, missing, and died of wounds 453. Nine men died of disease or other causes, which brought the total casualties in the American Expeditionary Force up to 462.

Thirty-Six members of the battalion were recommend for the Distinguished Service Cross, though only one of the recommendations was recognized by GHQ.

In promotions actually within the battalion, there was one Major promoted to Lieutenant Colonel, two Captains promoted to Major, four 1st Lieutenants promoted to Captains, and nine 2nd Lieutenants promoted to 1st Lieutenant.[22] In addition, six officers returned to the United States as instructors, all of whom received promotion there, and 20 non-commissioned officers were promoted to 2nd Lieutenants at the Army School at LANGRES, France.

Men from 31 different states were in the battalion on its return to the States.[23]

22. The manuscript inadvertently omits "promoted to first lieutenants, and four sergeants promoted to second lieutenants" (compare with White & Peavy).

23. It appears Captain Means drew some material - particularly these last five paragraphs - directly from the battalion history by White and Peavy. That would place composition of the D Company history sometime after the battalion history. Though undated, both were probably written in 1919 or 1920, just after disbanding the unit and discharging the men.

Appendix A:

ROSTER OF COMPANY D, 151ST MACHINE GUN BATTALION

MIDNIGHT, MARCH 31, 1919
COMPILED BY CAPTAIN M. A. MEANS

Captain, Infantry, USA
1. Means, Monroe A.

1st Lieutenants, Infantry, USA
1. Andres, William P.
2. Geiszel, John H.
3. Parkinson, Nellis P.

2nd Lieutenants, Infantry, USA
1. Rhoads, Roy G.
2. Johnson, William M., Jr.

1st Sergeant
1. Troop, Hiram E., 114375

Mess Sergeant
1. Stumpf, Charles F., 114379

Supply Sergeant
1. Stumpf, Charles F., 114379*

Supply Sergeant
1. Drawbaugh, Carlton J., 114234

Stable Sergeant
1. Zeiders, Geroge W., 114381

Corporals
1. Shaffer, Benjamin L., 114436
2. Hawthorne, Ira, 114344
3. Roberts, Fred, 114415
4. Denlinger, Jacob L., 114351
5. Rogers, Irl, 112195
6. Reich, Ivan G., 114349
7. Keagy, Charles M., 114398
8. Holbrook, Gilbert S., 114311 (Attached)
9. Mork, Clarence, 112307
10. Keenen, James P., 114429
11. Currier, Harry, 112137
12. Shipman, Robert L., 114306 (Absent AEF University)
13. Cramblett, Ernest L., 114298 (Absent sick, BH#90)
14. Caldwell, Richard A., 114365
15. Herr, Paul B., 114317

Cooks
1. Geisler, Roy W., 114425
2. Troop, Charles R., 114394
3. Schmeltzer, Frank J., 114303

Horseshoer
1. Connors, Maurice P., 114337

Sergeants
1. Peacock, Harry E., 114403
2. Gruger, Walter H., 114323
3. Demuth, Christopher H., 114310
4. Brenner, John D., 114334
5. Deetz, Robert E., 114377
6. Achey, Howard P., 114332
7. Knoke, William H., 112300
8. Murray, James E., 112310
9. Stauffer, Howard E., 114352
10. Humphreys, Harry S., 114397
11. Pennell, Walter R., 114413
12. Matt, Lewis J., 114410

Privates First Class
1. Anderson, Charles W., 114432
2. Armstrong, Benjamin F. W., 114347
3. Beamsderfer, Charles M., 114376
4. Bair, Edward A., 114335
5. Beck, David W., 114412
6. Dennis, Raymond E., 114342
7. Dickel, Robert A., 114319
8. Edgar, Cecil E., 112333
9. Fetter, Elwood I., 114299
10. Gatchell, Samuel H., 114360 (Trans. Fr., 204th Co. 102nd Bn. MPC So#66 HQ Dist., Paris.)
11. Geibe, Harry H., 114320
12. Grau, Richard, 114292
13. Hamaker, Harry A., 114330
14. Harnish, Walter H., 114385
15. Humphrey, Lee, 1580044
16. Imhoff, William C., 114417
17. Jones, Thurman, 1597896
18. Johnson, Edwin, 2034263
19. Karabetos, Gregoreos, 114277
20. Keller, David F., 114421
21. Kirsch, John F., 114378
22. Kuhlman, Edward L., 114329
23. Lapham, James W., 114287
24. Lime, Joseph J., 114339
25. McColley, Vernon E., 2986378
26. Mathews, Leonard, 1592816
27. Mearig, Maurice L., 114296

Saddler
1. Downs, Frank M., 114355

Mechanics
1. Musser, Leon B., 114300
2. May, Horace P., 114374
3. Frederick, Charles, 114435

Bugler First Class
1. Walker, Charles D., 1981816

Bugler
1. Inman, Edward, 2980350

Privates
1. Ahlstrom, Elmer E., 2052674
2. Anderson, George E., 2053198
3. Bale, Frank W., 2054249 (Trans. 3rd Army Repl. Depot Par. 7, SO#80, Mar 21/19)
4. Beach, Charles, 2043177
5. Bishop, Leverett E., 58935 (Trans. fr., Co. D, 144th Inf. SO#62, Hq. 36th Div. mar. 5/19)
6. Brostoff, Morris, 2025857
7. Childs, James T., 113710
8. Corrigan, Dee E., 99275
9. Devine, Percy C., 2980502
10. Dudley, Robert B., 114419
11. Fifield, Leonard L., 2052634
12. Fisher, Charles H., 2053396
13. Fornash, Zebedee, 1580123
14. Foulke, Rowan F., 114358
15. Frederick, Clyde G., 2052555
16. Hall, John F., 114395
17. Hamby, Lawrence, 113721
18. Hill, Jacob H., 2025883
19. Hoover, Andrew K., 112296
20. Imhoff, Bernell, 114366
21. Kelly, George, 2052824
22. Knox, George L., 114382
23. Knosp, Albert B., 114428
24. Leamon, Aaron R., 114305
25. Leaman, Lester, 114363

28. Myers, Joseph G., 114291
29. Orahood, Walter L., 114407
30. Patrick, James E., 114304
31. Peltier, Jerry C., 2043558
32. Pearson, Henry J., 114285
33. Resh, Samuel, 114328
34. Ryan, Earl E., 114345
35. Schmidt, Harry E., 114345
36. Sigman, James, 114436
37. Singleton, Luther, 114338
38. Siner, George, 1579922
39. Shrum, David P., 114278
40. Smith, David P., 114278**
41. Snavely, Royal, 114423
42. Spangler, Aud, 1579927
(In confinement)
43. Stoeckl, Louis Leo, 114336
44. Trimble, Ralph W., 114401
45. Williams, Algen H., 58946
46. Zatzke, William E., 2052466

Absent sick
1. Kapp, John W., 114340, Pvt. 1cl.
2. Wells, John S., 2254004, Pvt.

M. A. Means,
Captain, Infantry USA
Commanding.

26. Lenz, Charles, 2053044
27. Lubsen, Edward, 2980239
29. Luka, Harry W., 2025894***
30. McGinnis, Jah H. B., 114282
31. McKale, August, 2025981
32. McKlemurry, George, 1585262
33. Martin, Charles A., 114389
34. Meekins, Walter R., 114372
35. Meiser, Ray C., 2053127
36. Mihm, John H., 2052898
37. Miller, John J., 2984223
38. Miller, John L., 114283
39. Moyer, Frank A., 114283****
40. Obermeyer, Henry A., 2052550
41. Parks, Floyd C., 2053352
42. Reid, Reuben, 2052853
43. Rubino, Frank, 2985288
44. Sanders, Ernest, 1592853
45. Sarver, Harry W., 1579918
46. Sheldon, Orvel, 2986354
47. Sidwell, George W., 114434
48. Smith, Michael J., 2052573
49. Stevenson, Aurice C., 1585512
50. Stopka, Joseph, 1392180
51. Temples, William, 84537
52. Thompson, Joseph L., 3321417
53. Thompson, Martin A., 3322894
54. Wallace, Bradley E., 1585378
55. Ward, Elmer L., 1585379
56. Weatherly, Joseph B., 1585381
57. Williams, Harry M., 2025927
58. Withers, Veare R., 2043510

EDITOR'S NOTE:
The following typographical errors are reproduced from the manuscript.

**Repetition of Sergeant "Stumpf, Charles F., 114379"*
***Repetition of "David P., 114278"*
****Omission of "28." in the list of privates.*
*****Repetition of Serial Number "114283"*

CASUALTIES OF COMPANY D, 151ST MACHINE GUN BATTALION

COMPILED BY JOEL R. PARKINSON
INFORMATION WAS DRAWN FROM THE ACCOUNTS
OF PARKINSON, MEANS, AND WHITE & PEAVY.

Badonviller Sector

March 17, 1918
Private Sylvester Sullivan - Killed (accidentally shot)

May 26, 1918
2nd Lieutenant John F. Noxon - Wounded (gassed)
1st Sergeant Russel H. Dudley - Wounded (gassed)
Private Charles W. Anderson - Wounded (gassed)

June 18, 1918
1st Lieutenant M. A. Means - Gassed
(Means does not mention his own gassing)
Sergeant. John J. Kipphorn - Wounded
Sergeant Roy G. Rhoads - Wounded
Sergeant George L. Stark - Wounded
Corporal Walter R. Pennell - Wounded
Private Charles Beamsderfer - Wounded
Private David W. Beck - Wounded
Private Leverette E. Bishop - Wounded
Private Ernest Cramblet - Wounded
Private Jacob L. Denlinger - Wounded
Private Clarence Denlinger - Wounded
Private Frank M. Downs - Wounded
Private Rowan P. Foulke - Wounded
Private Burnell Imhoff - Wounded
Private Jay H. B. McGinnis - Wounded
Private Frank Myers - Wounded
Private Ramond Proffitt - Wounded

Private Charles J. Reemsnyder - Wounded
(later killed at St. Mihiel)
Private Irl Rogers - Wounded
Private Earl J. Ryan - Wounded
Private John W. Shay - Wounded
Private Robert Shipman - Wounded

Champagne

July 15-18, 1918
Private Edward W. Bair - Wounded
Private Robert Bond - Wounded
Private Raymond Bryson - Killed by shellfire
Private Joseph A. Earley - Wounded
Private William Imhoff - Wounded
Private G. Karabetos - Wounded
Private H. E. Loucks - Wounded
Private Wayne McLaughlin - Wounded
Private Charles L. Miller - Wounded
Private G. W. Rittenhouse - Wounded
Private George A. Rodman - Killed by shellfire (head blown off)

Chateau-Thierry Advance

July 23, 1918
Private Harry White - Died of pneumonia

July 25, 1918
Corporal A. H. Breitigan - Died of shellfire wounds (July 26)

July 26, 1918
Corporal Julius M. Lyons - Killed by shellfire
Private Clifford Boden - Wounded by shellfire
Private Sylvester Furlow - Wounded by shellfire
Private Aaron Jenkins - Died of shellfire wounds (July 28)
Private Benjamin E. Keenen - Wounded by shellfire
Private Henry J. Pearson - Wounded by shellfire
Private Charles R. Wagner - Wounded by shellfire
Private Harry R. Wright - Died of shellfire wounds (July 28)

July 27, 1918
Corporal John C. Kiehl - Wounded

Ourcq River Crossing

July 28-29, 1918
Sergeant Warren B. Frey - Wounded
Sergeant I. G. Weidman - Wounded
Corporal M. L. Moore - Killed in action
Corporal Fred Roberts - Wounded
Corporal Benjamin Shaffer - Wounded
Corporal J. H. Westerhoff - Wounded
Private Walter W. Brown - Wounded
Private Dewey Clark - Wounded
Private Martin S. Cover - Killed in action
Private David T. Davis - Killed in action
Private Carrol Fanus - Killed in action
Private H. M. Fawber - Wounded
Private Elwood Y. Fishel - Wounded
Private Samuel Gatchell - Wounded
Private Wilbur A. Gruver - Wounded
Private John F. Hall - Wounded
Private John Harkcom - Killed in action
Private Charles W. Houck - Wounded
Private Jospeh Kilpatrick - Wounded
Private Charles Kiscaddin - Wounded
Private P. D. Kissinger - Wounded
Private James W. Lapham - Wounded
Private Lester Leaman - Wounded
Private Lester L. Litner - Wounded
Private H. A. McCullom - Wounded
Private Walter Meekins - Wounded
Private Joseph L. Meither - Wounded
Private MecLeon B. Messer - Wounded
Private John R. Miller - Wounded
Private Joseph H. Myers - Wounded
Private Edward A. Nixdorf - Wounded
Private Samuel Resh - Wounded
Private Earl H. Ryan - Wounded
Private George W. Sidwell - Wounded
Private George Smith - Died of wounds
Private John Stiffel - Wounded
Private Fred E. White - Killed in action
Private John G. Walters - Killed in action
Private William J. Winnerling - Wounded
Mechanic Ernest F. Roth - Wounded

St. Mihiel Offensive

September 12, 1918
2nd Lieutenant John H. Geiszel - Wounded by shellfire
Corporal Frank A. Cramblet - Killed in action
Private William Dixon - Wounded
Private Charles Gleason - Wounded
Private Jacob P. Herr - Wounded
Private Leon M. Madlem - Wounded
Private James E. Patrick - Wounded
Private C. J. Reemsnyder - Killed in action by gunfire
Private William Taylor - Wounded

September 15, 1918
Corporal Gerald H. Gochnauer - Wounded (gassed)
Private Paul H. Harmon - Wounded (gassed)
Private Carl Werner - Wounded (gassed)

September 22, 1918
Private V. A. Munyon - Wounded

Meuse-Argonne Offensive

All of October, 1918
Sergeant Howard P. Achey - Wounded
Sergeant Clifford W. Dudley - Wounded
Private Blake Carpenter - Wounded
Private Herbert Churchill - Wounded
Private Raymond E. Dennis - Wounded
Private Paul B. Herr - Wounded
Private Lewis J. Matt - Wounded
Private Frank Seiders - Wounded
Private Chester H. Victor - Wounded (buried alive by shellfire)

The Race For Sedan

November 5, 1918
Private Earl Ryan - Wounded

November 8, 1918
Private Ralph W. Olds - Killed by shellfire

Summary of Company D Casualties

	Killed	Died of Wounds	Died Sick	Wounded	POW	Missing	Total
Badonviller	1	0	0	25	0	0	26
Champagne	2	0	0	9	0	0	11
Chateau-Thierry	1	3	1	6	0	0	11
Ourcq River	7	1	0	32	0	0	40
St. Mihiel	2	0	0	11	0	0	13
Meuse-Argonne	0	0	0	9	0	0	9
Race For Sedan	1	0	0	1	0	0	2
Company Total	14	4	1	93	0	0	112
Authorized Strength	172	172	172	172	172	172	172
Casualty Rate	8%	2%	0%	54%	0%	0%	65%

APPEDIX B:

THE 151ST MACHINE GUN BATTALION, 42ND RAINBOW DIVISION

A Battalion History and Citations of the Rainbow, August 13, 1917 to April 26, 1919 by Miller G. White, Jr. and Arthur H. Peavy

Organization and Training

The 151st Machine Gun Battalion was originally organized in August 1917 as one of two three-company machine gun battalions which were to form a part of a composite division of National Guard for service in Europe—the Division being designated the 42nd and, because of its composition, also termed the "Rainbow Division."[1]

This battalion was selected from the Second Georgia Infantry, which organization had served continuously in the Federal service since June 19, 1916, including five months' service on the Mexican border from October 22, 1916, to March 22, 1917. Companies B, C, and F, then forming the First Battalion, Second Georgia Infantry, were chosen as the three companies to form the new battalion.

The actual transfer was accomplished August 13, 1917, and the work of the entire battalion was directed toward preparations for the movement to the mobilization camp of the 42nd Division. After being brought to war strength by transfers within the First Georgia Brigade, of both officers and enlisted men in the required numbers, the entire battalion entrained at Camp Harris,

1. Douglas MacArthur dubbed the 42nd Division with this nickname when he described its components drawn from National Guard units as "stretching like a rainbow clear across the United States."

Macon, Georgia, on August 29, 1917, detraining September 1, 1917, at Camp Albert L. Mills, Long Island, with a total strength of 21 officers and 560 enlisted men.

After arrival at the mobilization camp of the division every effort was made to prepare the organization immediately for overseas service. New equipment was drawn, the organization completed, designations of companies being changed to A, B, and C (F Company becoming A Company under the new designation), and the Battalion started in on a period of training directed chiefly toward the physical development of the men for the hardships which it was anticipated they must endure in foreign service.

Two months of this training was completed before the Battalion was ordered overseas. On October 29, 1917, under orders from Headquarters, 42nd Division, the Battalion entrained at Garden City, L.I., proceeded by rail and ferry to Hoboken, N.J., and embarked that day on the U. S. Transport *Agamemnon*.

At the date of embarkation the Battalion carried a total strength of 25 officers and 545 enlisted men. The gain in officers had been made by the addition of three Reserve Corps Officers and a Dental Surgeon. The loss in enlisted strength had been occasioned by transfers of men to hospitals for various reasons and by the discharge of several men on account of physical disability.

The transport *Agamemnon*, carrying the 151st Machine Gun Battalion and other troops, sailed from Hoboken on October 31, 1917. The first eight days were calm and uneventful. The usual submarine lookouts, so necessary at that time, were constantly maintained, though no enemy craft was sighted during the entire voyage.

On the night of November 9 occurred the only event of the voyage which might be considered of interest. Shortly after dark the transport *Von Steuben*, sailing in convoy with the *Agamemnon* and two other transports, collided with the *Agamemnon*, burying her bow in the port side of the latter vessel and causing considerable damage.[2] The resulting hole, being fortunately almost entirely above the waterline, was quickly repaired by an efficient crew and progress was resumed with little delay. The conduct of the men at this time, when none of them were aware of the exact nature of the accident nor the extent of the damage, was remarkable in the extreme. They went quickly and quietly to their allotted places, remaining there until the signal that all was well had been received.[3]

On Monday, November 12th, land was sighted and before noon that day the *Agamemnon* was anchored in the harbor of Brest, France. On account of

2. This collision occurred at night as the four vessels in the convoy were routinely changing their relative positions in formation to make torpedoing more difficult (Reilly, 78).
3. A roll-call aboard the *Agamemnon* indicated that one man from the 151st Machine Gun Battalion was missing and presumed lost overboard. It later turned out that the poor guy was sitting on the ship's railing and the crash threw him safely onto the deck of the *Von Steuben*. Radio silence among the ships prevented immediate disclosure of his safety. Yet he happily returned to his outfit upon arrival at Brest (Reilly, 79).

transportation conditions and the lack of accommodations in the city itself, the men were held on board until November 17th when the entire battalion was loaded on lighters and put ashore at Brest with orders to entrain the same day.

In the trip from Brest to its first station in France, the Battalion gained its initial experience in traveling by freight train. Loading into box cars on the 17th of November, with three days' travel rations of canned goods and hard bread, the Battalion left Brest shortly after noon. One night's experience with from thirty-six to forty men in a French box car[4] and the novelty of the situation was gone. The men, unaccustomed to such conditions, were cramped and crowded and the trip was long and monotonous. After three days' travel the rations gave out. Except for what little food the men could purchase en route and the coffee served at one or two stations, they had nothing to eat during the last thirty-six hours of the trip.

After traveling four days and nights, the Battalion reached Vaucouleurs, France, at 7:00 o'clock on the night of November 21st, but remained in the train until morning of the 22nd. Detraining then, the Battalion was divided, Company C going to Vaux La Petite, marching, and Battalion Headquarters, with Companies A and B, taking station at Uruffe. The marches to these stations were final tests for everyone. Worn out after the long railway journey, and marching with heavy packs in the pouring rain, the members of the Battalion displayed then the grit and ability to endure unaccustomed hardships which was later to prove one of their greatest assets.

Arriving at these stations, the Battalion took up its first training program, remaining in the Vaucouleurs area until December 12, 1917. Under orders from the Commanding General, 42nd Division,[5] the Battalion commenced a march of 110 kilometers to its new station in the 7th (Rolampont) Area. Leaving Uruffe on the morning of December 12th, Battalion Headquarters, with Companies A and B, marched to Verseignes, while Company C proceeded from Vaux La Petite to Bure the same day. Marching on the 13th carried the Headquarters with Companies A and B to Doremy, and Company C to Germisay. On December 14th, marching in heavy snow storms, the entire battalion assembled at Manois where it remained at rest through Christmas, 1917.

December 26th, the Battalion again took up the march. The weather continued more than severe—freezing temperatures and heavy snowstorms making the entire march from this point to the final stations a trying hardship for the Southern men unaccustomed to such conditions. In spite of these difficulties, the march was carried out according to schedule. Battalion Headquarters, with two companies, spent the night of December 26th at Triex, while Company C took station at Blancheville, and proceeding on the 27th to Crenay, with

4. These boxcars were nicknamed "40 and 8s" because they presumably had a capacity for either 40 men or 8 horses. Of course, achieving this "capacity" meant that men were packed in like sardines.
5. At this time the commander was Major General William A. Mann. Major General Charles T. Menoher succeeded him three days later on December 15, 1917.

Company C stationed at Chaumont. December 28th carried the Battalion Headquarters and Company A to Vieux Moulin, with the two remaining companies at Laffonds.

During this time, owing to changes in tables of organization for a brigade machine gun battalion, the Battalion's strength had been increased to four companies by the addition of B Company, 149th Machine Gun Battalion, carried as attached.[6] In the original organization of the 42nd Division this company had been drawn from Company K, 4th Pennsylvania Infantry, to form part of a four-company divisional machine gun battalion. As part of the National Guard of Pennsylvania, this company had, like the original companies of the 151st Machine Gun Battalion, seen service on the Mexican border in 1916. When the Battalion reached Vieux Moulin on December 28th, Company B, 149th Machine Gun Battalion, was in station at Laffonds.

On January 4, 1918, the entire battalion, including the new company, was assembled at Villers sur Suize (Haute Marne) and went into more or less permanent billets for its final period of training before entering the lines. The entire march from the Vaucouleurs Area had been made only by undergoing the severest hardships. Every man who completed the march had proved his willingness to meet whatever demand might by made of him in the future.

The training period at Villers sur Suize lasted for five weeks, during which time the Battalion received its final equipment in Hotchkiss machine guns, helmets, gas masks, etc. This training period completed as much as possible the instruction of the men prior to their entry into the lines and was carried on in the same difficult weather which had been experienced during December.

The Luneville Sector

On February 18, 1918, Battalion Headquarters and Companies A and B proceeded to Rolampont and entrained, arriving and detraining at Berbevillers (Vosges) on February 19th, and marching the same day to Givrillers. On February 19th, Company C and Company B, 149th Machine Gun Battalion, entrained at Rolampont, arriving and detraining on the 20th at Moyen (Vosges) and joining the Battalion Headquarters at Givrillers the same day. The Battalion remained at this station until February 22nd when the four line companies were attached to the infantry regiments of the 84th Brigade, Companies A and B joining the 167th Infantry at Brouville, Company C proceeding to Baccarat and thence, on the 23rd, to join a battalion of the 168th Infantry at Neufmaisons, while Company B, 149th M.G. Battalion, on the 22nd, joined a reserve battalion of the 168th Infantry at Badmenil. Battalion Headquarters, with headquarters

6. Attachment of B Company, 149th Machine Gun Battalion, to the 151st Machine Gun Battalion actually did not occur until January 25, 1918 (Means).

company, took station at this time at Merviller, from which point the Battalion Commander, as Brigade Machine Gun Officer,[7] was to direct the machine gun operations throughout the 84th Infantry Brigade.

March 8th, the first companies of the Battalion actually entered the first line positions, Company C, working with the French, going into positions in the C. R.[8] Badonviller, while Company A, also in conjunction with French units and the 167th U.S. Infantry, took position a day or two later in the C. R. Ancerviller. On March 17th, Company B, 149th Machine Gun Battalion, operating with the infantry battalion to which it was attached,[9] relieved Company C at Badonviller. On the 18th Company B, 151st M.G. Battalion, in connection with its battalion of the 167th Infantry, relieved Company A at Ancerviller.

In this manner each company of the Battalion made one tour of duty in front line positions during the time that the 42nd Division occupied this sector with and under orders of the 128th French Infantry Division and the Sixth French Corps. With the exception of Company C, the occupation of this first sector of the front line was practically without incident. Company C had occasion to fire a protective barrage during a successful raid accomplished by the 168th Infantry, this being the first experience in overhead barrage fire of any company of the Battalion.

March 23rd, all units of the Division were relieved and the 151st Machine Gun Battalion proceeded by marching to Rambervillers, with one company (B) stationed at Bazien and joining the Battalion on the 24th at Rambervillers.

The Battalion was very fortunate during this first experience in actual warfare, suffering only three casualties: two being slightly wounded and returning to duty within a few weeks, while one soldier was severely wounded and died of wounds shortly afterwards.[10]

The Baccarat Sector

At the time of its relief from the Luneville Sector, the 42nd Division was under orders to proceed by marching to the Seventh (Rolampont) Area for additional equipment and further training before entering a more active sector on the Western Front. It was at this time, however, that the first phase of the German offensives of 1918 were gaining in violence.[11] The 42nd Division was placed under orders of the Commanding General, 6th French Corps,[12] the orders for movement to the Rolampont Area having been withdrawn. On

7. Major Cooper D. Winn.
8. "C.R." here and elsewhere stands for "Center of Resistance" (Parkinson).
9. Third Battalion, 168th Infantry Regiment.
10. This figure omits two men who were accidentally killed and three who died of sickness during this period of time.
11. The first German spring offensive opened along the Somme on March 21, 1918.
12. This was General Duport.

March 28th the entire battalion was ordered to proceed by marching to Badmenil and there to await further instructions.

On that date, March 28th, the final transfer of Company B, 149th Machine Gun Battalion, was completed. From that time on it became designated as Company D, 151st Machine Gun Battalion.

March 30th brought the new orders, and during the night of March 30-31st all four line companies of the Battalion, having been again attached to the infantry regiments, proceeded to new stations in the Baccarat Sector. Companies A and B were attached, as in the first case, to the 167th Infantry, and Companies C and D to the 168th Infantry. Battalion Headquarters, on March 21st, proceeded to Neufmaisons, at which place it took permanent station during the occupation of the Baccarat Sector. Companies A and B, in this new sector, had a rear position at Vacqueville, alternating in front line positions in either the C.R. Neuviller or C.R. Grand Bois. Companies C and D, with the 168th Infantry, had a rear position at Pexonne and alternated between that place and C.R.s Badonviller and Village Negre.

During the occupation of this sector the machine gun positions used were ones which had been established by French troops during the four previous years that this line had been maintained. Many of the positions were entirely inadequate either for offense or defense and several efforts were made to change these positions. The requested authority, however, could not be obtained until nearly the end of the stay of the Battalion in this sector and then only a few of the positions, on the right of the sector, were allowed to be changed. The trenches and dugouts, too, were decidedly run down and insufficient when the 42nd Division assumed control of the sector and much of the work of the troops was expended in repairing and constructing these trenches and dugouts.

The Battalion occupied the Baccarat Sector for two and a half months, during which time valuable experience was gained in trench warfare, in barrage and indirect fire work, and in various minor details necessary to perfect the training of the men for more active fronts. During May the companies then in the line experienced a heavy projector gas attack on May 27th and 28th. Company C, on the latter date, assisted very materially in breaking up an attempted enemy raid which followed the gas attack of several hours. In this gas attack the training of the men showed itself best, for Company C, being stationed in positions which were most heavily gassed, had only three casualties, while the infantry battalion to which it was attached suffered more than 200 casualties in the same period from gas.

Later, on June 15, 1918, Company C furnished one platoon of machine guns which took over and occupied the entire machine gun sector in the C.R. Chamois, relieving for this purpose the whole of the machine gun company of the 165th Infantry. The last few days of the Battalion's occupation of the trenches in the Baccarat Sector brought the most severe projector gas attack which any of the companies had experienced. Company D, then in the line and awaiting relief, suffered twenty-four casualties from gas at this time.[13]

On the night of June 18th, the first units of the 151st were relieved, Battalion Headquarters and Companies A and B marching that night to Menil. On the night of the 19th, Companies C and D were relieved and assembled at Neufmaisons while Headquarters took station at Domevre sur Durbion, Company B moving the same night to Padaux. On June 20th Company A joined Battalion Headquarters at Domevre and Companies C and D moved to Rambervillers. June 21st carried Company C to Dompierre and Company D to Thaon.

The Esperance-Souain Sector, Champagne

On June 23, 1918, the entire Battalion marched and assembled at Thaon where it entrained in two sections, Companies C and D with Headquarters in the first section and Companies A and B following in the second section. Vitry-le-Francois was the detraining point for the Battalion and all detrainments were completed on the morning of June 24th. The Battalion took station at St. Amand-sur-Fion with orders for two weeks' training on special maneuvers to be carried out in that vicinity.

Conditions at the front, however, caused an unexpected change in orders, and on the night of June 29, 1918, the entire battalion marched to Marson and thence, on the 30th, to Tilloy-et-Bellay. There it again took station for practice of an attack formation preparatory to a minor offensive operation which it was then intended the 42nd Division, assisted by two French divisions, should carry out on the Champagne front. Order of battle again necessitated a change in orders. Upon the request of the French General Staff for American reinforcements on the Champagne front, in anticipation of a new German offensive in that sector, the 42nd U.S. Division was placed at the disposal of General Gouraud,[14] commanding the 4th French Army.

July 3rd, acting under orders of General Gouraud, the 151st Machine Gun Battalion was sent to Suippes where it arrived on the morning of July 4th and went into bivouac for the day under cover of such shelter as the terrain afforded. That night the line companies were once more attached to infantry regiments. Companies A and B took up support positions in the Esperance-Souain Sector, north of Suippes, with battalions of the 167th Infantry. Company D took position in the support lines of the same sector with a battalion of the 168th Infantry[15] and Company C went into reserve with its battalion of the 168th Infantry at Camp 3.5, just back of the support line of this sector. Battalion Headquarters was established at Camp Nantivette, just north of Suippes.

13. This figure apparently lumps together gas casualties from two separate dates. Company D had three men gassed on May 26 (Means). Then 22 more were gassed (including Lieutenant Means - slightly gassed) on June 18 (Means).
14. General Henri Joseph Eugene Gouraud.
15. Third Battalion, 168th Infantry.

In these positions the Battalion remained from July 4th to 14th, during a period of comparative quiet. This period was utilized in familiarizing the officers and men of the Battalion with the plan of defense of the sector, the nature of the terrain ahead, and their respective duties in the event of an enemy attack. The French troops holding the first line positions ahead of our line continually carried out successful night and day raids on the enemy lines, capturing many prisoners and gaining much information which was to prove valuable to the defending troops later on.[16]

The Champagne-Marne Defensive

After having received two warnings of an impending enemy attack which failed to materialize, on the night of July 14th, shortly before midnight, information was given out by the French headquarters that the long expected German offensive was scheduled to commence at midnight.

Anticipating the enemy preparatory barrage, American and French artillery commenced a heavy barrage fire on the German front lines at midnight. Almost before our men could seek cover in the few available dugouts near their positions, the enemy barrage commenced. The artillery action was terrific, a barrage such as our men had never witnessed being placed blanket-like over the whole of the Allied front in that sector.

The men took to what cover the location afforded, but dugouts were so crowded that rather than suffocate in them many men went back to their frame barracks. Others, on account of the positions manned by their guns, were obliged to remain on duty in open trenches. It was these circumstances which caused such heavy casualties in the Battalion, even though during this first night's fighting no company of this Battalion occupied other than support positions, nor was any gun of the Battalion able to fire on the enemy when his attacking waves debauched at 4:00 o'clock on the morning of the 15th. The entire area was heavily shelled throughout that day with both shrapnel and gas. Company C, stationed at Camp 3.5 without cover for their stock, lost every cart mule they had and suffered heavy casualties. Battalion Headquarters, at Camp Nantivette, was forced to move under shell fire to positions in the woods directly back of Suippes where it remained until the Battalion was relieved.

July 16th, the enemy attack had spent itself on our front lines, gaining only the extreme outposts of the French positions in our front. Company C was directed to move from its reserve position at Camp 3.5 to a position in the intermediate line ahead, which it held until relieved from the sector. The entire

16. These raids were vital to General Gouraud's plan of defense at Champagne. German prisoners taken were interrogated to ascertain the time of the looming attack. Based on this intelligence Gouraud would move most of his troops out of the front line trenches at the last minute so the brunt of German artillery would be wasted on unoccupied fortifications.

action was the most severe the Battalion had then experienced. During the time that the artillery action continued, which was continuous from the beginning, on the night of the 14th, the men were practically without food except for their reserve rations. Liaison with the field kitchens, which obtained their rations from the infantry supply companies, demonstrated the impracticability of detaching the line companies of the Battalion from their own headquarters for combat purposes.

That attack lasted well through July 15th and gradually subsided during the 16th with the enemy holding practically no advantage and the Allied lines at that point entirely intact. Heavy shelling continued on both sides during the 17th and 18th. On the night of the 18th, or morning of the 19th, the Battalion received orders for its relief, to be completed before daylight of that day. The difficulties of accomplishing this relief are difficult of description. The companies were practically without transportation, they received their moving orders too late for them to obtain the necessary carts and animals from the echelon, and were forced, in order to comply with these orders, to leave their positions and march under heavy shell fire the entire distance to Camp Noblotte, which was the assembling point for the Battalion and located some fifteen kilometers distant. In spite of these difficulties, however, the relief was accomplished. The men themselves, worn though they were with the strain of the preceding four days, carried their equipment, including guns, tripods and much of their ammunition.[17]

The Champagne-Marne defensive was a terrific, trying experience, but it thoroughly completed the training of this Battalion, preparing the men for the hard fighting they were soon to undergo. Every man conducted himself with gallantry under these trying conditions.

In casualties during this action, the Battalion lost twelve killed in action, gassed forty-one, and sixteen men wounded by shell fire.

The Aisne-Marne Offensive

By noon of July 19th the entire battalion had assembled in barracks at Camp Noblotte, where it remained until the night of July 20th. Then, under orders to entrain on July 22nd at Coolus, it completed the first stage of the march to that point, billeting on July 21st at Sarry, a few kilometers from Chalons. On the night of the 21st, while enemy planes made a strong air raid on Chalons, Headquarters and Companies A and B completed the march to Coolus and entrained early on the morning of July 22nd, arriving and detraining that night at Lizy-sur-Ourcq, and taking station the same night, Headquarters and

17. Due to the initiative of 2nd Lieutenant John H. Geiszel in charge of Company D's trains, he was able to bring forward the mule carts and wagons that night. Then Company D alone was able to move under cover of darkness without having to carry all their equipment and ammo by hand the whole distance to the rear (Means).

Company A at Sameron, Company B at Ussy. On the night of the 23rd, Companies C and D entrained at Coolus, arriving and detraining at La Ferte on the morning of the 24th, and taking station, Company D at Jaignes, Company C at Changis.

While at these stations the companies of the Battalion were once more detached from Battalion Headquarters, A and B being placed under command of the 167th Infantry, and C and D with the 168th Infantry.

On the night of July 24th, the entire battalion, with their respective infantry battalions, loaded on camions. After an all-night ride, during which the men had no chance for sleep owing to the rough roads and crowded trucks, arrived and unloaded near Epieds, with their equipment and machine guns, but with no animals to draw the carts. The entire field and combat train, together with all cart mules, were left behind to make the trip up by road.

After unloading, Companies A and D marched, drawing their machine gun carts by hand,[18] to reserve positions near Courpoil, at which latter place headquarters was established. Companies B and C stopped for a brief rest in the woods near Courpoil and then were ordered to the front line in the Bois de Fere, north of Courpoil, which positions they took, relieving elements of the 28th U.S. Division without reconnaissance.

Remaining in open positions, under heavy harassing fire from enemy batteries throughout the night of July 25th, Company C, operating with a battalion of the 168th Infantry, commenced its advance with the first wave of infantry at about 10 o'clock in the morning, with a line running east and west through Croix Rouge Farm as its first day's objective. B Company, with a battalion of the 167th Infantry, commenced its advance with the first wave of infantry, Croix Rouge Farm and vicinity being its objective for that day. In making this advance, the orders to attack were received at 5:00 P.M., with instructions to attack at 5:15 P.M. The orders were carried out, but the attack was made through thick woods, alive with German machine guns, over a terrain utterly strange to the men who had never before experienced offensive warfare nor open fighting of this kind.[19] That both of these companies stuck with their infantry companies and reached the prescribed objectives before nightfall of that day speaks well for the training the men had received, and for their ability to face danger and conditions which they had never before experienced.

In the case of Company B, the company was divided into three separate platoons, one platoon working with each infantry company and advancing in the first wave of the attack. Both companies suffered heavy losses, and, owing to the terrain and the manner in which they were employed, were unable to assist the infantry in attack, being little or no value until the objectives were attained. A platoon of Company B reached the Croix Rouge Farm with the

18. Actually, Company D had left their mule carts behind and the men lugged all guns, tripods, and ammo to the front by foot (Means; Parkinson). Probably the other companies did the same.
19. This fight was like Belleau Wood all over again, though on a smaller scale.

first units of infantry and were then able to materially assist in holding the captured objective.

On the 27th, Companies A and D, working with their respective infantry battalions, took up the advance with Companies B and C following in close support. The advance on the 27th met with little resistance and that night all companies were in fox holes just south of the Ourcq River.

On the 28th, the advance was continued to the Ourcq under heavy shell fire and machine gun fire from the enemy. This day's work again demonstrated the impracticability of operating machine guns in the manner that our companies were used here. For Companies A and D were never able, during the actual advance, to assist the infantry with their fire and both companies suffered heavy losses in the valley of the Ourcq and around Sergy. Remaining in these positions during the night of the 28th, these companies, closely supported by the other two companies, were able to assist the infantry a little in holding the acquired positions. But during the attack on Hill 212 and Sergy but little assistance could be rendered, although each time the infantry attacks were launched the machine guns accompanied them.

Enemy artillery poured a continual rain of shells on our lines, causing more casualties, while enemy avions hovered unmolested by Allied planes over our front lines and played their machine guns on the unprotected lines continuously.

It was at this time that the Battalion Commander requested authority to assemble his Battalion in positions on a hillside just south of what then constituted the front lines. This position was such that an assembled machine gun battalion, operating under one command, could have supported the infantry attacks at that place with a concentrated overhead machine gun barrage, which could undoubtedly have simplified the capture of those stubbornly held enemy positions on Hill 212 and around Sergy. But this opportunity to demonstrate the efficiency of a machine gun battalion working as a battalion was not granted and the companies remained scattered along the line with the infantry troops.

During this time liaison with the company kitchens in rear had been completely lost and repeated efforts of the mess sergeants to locate and feed their companies in the line failed. Rations at that time were drawn through the infantry regiments, the Battalion field train was divided among the four companies, and practically no food reached the front line companies during the period from July 27th to August 2nd.

July 30th, Company B, having been in front line positions for six days, continuously under heavy fire and decidedly crippled, was relieved and retired to the woods north of Courpoil where the rear Battalion Headquarters had been established. This company, however, was allowed only a single day of rest, for on the morning of August 1st it was again moved up to the front line, relieving Company A. Company A, upon relief, was immediately attached to a battalion of the 47th Infantry of the 4th Division, which had entered the line at that point, and accompanied that battalion in its unsuccessful attack on Hill 212.

Finally, after five days of bloody fighting, almost without food or water, exposed to every type of enemy fire and exposure, the lines were successfully advanced in this new advance toward Fismes for the first few kilometers. The companies were relieved while in the Foret de Nesles and retired to reserve positions in the woods north of Beuvardes, with Battalion Headquarters established at Croix Blanche Farm.

August 6th, Brigadier General MacArthur assumed command of the 84th Infantry Brigade, immediately ordering the 151st Machine Gun Battalion to assemble under its own command. Accordingly, the Battalion assembled in the woods to which the companies had retired and remained in this position until August 10th when, under orders from Division Headquarters, the entire Battalion marched to La Charite, in the vicinity of Chateau Thierry, and bivouacked that night in the open. On August 11th, it resumed the march, finally taking station for a two-day rest on the afternoon of August 11th at Bouresches.

The Aisne-Marne Offensive, so far as this Battalion was concerned, was ended August 5th. In it the operations finally and positively proved, to those who were in a position to witness them, that the work of a machine gun battalion in attack in open warfare was certainly of little assistance to attacking troops when the organization is divided among several small commands and advanced with the first line of the infantry. Undoubtedly, this Battalion suffered a great deal heavier loss than would have been the case had other methods of employing the machine guns been used. Certain it was that the effectiveness of the machine guns would have been left to a considerably greater extent if they had been employed in overhead supporting fire rather than the effort that was made to place them in the first infantry wave, working under infantry company or battalion commanders. The failure, under the methods used, to get needed food and supplies to the fighting line also demonstrated the impracticality of operating machine gun companies under other than their own headquarters.

In casualties during this offensive, the Battalion lost twenty-seven killed in action, five died of wounds, twenty-three gassed, and one hundred and forty-seven wounded by shell or machine gun fire.

In the Bourmont Training Area

After a brief rest at Bouresches, the Battalion received orders, on the night of August 13th, to move on the 14th to station at Chamigny. There Headquarters and Company B were stationed with Companies A, C, and D at Tanqueaux, about one kilometer away.

At this point the first leaves which had ever been granted the Battalion were permitted, ten percent of the strength being granted forty-eight hours' leave of absence in Paris.

On August 17th, Headquarters, with Company A and Company B, entrained at La Ferte-sous-Jouarre, arriving and detraining on the night of the 18th at Damblain and marching that night to billets at Sauville (Vosges). Companies C and D, entraining at La Ferte a day later, arrived and detrained at Bourmont on the 24th, joining the Battalion at Sauville the same day.

In this area the Battalion settled down in more or less permanent billets with orders to carry out a five weeks' training schedule. A few days were allowed in which to clean up both clothes, equipment, and men. A certain amount of new equipment was drawn and comfortable billets were secured before the actual training was commenced. It was also expected that in this area, during the five weeks of rest, the seven-day leaves authorized by G.H.Q. for organizations in France more than four months would be granted.

The training was taken up and the Battalion commenced a series of practice maneuvers of an attack formation in support of an infantry battalion, according to instructions from higher headquarters. This training was brought to a sudden close, for on the 29th of August unexpected orders were received for the Battalion to move that night.

After hurried preparations, the Battalion cleared Sauville at 9:30 P.M., August 29th, in the pouring rain, arriving on the morning of August 30th at Bulgneville, where it remained in bivouac during that day, moving again at sundown to Gironcourt. At Gironcourt orders were received suspending the movement of the organization and the Battalion remained at that point until September 4th when it again took up the march. It bivouacked at Battigny on the 5th and moved again that night to Thuilly aux Groesles where billets were secured and the Battalion remained until the night of the 7th.

The St. Mihiel Offensive

Marching on the night of the 7th of September carried the Battalion to bivouacs four kilometers south of Toul, where it remained during the 8th and marched that night through Toul to bivouacs in the woods near Sanzey. A short move again on the night of the 9th placed the Battalion in concealment in the forest in rear of the lines around Seicheprey and it was at this place that the orders covering the St. Mihiel Offensive were received.

According to the orders received, the 151st Machine Gun Battalion was to attack in support of the 84th Infantry Brigade on the right of the division sector. On the 10th the Battalion Commander and the four company commanders went to their prospective positions of attack to reconnoiter the ground, select such emplacements as were possible, and prepare the necessary fire data. On the 11th, in a downpour of rain, the Battalion moved to its positions in the jump-off trench. All companies were located in their positions before midnight. The Battalion advanced P.C. was established in the rear of the jump-off between Beaumont and Flirey, with the field and combat trains under cover near Mandres.

In this offensive, the Battalion, for the first time, was able to act as an individual organization under its own commander and was not divided between the two infantry regiments and placed under the command of the infantry battalion commanders.

The attack itself commenced with a preparatory artillery barrage at 1:00 A.M. The first wave of the attacking infantry, advancing with tanks, went over at 5:00 A.M. under cover of an overhead barrage from our machine guns. The machine gun companies themselves took up the advance between the first and second waves of infantry, holding themselves in readiness to support or protect any portion of the line which might have been held up. The attack progressed rapidly to the first day's objective and the Battalion dug in with the first line of infantry slightly north of Essey before nightfall of the 12th.

In the meantime the field and combat echelon had moved up to the original jump-off trench and sent the field kitchens on to Essey, thus enabling ration parties to convey hot food to the men in the front lines. Liaison was maintained with the train at all times and throughout this advance the men were satisfactorily fed and the ammunition supply maintained at the maximum.

On the 13th, the advance was resumed and by noon of that day the final objectives had been attained and the Battalion was established in the front line at St. Benoit. The Battalion advanced P.C. was established at the Chateau St. Benoit, while the field and combat trains moved to Pannes, by the cream of the German Army.[20]

The Essey-Pannes Sector

In the period that followed the completion of the St. Mihiel Offensive, the Battalion occupied positions in the line of what was known as the Essey-Pannes Sector. During this time the lines were consolidated, wire was put out, splinter-proof shelter prepared, and the sector made more or less permanent. The enemy continued to lay intermittent, harassing artillery fire over the entire front, but the work of organization was never seriously hindered.

On one occasion during this occupation the entire battalion took part in a covering, overhead barrage during a very successful double raid carried out by the 167th and 168th Infantry.[21] This barrage again demonstrated what had

20. The meaning of this latter clause is uncertain.

21. On the night of September 21-22, the 168th Infantry raided Marimbois Farm under the machine gun fire of Company D. The 167th Infantry raided the village of Haumont under the machine gun fire of Company B (Parkinson).

already been well proven in the St. Mihiel Offensive - that a machine gun battalion could work more successfully and furnish greater assistance to the infantry, acting as a battalion and firing over the heads of the advancing infantry, than by working as individual companies with infantry battalions.

The occupation of the Essey-Pannes Sector came to an end on September 27th when the Battalion was relieved and moved to Marbotte Barracks (near Apremont), after spending two nights (September 28th and 29th) in a rest camp at Nonsard. At Marbotte Barracks the Battalion loaded on camions and moved to Seraucourt, which point was reached on October 1st, and where the Battalion remained in billets until October 4th. On the 4th the movement was again commenced, arriving at Brabant the morning of the 5th and marching again that night to reach bivouacs in the Bois de Montfaucon on the 6th. From October 6th to 10th the Battalion remained in this bivouac, subject to occasional harassing fire from enemy batteries.

Casualties in the St. Mihiel Offensive and subsequent occupation of the Essey-Pannes Sector were, in comparison with the two previous major engagements participated in by this Battalion, extremely light. In the entire period from September 12th to 27th, the losses totaled only six killed in action, forty-seven wounded, and one died of wounds.

The Meuse-Argonne Offensive
First Phase

On October 10th, orders were received for the Battalion to move into positions in rear of the line then held by the First Division near Exermont. The 42nd Division had been placed under command of the Fifth Corps and was to take up the advance through the Argonne which had been carried to that point by other divisions of the Fifth Corps. Accordingly, on October 10th, the entire battalion moved to billets at Eclisfontaine. On the 11th, in accordance with instructions from higher headquarters, a reconnaissance party of the Battalion and company commanders reported to Headquarters, 2nd Infantry Brigade of the First Division, where a guide was secured who carried the party to the positions occupied by the machine gun companies of that brigade which our companies were to relieve.

It was learned here that the 2nd Brigade had been using their machine gun companies in the same manner that they had been used in the 42nd Division in the Aisne-Marne Offensive, the method being to attach a machine gun company to each infantry battalion. As it was not intended to employ our companies in that manner, the positions and information gained by this reconnaissance were of little value. Instead of taking over the exact positions occupied by the companies to be relieved, a "relief line" was agreed upon. On October

12th Companies B and D were sent up to this line, taking positions under heavy shell fire in the vicinity of Hill 263 and in front of Exermont. Companies A and C were placed in reserve positions in the Exermont valley, with the field and combat trains remaining in station at Eclisfontaine. All of these movements were made under heavy shell fire which, in fact, continued throughout this period.

Scarcely had the Battalion been disposed in these positions when orders were received for the Battalion to prepare to deliver a protective barrage in support of an infantry attack. The 84th Infantry Brigade, attacking in liaison with the 32nd Division on its right, was to reduce a portion of the Bois de Romagne, including Hills 288 and 242, in an effort to break the German line of defenses known as the Kriemhilde Stellung, the attack working in the general direction of Landres-et-St. Georges. Accordingly, on the 13th, careful reconnaissance was made by all officers of the Battalion and positions for all guns were selected on the forward slope of Hill 263. This position furnished almost a clear field of fire over the trenches and positions as far back as Landres-et-St. Georges.

The artillery preparation for this attack commenced shortly after 5:00 o'clock on the afternoon of October 13th. That night our companies prepared positions for each gun on the selected slope, each gun being well dug in and protected as much as possible from the enemy shell fire to which it would be exposed. Skeleton crews of three men per gun were left in these positions, the remainder of the men being placed under cover behind Hill 263 where they could readily and quickly replace men in the gun positions who bacame casualties.

From these positions, on October 14th, the entire Battalion fired a terrific preparatory barrage prior to the infantry advance. When the infantry attack was launched at 8:00 A.M., our guns continued to fire a protective barrage overhead. This attack was held up by terrific machine gun fire of the enemy from Hill 288 and the Cote de Chatillon, which our artillery had been unable to entirely suppress and which fire necessitated a change in the brigade plan of attack.

When the new attack was launched, our Battalion was assigned the duty of covering the advace of the infantry which was to reduce the enemy stronghold on Cote de Chatillon. On this occasion, the opportunity came to employ every gun of the Battalion in one terrific barrage covering the advance of our infantry. The terrain was exceedingly well adapted to the work in hand. When the attack was commenced, our guns covered practically every foot of the enemy trenches included in the infantry's objective with an intense and continuous fire. The enemy was kept under cover so perfectly that the attacking troops were able to advance almost to their objective before they were subjected to any German rifle or machine gun fire. On this occasion the attack was successful and our Battalion proceeded to organize their position in the newly gained territory.

These two operations of the Battalion had afforded opportunity to demonstrate once more that machine guns were of infinitely more value to attacking troops when they were employed to furnish a protective cover barrage than when divided among and advancing with the first waves of assault battalions. In the attack on Cote de Chatillon the machine guns were by far more useful than they had ever before been, so far as assisting the attacking troops while advancing with them. These operations, in fact, were successful in the employment of the machine guns to such an extent that after the reduction of Hill 288 and the Cote de Chatillon the Commanding General, Fifth Army Corps,[22] called a conference of all machine gun battalion commanders in the Corps in order to acquaint them with the methods employed in this attack.[23]

During all the operations in this phase of the Meuse-Argonne fighting, the liaison with field and combat trains of the Battalion had been perfectly maintained in spite of every difficulty of impassible roads and incessant enemy shell fire. Men in the front line positions were fed, almost without exception, twice a day, and the ammunition supply was never in doubt, though both food and ammunition had to be carried to the lines through a valley subject at all times to heavy fire from enemy batteries.

Second Phase

The first phase of this Battalion's operations in the Argonne having been completed with the reduction of the Cote de Chatillon, it was expected that the 42nd Division would continue the advance as soon as sufficient artillery and supporting troops could be brought forward. With this idea in mind, the work of the Battalion in consolidating the sector was directed chiefly toward the preparation of positions from which supporting fire similar to that employed in the first phase could be given over the heads of the attacking troops. During the period, October 16th to 30th, Battalion Headquarters, with field and combat trains, was stationed at Exermont while the companies were partially relieved and returned to support positions in this vicinity. Company D, remaining in the line the entire period, continued the work of preparing the positions for a new advance. The remaining companies successfully worked on similar positions, keeping a portion of their guns in the line for defensive work.

Orders were changed, however, and the 2nd Division was directed to take positions which had been prepared under direction of the then Division Machine Gun Officer of the 42ndDivision, and to fire the barrage which that officer had planned. The guns of the 42nd Division, including those of our Battalion, were also ordered to remain in positions similar to those they had prepared and to fire a protective barrage with the machine guns of the 2nd Division in the attack to be made.

22. Major General Charles P. Summerall.

23. Summerall called the meeting, but Major Cooper D. Winn, commander of the 151st Machine Gun Battalion, was the "instructor" in these proven new tactics.

Accordingly, on the night of October 31st, all companies of the 151st Machine Gun Battalion returned to their positions in the line north of Exermont. When, on November 1st, the 2nd Division launched its attack on the enemy line running north of Landres-et-St. Georges, our Battalion was in position and fired a continuous preparatory barrage before the actual attack commenced, and an overhead, moving barrage after the infantry advance debauched, continuing this latter fire as long as safe clearance over the infantry could be had.

When the 2nd Division's advancing waves had gone beyond the reach of our guns, the Battalion was relieved automatically and retired to Exermont where the entire battalion assembled and remained in bivouac during the day and night of November 1st.

Third Phase

Upon its relief by the 2nd Division the 42nd Division had been placed under command of the Commanding General, First Corps.[24] Under orders resulting, this Battalion was moved, on the morning of November 2nd, toward Sommerance. Due to crowded roads and impassable traffic conditions, the orders were changed after the movement was commenced and the Battalion went into bivouac that night on a hillside south of Sommerance in the pouring rain.

New orders, on November 3rd, moved the Battalion to bivouac near Imecourt and on the 4th to bivouac along the Haraucourt-Fontenoy Road, where orders were received for the Division to again enter the front lines on the 5th, the lines then resting just north of St. Pierremont.

Pursuant to these new orders for attack, our Battalion moved forward on the 5th, the line companies taking up their positions with the infantry north of St. Pierremont, while the field and combat trains moved up to St. Pierremont and went into billets there. The advance of the infantry commenced almost as soon as our troops reached the line. The enemy retreated so rapidly after the attack of November 1st that the lines on this day met with practically no resistance and the advance consisted more of a pursuit than of an attack. Our companies, in order to keep up with rapidly advancing infantry, carried their machine gun carts with them and the work on this advance presented its chief difficulty in the movement itself.

The infantry was advancing in rapid pursuit, roads and bridges had been destroyed by mines at every possible point by the retreating Germans, and it was often necessary for the men to lift the carts themselves. On one occasion a bridge had been destroyed and as a last resort an old mill race was utilized as a bridge, all the machine gun carts being carried safely across in this manner.

Night of November 5th found the advancing lines in the vicinity of Stonne where they remained overnight, again taking up the pursuit of the enemy on

24. Major General Joseph Theodore Dickman.

the 6th and advancing as far as Bulson on the left and Haraucourt on the right. Our comanies had, in fact, advanced more rapidly than the first waves of infantry - Companies C and D, working on the right of the division sector, being the first American troops to reach the town of Haraucourt. On the night of November 6th, the entire Battalion was assembled in the vicinity of Bulson and remained there until the 7th when the advance was carried forward to Thelonne. Here the Battalion Commander, with one company commander,[25] went forward on a reconnaissance trip with a view to a further advance by the Battalion. In so doing they reached the heights immediately overlooking the Meuse River.

On the night of the 7th, the entire battalion was billeted in the town of Thelonne at which place they were subjected to a heavy artillery fire from enemy batteries and suffered several casualties.

November 8th, the Battalion was at last relieved from the line, retiring to reserve bivouac on the Bulson-Haraucourt road for that night.

During the advance from St. Pierremont to Thelonne, the difficulties of supplying the front line companies with food had been even greater than those encountered by the Battalion itself. The field and combat trains, endeavoring to follow the line of the advance, met with every imaginable obstacle. Roads, deep in mud from weeks of rain, plowed by shell fire, and in places entirely wiped out by mines, were crowded and jammed with troops, trains, and artillery of three divisions.[26]

November 6th, the field kitchens and ration carts, having been on the road all the previous night and all that day, finally made the town of Stonne shortly before midnight, from which point rations were sent forward to the line in small carts. The combat train had been jammed along the road by the crowded traffic. Escort wagons, endeavoring to reach ration and forage dumps, were held for hours without moving. It was only by continual effort on the part of officers and men in charge of these trains that even a portion of them finally reached the hill south of Bulson on the night of the 6th and morning of the 7th. In spite of these difficulties, the men had been well fed in the front line throughout the drive and the difficulties of transportation were overcome. A portion of the train had, however, been compelled to remain at St. Pierremont as higher authorities, in endeavoring to clear roads of unnecessary traffic, had ordered all vehicles other than those carrying food, ammunition, and wounded off the road entirely.

November 9th, the Battalion was finally relieved from the line and moved back to Grandes Armoises. It was joined on the night of the 10th by that portion of the train which had remained at St. Pierremont, joining the Battalion at

25. Winn had taken Captain Travis of Company C with him (Parkinson).

26. These three were the 1st, 42nd, and 77th Divisions. The 42nd and 77th Divisions were advancing to Sedan on the left and right of the First Corps, respectively. A brigade of the 1st Division was moving laterally across the sector for the First Corps in an attempt to reach Sedan first (Dickman). Clogged roads and confusion briefly reigned due to the 1st Division.

Grandes Armoises. Thus the Meuse-Argonne Offensives came to an end for this Battalion after more than a month of gruelling work, hard fighting, and exposure to every kind of weather and enemy fire.

The casualty reports of the Battalion for this period from October 10th to November 10th furnish the final proof that the method we employed in this offensive was the only proper one for machine gun battalions, and by far the most successful from every standpoint. The actual losses of the Battalion included two killed in action, four died of wounds, and fifty-four wounded by shell or machine gun fire.

The Army of Occupation

On the night of November 10th, while in billets at Grandes Armoises, orders were received for the Battalion to move on November 11th to Germont. It was during this movement that the first word of the signing of the Armistice was received.

After remaining at Germont the night of the 11th and all day of the 12th, orders were received at 12:30 P.M., November 13th, for the Battalion to move at 1:00 P.M. the same day to Alliepont, at which latter place it remained during the night of the 13th, moving again on the 14th to bivouac in the vicinity of Landres-et-St. Georges. On the 16th, movement carried the entire Battalion to billets at Brandeville and it was at this place, on the 17th, that the 42nd Division was officially announced as a part of the American Army of Occupation.

The following few days at Brandeville were spent in hurried preparations for the march into Germany. Partially new equipment was drawn, new clothing issued as far as possible, animals were drawn to fill out the full complement of the Battalion, and on November 20th the movement to Germany commenced.

The first day's march, that of November 20th, carried the organization to billets at Ires les Pres, near Montmedy, from which station the march was continued on the 21st, passing out of France and into Belgium, and billeting that night at Vieux Virton. Movement again on the 22nd placed the Battalion in Guelff, Belgium, near Arlon, and on November 23rd the first stage of the march was completed and the Battalion placed in comfortable billets in the town of Simmern (Septfontaines), Luxembourg. Here we remained in billets at rest for a week.

The second and hardest stage of the march to the Rhine commenced December 1st with a long hike to Heisdorf and thence on the 2nd to Mantern-ach, Luxembourg. On December 3rd the Battalion passed out of Luxembourg, billeting that night with Headquarters and two companies at Eisenoch, while the remaining two companies remained at Menningen, Germany. There followed six days of hard marching through the successive towns of Idesheim, Gindorf, Bettenfeld, Waldkonigin, Boxberg (where the Battalion was divided,

Headquarters with two companies stationed at Boxberg, with one company at Beinhausen and one at Neichen) and ending at Boos.

This marching, from Simmern, Luxembourg, to Boos, Germany, was one of te hardest on both men and animals that the Battalion had ever experienced. At the end of every night's march, wagons had to be unloaded and sent from five to ten kilometers to draw rations and forage. Shoes wore out and no new ones were obtainable. Mules, insufficiently fed and greatly over-worked, gave out on the steep, slippery hills and in nearly every day's march it was necessary to double-back with various teams in order to get the train to its destination. But through it all the men displayed the same ability to go the limit, to endure any hardship, and to carry out orders of whatever nature, that carried them so successfully through nine months of almost continuous front line work.

After remaining at Boos for a short rest, the Battalion again took up the march on December 14th, proceeding that day to Bell, Germany, and on the 15th to Waldorf. This latter town was intended as the final station of this battalion in the Division Area while in Germany. The town was small, accommodations for men and officers were insufficient, and on the 17th Company A was moved to billets at Gonnersdorf. This arrangement still proved unsatisfactory for permanent station and after an inspection by the Commanding General, 84th Infantry Brigade, the Battalion was ordered to move to Kripp on the Rhine - to which place the movement was completed on December 20th.

At Kripp splendid billets were obtained for all the men and officers. Headquarters was established in the beautiful home of an Italian Count[27] and everything was arranged for the expected long stay in German territory. While at Kripp the men were thoroughly drilled in military courtesy and close order drill, new clothes and equipment were issued, and passes - those long delayed seven days leaves - were at last granted.

In this comfortable place the Battalion remained throughout the months of January, February, and March. It was reviewed and inspected on March 16th by the Commander-in-Chief of the American Expeditionary Forces.[28] Finally, on April 5th, after having turned in all but mobile personal equipment, the Battalion departed for Brest and the United States.

Leaving the American Expeditionary Forces

On April 5th the Battalion moved by marching to Sinzig, Germany, and entrained for a three day ride on its last freight train - this time an American train with kitchen cars which permitted the serving of hot meals en route. Arriving and detraining at Brest, France, on April 8th, the Battalion was placed at Camp Pontanezen, Brest, for preparation for embarkation.

27. The Count Ta Vegge (Parkinson).
28. General John J. Pershing.

After a few days' hard work and numerous inspections, the Battalion was pronounced ready for embarkation. On April 13, 1919, operating under the provisions of Embarkation Order No. 173, Headquarters Base Section No, 5, S. O. S., an advance party consisting of the Battalion Commander, Adjutant, Supply Officer, a Mess Officer, and a Police Officer, and eighty-four men, left Camp Pontanezen and embarked on the *U.S.S. Minnesota*. On the 14th, the remainder of the Battalion marched to Brest and embarked on the same battleship.

April 15th, the Battalion said farewell to France. At 3:35 that afternoon the ship weighed anchor and sailed for the United States with orders to proceed to Newport News, Virginia.

After a quiet voyage, during which only a few days of rough weather were encountered, the Battalion debarked at Hoboken, New Jersey, having received orders on Wednesday, April 23rd, to change to that port instead of Newport News.

Demobilization

Arriving and debarking at Hoboken, N.J., April 26th, the Battalion proceeded that night to Camp Merritt, N.J. The work of demobilization commenced on Monday, April 28th. Here the Battalion was split up, detachments of men being sent as casuals to Camp Dix, N.J., Fort Russell, Wyo., Camp Custer, Mich., and smaller detachments to Upton and other camps for discharge.

The Battalion organization itself was not lost at this point, however. Headquarters and the remaining men of Headquarters Company and Companies A, B, C, and D were sent to Camp Gordon, Ga., for final demobilization and discharge. The Battalion left Camp Merritt on May 7th and proceeded to Macon, Ga., arriving at the latter point on the 9th, with 17 officers and 248 enlisted men.

At Macon a warm reception had been arranged and for the first time the men of the Battalion realized how wonderful a backing the people of Macon and Georgia had given them. Macon was decorated from head to foot in the Rainbow colors and "Welcome" signs greeted us everywhere. It seemed as though the entire population of Georgia was there to welcome the soldiers home and if pure noise is any sign of joy, the people as well as the soldiers were beside themselves. An effort was made to have the Battalion parade through certain of the downtown district's streets and, in fact, the men were finally formed in some sort of column and started off. But the men and their many friends and relatives were almost too anxious to get together and it is feared that as a military formation this parade would have exacted much criticism from army officers had they been there to see.

The first hilarious welcome over, the entire Battalion was entertained at a beautifully arranged luncheon at the Hotel Lanier, served by the ladies of the 151st Machine Gun Battalion Auxiliary. After this luncheon the crowd adjourned to the small park before the City Auditorium, which was dedicated to the Battalion as ground on which to erect the monument to its dead.

Entertainments continued throughout the afternoon - every man and officer of the Battalion, whether Macon was his home or not, was the guest of a Macon home and was made to feel that on that particular day the city and all that was in it was his.

One feature of the welcome which impressed every soldier of the Battalion was their reception by ex-members of the Battalion who had been returned home prior to that time as casualties. Men there were whom we had thought dead, who had been carried as dead or missing on all our reports, and who greeted us here as calmly as though they had never seen a battlefield. They were men who had almost made the greatest sacrifice in the cause of liberty - and it was the smiling welcome of these men which impressed us most and made us realize how much we had to be thankful for in that we could return with a whole body and good health.

The entertainment was brought to a close that night by a dance on one of the city streets where, with good music to urge them on, everyone danced off the stored up energy which the excitement and kaleidoscopic program of the day had generated.

It was with real regret that the Battalion again loaded on the 10th for the final trip to Gordon. Among cheers from the crowds and promises of a speedy return, they bid farewell to Macon for the second time since the Battalion's organization, though this time it was with far more joyful men that we looked forward to this new journey.

Arriving in Atlanta, Ga., on the morning of the 10th, the Battalion was again given a warm welcome, and after a short parade through Atlanta's business section, was entertained at a luncheon at the Capitol City Club. The Governor of the State and other prominent men made short addresses of welcome to the men, extending thanks to them for their services in foreign fields.

After this luncheon the Battalion was formed (for the last time in its existence) and marched back to the train. Arriving at Camp Gordon in the afternoon of the 10th, the 151st Machine Gun Battalion detrained at that place and within two hours of its arrival had ceased to exist. The men were assigned to various casual companies for discharge, officers were given quarters in one barrack, and Thursday, May 15th, every enlisted man of the Battalion had joyfully received his discharge and departed for his own home.

Summary

Consolidating the foregoing, and adding brief statistical facts which the records of the Battalion disclose, the following is a summary of the activities of the Battalion since its organization.

Organized in August, 1917, as a three-company machine gun battalion, and joining the 42nd Division at Camp Mills, on September 1, 1917, the Battalion sailed for overseas service October 31, 1917. After a short period of training the Battalion entered the lines at Lorraine in February, 1918, where it served almost continually until June 18. During this time it was increased to a four-company Battalion by the addition of a company from the 149th Machine Gun Battalion.

During its service of nearly eighteen months with the American Expeditionary Forces, the Battalion, or elements thereof, was in actual contact with the enemy under battle conditions for 167 days, was in range of the enemy's artillery for 194 days, established headquarters in 77 different localities, moved by rail on French Unit Type trains five times and by rail on an American train once, by camion twice, and marched approximately twelve hundred kilometers. It participated in four major engagements and is credited with having served in ten separate engagements, including various occupations of more or less quiet sectors. It served as a unit in the American Army of Occupation 140 days.

In casualties the Battalion lost, from March 1st to November 11th, 47 killed in action, 10 died of wounds, 1 missing in action and never accounted for, and 385 wounded in action (including gassed), making the total battle casualties in killed, died of wounds, missing and wounded, 443, while 9 men who died of disease or other causes brought the total casualties while serving with the American Expeditionary Forces up to 452.[29]

Thirty-Six members of the Battalion were recommend for the award of the Distinguished Service Cross, though only one of the recommendations was recognized by G.H.Q.

In promotions, actually within the Battalion, was one major promoted to lieutenant colonel, two captains promoted to major, four first lieutenants promoted to captain, nine second lieutenants promoted to first lieutenants, and four sergeants promoted to second lieutenant. In addition, six officers returned to the United States as instructors, all of whom received promotion upon arrival in the United States, and twenty non-commissioned officers were promoted to second lieutenant at the Army Candidate's School at Langres, France.

29. There are several minor discrepancies between the figures given in the last two paragraphs and those provided by Captain Means (Means). Presumably the battalion numbers are more accurate here, coming from sources within the battalion headquarters with direct access to the appropriate records. However, Captain Means was firsthand and is probably more reliable when it comes to events and conditions in the field during actual movement and combat. Those facts that can be independently confirmed tend to bear out these two assumptions.

Though with an original authorized strength of only 581 officers and men, which was increased later to 764, the Battalion has had on its rolls since the date of organization the names of 1,237 officers and enlisted men. Composed originally of all Georgia men, the Battalion returned to the United States with only 236 of its original members and with men on its rolls from thirty-one different States.

At the End of the Rainbow

Our service as a Battalion, as a part of the Rainbow, comes to a close. To all appearances this is the end - but the memories which each man carries with him, as he again takes up the thread of civilian life, will never grow dim: the hardships and dangers - the long, monotonous days of rain and mud and the cold - the delightful little periods of rest in the picturesque villages of France - the comfortable tour of duty in Germany - and lastly, the wonderful joy of our home-coming, will live forever in our minds and hearts, and the bond of fellowship which grew up in those trying days between the men of the Rainbow will go down to their posterity as something which time cannot destroy.[30]

And may each man, as he returns to his home and the loved ones who waited so patiently and so courageously for his return, find there the true gold which lies at the end of the Rainbow.

30. This has certainly been true for the Parkinson family. Many of Lieutenant N. P. Parkinson's grandchildren and great-grandchildren are still cognizant and proud of their heritage as Rainbow Division "posterity."

DEDICTATED TO THE MEMORY OF OUR FALLEN COMRADES

List of Names of Men of the 151st Machine Gun Battalion Killed in Action, Died of Diseases, and Accidentally Killed

HQ Company

Killed in Action
James M. Oliver, Sgt., Orchard Hill, Ga., July 15, 1918.
(On duty with Company C)

Company A

Killed in Action
Thomas H. Blissett, Pvt., Juliette, Ga., July 26, 1918.
Jesse D. Bridges, Pvt., Albany, Ga., July 30, 1918.
Robert D. Collins, Pvt., Bonair, Ga., July 30, 1918.
Herman K. Davis, Pvt., Zebulon, Ga., July 29, 1918.
Frank Enters, Pvt., Wrightsville, Ga., July 29, 1918.
Bernard F. Green, Corp., Bradley, Ga., July 30, 1918.
Paul Hern, Pfc., Macon, Ga., July 28, 1918.
Thos. W. Hollis, Pvt., Forsyth, Ga., July 30, 1918.
Frank M. Hunt, Pfc., Milner, Ga., July 30, 1918.
Otis Knight, Pvt., Macon, Ga., July 30, 1918.
Ernest P. McWilliams, Pvt., Macon, Ga., July 30, 1918.
Clifford I. Phillips, Pvt., Wamacraw, Ore., July 30, 1918.
Jack Taylor, Pvt., Weiser, Idaho, July 30, 1918.
Melvin Wilson, Pvt., Midvalde, Idaho, July 30, 1918.

Accidentally Killed
Edgar Coots, Pvt., Columbus, Ga., July 1, 1918.

Died of Disease
Normand H. Hawkinson, Pvt., Gooding, Idaho, June 22, 1918.
Delbert W. Sawyer, Pvt., Gooding, Idaho, February 22, 1911 (typo)
Ben Whitt, Pvt., no record, December, 1918.

Died of Wounds
John Morteson, Pvt., Michigan, November 18, 1918.

Company B

Killed in Action
Calvin C. Climer, Pvt., Cleveland, Tenn., July 29, 1918.
Otis E. Cook, Pvt., Griffin, Ga., September 13, 1918.
Daniel P. Hudson, Pfc., Dexter, Ga., July 15, 1918.
Emmett L. Martin, Pvt., Barnsville, Ga., July 27, 1918.
James G. Mason, Pvt., Dublin, Ga., July 28, 1918.
Paul B. Minter, Sgt., Monticello, Ga., July 27, 1918.
George F. Robertson, Pvt., Brakenbau, Okla., July 15, 1918.
Guerry J. Temple, Pvt., Blakely, Ga., July 15, 1918.
Madie R. Ware, Pvt., Abbeville, Ga., September 13, 1918.
Thomas G. Whitaker, Pvt., Miller City, Ga., Sept. 22, 1918.

Accidentally Killed
Homer J. Terry, Pvt., Poterdale, Ga., February 22, 1918.

Died of Disease
Frank L. Adkins, Pvt., Vienna, Ga., March 8, 1918.

Died of Wounds
Clarles B. Long, Sgt., Macon, Ga., November 9, 1918.
Willie C. Murray, Corp., Unadilla, Ga., Rec., A., July 27, 1918.
Clifford Evans, Pvt., no record, Rec. 1 A, March 19, 1918.
Gussie Rich, Pvt., Union, Ky., Rec. 1 A, Sept. 13, 1918.

Company C

Killed in Action

Troy D. Barnett, Sgt., Hampton, Ga., Nov., 5, 1918.
Delmar M. Howard, Pfc., Mystic, Ga., July 16, 1918.
Jarvis W. Moore, Corp., Macon, Ga., October 18, 1918.
Roy S. Ratley, Corp., Leslie, Ga., July 16, 1918.
Carl Thompson, Pvt., Columbus, Ga., July 27, 1918.
Earl S. Wadsworth, Mech., Macon, Ga., July 16, 1918.
Mark Mosco, Pvt., no record, July 16, 1918.
George W. Miller, Pvt., Gooding, Idaho, July 15, 1918.
Harry C. Deanor, Pvt., Pontiac, Mich., Sept. 12, 1918.

Died of Disease

Freeman C. Mills, Bug., Macon, Ga., November, 1918.
Joseph E. Tucker, Pvt., Brinson, Ga., January 25, 1918.

Died of Wounds

Clarence D. Fordham, Corp., Dublin, Ga., Rec. 1 A, July 25, 1918.
Dewey Weeks, Pvt., Meig, Ga., Rec. 1 A, July 30, 1918.
George L. Weeks, Pvt., Eastman, Ga., rec. 1 A, July 16, 1918.

Company D

Killed in Action

Raymond Bryson, Pfc., Lancaster, Pa., July 18, 1918.
Abraham Breitigan, Corp. Lititz, Pa., July 26, 1918.
Martin Cover, Pfc., Ephrata, Pa., July 28, 1918.
Julius M. Lyons, Pfc., Lancaster, Pa., July 26, 1918.
Martin L. Moore, Corp., New Holland, Pa., July 28, 1918.
John G. Walter, Pfc., Lancaster, Pa, July 28, 1918.
Carroll Fanus, Pvt., Harrisburg, Pa., July 28, 1918.
John A. Harkcom, Pvt., Hew Holland, Pa., July 29, 1918.
Charles J. Reemsnyder, Pfc., Ephrata, Pa., Sept. 12, 1918.
Frank Cramblett, Pvt., Gooding, Idaho, Sept., 12, 1918.
David T. Davis, Pvt., Idaho, July 28, 1918.
George A. Rodman, Pvt., Denair, Cal., July 15, 1918.
Aaron Jenkins, Pvt., Covington, Ky., July 28, 1918.
Fred White, Pvt., no record, July 28, 1918.
Ralph W. Olds, Pvt., Detroit, Mich., Nov. 8, 1918.

Accidentally Killed

Sylvester Sullivan, Pfc., Harrisburg, Pa., March 17, 1918.

Died of Disease
Harry White, Pvt., Harrisburg, Pa., July 23, 1918.

Died of Wounds
George Smith, Pvt., Rapid City, S.D., Rec., A, July 28, 1918.
Harry Wright, Pvt., no record, Rec. 1 A, July 28, 1918.

Summary of 151st Machine Gun Battalion Casualties Compiled by Joel R. Parkinson

	Killed	Died of Wounds	Died Sick	Gassed, Wounded	Missing	Total
Luneville Sector	0	1	5	2	?	8
Baccarat Sector	0	0	1	27	?	28
Champagne	12	1	0	57	?	70
Aisne-Marne	27	5	1	170	?	203
St. Mihiel	6	1	0	47	?	54
Meuse-Argonne	2	4	1	54	?	61
Other Periods	0	0	1	28	?	29
Battalion Total	47	12*	9	385	1	454
Reported in List of Dead	47	10*	9	--	1	452
Reported by White/Peavy	47	10*	9	385	1	452
Reported by Means	47	10*	9	395**	1	462
Authorized Strength	764	764	764	764	764	764
Casualty Rate	6%	1%	1%	50%		59%

These casualty figures display a clear learning curve for the 151st Machine Gun Battalion. Casualties steadily increased as the Battalion went from quiet sector to active defense to aggressive offense. Then casualties decreased as commanders figured out how to use machine guns effectively as a unit rather than scattering them among the infantry.

*Discrepancies in the number reported who died of wounds might be due to one of two factors: (1) Whether or not the figure includes men killed accidentally. (2) Whether or not those believed to have died, but who later turned out to be recovering back home, are included.

** The number of wounded reported by Captain Means is either incorrect or might include men from Company D (like himself) who were slightly injured without leaving duty and therefore not included in the official battalion records.

BIBLIOGRAPHY

Personal On Nellis P. Parkinson

Parkinson, Joel R. *Presbyterians, Patriots and Pioneers: The Parkinson Family History.* (Alliance, OH: unpublished manuscript, 1999).

Parkinson, Nellis P. *The Parkinson Family History.* (Clarendon Hills, IL: unpublished typed notes, 1970).

Platoon

Parkinson, Lieutenant Nellis P. *A Narrative of My Personal Experiences In the World War Written For My Sons From My War Diary.* (Decatur, IL: unpublished typed manuscript, 1930). This memoir, with slight editing of spelling and punctuation, provided the narrative text of this book. Lieutenant Parkinson's account is detailed, broad, informative, and fabulous.

Company D

Geiszel, Lieutenant John H. Unpublished marginal notes written in *The American Heritage History of World War I*, narrative by S. L. A. Marshall. (American Heritage Publishing, 1964). These private recollections and reflections are pithy and unrestrained in expression.

Geiszel, Lieutenant John H. Unpublished marginal notes written in *Fragments From France*, by Captain Bruce Bairnsfather. (New York: G. P. Putnam's Sons, 1917).

Means, Captain Monroe A. *Narrative of the Activities of D Company, 151st Machine Gun Battalion, 42nd Rainbow Division in the American Expeditionary Forces.* (Unpublished and undated typed manuscript, circa 1919). Includes casualties for each engagement and roster of D Company as of March 31, 1919. Most of Means' material is redundant with Parkinson's more detailed account. Yet Means is invaluable as independent confirmation of what Parkinson recorded.

151st Machine Gun Battalion

White, Miller G., Jr., and Peavy, Arthur H. *The 151st Machine Gun Battalion, 42nd (Rainbow) Division: A Battalion History and Citations of the Rainbow, August 13, 1917 to April 26, 1919.* (Unpublished and undated typed manuscript, circa 1919). Includes list of the dead for the Battalion. Most of this brief history is redundant with those of Means and Parkinson. A drawback is that no names are given in the narrative except for Gouraud and MacArthur. White was a sergeant with Battalion headquarters.

84th Brigade

Amerine, William H. *Alabama's Own In France: War Stories of the 167th U.S. Infantry.* (New York: Eaton & Gettinger, 1919).

MacArthur, Douglas. *Reminiscences.* (New York: McGraw-Hill Book Company, 1964).

Robb, Chaplain Winfred E. *The Price of Our Heritage: In Memory of the Heroic Dead of the 168 Infantry*. (Des Moines, IA: American Lithographing and Printing Co., 1919). Photos and short biographical sketches of the men of the 168th Infantry Regiment who were killed in action.

Taber, John H. *The Story of the 168th Infantry*. (Iowa City, IA: State Historical Society of Iowa, 1925).

42nd Rainbow Division

Cheseldine, Captain R. M. *Ohio In the Rainbow: Official History of the 166th Infantry, 42nd Division, In the World War*. (Columbus, OH: F. J. Heer Printing Company, 1924).

Collins, Louis L. *History of the 151st Field Artillery, Rainbow Division: Minnesota In the World War, Volume I*. (Saint Paul, MN: Minnesota War Records Commission, 1924).

Langille, Leslie. *Men of the Rainbow: A Graphic Description of the Part This Military Unit Played In the World War, Interspersed With Humor and Pathos*. (Chicago, IL: The O'Sullivan Publishing House, 1933).

Reilly, Brigadier General Henry J. *Americans All: The Rainbow At War, Official History of the 42nd Rainbow Division In the World War*. (Columbus, OH: F. J. Heer Printing Company, 1936). Massive. Absolutely essential to the study of the Rainbow Division in WWI. Reilly commanded the 149th Field Artillery and later the 83rd Infantry Brigade.

Wolf, Walter B. *A Brief Story of the Rainbow Division*. (New York: Rand McNally & Co., 1919). Short and sweet by the 84th Brigade Adjutant.

Corps, Army, and A.E.F.

Adams, Myron E. *The Fort Sheridan Association: The History and Achievements of the Fort Sheridan Officers' Training Camps*. (Fort Sheridan, IL: The Fort Sheridan Association, 1920).

Adler, Major J. O. (editor). *History of the Seventy-Seventh (77th) Division, August 25th, 1917 - November 11th, 1918*. (New York: The 77th Division Association, 1919).

Dickman, Major General Joseph T. *The Great Crusade: A Narrative of the World War*. (New York: D. Appleton and Company, 1927). Dickman was a competent and conscientious 3rd Division, corps, and army commander. The narrative of events is very brief, but some of his larger insights are worthwhile.

Liggett, Major General Hunter. *Commanding an American Army: Recollections of the World War*. (Boston, MA: Houghton Mifflin Company, 1925). By a corps and later army commander in the A.E.F.

Pershing, General John J. *My Experiences In the World War*. (New York: Frederick A. Stokes Company, 1931). General overview of America in WWI by the commander of the A.E.F.

Randall, Roy Oscar and Baxter, John Sydney (editors). *Why America Won the War: A Photographic History*. (Chicago, IL: Union Book & Publishing Company, 1922).

Government Manuals

Army War College. *Machine-Gun Drill Regulations (Provisional) 1917*. (Washington, DC: Government Printing Office, 1918).

Manual of Equipment For Machine Gun Companies: Hotchkiss Machine Gun Model 1914, Saint-Etienne Tripod Model 1915, Hotchkiss Tripod Model 1916, Gun Cart Model 1907, Ammunition Cart Model 1907. (France: A.E.F., Ordinance Department, Automatic Arms Division, May 1918).

Manual of the Automatic Pistol Caliber .45, Model of 1911. (War Plans Division, May 1918).

Ordnance Department. *Handbook of the Vickers Machine Gun Model of 1915 and Mark IV Tripod*. (Washington, DC: Government Printing Office, June 7, 1918).

Regulations For Machine Gun Companies Equipped With Hotchkiss Machine Guns, Model 1914, on Tripod Mounts, Model 1915, Omnibus Type: Volume II, Matériel. (Paris, France: Imprimerie Nationale, 1917).

Supplement To Machine Gun Drill Regulations (Provisional) 1917 and Provisional Machine Gun Firing Manual 1917. (France: General Headquarters, American Expeditionary Forces, August, 1918).

Orders (arranged chronologically)

War Department. *General Orders No. 94*, July 16, 1917.

Commission Letter For Second Lieutenant Nellis P. Parkinson, November 27, 1917.

Headquarters Fort Sheridan Training Camp, *Special Orders No. 83*, November 27th, 1917. Orders for Parkinson and others to proceed to Hoboken, New Jersey, for transport to France.

Headquarters Port of Embarkation, Hoboken, New Jersey, *Special Orders No. 135*, December 19th, 1917. Orders of Embarkation for Parkinson.

Headquarters Second Corps Schools, American Expeditionary Forces, *Special Orders No. 30*, March 9, 1918. Orders for Parkinson and other officers to report to the Eighth French Army for a tour of duty of two weeks and then assignment to the 42nd Division as of March 24, 1918.

Headquarters 42nd Division, *Special Orders No. 85*, March 29, 1918. Parkinson's assignment to the 151st Machine Gun Battalion.

Headquarters 151st Machine Gun Battalion, *Special Orders No. 78*, March 30th, 1918. Parkinson's assignment to Company D for duty.

Headquarters 151st Machine Gun Battalion, 2nd Lieutenant J. A. Turner, *Informal Memo*, August 9, 1918. Orders for Lieutenants Wingo, Olson, Parkinson, and Andres to report to the Surgeon at Croix Blanche Farm, for physical examination prior to promotion.

Headquarters 42nd Division, Major General Charles T. Menoher, *Citation of the 42nd Division*, August 13, 1918. Enumerates the accomplishments of the Division on the anniversary of its organization.

Headquarters 151st Machine Gun Battalion, *Special Orders No. 117*, August 24, 1918. Assigns Parkinson to command a contingent of enlisted men sent to Division Signal School.

Headquarters Fourth Army Corps, *Field Order No. 14*, "Secret", September 8, 1918. General Dickman's plan of attack for St. Mihiel.

G.H.Q., American Expeditionary Forces, *Special Orders No. 262*, September 19, 1918. Promotion of Andres and Parkinson from Second to First Lieutenants.

Headquarters 151st Machine Gun Battalion, *Special Orders No. 14*, February 11, 1919. Parkinson's 14 day leave in France.

Headquarters 42nd Division, *General Order No. 21-G*, April 2, 1919. Citation of the Division by Major General Flagler.

Headquarters Camp Custer, Michigan, *Special Orders No. 128*, May 9, 1919. Parkinson's 15 day leave of absence prior to discharge.

Headquarters Camp Custer, Michigan, *Demobilization Special Orders No. 124*, May 26, 1919. Parkinson's honorable discharge from the U. S. Army.

Selected Secondary Sources

Bairnsfather, Captain Bruce. *Fragments From France*. (New York: G. P. Putnam's Sons, 1917). Classic cartoons about trench warfare by a British officer who was there.

Dooly, William G., Jr. *Great Weapons of World War I*. (New York: Walker and Company, 1969).

Ellis, John. *Eye-Deep In Hell: Trench Warfare In World War I*. (New York: Pantheon Books, 1976).

Ford, Roger. *The Grim Reaper: Machine-Guns and Machine-Gunners In Action*. (New York: Sarpedon, 1996).

Headquarters, Department of the Army. *FM 90-2: Battlefield Deception*. (Washington, DC: October 1988). Theory and practice of deception in warfare.

Manchester, William. *American Caesar: Douglas MacArthur, 1880-1964* (Boston, MA: Little, Brown and Company, 1978).

Marshall, S. L. A. *The American Heritage History of World War I*. (American Heritage, 1964). Generally a good overview of the whole war, although Lieutenant Geiszel detected several factual errors concerning events of which he had first-hand knowledge.

Messenger, Charles. *Trench Fighting 1914-18*. (New York: Ballantine's Books, 1972).

Perret, Geoffrey. *Old Soldiers Never Die: The Life of Douglas MacArthur*. (New York: Random House, 1996).

Peterson, H. C. *Propaganda For War: The Campaign Against American Neutrality, 1914-1917*. (Norman, OK: University of Oklahoma Press, 1939).

Reynolds, Francis J. and Churchill, Allen L. (editors). *World's War Events: Recorded By Statesmen, Commanders, Historians and By Men Who Fought Or Saw the Great Campaigns*. (New York: P. F. Collier & Son, 1919). Includes the terms of the Armistice and the text of the Versailles Treaty.

Stallings, Laurence. *The Doughboys: The Story of the AEF, 1917-1918*. (New York: Harper & Row, 1963). Stallings was a Marine lieutenant who was seriously wounded at Belleau Wood.

INDEX